Microsoft®

Access 97

Illustrated PLUS Edition

Microsoft®

Access 97
Illustrated PLUS Edition

Elizabeth Eisner Reding
Lisa Friedrichsen

COURSE
TECHNOLOGY

ONE MAIN STREET, CAMBRIDGE, MA 02142

an International Thomson Publishing company I(T)P®

Cambridge • Albany • Bonn • Boston • Cincinnati • London • Madrid • Melbourne • Mexico City
New York • Paris • San Francisco • Singapore • Tokyo • Toronto • Washington

Microsoft Access 97—Illustrated PLUS Edition

is published by Course Technology

Managing Editor:	Nicole Jones Pinard
Product Manager:	Jeanne Herring
Production Editor:	Daphne Barbas
Developmental Editor:	Rachel Bunin
Composition House:	GEX, Inc.
QA Manuscript Reviewers:	Greg Bigelow, Chris Hall, John McCarthy, Brian McCooey, Jeff Goding
Text Designer:	Joseph Lee
Cover Designer:	Joseph Lee

© 1998 by Course Technology — I(T)P®

For more information contact:

Course Technology
One Main Street
Cambridge, MA 02142

International Thomson Publishing Europe
Berkshire House 168-173
High Holborn
London WC1V 7AA
England

Thomas Nelson Australia
102 Dodds Street
South Melbourne, 3205
Victoria, Australia

Nelson Canada
1120 Birchmount Road
Scarborough, Ontario
Canada M1K 5G4

International Thomson Editores
Campos Eliseos 385, Piso 7
Col. Polanco
11560 Mexico D.F. Mexico

International Thomson Publishing GmbH
Königswinterer Strasse 418
53277 Bonn
Germany

International Thomson Publishing Asia
211 Henderson Road
#05-10 Henderson Building
Singapore 0315

International Thomson Publishing Japan
Hirakawacho Kyowa Building, 3F
2-2-1 Hirakawacho
Chiyoda-ku, Tokyo 102
Japan

ISBN 0-7600-5157-7

Printed in the United States of America

10 9 8 7 6 5 4 3 2 1

Illustrated Series™ Team

At Course Technology we believe that technology will transform the way that people teach and learn. We are very excited about bringing you, instructors and students, the most practical and affordable technology-related products available.

▶ The Development Process

Our development process is unparalleled in the educational publishing industry. Every product we create goes through an exacting process of design, development, review, and testing.

Reviewers give us direction and insight that shape our manuscripts and bring them up to the latest standards. Every manuscript is quality tested. Students whose backgrounds match the intended audience work through every keystroke, carefully checking for clarity and pointing out errors in logic and sequence. Together with our own technical reviewers, these testers help us ensure that everything that carries our name is as error-free and easy to use as possible.

▶ The Products

We show both how and why technology is critical to solving problems in the classroom and in whatever field you choose to teach or pursue. Our time-tested, step-by-step instructions provide unparalleled clarity. Examples and applications are chosen and crafted to motivate students.

▶ The Illustrated Series™ Team

The Illustrated Series™ Team is committed to providing you with the most visual introduction to microcomputer applications. No other series of books will get you up to speed faster in today's changing software environment. This book will suit your needs because it was delivered quickly, efficiently, and affordably. In every aspect of business, we rely on a commitment to quality and the use of technology. Each member of the Illustrated Series™ Team contributes to this process. The names of all our team members are listed below.

The Team

Cynthia Anderson	Mary-Terese Cozzola	Jeanne Herring	Elizabeth Eisner Reding
Chia-Ling Barker	Carol Cram	Meta Chaya Hirschl	Art Rotberg
Donald Barker	Kim T. M. Crowley	Jane Hosie-Bounar	Neil Salkind
Ann Barron	Catherine DiMassa	Steven Johnson	Gregory Schultz
David Beskeen	Stan Dobrawa	Bill Lisowski	Ann Shaffer
Ann Marie Buconjic	Shelley Dyer	Chet Lyskawa	Dan Swanson
Rachel Bunin	Linda Eriksen	Kristine O'Brien	Marie Swanson
Joan Carey	Jessica Evans	Tara O'Keefe	Jennifer Thompson
Patrick Carey	Lisa Friedrichsen	Harry Phillips	Sasha Vodnik
Sheralyn Carroll	Jeff Goding	Nicole Jones Pinard	Jan Weingarten
Brad Conlin	Michael Halvorson	Katherine T. Pinard	Christie Williams
Pam Conrad	Jamie Harper	Kevin Proot	Janet Wilson

Preface

Welcome to *Microsoft Access 97 – Illustrated PLUS Edition!* This book in our highly visual new design offers new users a comprehensive hands-on introduction to Microsoft Access 97 and is appropriate for a full semester course.

▶ Organization and Coverage

This book is divided into two sections: two units on Microsoft Windows 95 and sixteen units on Microsoft Access 97. The Windows 95 section provides a brief introduction to the Windows 95 environment and helps students learn basic Windows skills. The next section concentrates on Access 97 and moves from beginning coverage to the most advanced topics.

This book has been approved by Microsoft as courseware for the Certified Microsoft Office User (CMOU) program. After completing the tutorials and exercises in this book, you will be prepared to take the Expert level CMOU Exam for Microsoft Access 97. By passing the certification exam for a Microsoft software program you demonstrate your proficiency in that program to employers. CMOU exams are offered at participating test centers, participating corporations, and participating employment agencies. For more information about certification, please visit the CMOU program World Wide Web site at http://www.microsoft.com/office/train_cert/.

▶ About this Approach

What makes the Illustrated approach so effective at teaching software skills? It's quite simple. Each skill is presented on two facing pages, with the step-by-step instructions on the left page, and large screen illustrations on the right. Students can focus on a single skill without having to turn the page. This unique design makes information extremely accessible and easy to absorb, and provides a great reference for students after the course is over. This hands-on approach also makes it ideal for both self-paced or instructor-led classes. The modular structure of the book also allows for great flexibility; you can cover the units in any order you choose.

Each lesson, or "information display," contains the following elements:

This icon indicates a CourseHelp 97 slide show is available for this lesson. See the Instructor's Resource Kit page for more information.

Each 2-page spread focuses on a single skill.

Concise text that introduces the basic principles in the lesson and integrates the brief case study.

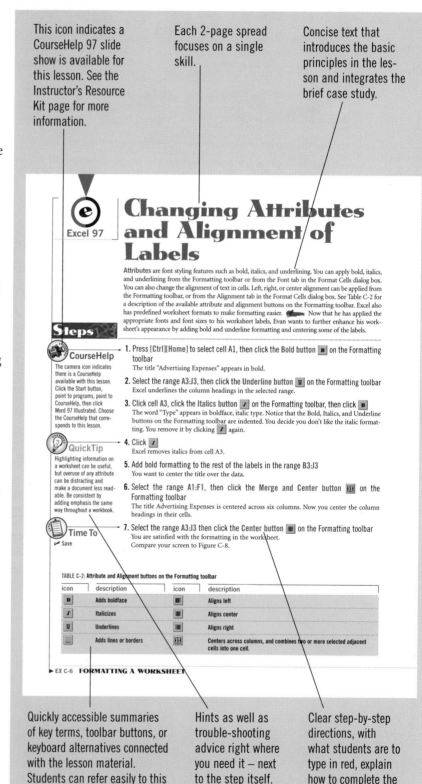

Quickly accessible summaries of key terms, toolbar buttons, or keyboard alternatives connected with the lesson material. Students can refer easily to this information when working on their own projects at a later time.

Hints as well as trouble-shooting advice right where you need it – next to the step itself.

Clear step-by-step directions, with what students are to type in red, explain how to complete the specific task.

Every lesson features large, full-color representations of what the screen should look like as students complete the numbered steps.

The innovative design draws the students' eyes to important areas of the screens.

Brightly colored tabs above the program name indicate which section of the book you are in. Useful for finding your place within the book and for referencing information from the index.

FIGURE C-8: Worksheet with formatting attributes applied

Title centered across columns

Buttons indented

Center button

Column headings centered, bold, and underlined

Excel 97

CLUES TO USE

Using AutoFormat

Excel provides 16 preset formats called AutoFormats, which allow instant formatting of large amounts of data. AutoFormats are designed for worksheets with labels in the left column and top rows and totals in the bottom row or right column. To use AutoFormatting, select the data to be formatted—or place your mouse pointer anywhere within the range to be selected—click Format on the menu bar, click AutoFormat, then select a format from the Table Format list box, as shown in Figure C-9.

FIGURE C-9: AutoFormat dialog box

List of AutoFormats

Sample of selected format

FORMATTING A WORKSHEET EX C-7

Clues to Use Boxes provide concise information that either expands on the major lesson skill or describes an independent task that in some way relates to the major lesson skill.

The page numbers are designed like a road map. EX indicates the Excel section, C indicates Excel Unit C, and 7 indicates the page within the unit. This map allows for the greatest flexibility in content — each unit stands completely on its own.

Other Features

The two-page lesson format featured in this book provides the new user with a powerful learning experience. Additionally, this book contains the following features:

▶ **Real-World Case**

The case study used throughout the textbook, a fictitious company called Nomad Ltd, is designed to be "real-world" in nature and introduces the kinds of activities that students will encounter when working with Microsoft Access 97. With a real-world case, the process of solving problems will be more meaningful to students.

▶ **End of Unit Material**

Each unit concludes with a Concepts Review that tests students' understanding of what they learned in the unit. A Skills Review follows the Concepts Review and provides students with additional hands-on practice of the skills they learned in the unit. The Skills Review is followed by Independent Challenges, which pose case problems for students to solve. At least one Independent Challenge in each unit asks students to use the World Wide Web to solve the problem as indicated by a Web Work icon. The Visual Workshop that follows the Independent Challenges helps students to develop critical thinking skills. Students are shown completed database objects and are asked to create them in an existing database.

Instructor's Resource Kit

The Instructor's Resource Kit is Course Technology's way of putting the resources and information needed to teach and learn effectively into your hands. With an integrated array of teaching and learning tools that offer you and your students a broad range of instructional options, we believe this kit represents the highest quality and most cutting edge resources available to instructors today. Many of these resources are available online at www.course.com. The resources available with this book are:

CourseHelp 97 CourseHelp 97 is a student reinforcement tool offering online annotated tutorials that are accessible directly from the Start menu in Windows 95. These on-screen "slide shows" help students understand the most difficult concepts in a specific program. Students are encouraged to view a CourseHelp 97 slide show before completing that lesson. This text includes the following CourseHelp 97slide shows:
• Planning a Database
• Sorting Records
• Filtering Records
Adopters of this text are granted the right to post the CourseHelp 97 files on any standalone computer or network.

Course Test Manager Designed by Course Technology, this cutting edge Windows-based testing software helps instructors design and administer tests and pre-tests. This full-featured program also has an online testing component that allows students to take tests at the computer and have their exams automatically graded.

Course Faculty Online Companion This new World Wide Web site offers Course Technology customers a password-protected Faculty Lounge where you can find everything you need to prepare for class. These periodically updated items include lesson plans, graphic files for the figures in the text, additional problems, updates and revisions to the text, links to other Web sites, and access to Student Disk files. This new site is an ongoing project and will continue to evolve throughout the semester. Contact your Customer Service Representative for the site address and password.

Course Student Online Companion This book features its own Online Companion where students can go to access Web sites that will help them complete the Web Work Independent Challenges. This page also contains links to other Course Technology student pages where students can find task references for each of the Microsoft Office 97 programs, a graphical glossary of terms found in the text, an archive of meaningful templates, software, hot tips, and Web links to other sites that contain pertinent information. These new sites are also ongoing projects and will continue to evolve throughout the semester.

Student Files To use this book students must have the Student Files. See the inside front or inside back cover for more information on the Student Files. Adopters of this text are granted the right to post the Student Files on any stand-alone computer or network.

Instructor's Manual This is quality assurance tested and includes:
• Solutions to all lessons and end-of-unit material
• Unit notes with teaching tips from the author
• Extra Independent Challenges
• Transparency Masters of key concepts
• Student Files
• CourseHelp 97

The Illustrated Family of Products

This book that you are holding fits in the Illustrated Series – one series of three in the Illustrated family of products. The other two series are the Illustrated Projects Series and the Illustrated Interactive Series. The Illustrated Projects Series is a supplemental series designed to reinforce the skills learned in any skills-based book through the creation of meaningful and engaging projects. The Illustrated Interactive Series is a line of computer-based training multimedia products that offer the novice user a quick and interactive learning experience. All three series are committed to providing you with the most visual and enriching instructional materials.

Brief Contents

Contents

Windows 95

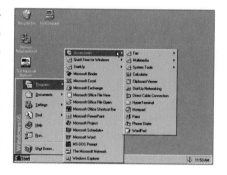

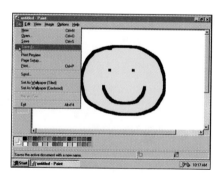

Access

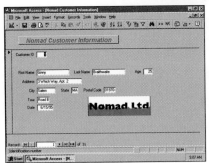

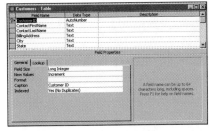

Contents

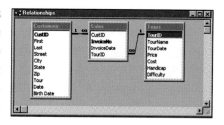

Developing Forms with Subforms

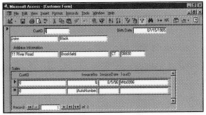

Creating Complex Reports

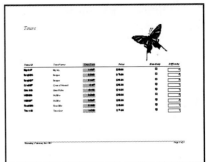

Contents

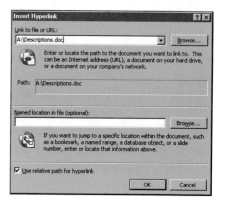

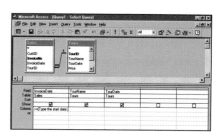

Managing Database Objects   AC L-1

Creating Macros   AC M-1

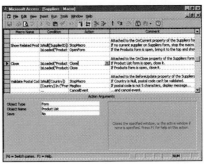

Creating Modules   AC N-1

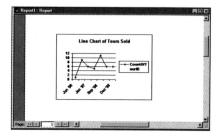

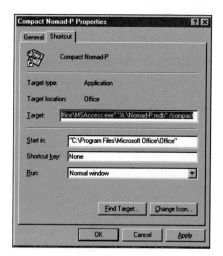

Getting
Started with Microsoft Windows 95

Objectives

▶ **Start Windows and view the desktop**
▶ **Use the mouse**
▶ **Start a program**
▶ **Resize a window**
▶ **Use menus and toolbars**
▶ **Use dialog boxes**
▶ **Use scroll bars**
▶ **Get Help**
▶ **Close a program and shut down Windows**

Microsoft Windows 95 is an operating system that controls the basic operation of your computer and the programs you run on it. Windows has a graphical user interface (GUI) which means you can use pictures (called icons) in addition to words to carry out tasks and operations. Windows 95 also helps you organize the results of your work (saved as files) and coordinates the flow of information among the programs, files, printers, storage devices, and other components of your computer system. ◢— This unit introduces you to basic skills that you can use in all Windows programs.

Starting Windows and Viewing the Desktop

Microsoft Windows 95 is an operating system designed to help you get the most out of your computer. You can use Windows 95 to run **programs**, also known as **applications**, which are software tools you use to accomplish tasks. When you first start Windows, you see the **desktop**, which is the area on your screen where you organize your computer work. See Figure A-1. The small pictures you see on the desktop are called icons. Icons represent a program you use to carry out a task, or a document, or a set of files or documents. The **My Computer** icon represents a program you use to organize the files on your computer. The **Recycle Bin** icon represents a storage area for deleted files. Below the desktop is the taskbar, which shows you the programs that are running (at the moment, none are running). At the left end of the taskbar is the **Start button**, which you use to start programs, find files, access Windows Help and more. Use Table A-1 to identify the icons and other key elements you see on your desktop. ◀━━━━ If Windows 95 is not currently running, follow the steps below to start it now.

Steps

1. **Turn on your computer and monitor**

   Windows automatically starts, and the desktop appears as shown in Figure A-1. If you are working on a network at school or at an office, you might see a password dialog box. If so, continue to step 2.

2. **Type your password, then press [Enter]**

   If you don't know your password, see your instructor. Once the password is accepted, the Windows desktop appears on your screen, as shown in Figure A-1.

FIGURE A-1: Windows desktop

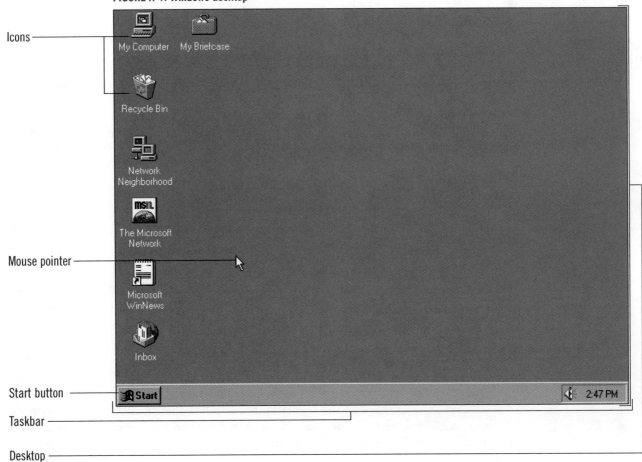

Icons

Mouse pointer

Start button

Taskbar

Desktop

CLUES TO USE

More about operating systems

Windows95 is one of several operating systems. The operating system you use depends to some degree on the kind of computer you are using. For example, the Apple Macintosh computer uses an operating system that only runs on Macintosh computers. Other computers might run other operating systems such as UNIX and OS/2. Each operating system has its own unique features and benefits, causing different user communites to prefer one over the other based on

their computing needs. Before Windows, many personal computers ran an operating system called MS-DOS. This character-based operating system required that you enter commands very carefully when you used the computer. With the development of Windows (and more powerful computers), personal computers can now run programs that take advantage of a graphical user interface. As a result computers have become easier to use.

TABLE A-1: Elements of the Windows desktop

desktop element	description
Icon	Picture representing a task you can carry out, a program you can run, or a document
Mouse pointer	Arrow indicating the current location of the mouse on the desktop
Taskbar	Area that identifies any programs currently open (that is, running); by default, the taskbar is always visible
Start button	Provides main access to all Windows operations and programs available on the computer

Using the Mouse

The mouse is a handheld input device that you roll on a smooth surface (such as your desk or a mousepad) to position the mouse pointer on the Windows desktop. When you move the mouse, the mouse pointer on the screen moves in the same direction. The buttons on the mouse, shown in Figure A-2, are used to select icons and commands. You also use the mouse to select options and identify the work to be done in programs. Table A-2 shows some common mouse pointer shapes. Table A-3 lists the five basic mouse actions. ◢ Begin by experimenting with the mouse now.

Steps

1. **Locate the mouse pointer** ▷ **on the Windows desktop and then move the mouse across your desk**
   Watch how the mouse pointer moves on the desktop in response to your movements. Practice moving the mouse pointer in circles, and then back and forth in straight lines.

2. **Position the mouse pointer over the My Computer icon**
   Positioning the mouse pointer over an icon is called **pointing**.

3. **With the pointer over the My Computer icon, press and release the left mouse button**
   Unless otherwise indicated, you will use the left mouse button to perform all mouse operations. Pressing and releasing the mouse button is called **clicking**. When you position the mouse pointer over an icon and then click, you **select** the icon. When an icon is selected, both it and its title are highlighted. Practice moving an icon by **dragging** it with the mouse.

4. **With the icon selected, press and hold down the left mouse button, then move the mouse down and to the right and release the mouse button**
   The icon becomes dimmed and moves with the mouse pointer. When you release the mouse button, the icon relocates on the desktop. Next, you will use the mouse to display a pop-up menu.

5. **Position the mouse pointer over the My Computer icon, then press and release the right mouse button**
   Clicking the right mouse button is known as **right-clicking**. Right-clicking an item on the desktop displays a **pop-up menu**, as shown in Figure A-3. This menu displays the commands most commonly used for the item you have clicked.

6. **Click anywhere outside the menu to close the pop-up menu**
   Now use the mouse to open a window.

7. **Position the mouse pointer over the My Computer icon, then press and release the left mouse button twice quickly**
   Clicking the mouse button twice quickly is known as **double-clicking**. Double-clicking this icon opens a window. The My Computer window displays additional icons that represent the drives and system components that are installed on your computer.

8. **Click the Close button ⊠ in the upper-right corner of the My Computer window**

FIGURE A-2: **The mouse**

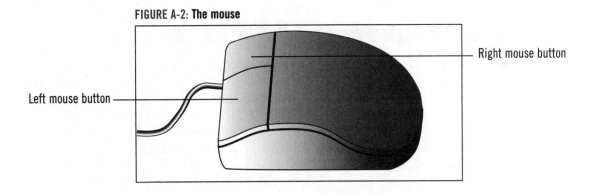

Left mouse button

Right mouse button

FIGURE A-3: **Displaying a pop-up menu**

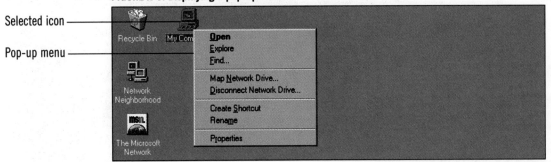

Selected icon

Pop-up menu

TABLE A-2: **Common mouse pointer shapes**

shape	used to
▷	Select items, choose commands, start programs, and work in programs
I	Position mouse pointer for editing or inserting text; called the insertion point or cursor
⌛	Indicate Windows is busy processing a command
↔	Change the size of a window; appears when mouse pointer is on the border of a window

TABLE A-3: **Basic mouse techniques**

technique	what to do
Pointing	Move the mouse to position the mouse pointer over an item on the desktop
Clicking	Press and release the left mouse button
Double-clicking	Press and release the left mouse button twice quickly
Dragging	Point to an item, press and hold the left mouse button, move the mouse to a new location, then release the mouse button
Right-clicking	Point to an item, then press the right mouse button

Windows 95

Starting a Program

Clicking the Start button on the taskbar displays the all-important Start menu. You use the Start menu to start a program, find a file, or display help information. Table A-4 describes the **default** categories of items available on this menu that are installed with Windows 95. As you become more familiar with Windows you might want to customize the Start menu to include additional items that you use most often. Begin by starting the **WordPad** program, an Accessory that comes with Windows 95. You can use WordPad to create and edit simple documents. See Table A-5 for a description of other popular Windows Accessories.

Steps

1. Position the mouse pointer over the **Start button** on the taskbar, then click
The Start menu appears. Next, you need to open the Programs submenu.

2. Point to **Programs**
An arrow next to a menu item indicates a **cascading menu**. Pointing at the arrow displays a submenu from which you can choose additional commands, as shown in Figure A-4.

3. Point to **Accessories**
This is the Accessories menu, containing several programs to help you complete day-to-day tasks. You want to Start WordPad, which should be at the bottom of the list.

4. Click **WordPad**
The WordPad program opens and a blank document window appears, as shown in Figure A-5. WordPad is a simple word processor provided with Windows 95 that you can use to write and edit documents. Note that when a program is open, a program button appears on the taskbar indicating that it is open. An indented button indicates the program that is currently active. Leave the WordPad window open for now, and continue to the next lesson.

TABLE A-4: Start menu categories

category	description
Programs	Opens programs included on the Start menu
Documents	Opens documents most recently opened and saved
Settings	Allows user preferences for system settings, including control panels, printers, Start menu, and taskbar
Find	Locates programs, files, and folders not included on the Start menu
Help	Displays Windows Help information by topic, alphabetical index, or search criteria
Run	Opens a program or file based on a location and filename that you type or select
Shut Down	Provides options to shut down the computer, restart the computer in Windows mode, restart the computer in MS-DOS mode, or log on to the system as a different user

FIGURE A-4: Cascading menus

Arrow indicates cascading menu will open

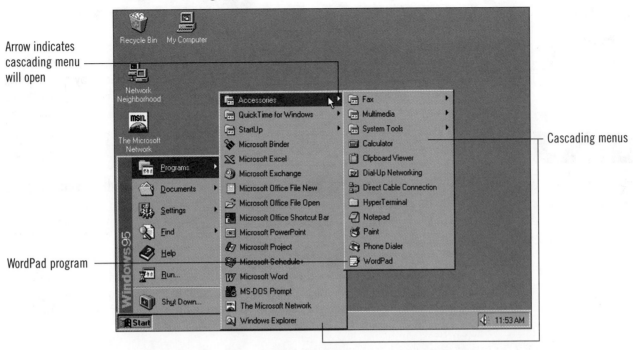

Cascading menus

WordPad program

FIGURE A-5: WordPad document window

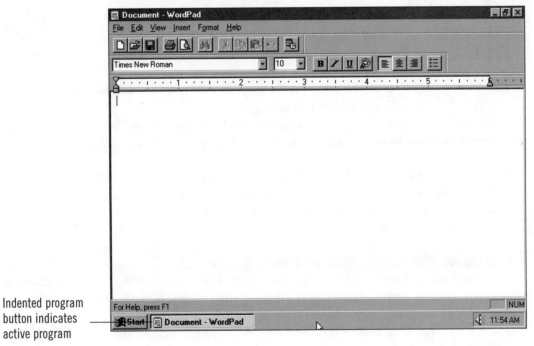

Indented program button indicates active program

TABLE A-5: Common Windows Accessories

accessory	description
Calculator	Use to add, subtract, divide, and multiply numbers
Paint	Use to draw and edit graphic images
WordPad	Use to create and edit documents

Windows 95

Resizing a Window

The Windows desktop can quickly get cluttered with icons and windows. One of the ways to keep your desktop organized is by changing the size of the windows. Each window is surrounded by a standard border and sizing buttons that allow you to change the size of windows by minimizing, maximizing, and restoring windows as needed. You can also drag a window's border to size it. See the related topic "More about sizing windows" for more information. ➤ Practice sizing the WordPad window now.

Steps

1. **In the WordPad window, click the Maximize button ▣, if the WordPad window does not already fill the screen**
   When a window is maximized, it takes up the whole screen.

2. **Click the Restore button ▣ in the WordPad window**
   The Restore button returns a window to its previous size, as shown in Figure A-6. The Restore button only appears when a window is maximized. In addition to minimizing, maximizing, and restoring windows, you can also change the dimensions of any window. Next, experiment with changing the dimensions of the WordPad window.

3. **Position the pointer on the right edge of the WordPad window until the pointer changes to ↔ , then drag it to the right**
   The width of the window increases. You can size the height and width of a window by dragging any of the four sides individually. You can also size the height and width of the window simultaneously by dragging the corner of the window.

4. **Position the pointer in the lower-right corner of the WordPad window, as indicated in Figure A-6, then drag down and to the right**
   The height and width of the window are increased at the same time. You can also position a restored window wherever you wish on the desktop by dragging its title bar.

5. **Click the title bar on the WordPad window and drag up and to the left**
   The window is repositioned on the desktop. At times, you might wish to close a program's window, yet keep the program running and easily accessible. You can accomplish this by minimizing a window.

6. **In the WordPad window, click the Minimize button ▣**
   When you minimize a window, it shrinks to a program button on the taskbar, as shown in Figure A-7. The WordPad program is still open and running; however, it is not active.

7. **Click the WordPad program button on the taskbar to restore the window to its previous size**
   The WordPad program is now active; this means that any actions you perform will take place in this window. Next, return the window to its full size.

8. **Click the Maximize button ▣ in the upper-right corner of the WordPad window**
   The window fills the screen. Leave the WordPad window maximized and continue with the next lesson.

FIGURE A-6: Restored WordPad window

Title bar ————

Sizing buttons ————

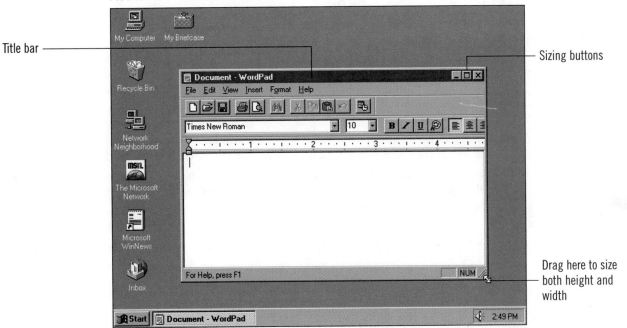

Drag here to size both height and width

FIGURE A-7: Minimized WordPad window

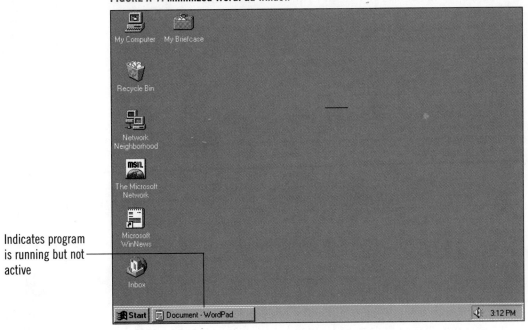

Indicates program is running but not active

More about sizing windows

More programs contain two sets of sizing buttons: one that controls the file which can be a document, spreadsheet, database, or presentation window within the program. The program sizing buttons are located in the title bar; the file sizing buttons are located below them in the menu bar. See Figure 1-8. When you minimize a file window within a program, the file window is reduced to an icon in the lower-left coner of

program window. The size of the program window remains intact.

Program window sizing buttons

FIGURE A-8: Program and file window sizing buttons

File window sizing buttons

Using Menus and Toolbars

A **menu** is a list of commands that you use to accomplish certain tasks. You've already used the Start menu to start WordPad. Each Windows program also has its own set of menus, which are located on the **menu bar** along the top of the program window. The menus organize commands into groups of related operations. See Table A-6 for examples of what you might see on a typical menu. Some of the commands found on a menu can also be carried out by clicking a button on a **toolbar**. Toolbar buttons provide you with convenient shortcuts for completing tasks. Open the Control Panel program, then use a menu and toolbar button to change how the window's contents are displayed.

Steps

1. **Click the Start button on the taskbar, point to Settings, then click Control Panel**
   The Control Panel window contains icons for various programs that allow you to specify your preferences for how your computer environment looks and performs.

2. **Click View on the menu bar**
   The View menu appears, displaying the View commands, as shown in Figure A-9. When you click a menu name, a general description of the commands available on that menu appears in the status bar. On a menu, a check mark identifies a feature that is currently selected (that is, the feature is enabled). To disable the feature, you click the command again to remove the check mark. A bullet mark can also indicate that an option is enabled. To disable this option, however, you must select another option in its place. In the next step, you will select a command.

3. **On the View menu, click Small Icons**
   The icons are now smaller than they were before, taking up less room in the window. You can also use the keyboard to access menu commands. Next, open the View menu by pressing [Alt] on the keyboard and then the underlined letter of the menu on the menu bar.

4. **Press and hold [Alt], then press [V] to open the View menu, then release both keys**
   The View menu appears. Notice that a letter in each command is underlined. You can select these commands by pressing the underlined letter. Now, select a command using the keyboard.

5. **Press [T] to select the Toolbar command**
   The Control Panel toolbar appears below the menu bar. This toolbar includes buttons for the commands that you use most frequently while you are in the Control Panel program. When you position the mouse pointer over a button, the name of the button – called a ToolTip – is displayed. Pressing a button displays a description of the button in the status bar. Use the ToolTip feature to explore a button on the toolbar.

Trouble?

If you cannot see the Details button on the toolbar, you can resize the Control Panel window by dragging the right border to the right until the button is visible.

6. **On the Control Panel toolbar, position the pointer over the Details button as shown in Figure A-10, then click**
   The Details view includes a description of each Control Panel program. If you were to click the View menu now, you would see that the Details command is now checked.

FIGURE A-9: View menu on Control Panel menu bar

Menu bar

Commands in menu

Description of menu in status bar

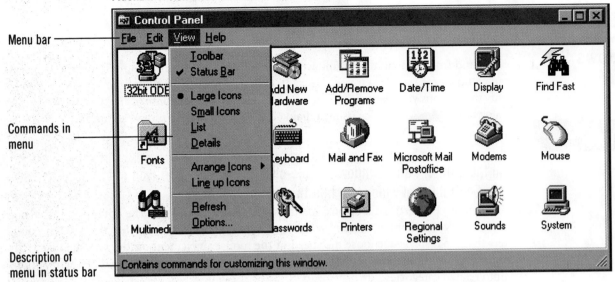

FIGURE A-10: Control Panel toolbar

Toolbar

ToolTip

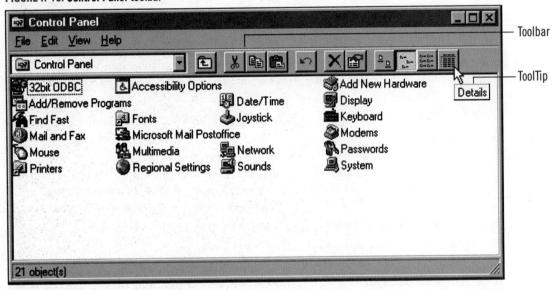

TABLE A-6: Typical items on a menu

item	description
Dimmed command	A menu command that is not currently available
Ellipsis	Choosing this menu command opens a dialog box that allows you to select different or additional options
Triangle	Choosing this menu command opens a cascading menu containing an additional list of menu commands
Keyboard shortcut	A keyboard alternative for executing a menu command
Underlined letter	Pressing the underlined letter executes the menu command

Using Dialog Boxes

A command from a menu that is followed by an ellipsis (...) requires more information before it can complete its task. When you select this type of command a **dialog box** opens for you to specify the options you want. See Figure A-11 and Table A-7 for some of the typical elements of a dialog box. ◄━━━ Practice using a dialog box to control your mouse settings.

Steps

1. In the Control Panel window, double-click the **Mouse icon** (you might need to resize the Control Panel window to find this icon)
   The Mouse Properties dialog box opens, as shown in Figure A-12. The options in this dialog box allow you to control the way the mouse buttons are configured, select the types of pointers that are displayed, choose the speed of the mouse movement on the screen, and specify what type of mouse you are using. **Tabs** at the top of the dialog box separate these options into related categories.

2. Click the **Buttons tab** if it is not the frontmost tab, then in the Button configuration area, click the **Left-handed radio button** to select it
   If the Left-handed radio button is already selected, click the Right-handed radio button. Use this option to specify which button is primary (controls the normal operations) and which is secondary (controls the special functions, such as context-sensitive pop-up menus). Next, select an option which shows pointer trails when you move the mouse.

3. Click the **Motion tab**, then in the Pointer trail area click the **Show pointer trails** check box to select it
   This option makes the mouse pointer easier to see on certain types of computer screens such as laptop computers. The slider feature, located below the check box, lets you specify the degree to which the option is in effect, in this case, the length of the pointer trail.

4. Drag the **slider** below the check box all the way to the right
   As you move the mouse, notice the longer pointer trails.

5. Click the other tabs in the Mouse Properties dialog box and experiment with the options that are available in each category
   Finally, you need to select a command button to carry out the options you've selected. The two most common command buttons are OK and Cancel. Clicking OK accepts your changes and closes the dialog box; clicking Cancel leaves the settings intact and closes the dialog box. The third command button in this dialog box is Apply. Clicking the Apply button accepts the changes you've made and keeps the dialog box open so that you can select additional options. Because you might share this computer with others, it's important to return the dialog box options back to the original settings.

6. Click **Cancel** to leave the original settings intact and close the dialog box

QuickTip
You can also use the keyboard to carry out commands in a dialog box. Pressing [Enter] is the same as clicking OK; pressing [Esc] is the same as clicking Cancel.

FIGURE A-11: Dialog box elements

Spin box

Radio button

Check box

List box

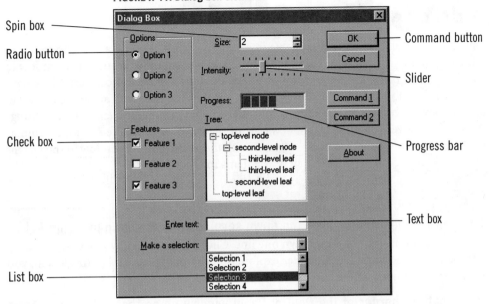

Command button

Slider

Progress bar

Text box

FIGURE A-12: Mouse Properties dialog box

Tabs

Button
configuration area

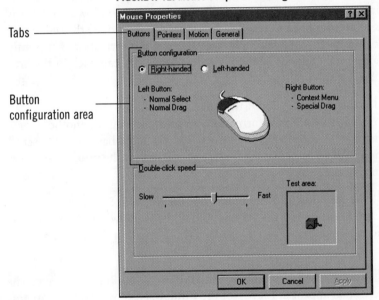

TABLE A-7: Typical items in a dialog box

item	description	item	description
Check box	Clicking this square box turns a dialog box option on or off	**List box**	A box containing a list of items; to choose an item, click the list arrow, then click the desired item
Text box	A box in which you type text	**Spin box**	Allows you to scroll or type numerical increments
Radio button	Clicking this small circle selects a single dialog box option	**Slider**	Allows you to set the degree to which an option is in effect
Command button	Clicking this button carries out a command in a dialog box	**Progress bar**	Indicates how much of a task is completed

Using Scroll Bars

When you cannot see all of the items available in a window, scroll bars will appear on the right and/or bottom edges of the window. Using the scroll bars, you can move around in a window to display the additional contents of the window. There are several ways you can scroll in a window. When you need to scroll only a short distance, you can use the scroll arrows. Clicking in the scroll bar above or below the scroll box scrolls the window in larger increments, while dragging the scroll bar moves you quickly to a new part of the window. See Table A-8 for a summary of the different ways to use scroll bars. ➤ With the Control Panel window in the Details view, you can use the scroll bars to view all of the items in this window.

Steps

1. In the Control Panel window, click the **down scroll arrow**, as shown in Figure A-13
   Clicking this arrow moves the view down one line. Clicking the up arrow moves the view up one line at a time. So that you can better explore other scrolling features in this lesson, you will resize the window to show fewer items.

2. Drag the **bottom border** of the Control Panel window up so that only 6 or 7 items appear in the window
   Notice that the scroll box appears smaller than in the previous step. The size of the scroll box changes to reflect the amount of items available, but not displayed in a window. For example, a larger scroll box indicates that a relatively small amount of the window's contents is not currently visible; therefore you need to scroll only a short distance to see the remaining items. A smaller scroll box indicates that a relatively large amount of information is currently not visible. To see the additional contents of the resized window, you can click in the area below the scroll box in the vertical scroll bar.

3. Click the area below the scroll box in the vertical scroll bar
   The view moves down one window full of information; for example, you see another 6 or 7 items further down in the window. Similarly, you can click in the scroll bar above the scroll box to move up one window full of information. Next, you will display the information that appears at the very bottom of the window.

4. Drag the **scroll box** all the way down to the bottom of the vertical scroll bar
   The view displays the items that appear at the very bottom of the window. Similarly, you can drag the scroll box to the top of the scroll bar to display the information that appears at the top of the window.

5. Drag the **scroll box** all the way up to the top of the vertical scroll bar
   This view displays the items that appear at the top of the window. Next, you will explore the horizontal scroll bar, so you can see all of the icons near the right edge of the window.

6. Click the area to the right of the scroll box in the horizontal scroll bar
   The far right edge of the window comes into view. Next, you will redisplay the left edge of the window.

7. Click the area to the left of the scroll box in the horizontal scroll bar

8. Resize the Control Panel window so that the scroll bars no longer appear

Trouble?

If you cannot see both the vertical and horizontal scroll bars, make the window smaller (both shorter and narrower) until both scroll bars appear.

FIGURE A-13: Control Panel window in Details view

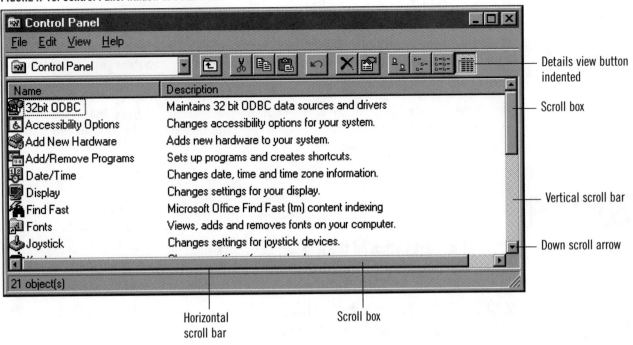

Details view button indented
Scroll box
Vertical scroll bar
Down scroll arrow
Horizontal scroll bar
Scroll box

TABLE A-8: Using scroll bars in a window

to	do this
Move down one line	Click the down arrow at the bottom of the vertical scroll bar
Move up one line	Click the up arrow at the top of the vertical scroll bar
Move down one window	Click in the area below the scroll box in the vertical scroll bar
Move up one window	Click in the area above the scroll box in the vertical scroll bar
Move up a greater distance in the window	Drag the scroll box up in the vertical scroll bar
Move down a greater distance in the window	Drag the scroll box down in the vertical scroll bar
Move a short distance side to side in a window	Click the left or right arrows in the horizontal scroll bar
Move to the right one screenful	Click in the area to the right of the scroll box in the horizontal scroll bar
Move to the left one screenful	Click in the area to the left of the scroll box in the horizontal scroll bar
Move left or right a greater distance in the window	Drag the scroll box in the horizontal scroll bar

Windows 95

Getting Help

Windows 95 comes with a powerful online Help system that allows you to obtain help information in several ways, depending on your current needs. The Help system provides guidance on many Windows features, including detailed steps for completing a procedure, definitions of terms, lists of related topics, and search capabilities. You can also receive assistance in a dialog box; see the related topic "More about Help" for more information. ◆━━━ In this lesson, you'll get Help on how to start a program. You'll also get information on the taskbar. You start the online Help system from the Start menu.

Steps

1. **Click the Start button on the taskbar, then click Help**
   The Help Topics dialog box opens, as shown in Figure A-14. Verify that the Contents tab is selected.

2. **Click the Contents tab if it isn't the frontmost tab, double-click How To in the list box, then double-click Run Programs**
   The Help window displays a selection of topics related to running programs.

3. **Click Starting a program, then click Display**
   A Windows Help window opens. At the bottom of the window, you can click the Related Topics button to display a list of topics that may also be of interest. Some help topics also allow you to display additional information about important words; these words are identified with a dotted underline.

4. **Click the dotted underlined word taskbar**
   A pop-up window appears with a definition of the underlined word.

5. **Read the definition, then click anywhere outside the pop-up window to close it**

6. **Click the Help Topics button to return to the Help Topics window**
   You can use the Find tab to search for a specific word or phrase for which you want to display help topics. As you type the word or phrase in the first list box, any available words that match appear in the second list box. In the next step, search for help topics on the word "taskbar."

7. **Click the Find tab, then in the first list box, type taskbar**
   Two word matches are displayed in the second list box, as shown in Figure A-15. The third list box displays help topics related to the selected word.

8. **In the third list box, click Customizing the taskbar or Start menu, then click Display**
   The Help window that appears lists the steps for completing this task. Close the Windows Help window for now.

9. **In the Windows Help window, click the Close button ⊠ in the upper-right corner of the window**
   Clicking the Close button closes the active window.

FIGURE A-14: **Help Topics dialog box**

Click this tab to
display an alpha-
betical index of
Help topics

Click this tab to
search for words
and phrases in
the Help topics

Prints contents of
help topic on a
printer connected
to your computer

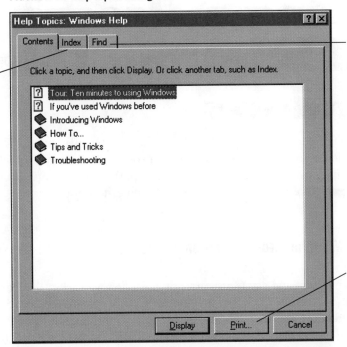

FIGURE A-15: **Find tab in Help Topics dialog box**

Type the word you
are searching for
here

List word matches

Lists the help
topics for word
matches

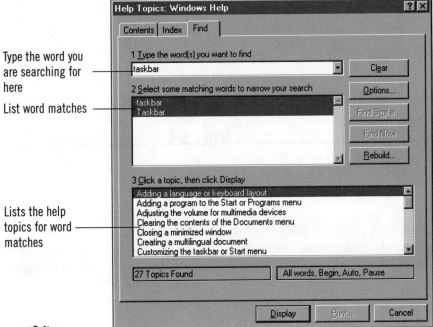

More about Help

To receive online help in a dialog box, click the Help button ☒ in the upper-right corner of the dialog box. The mouse pointer changes to ☒. Click the Help pointer on the item for which you need additional information. A pop-up window provides a brief explanation of the selected feature. You can also click the right -mouse button on an item in a dialog box. Then click the What's This? button to display the help explanation. In addition, when you click the right mouse button in a help topic window, you can choose commands to annotate, copy, and print the contents of the topic window. From the Help pop-up menu, you can also choose to have topic windows always appear on top of the currently active window, so you can see help topics while you work.

Closing a Program and Shutting Down Windows

When you are finished working with Windows, close all the open programs and windows, and then exit Windows using the Shut Down command on the Start menu. Do not turn off the computer while Windows is running; you could lose important data if you turn off your computer too soon. ➤ Close all your active programs and exit Windows.

Steps

1. Click the **WordPad program button** on the taskbar to make the WordPad program active

   To close a program and any of its currently open files, you select the Exit command on the File menu. You can also click the Close button in the program window. See the related topic "Closing programs and files with the Close button" for more information. If you have made any changes to the open files, you will be prompted to save your changes before the program quits. Some programs also give you the option of choosing the Close command on the File menu. This command closes the active file but leaves the program open, so you can continue to work in it. In the next step, you will quit the WordPad program and return to the Windows desktop.

QuickTip

Some programs allow you to close multiple files simultaneously by pressing [Shift], then clicking File on the menu bar. Click Close All to close all open files at once.

2. Click **File** on the menu bar, then click **Exit**

3. If you see a message asking you to save changes to the document, click **No**

4. In the Control Panel window, click the **Close button** ☒ in the upper-right corner of the window

   The Control Panel window closes. *Complete the remaining steps to shut down Windows and your computer only if you have been told to do so by your instructor.*

5. Click the **Start button** on the taskbar, then click **Shut Down**

   The Shut Down Windows dialog box opens, as shown in Figure A-16. In this dialog box, you have the option to shut down the computer, restart the computer in Windows mode, restart the computer in MS-DOS mode, or log on to the computer as another user.

6. Verify that the first option, "Shut down the computer?," is selected

7. If you are working in a lab click **No**; if you are working on your own machine or if your instructor told you to shut down Windows, click **Yes** to exit Windows and shut down the computer

FIGURE A-16: Shut Down Windows dialog box

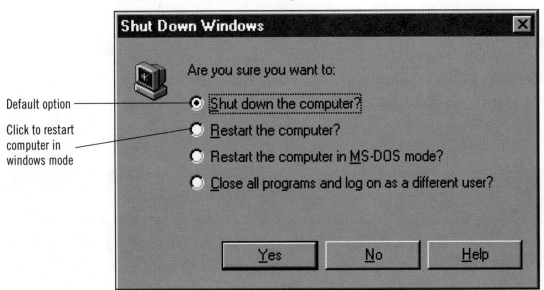

Default option ——

Click to restart
computer in
windows mode

Closing programs and files with the Close button

You can also close a program and its open files by clicking the Close button ☒ on the title bar in the upper-right corner of the program window. If there is a second set of sizing buttons in the window, the Close button that is located on the menu bar will close the active file only, leaving the program open for continued use.

Practice

▶ Concepts Review

Without referring to the unit material, identify each of the items in Figure A-17.

FIGURE A-17

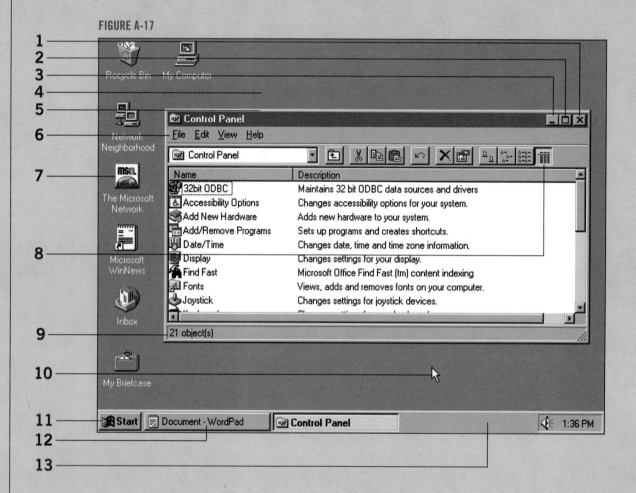

Match each of the statements with the term it describes.

14. **Displays Start button**
15. **Dialog box**
16. **Taskbar**
17. **Mouse**
18. **Title bar**
19. **Minimize button**
20. **Icon**

a. Shrinks a window to a button on the taskbar
b. Displays the name of the window or program
c. Displays list of programs you can run
d. Requests more information that you supply before carrying out command
e. Displays Start button and currently open programs
f. Lets you point to and make selections
g. Graphic representation of program you can run

Skills Review

1. **Start Windows and identify items on the screen.**
   a. Turn on the computer, if necessary.
   b. After Windows loads, try to identify as many items on the desktop as you can, without referring to the lesson material. Then compare your results with Figure A-1.
2. **Practice dragging, maximizing, restoring, sizing, and minimizing windows.**
   a. Drag the Recycle Bin icon to the bottom of the desktop.
   b. Double-click the My Computer icon to open the My Computer window.
   c. Maximize the window, if it is not already maximized.
   d. Restore the window to its previous size.
   e. Size the window by dragging the window borders until you see both horizontal and vertical scroll bars.
   f. Size the window until the horizontal scroll bar no longer appears.
   g. Click the Minimize button. Now try restoring the window.
3. **Run a program.**
   a. Click the Start button on the taskbar, then point to Programs.
   b. Point to Accessories, then click Calculator.
   c. Minimize the Calculator program.
4. **Practice working with menus and dialog boxes.**
   a. Click the Start button on the taskbar, then point to Settings, then click Control Panel.
   b. Click View on the menu bar, then click Toolbar twice to practice hiding and displaying the toolbar.
   c. Double-click the Display icon.
   d. Click the Appearance tab.
   e. Write down the current settings you see in this dialog box.
   f. Try out different selections in this dialog box to change the colors on your desktop and click the Apply button.
   g. Return the options to their original settings and click OK to close the dialog box.
5. **Use online Help to learn more about Windows.**
   a. Click the Start button on the taskbar, then click Help.
   b. Click the Contents tab.
   c. Double-click Introducing Windows.
   d. Double-click each of the following topics (click Help Topics to return to the Contents window after reading each topic):
   Welcome, then A List of What's New, then A new look and feel
   Getting Your Work Done, then The basics
   Keyboard Shortcuts, then General Windows keys
   Using Windows Accessories, then For General Use
   Using Windows Accessories, then For Writing and Drawing
6. **Close all open windows.**
   a. Click the Close button to close the Help topic window.
   b. Click File on the menu bar, then click Exit to close the Control Panel window.
   c. Click Calculator in the taskbar to restore the window.
   d. Click the Close button in the Calculator window to close the Calculator program.
   e. Click the Close button in the My Computer window to close the window.
   f. If you are instructed to do so by your instructor, use the Shut Down command on the Start menu to exit Windows. Otherwise, be sure all windows and programs are closed and you have returned the desktop to its original appearance as it appeared before you began this unit.

Windows 95

▶ Independent Challenges

1. Microsoft Windows 95 provides an extensive help system designed to help you learn how to use Windows effectively. In addition to step-by-step instructions, there are also tips that you can try to gain even greater confidence as you become acquainted with Windows features. In this challenge, you start Help, double-click Tips and Tricks, then double-click Tips of the Day. Read each of the following topics (click Help Topics to return to the Contents window after reading each topic):

> Getting your work done
> Personalizing Windows
> Becoming an expert
> Optional: If you have a printer connected to your computer, click the Print button to print the tips described in each Help topic window.
> Close all the Help topic windows and return to the desktop.

2. Use the skills you have learned in this unit to create a desktop that looks like the desktop in Figure A-18. It's OK if your desktop contains more items than in this figure.

FIGURE A-18: Shut Down Windows dialog box

Be sure to return your settings and desktop back to their original arrangement when you complete this challenge.

Managing

Files, Folders, and Shortcuts

Objectives

- ► **Format a disk**
- ► **Create a Paint file**
- ► **Save a Paint file**
- ► **Work with multiple programs**
- ► **Understand file management**
- ► **View files and create folders with My Computer**
- ► **Move and copy files using My Computer**
- ► **View files and rename folders with Windows Explorer**
- ► **Delete and restore files**
- ► **Manage files on the desktop**

In this unit, you will explore the file management features of Windows 95.
In this unit you will learn how to format a floppy disk, so that
you can permanently store your work. You will then create and save files
using a drawing program called Paint. Next, you will learn how to use
the Clipboard to copy and paste your work from one program to another.
Then, you will learn two methods for managing the files you create: using
My Computer and Windows Explorer. Finally, you will learn how to work
more efficiently by managing files directly on your desktop.

Formatting a Disk

When you use a program, your work is temporarily stored in your computer's random access memory (RAM). When you turn off your computer, the contents of RAM are erased. To store your work permanently, you must save your work as a file on a disk. You can save files either on an internal **hard disk** (which is built into your computer, usually drive C) or on a removable 3.5 or 5.25 inch **floppy disk** (which you insert into a drive on your computer, usually drive A or B). Before you can save a file on a floppy disk, you must prepare the disk to receive your file by first **formatting** the disk. ➤ To complete the steps below, you need a blank disk or a disk containing data you no longer need. Formatting erases all data on a disk, so be careful which disk you use.

Steps

1. Place a blank, unformatted disk in drive A:
If your disk does not fit in the drive A, try drive B and substitute drive B wherever you see drive A.

2. Double-click the **My Computer icon** on the desktop
The My Computer window appears, as shown in Figure B-1. This window displays all the drives and printers that you can use on your computer; depending on your computer system, your window might look different. You can use My Computer for managing your files as well as for formatting your disk. You will learn more about My Computer later in this unit. For now, locate the drive that contains the disk you want to format in the My Computer window.

3. Right-click the **3½ Floppy (A:) icon**
This icon is usually the first icon in the upper-left corner of the window. Clicking with the right mouse button displays a pop-up menu of commands that apply to using drive A, including the Format command.

4. Click **Format** on the pop-up menu
The Format dialog box opens, as shown in Figure B-2. In this dialog box, you specify the capacity of the disk you are formatting and the kind of formatting you want to do. See Table B-1 for a description of formatting options.

5. Click the **Full radio button**, then click **Start**
Windows is now formatting your disk. By selecting the Full option, you ensure that the disk can be read by your computer. Once a disk is formatted you will not need to format it again. After the formatting is complete, you see a summary about the size of the disk. Now that the disk is formatted, you are ready to save files on it. From now on, we will refer to this disk as your **Work Disk**. Before you continue with this unit, close each of the open dialog boxes.

6. Click **Close** in the Format Results dialog box, then click **Close** in the Format dialog box
You can keep the My Computer window open for now; you will return to it later in this unit.

Trouble?

Windows cannot format a disk if it is write-protected, therefore, you need to remove (on a 5.25 disk) or move (on a 3.5 disk) the write-protect tab to continue. See Figure B-3 to locate the write-protect tab on your disk.

FIGURE B-1: My Computer window

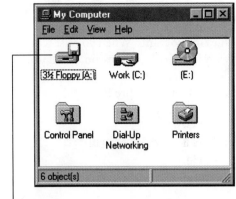

Drive containing disk

FIGURE B-2: Format dialog box

Click to format a new, blank disk

FIGURE B-3: Write-protect tabs

Write-protected tabs

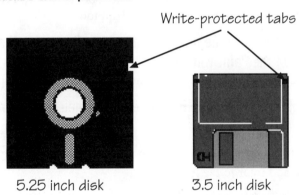

5.25 inch disk   3.5 inch disk

TABLE B-1: Formatting options

Option	Description
Capacity	Click the Capacity list arrow to specify the amount of information your disk is made to hold; for a high-density disk, choose 1.44 Mb, for double-density disks, choose 720Kb
Quick (erase)	Choose this option if your disk contains files that you want to erase; it takes less time than the Full option
Full	Choose this option if you are using a new, blank disk; this option initializes, as well as formats, the disk, requiring more time to complete than the Quick option
Copy System	Use this option when you want to make the disk you are formatting bootable; this means you will be able to start Files Only
Label	Choose this option to give your disk a name; this will help you keep track of the files you save on a disk

Creating a Paint File

Most of your work on a computer involves creating files in programs. When you use a program, you can use many of the Windows skills you have already learned. In this lesson, you'll work with **Paint**, a drawing program located on the Accessories submenu that you use to create simple graphics. Launch Paint and create the drawing shown in Figure B-4.

Steps

1. **Click the Start button on the taskbar, point to Programs, point to Accessories, then click Paint**
   The Paint program window opens. Notice the title and menu bars across the top of the screen. Along the left side of the window is the Toolbox. The white rectangular area, called the **drawing area**, is where you draw. The **color palette**, which contains the colors you use to paint with, is at the bottom of the window.

2. **Click the maximize button, if necessary, to maximize the window, then click the Brush tool**
   A Linesize box appears under the Toolbox where you choose the line size of the brush stroke you want. The Brush tool is a freehand drawing tool that you will control with your mouse. See Table B-2 for description of each of the Paint tools.

3. **In the Linesize box, click the thickest line width, then move the mouse pointer on the drawing area of the Paint window**
   Your pointer changes to and you are now ready to create a simple picture.

4. **Press and hold the left mouse button, drag the mouse in a large circle, then release the mouse button**

5. **Add eyes and a mouth inside the circle to create a smiling face**
   Next, you will add color to the image.

Trouble?

If you make a mistake while painting, choose Undo from the Edit menu.

6. **Click the Fill With Color tool , click the bright yellow color in the bottom row of the color palette as shown in Figure B-4, then click on your smiling face with the Fill With Color pointer**
   The Fill With Color tool fills the area with the currently selected color and your drawing is complete; compare it to Figure B-4. Don't worry if your file looks slightly different. In the next lesson, you will save your work.

FIGURE B-4: Paintbrush window with graphic

Toolbox

Fill with color
pointer

Color palette

TABLE B-2: Paint Toolbox tools

Tool	Description	Tool	Description
Free-Form Select	Selects a free-form section of the picture to move, copy, or edit	Airbrush	Produces a circular spray of dots
Select	Selects a rectangular section of the picture to move, copy, or edit	Text	Inserts text in to the picture
Eraser/Color Eraser	Erases a portion of the picture using the selected eraser size and foreground color	Line	Draws a straight line with the selected width and foreground color
Fill With Color	Fills closed shape or area with the current drawing color	Curve	Draws a wavy line with the selected width and foreground color
Pick Color	Picks up a color off the picture to use for drawing	Rectangle	Draws a rectangle with the selected fill style; also used to draw squares by holding down [Shift] while drawing
Magnifier	Changes the magnification; displays list of magnifications under the toolbar	Polygon	Draws polygons from connected straight-line segments
Pencil	Draws a free-form line one pixel wide	Ellipse	Draws an ellipse with the selected fill style; also used to draw circles by holding down [Shift] while drawing
Brush	Draws using a brush with the selected shape and size	Rounded Rectangle	Draws rectangles with rounded corners using the selected fill style; also used to draw rounded squares by holding down [Shift] while drawing

CLUES TO USE

Reversing actions

With the Undo feature (available in most Windows applications), you can reverse the result of the last action. For example, if you are creating a drawing in Paint and you draw a rectangle when you intended to draw a straight line, you can click Edit on the menu bar and then click Undo. In this case, this command will remove the rectangle from the graphic, so you can click a new tool and try again.

Saving a Paint File

Much of your work with Windows will involve saving different types of files. The files you create using a computer are stored in the computer's random access memory (RAM). **RAM** is a temporary storage space that is erased when the computer is turned off. To store a file permanently, you need to save it to a disk. You can save your work to a 3.5 inch disk, also know as a **floppy disk**, which you insert into the drive of your computer (i.e., drive A or B), or a hard disk, which is built into your computer (usually drive C). ◄━━ Now, save the Paint file you created in the last lesson.

Steps

1. Click **File** on the menu bar, then click **Save As**, as shown in Figure B-5
   The Save As dialog box opens, as shown in Figure B-6. In this dialog box, you give your work a file name and specify where you want the file saved. Specify the location first.

2. Click the **Save In list arrow**, click **3½ Floppy (A:)** (or whichever drive contains your Work Disk), then click the **Save as type list arrow** and click **16 color Bitmap**
   The drive containing your Work Disk is now active. This means that the file you save will be saved on the disk in this drive.

3. Double-click the text in the File Name box, type **My first Paint file**, then click **Save**
   Your drawing is now saved as a Paint file with the name "My first Paint file" on your Work Disk in drive A. When you name a file, you can type up to 255 characters (including spaces and punctuation) in the File Name box. You can also use both upper and lowercase.

FIGURE B-5: Text toolbar

Font box ———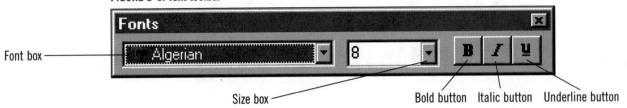

Size box ——— Bold button Italic button Underline button

FIGURE B-6: Completed drawing

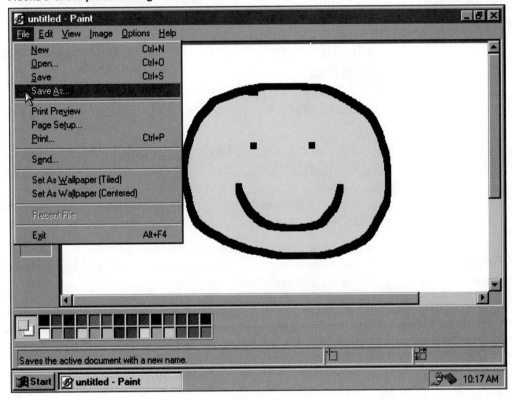

FIGURE B-7: Click to select a new location for a file

Click to select a new location for a file ———

Existing files (if any) appear in list ———

Enter filename ———

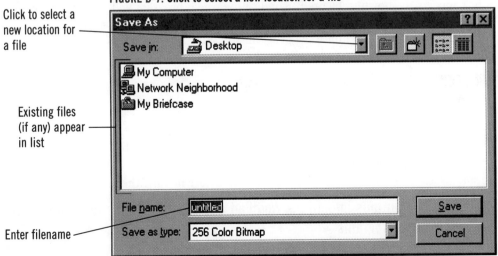

Working with Multiple Programs

Occasionally, you might want to work with more than one program at a time. For example, perhaps you have created a graphic file that you want to include with text in a document file. With Windows 95 you can copy objects onto the Clipboard. The Clipboard is a temporary area in your computer's memory for storing text or graphics. Once you place something on the Clipboard, you can paste it into other locations. Using the taskbar or keyboard, you can switch to another program quickly so that you can paste the contents of the Clipboard into another file without closing the original program. ◄━━━ Next, you will copy the logo graphic you created in the previous lesson into a WordPad document.

Steps

1. **Click the Start button** on the taskbar, point to Programs, point to **Accessories**, then click **WordPad**

   The WordPad program window opens. If the WordPad program window does not fill your screen, click the Maximize button. The blinking insertion point, also called the cursor, indicates where the text you type will appear.

2. In the WordPad window, type **This is the new logo I created for our company brochure.**, then press **[Enter]** twice

   Pressing [Enter] once places the insertion point at the beginning of the next line. Pressing [Enter] again creates a blank line between the first line of text and the graphic you will copy from the Paint program.

3. Click the **Paint program button** on the taskbar

   The Paint program becomes the active program in the window. Next, you will select the logo graphic in the Paint window.

4. Click the **Select tool** ▣, then drag a rectangle around the entire graphic

   When you release the mouse button, the dotted rectangle indicates the contents of the selection. The next action you take will affect the entire selection.

5. Click **Edit** on the menu bar, then click **Copy**

   The selected logo graphic is copied to the Clipboard. When you copy an object onto the Clipboard, the object remains in its original location, and is also available to be pasted into another location. Now you will switch to the WordPad window using the keyboard.

6. Press and hold down **[Alt]**, press **[Tab]** once, then release **[Alt]**

   A box appears, as shown in Figure B-8, indicating which program will become active when you release the Alt key. If you have more than two programs open, you press the Tab key (while holding down [Alt]) until the program you want is selected. The WordPad program becomes the active program in the window.

7. Click **Edit** on the menu bar, then click **Paste**

   The contents of the Clipboard, in this case the Paint graphic, are pasted into the WordPad window at the location of the insertion point.

8. Click **File** on the menu bar, then click **Save As**, and save the file to your **Work Disk** with the name **My WordPad** file

   Be sure to select the Work Disk in the Save In box before naming the file.

9. Click the **Close buttons** in both the WordPad and Paint programs to close the open files and exit the programs

   You return to the desktop and the My Computer window.

Trouble?

If you make the wrong program active, hold down [Alt] and press [Tab] to redisplay the box. Then (while holding down [Alt]), press [Tab] to move the selection box from program to program. When the program you want to make active is selected, then release both keys.

FIGURE B-8: Using the keyboard to switch between programs

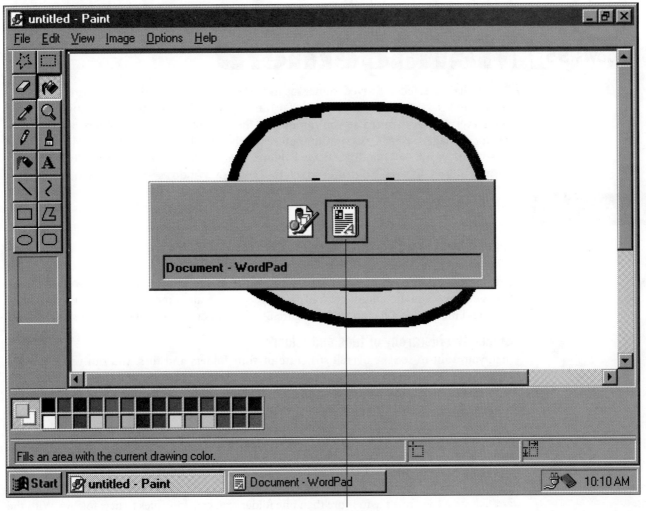

Indicates which
program will
become active

Windows 95

Understanding File Management

After you have created and saved numerous files while working in various programs, it can be a challenge to keep track of all of your files. Fortunately, Windows 95 provides the tools you need to keep everything organized so you can quickly locate the files you need. There are two main tools for managing your files: My Computer (which you have already opened when you formatted your Work Disk) and Windows Explorer. You'll learn more about Windows Explorer later in this unit. ◀━━━ No matter which tool you use, Windows 95 gives you the ability to:

Details

Create folders in which you can save your files
Folders are areas on your disk (either a floppy disk or a hard disk) in which you can save files. For example, you might create a folder for your documents and another folder for your graphics. Folders can also contain additional folders, so you can create a more complicated structure of folders and files, called a hierarchy. See Figure B-9 for an example of your Work Disk hierarchy.

Examine the hierarchy of files and folders
When you want to see the overall structure of your folders and files, you can use either My Computer or Windows Explorer. By examining your file hierarchy with these tools, you can better organize your files by adding new folders, renaming folders, deleting folders, and adjusting the hierarchy to meet your needs. Figures B-10 and B-11 illustrate sample hierarchies for your Work Disk, one using My Computer and the other using Windows Explorer.

Copy, move, delete, and rename files
For example, if you decide that a file belongs in a different folder, you can move the file to another folder. You can also rename a file if you decide a new name is more descriptive. If you want to keep a copy of a file in more than one folder, you can copy files to new folders. With the same files in two different folders, you can keep track of previous versions of files, so that they are available in the event of data loss. You can also delete files you no longer need, as well as restore files you delete accidentally.

Locate files quickly with the Windows 95 Find feature
With Find you can quickly locate files by providing only partial names or by other factors, such as by file type (for example, a WordPad document, a Paint graphic, or a program) or by the date the file was created or modified.

Preview the contents of a file without opening the file in its program
For example, if after locating a particular file, you want to verify that it is the file you want, you can use the Preview feature to quickly look at the file. The Preview feature saves you time because you do not need to wait for the program to open the file. Other options help you get additional information about your files so you can better organize your work.

FIGURE B-9: Sketch of Work Disk hierarchy

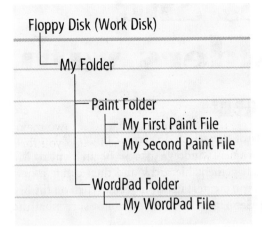

Floppy Disk (Work Disk)

└─ My Folder

    ┌─ Paint Folder
    │   ├─ My First Paint File
    │   └─ My Second Paint File
    │
    └─ WordPad Folder
       └─ My WordPad File

FIGURE B-10: Sample hierarchy in My Computer

Contents of My Folder

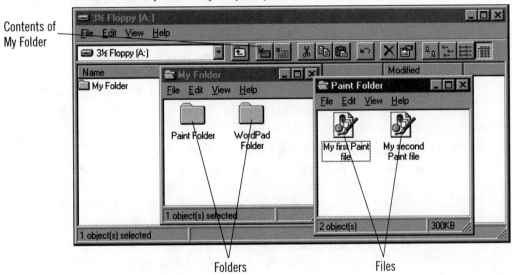

Folders   Files

FIGURE B-11: Sample hierarchy in Windows Explorer

Folders

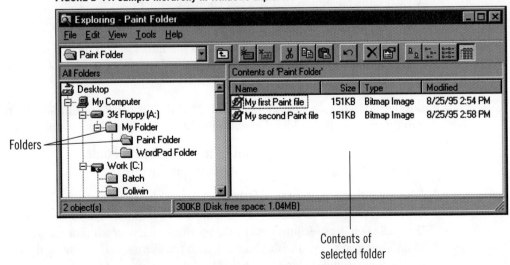

Contents of selected folder

Windows 95

Viewing Files and Creating Folders with My Computer

The My Computer window displays the contents of the selected drive or folder. When you double-click a drive or folder, its contents appear in a new window. ◄━━ Begin by using My Computer to move around in the system's file management hierarchy and then create a new folder on your Work Disk that will contain the files you create. First, you need to turn on the My Computer toolbar if it is not currently displayed. See Figure B-12 if you're not sure what the toolbar looks like.

Steps

1. **Click the Maximize button** in the My Computer window, if My Computer does not already fill the screen
   If your toolbar is visible, skip Step 2 and continue with Step 3.

2. Click **View** on the menu bar, then click **Toolbar**

3. Click the drive list arrow, then click the drive icon for your hard disk
   Now you are ready to view the hierarchy of your hard drive. You can do this using any one of the four view buttons on the My Computer toolbar.

4. Click the **Details button** 🏢 on the My Computer toolbar
   In addition to the drive and folder icons, Details view also displays the type of drive or folder, the amount of total available space on the hard disk, and the remaining free space, as shown in Figure B-12. The List button provides a slightly smaller amount of information, but still mostly text-based. Let's try viewing the files and folders using a more graphical view.

5. Click the **Large Icons button** 🔲 on the My Computer toolbar
   This view offers less information but provides a large, clear view of the contents of the disk.

6. Click the **Small Icons button** 🔳 on the My Computer toolbar
   This view provides the same amount of information as the large icons except that the icons are smaller and take up less space in the window. Next, you want to display the contents of My Computer again, so that you can choose another drive.

7. Click the **Up One Level button** 🗁 on the My Computer toolbar
   Clicking the Up One Level button displays the next level up the file hierarchy, in this case My Computer. Now, you are ready to create a folder on your Work Disk so you need to select the drive that contains your Work Disk.

8. Double-click the **3½ Floppy (A:) icon** (or B if that drive contains your Work Disk)
   You can now create a folder that will contain the files you create in this unit.

9. Click **File** on the menu bar, point to **New**, then click **Folder**
   A new folder is created on your Work Disk. Finally, give the folder a unique name.

10. Type **My Folder**, then press **[Enter]**
    Verify that the contents contained in the window are the same as those shown in Figure B-13. Depending on the selections used by the previous user, your window might not match the one in the illustration. If you wish, you can match the illustration by resizing the window, displaying the toolbar, and clicking the Details button.

Toolbar

FIGURE B-12: Using Details view to examine the hard disk

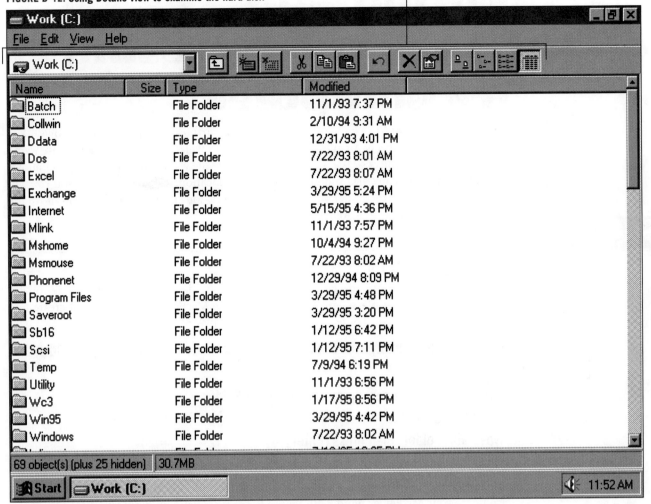

FIGURE B-13: New folder in A: window

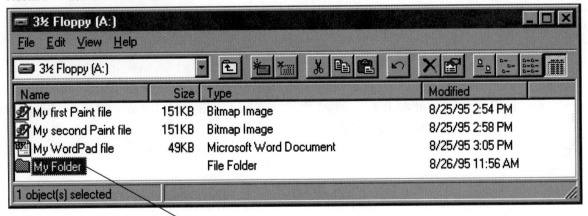

New folder

MANAGING FILES, FOLDERS, AND SHORTCUTS W B-13

Moving and Copying Files Using My Computer

At times you might want to change the hierarchy of your files within a particular drive. For example, to better organize your files, you might decide to place files in a folder whose name reflects the name of a project or the program in which the file was created. My Computer allows you to quickly move or copy files and folders to another location. In this lesson you will create two folders within the folder you created in the previous lesson. Then you will move the appropriate files into these new folders.

Steps 1 2 3 4

1. Double-click the **My Folder** to open it

The My Folder window opens. Before you can create a folder, you have to make sure you are creating it in the right place—in this case within the My Folder. Now you will create two folders, one named Paint Folder and the other named WordPad Folder.

2. Right-click in an empty area of the My Computer window (away from files, folder, and buttons)

3. Point to **New** in the pop-up menu, then click **Folder**

A new folder appears in the My Computer window. Next, you'll name it.

4. Type **Paint Folder**, then press **[Enter]**

Now you need to repeat these steps to create another folder.

5. Repeat Steps B-4 to create a folder named **WordPad Folder**

Compare your My Folder window to Figure B-14. Next, you will move the Paint files to the Paint Folder, removing them from the original location at the root of drive A:.

6. In the 3½ Floppy (A:) window, click **My first Paint file**, then press **[Shift]** and click **My second Paint file**, then drag both files on top of the Paint Folder icon in the My Folder window

Windows displays the Moving window which shows the names of the files being moved and how much of the move operation is complete. See Table B-3 for a description of the different file selection techniques. Instead of dragging files or folders to a new location, you can use the cut, copy, and paste commands on the Edit menu or the Cut, Copy, and Paste toolbar buttons. Next, you will move the WordPad file to the WordPad folder.

7. Click **My WordPad file** to select it, then drag the file over the **WordPad Folder** icon and release the mouse button

The My WordPad file is moved to the WordPad Folder. Next, you will close all of the open windows including the 3½ Floppy (A:) window.

8. Click the **Close buttons** in all open windows

All open windows are closed and you return to the Windows desktop.

QuickTip

To cut a selected file, you can press [Ctrl] [X]. To copy a selected file, you can press [Ctrl] [C]. To paste a selected file, you can press [Ctrl] [V].

FIGURE B-14: Contents of My Folder

Newly created folder

Newly created folder

Windows 95

TABLE B-3: File/folder selection techniques

To Select This	Use This Technique
Individual objects not grouped together	Click the first object you want to select, then press [Ctrl] as you click each additional object you want to add to the selection
Objects grouped together	Click the first object you want to select, then press [Shift] as you click the last object in the list of objects you want to select; all the objects listed between the first and last objects are selected

Using Edit commands to copy and move files

An alternative to dragging files is to use the Cut, Copy, or Paste commands on the Edit menu or the Cut, Copy and Paste buttons on the toolbar. The Cut and Copy commands or Cut and Copy buttons place the selected files on the Clipboard.

Once on the Clipboard, the files can be pasted into the destination folder with the Paste command or Paste button . Be sure to select the destination folder before you paste your files. You can also use keyboard shortcuts to cut, copy, and paste files.

MANAGING FILES, FOLDERS, AND SHORTCUTS   W B-15

Viewing Files and Renaming Folders with Windows Explorer

You've seen how to view, copy, and move files and create folders with My Computer. Windows 95 also provides another tool, Windows Explorer, that is particularly useful when you need to establish a hierarchy or move and copy files between multiple drives. You can also use Windows Explorer to view files without opening them. ◀━━━ In this lesson, you will copy a folder from your Work Disk onto the hard drive, and then rename it.

Steps

1. **Click the Start button, point to Programs, click Windows Explorer, then click the Maximize button in the Windows Explorer window**

   The Windows Explorer window appears, as shown in Figure B-15. You can see right away that unlike My Computer, the window is divided into two sides called panes. The left pane displays the drives and folders on your computer. The right pane displays the contents of the drive or folder selected in the left pane. A plus sign next to a folder in the left pane indicates there are additional files or folders located within a drive or folder. A minus sign indicates that all folders of the next level of hierarchy are displayed.

2. **In the left pane, right-click the hard drive icon, then click Properties on the pop-up menu**

   The Properties dialog box opens with the General tab the frontmost tab. Here, you see the capacity of your hard drive and how much free space you have available. After you've examined the properties of your hard drive you can close this window.

3. **Click the Close button in the Properties dialog box**

   Next, you will use Windows Explorer to examine your Work Disk.

4. **In the left pane double-click the 3½ Floppy (A:) icon**

   The contents of your Work Disk are displayed in the right pane as shown in Figure B-16. The plus sign next to My Folder indicates that it contains additional folders. Try expanding My Folder in the next step.

5. **In the left pane, click the plus sign next to My Folder**

   The folders contained within the My Folder now appear in the left pane.

6. **In the left pane, click the WordPad folder**

   The contents of the WordPad folder appear in the right pane of Windows Explorer. In the next step, you'll copy the WordPad folder to the hard drive in order to have a backup copy for safe keeping.

7. **In the left pane, drag the WordPad folder on top of the icon for the hard drive, then release the mouse button**

   The WordPad folder and the file in it are copied to the hard disk. Check to see if the copy of this folder is on the hard drive.

8. **In the left pane, click the icon representing your hard drive**

   The WordPad Folder should now appear in the list of folders in the right pane. You might have to scroll to find it. Now let's rename the folder so you can tell the original folder from the backup.

9. **Right-click the WordPad folder in the right pane, click Rename in the pop-up menu, then type Backup WordPad Folder and press [Enter]**

   Leave the Windows Explorer window open and continue with the next lesson.

FIGURE B-15: Windows Explorer window

Menu bar —

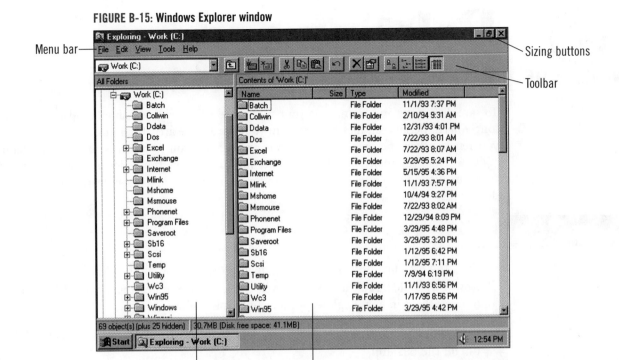

Sizing buttons

Toolbar

Left pane   Right pane

FIGURE B-16: Contents of your Work Disk

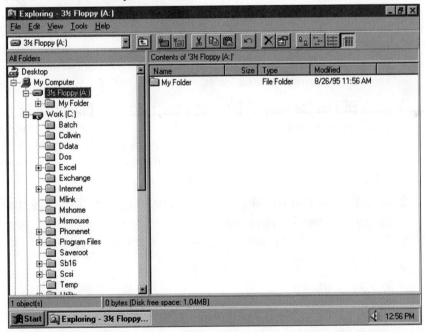

Quick View

At times you might want to preview a document to get an idea of what is in the file before opening it. It is much faster to preview the document using either My Computer or Windows Explorer than opening the program in which the file was created, then opening the file. To preview the file, simply right-click the selected file, then click Quick View on the pop-up menu. A preview of the file appears in the Quick View box. If the Quick View command does not appear on the pop-up menu, it means that this feature was not installed on your computer; see your instructor or technical support person for additional information.

Deleting and Restoring Files

To save disk space and to manage your files more effectively, you should delete files you no longer need. Because all files deleted from your hard drive are stored in the Recycle Bin (until you remove them permanently), you can restore files you might have deleted accidentally. There are many ways to delete files in Windows 95. In this lesson, you'll use two different methods for removing files you no longer need. Then you will learn how to restore a deleted file.

1. Click the **Restore button** on the Windows Explorer title bar

Now you should be able to see the Recycle Bin icon on your desktop. If you can't see it, resize or move the Windows Explorer window until it is visible.

2. Drag the folder called **Backup WordPad Folder** from the right pane to the **Recycle Bin** on the desktop

The folder no longer appears in the Windows Explorer window because you have moved it to the Recycle Bin. The Recycle Bin looks as if it contains paper. If you see an "Are you sure you want to delete" confirmation box, click No and see the Trouble? on the next page. Next, you will examine the contents of the Recycle Bin.

3. Double-click the **Recycle Bin** icon on the desktop

The Recycle Bin window appears, as shown in Figure B-17. Depending upon the number of files already deleted on your computer, your window might look different. The folder doesn't appear in the Recycle Bin window but the file does. Use the scroll bar if you can't see it. Next, you'll try restoring a deleted folder.

4. Click **Edit** on the Recycle Bin menu bar, then click **Undo Delete**

The Backup WordPad folder is restored and should now appear in the Windows Explorer window. You might need to move or resize your Recycle Bin window if it blocks your view of the Windows Explorer window. Next, you can delete the Backup WordPad folder for good using a Windows Explorer toolbar button.

5. Click the **Backup WordPad Folder** in the left pane, then click the **Delete button** ☒ on the Windows Explorer toolbar

The Confirm Folder Delete dialog box opens as shown in Figure B-18.

6. Click **Yes**

When you are sure you will no longer need files you've moved into the Recycle Bin, you can empty the Recycle Bin. You won't do this now, in case you are working on a computer that you share with other people. But, when you're working on your own machine, simply right-click the Recycle Bin icon, then click Empty Recycle Bin in the pop-up menu.

Leave both the Recycle Bin and the Windows Explorer windows open and continue to the next lesson.

Trouble?

If you are unable to recycle a file, it might be because your Recycle Bin is full, or too small, or the properties have been changed so that files are not stored in the Recycle Bin, they are deleted right away. Right-click the Recycle Bin icon, then click Properties on the pop-up menu to change the settings for storage and capacity.

FIGURE B-17: Contents of Recycle Bin

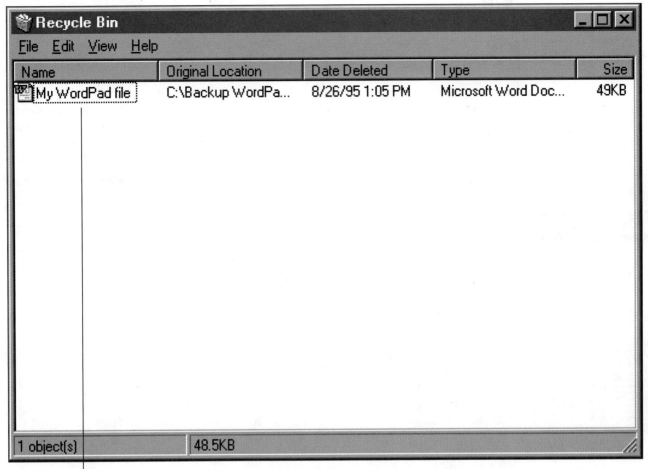

File you just
deleted

FIGURE B-18: Confirm Folder Delete dialog box

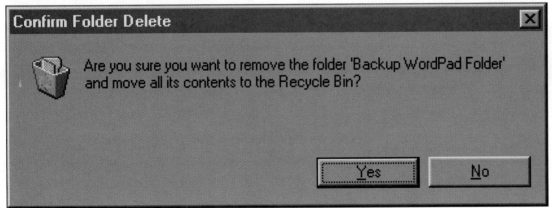

Important note about deleting files on a floppy disk

You cannot restore files deleted from a floppy disk. Once a file on a floppy disk is sent to the Recycle Bin, it is permanently removed from the floppy disk and cannot be retrieved.

Managing Files on the Desktop

Windows 95

You've now learned two different tools for managing files in Windows 95: My Computer and Windows Explorer. There is yet another Windows 95 feature you can use to make it easier to access files, folders, or programs you frequently use. A pop-up menu on the Windows desktop allows you to create folders and shortcuts on the desktop itself. **Shortcuts** are icons that point to an object that is actually stored elsewhere in a drive or folder. When you double-click a shortcut, you open the object without having to find its actual location. ◄━━ In this lesson, you will create a shortcut to the My WordPad file. Creating shortcuts to files you use frequently and placing them on the desktop allows you to work more efficiently.

Steps

QuickTip

Windows 95 enables you to customize your desktop to suit your work habits. For example, you can create a folder on the desktop that you can use to store all of your shortcuts. You can even create a shortcut folder on the desktop.

1. In the left pane of the Windows Explorer window, click the **WordPad folder**
   You need to select the file you want to create a shortcut to, first.

2. In the right pane, right-click the **My WordPad file**
   A pop-up menu appears as shown in Figure B-19.

3. Click **Create Shortcut** in the pop-up menu
   The file named Shortcut to My WordPad file appears in the right pane. Now you need to move it to the desktop so it will be at your fingertips whenever you need it. If you drag it using the left mouse button you will copy it to the desktop. If you drag it using the right mouse button you will have the option to copy or move it. Let's try dragging it using the right mouse button.

4. Right-drag the **Shortcut to My WordPad** file to an empty area of the desktop
   When you release the mouse button a pop-up menu appears.

5. Click **Move Here** in the pop-up menu
   A shortcut to the My WordPad file now appears on the desktop as shown in Figure B-20. When you double-click this shortcut icon, you will open both WordPad and the My WordPad file document. Now let's delete the shortcut icon in case you are working in a lab and share the computer with others. Deleting a shortcut does not delete the original file or folder to which it points.

6. On the desktop, click the **Shortcut to My WordPad file**, then press **[Delete]**; click Yes to confirm the deletion
   The shortcut is removed from the desktop and now appears in the Recycle Bin; however, the file itself remains intact in the WordPad folder. (See the Windows Explorer window to make sure it's still there.)

7. Close all open windows

FIGURE B-19: Pop-up menu

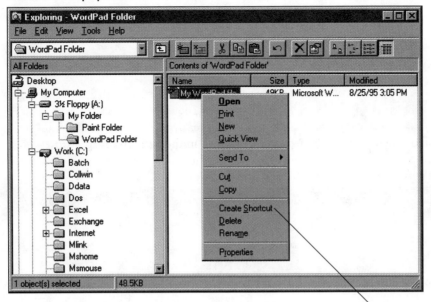

Click to create a
shortcut to the file

FIGURE B-20: Shortcut on desktop

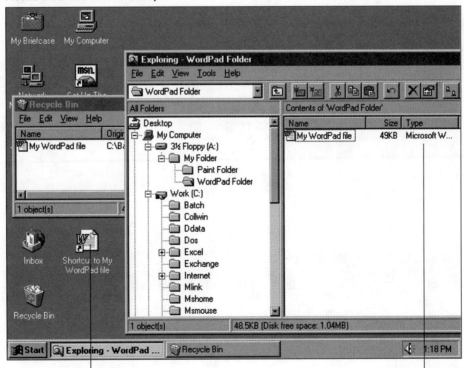

Shortcut located
here

File that shortcut is
based on is still on
your Work Disk

Adding shortcuts to the Start menu

If you do not want your desktop to get cluttered with icons, but you would still like easy access to certain files, programs, and folders, you can create a shortcut on the Start menu or any of its cascading menus.

Drag the file, program, or folder that you want to add to the Start menu from the Windows Explorer window to the Start button. The file, program, or folder will appear on the first level of the Start menu.

MANAGING FILES, FOLDERS, AND SHORTCUTS W B-21 ◄

Practice

► Concepts Review

Label each of the elements of the Windows Explorer window shown in Figure B-21.

FIGURE B-21

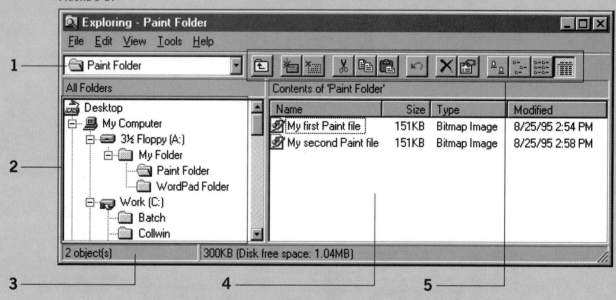

Match each of the descriptions with the correct term.

6. RAM   a. Permanent storage of your work in programs
7. Folders   b. Temporary location of your work as you use a program
8. Files   c. Temporary location of information you wish to paste into another program
9. Hierarchy   d. Storage area for organizing files or folders by type, project, or whatever you wish
10. Clipboard   e. Structure of files and folders revealing organization of a disk

Select the best answer from the list of choices.

11. To prepare a floppy disk to receive your files, you must first do which of the following?
    a. Copy work files to the disk   b. Format the disk
    c. Erase all the files that might be on the disk   d. Place the files on the Clipboard

12. To view the contents of a folder, you can use which of the following tools?
    a. The desktop   b. Windows Explorer   c. My Computer   d. Either b or c

13. You can use the My Computer program to:
    a. Create a drawing of your computer.   b. View the contents of a folder.
    c. Customize the Start menu.   d. Determine what programs begin automatically when you start Windows.

14. While you are working in a program, where is your work stored?
    a. On a hard drive   b. In RAM   c. In the monitor   d. On the Clipboard

15. **What is the correct sequence for starting the Paint program?**
    - **a.** Double-click the Paint shortcut on the desktop
    - **b.** Click Start, Programs, Accessories, Paint
    - **c.** Click Start, Programs, Paint
    - **d.** Click Start, Accessories, Paint

16. **Which of the following best describes the WordPad program?**
    - **a.** A program for pasting in graphics
    - **b.** A program for performing complex financial analysis
    - **c.** A program that is a simple text editor for creating basic documents
    - **d.** A program for creating graphics

17. **For most Windows programs, the Save As command is located on which menu?**
    - **a.** File
    - **b.** Edit
    - **c.** Help
    - **d.** Save

18. **Which of the following is NOT a way to move files from one folder to another?**
    - **a.** Opening the file and using the Save As command to save the file in a new location.
    - **b.** In My Computer or the Windows Explorer, drag the selected to the new folder.
    - **c.** Use the Cut and Paste commands on the Edit menu while in the My Computer or the Windows Explorer windows.
    - **d.** Use the [Ctrl] [X] and [Ctrl] [V] keyboard shortcuts while in the My Computer or the Windows Explorer windows.

19. **Which of the following is a way to rename the selected file in either the My Computer window or the Windows Explorer window?**
    - **a.** Click Edit on the menu bar, then click Rename.
    - **b.** Click File on the menu bar, then click Rename.
    - **c.** Click the Rename button on the toolbar.
    - **d.** You can only rename files in the program in which the file was created.

20. **In which of the following can you view the hierarchy of drives, folder, and files in a split pane window?**
    - **a.** The Windows Explorer window
    - **b.** The Programs window
    - **c.** The My Computer window
    - **d.** The WordPad window

► Skills Review

1. **Format a disk.**
   - **a.** Insert a new blank disk in a drive.
   - **b.** Open My Computer and use the right mouse button to click on the drive.
   - **c.** Format the disk using the Format command on the pop-up menu. Check that the capacity and format type are correct.

2. **Create a WordPad file.**
   - **a.** Launch WordPad.
   - **b.** Type a short description of your artistic abilities and press [Enter] several times to create extra space between the text and the graphic you are about to create.
   - **c.** Insert your Work Disk in the appropriate disk drive, then save the document as My New Document to the My Folder on your Work Disk.
   - **d.** Minimize the WordPad program.

3. **Create and save a Paint file.**
   - **a.** Launch Paint.
   - **b.** Create your own unique, colorful design using several colors. Use a variety of tools. For example, create a filled circle and then place a filled square inside the circle. Use the Text button to create a text box in which you type your name.
   - **c.** Save the picture as My Art to the My Folder on your Work Disk.
   - **d.** Select the entire graphic and copy it onto the Clipboard.

    e. Switch to the WordPad program.

    f. Place the insertion point below the text and paste the graphic into your document.

    g. Save the changes to your WordPad document.

    h. Switch to the Paint program.

    i. Using the Fill With Color button, change the color of a filled area of your graphic.

    j. Save the revised graphic with a new name, My Art2 to the My Folder on your Work Disk.

    k. Select the entire graphic and copy it to the Clipboard.

    l. Switch to the WordPad program and above the picture type "This is an improved graphic."

    m. Select the old graphic by clicking the picture, then paste the new contents of the Clipboard. The new graphic replaces the old graphic that was selected.

    n. Save the changed WordPad document with a new name, My Second Document to the My Folder on your Work Disk.

    o. Exit the Paint and WordPad programs.

4. Manage files and folders with My Computer.

    a. Open My Computer.

    b. Be sure your Work Disk is in either drive A or drive B.

    c. Double-click the drive icon that contains your Work Disk to prepare for the next step.

5. Create new folders on the Work Disk and on the hard drive.

    a. Create a folder called My Review Folder on your Work Disk by clicking File, New, then clicking Folder.

    b. Open the folder to display its contents in a separate window.

    c. Create another folder (at the root of C on the hard drive) called My Temporary Folder.

    d. In the My Review Folder window, click File, New, then click Folder. Create two new subfolders (under My Review Folder), one called Documents and the other called ArtWork.

    e. In the My Computer window, double-click the drive C icon to display the contents of your hard drive in a new window.

6. Move files to the new folders in the My Review Folder.

    a. Open the ArtWork folder on your Work Disk.

    b. From the root of the Work Disk, drag the two Paint files into the ArtWork folder window on your Work Disk. Close the ArtWork folder window.

    c. Open the Documents folder on your Work Disk.

    d. From the root of the Work Disk, drag the two WordPad files into the Documents folder window on your Work Disk. Close the Documents folder window.

    e. Close all of the open windows in My Computer.

7. Copy files to the My Temporary Folder on the hard drive.

    a. Open the Windows Explorer.

    b. Copy the four WordPad and Paint files from the folders on the Work Disk to the My Temporary Folder.

8. Delete files and folders.

    a. Drag the My Temporary Folder to the Recycle Bin icon.

    b. Click the My Review Folder and press [Del]. Then confirm that you want to delete the file.

    c. Double-click the Recycle Bin icon and restore the My Temporary Folder and its files. Delete the folder again.

9. Create a shortcut that opens Windows Explorer.

    a. Use Windows Explorer to locate the Windows folder on your hard drive. In the right side of the window, scroll through the list of objects until you see a file called Explorer.

    b. Drag the Explorer file to the desktop.

    c. Close the Windows Explorer.

    d. Double-click the new shortcut to test the shortcut for starting Windows Explorer. Then close the Explorer again.

    e. Delete the shortcut for Windows Explorer. Then use the Start button to verify that the Windows Explorer program is still available on the Programs menu.

Independent Challenges

1. It is important to develop a sound, organized plan when you manage files and folders. Practice your skills by organizing the following list of names into a coherent and logical hierarchy. Begin by identifying folders. In each folder, identify the files you could expect to find in them. Sketch a hierarchical structure like the one you would see in the right side of a Windows Explorer window.

- Projects
- My Resume
- Recommendation letter
- First Qtr Bulletin
- Marketing
- Finance
- Sales 95
- Sales 96
- Personal
- Employee Profile article
- Sales 94
- Project Plan Second Qtr
- Project Plan First Qtr
- Sales Summary
- Performance Review 1996

2. It is important to develop a sound, organized plan when you manage files and folders. Practice your skills by organizing the following list of names into a coherent and logical hierarchy. Begin by identifying folders. Then in each folder, identify the files you could expect to find in them. Sketch the series of windows containing the folders and files you would display using My Computer. For example, one of the windows might represent the contents of a folder designated for non-work related files.

- Projects
- My Resume
- Recommendation letter
- First Qtr Bulletin
- Marketing
- Finance
- Sales 95
- Sales 96
- Personal
- Employee Profile article
- Sales 94
- Project Plan Second Qtr
- Project Plan First Qtr
- Sales Summary
- Performance Review 1996

3. On your computer's hard drive (at the root of C:), create a folder called My Review Folder. Then using the files on your Work Disk, create the file hierarchy indicated below. Follow these guidelines to create the files you need to place in the correct folders.

1. Create a new file using WordPad that contains a simple list of things to do. Save the file as To Do List.
2. Create two copies of any WordPad files and rename them New WordPad Article and Copy of Article.
3. Copy any Paint file and rename the copy Sample Logo.
4. Copy the To Do List, and rename the copy Important.

After you have placed the files in their correct folders, copy the My Review Folder (and its contents) to your Work Disk. Then on your hard drive, delete the My Review Folder. Using the Recycle Bin icon, restore the file called Important. To remove all your work on the hard drive, delete this file again.

4. To make working with files on a floppy disk easier, create a shortcut to a Windows Explorer window that displays the contents of a disk in the drive that currently contains your Work Disk. (*Hint*: Open Windows Explorer as shown in Figure B-23 and drag the icon representing your floppy drive to the desktop). Next, capture a picture of your desktop (with the new shortcut) onto the Clipboard by pressing the [Prnt Scrn] key (located on the upper-right side of your keyboard). With the picture on the Clipboard, open the Paint program and paste the contents of the Clipboard into the drawing window as shown in Figure B-24. Save the Paint file as My Desktop Picture on your Work Disk. Finally, delete the shortcut.

FIGURE B-22

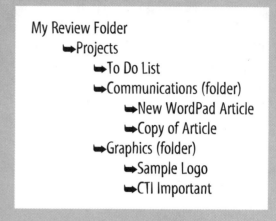

Getting
Started with Access 97

Objectives

- ► **Define database software**
- ► **Start Access 97**
- ► **View the Access window**
- ► **Open a database table**
- ► **Enter and edit records**
- ► **Preview and print a datasheet**
- ► **Get Help**
- ► **Close a database and exit Access**

In this unit, you will learn the basic features of Access, a popular database program, and the various components of a database. You will also learn how to use different elements of the Access window, and how to enter and edit records in a table. Finally, you will learn to use the extensive on-line Help system available in Access. ◢ Michael Belmont is the Travel Division manager at Nomad Ltd, an outdoor gear and adventure travel company. Recently, Nomad switched to Access from a paper-based system for storing and maintaining customer records. Michael will use Access to maintain customer information for Nomad.

Defining Database Software

Access is a database program that runs in the Windows environment. A **database** is a collection of data related to a particular topic or purpose (for example, customer data). Information in a database is organized into **fields**, or categories, such as customer name. A group of related fields, such as all the information on a particular customer, is called a **record**. A collection of related records is called a **table**. A database, specifically a **relational database**, is a collection of one or more related tables that can share information. Figure A-1 shows the structure of a database. Traditionally, businesses kept track of customer information using index cards, as illustrated in Figure A-2. However, with an electronic database, like Access, businesses can store, retrieve, and manipulate data more quickly and easily.

With database software Michael Belmont can:

Enter data quickly and easily

With Access, Michael can enter information on Nomad's customers faster and more accurately than he could using the paper-based method. He can enter data using screen **forms**, which contain **controls** such as check boxes, list boxes, and option buttons, to facilitate data entry. Figure A-3 shows customer information in an Access form.

Organize records in different ways

Michael can review his data sorted by any field, and see records that meet specific criteria by filtering the data. After Michael specifies a sort order, Access automatically keeps records organized, regardless of the order in which they are entered.

Locate specific records quickly

By creating a **query**, a definition of the records he wants to find, Michael can instruct Access to locate the record or records that meet certain conditions. A query can be saved for future use.

Eliminate duplicate data

Access ensures that each record is unique by assigning a **primary key** field to each table. It is not possible for two records in a table to have the same data in their primary key field. Using the paper system, Michael could have duplicate customer records if he forgot that an index card already existed for a particular customer.

Create relationships among tables in a database

Access is a relational database, which allows information within its tables to be shared. This means that Michael needs to enter a customer name only once and it will be referenced in other tables in Nomad's database.

Create reports

Generating professional reports is easy with Access. Michael can produce reports to illustrate different relationships among the data and share these reports with other Nomad employees.

Change the appearance of information

Access provides powerful features for enhancing table data and creating charts so that information is visually appealing and easy to understand.

FIGURE A-1: Structure of a database

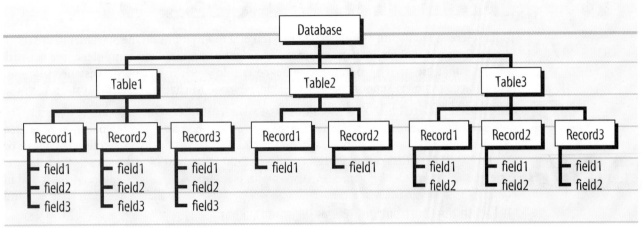

FIGURE A-2: Customer information on an index card

Ginny Braithwaite
3 Which Way, Apt. 2
Salem, MA 01970
(508) 555-7262

Bike tour-Road bike
Loved our ad; thinks Nomad is a wonderfully run company.
She loves our environmentally-friendly attitude!

FIGURE A-3: Customer information in an Access form

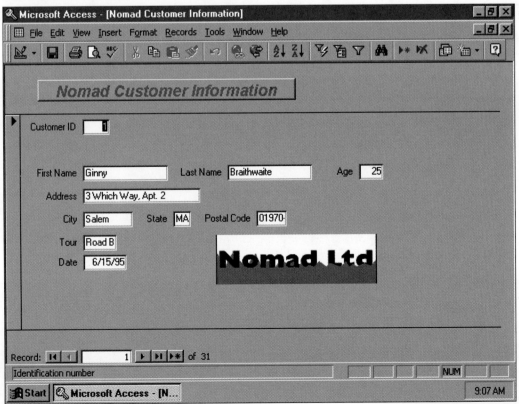

Access 97

Starting Access 97

To start Access, you use the Windows 95 taskbar. Point to Programs on the Start menu, then click Microsoft Access. A slightly different procedure might be required for computers on a network and those that use utility programs to enhance Windows 95. If you need assistance, ask your instructor or technical support person for help. ◢◣◣ Michael first needs to start Access so that he can begin to learn how to use it.

1. **Locate the Start button** [Start] **on the taskbar**
   The Start button is on the left side of the taskbar and is used to start, or **launch**, programs on your computer.

2. **Click the Start button** [Start]
   Microsoft Access is located in the Programs group—located in the Start menu.

3. **Point to Programs**
   All the programs, or applications, found on your computer can be found in this area of the Start menu.
   Microsoft Access appears in the Program list as shown in Figure A-4.

Trouble?

If you can't locate Microsoft Access in the Programs list, point to Microsoft Office, then click Microsoft Access to start Access.

4. **Click Microsoft Access**
   Access opens and displays the Access window. A Microsoft Access dialog box opens in which you select whether to open a new or existing database. For now, you just want to view the Access window.

5. **Click Cancel**
   The dialog box closes and a blank Access window appears. In the next lesson, you will familiarize yourself with the elements of the Access window.

If you had a previous installation of
Office on your computer, your screen
may contain the Office 97 shortcut bar.

FIGURE A-4: Microsoft Access program selected

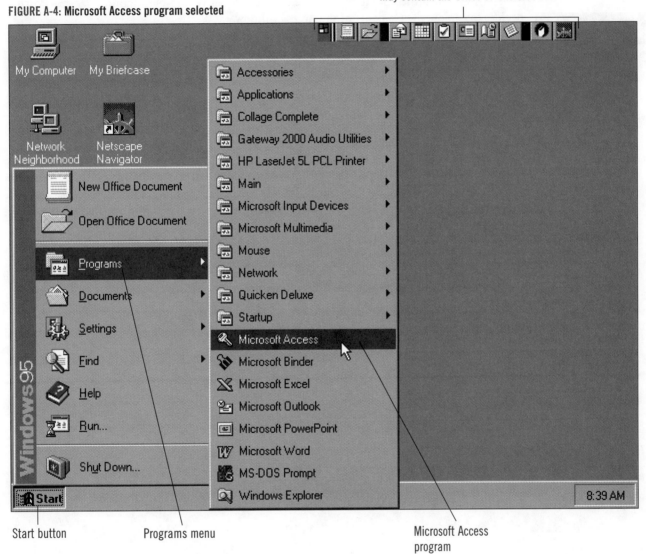

Start button   Programs menu   Microsoft Access
                                                                 program

Viewing the Access Window

When you start Access, the screen displays the **startup window**, the area from which you carry out all database operations. The Access window contains many elements that help you enter and manipulate the information in your database. Some of these elements, which are described in Table A-1 and identified in Figure A-5, are common to all Windows programs. ⬤➤⬤ Michael decides to explore the elements of the Access window.

Steps

Trouble?

All lessons from this point on assume you have Access running. If you need help, refer to the previous lesson, "Starting Access 97," or ask your technical support person or instructor for assistance.

1. **Click the Maximize button** 🔲, if the Access window does not fill the screen

2. **Look at each of the elements shown in Figure A-5**
   You browse through the commands in the File menu.

3. **Click File on the menu bar**
   The File menu opens, as shown in Figure A-6. The File menu has commands for opening a new or existing database, saving a database in a variety of formats, and printing. At the bottom of the File menu, the four most recently opened databases are listed. Because there are so many components in a database, menu commands vary depending on which database element is currently in use.

4. **Press [Esc] twice to close the File menu**
   Pressing [Esc] once closes the File menu, but File on the menu bar is still highlighted. Pressing [Esc] the second time deselects the menu name.

5. **Review the Database toolbar to see what commands are available**
   Many of the buttons on this toolbar can be found within commands on the File menu, and the remaining buttons can be found in other menu commands.

TABLE A-1: Elements of the Access window

element	description
Menu bar	Contains menus used in Access
Startup window	Area from which database operations take place
Status bar	Displays messages regarding operations and displays descriptions of toolbar buttons
Title bar	Contains program and filename of active database
Database toolbar	Contains buttons for commonly performed tasks

CLUES TO USE

Finding out about buttons and menu commands

If you don't know what a toolbar button does, read its ToolTip—its name—by placing your mouse pointer over its button face. Even though a button is dimmed and not active in a certain window, you can still access its ToolTip.

FIGURE A-5: Access window

Title bar

Menu bar

Database toolbar

Startup window

Status bar

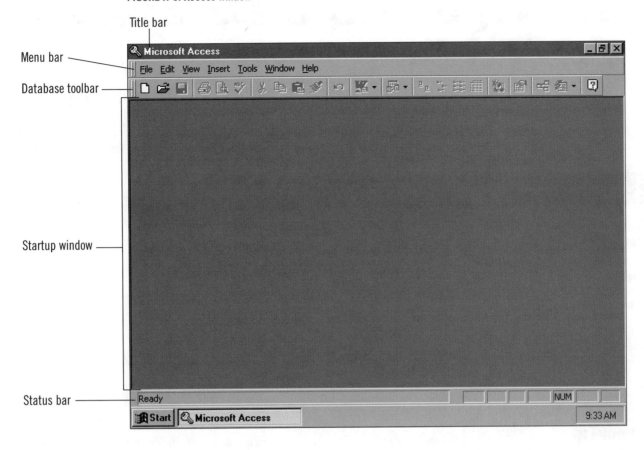

FIGURE A-6: File menu in startup window

Recently opened
databases are
listed at the bottom
of this menu; your
file list may differ

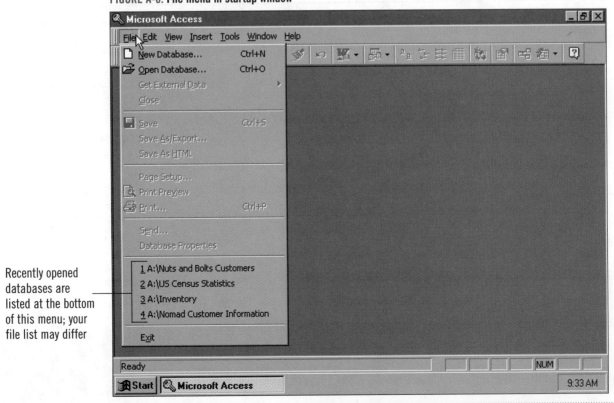

Opening a Database Table

After you open a database, Access displays the database window. The **database window** provides access to all objects in the database. Table A-2 describes the objects—such as tables, forms, and reports—that help you use the information in a database. A database **table** is a collection of related records within a database; a single database can contain multiple tables. Michael wants to open a database and review the table containing information about Nomad's products to see how it is structured.

Steps

QuickTip

Make a copy of your Student Disk before you use it.

1. **Place your Student Disk in the appropriate drive**
   To complete the units in this book, you need a Student Disk. See your instructor for a copy of the Student Disk, if you do not already have one.

2. **Click the Open Database button [icon] on the Database toolbar**
   Access displays the Open Database dialog box. Depending on the databases stored on your disk, your dialog box might look slightly different from the one shown in Figure A-7.

3. **Click the Look in list arrow, then click the drive that contains your Student Disk**
   A list of the files on your Student Disk appears in the Look in list box.

4. **In the File name list box, click Inventory if it's not already selected**

QuickTip

To open a database file quickly, you can double-click the filename in the File name list box of the Open dialog box.

5. **Click Open**
   The Database window for the file Inventory opens, as shown in Figure A-8. The top of the Database window contains the **object buttons** for the Access database objects (which are described in Table A-2). Each object button appears on its own **tab**. The Tables tab is currently the front-most tab in the dialog box. The window lists the tables in the selected database (in this case, the Inventory database contains only one table, Products). The command buttons at the right side of the window allow you to open an existing table, design your own table, or create a new table. You want to open the Products table, which is already selected.

6. **Click Open**
   A window for the Products table opens. The table contains information for 17 Nomad products. Each row is a record and the information is organized by fields arranged in columns.

TABLE A-2: Database objects

object	description
Table	Stores related data in rows (records) and columns (fields)
Query	Asks a question of data in a table; used to find qualifying records
Form	Displays table data in a layout of fields on the screen
Report	Provides printed information from a table, which can include calculations
Macro	Automates database tasks, which can be reduced to a single command
Module	Automates complex tasks using a built-in programming language

FIGURE A-7: Open dialog box

Your list of filenames might be different

Click to display list of available storage areas

Open dialog box toolbar

Click to open selected file

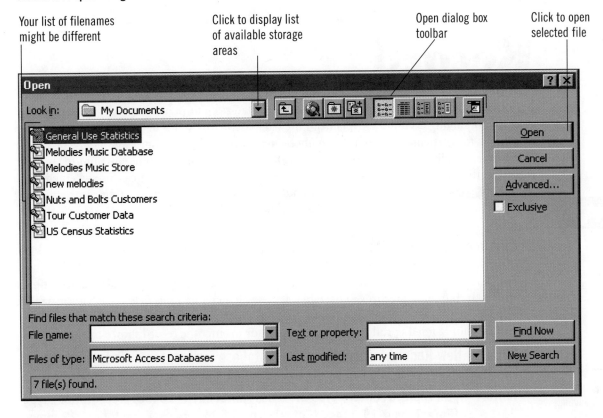

FIGURE A-8: Database window

Tables list box

Object button tabs

Command buttons allow you to open, design, or create a table

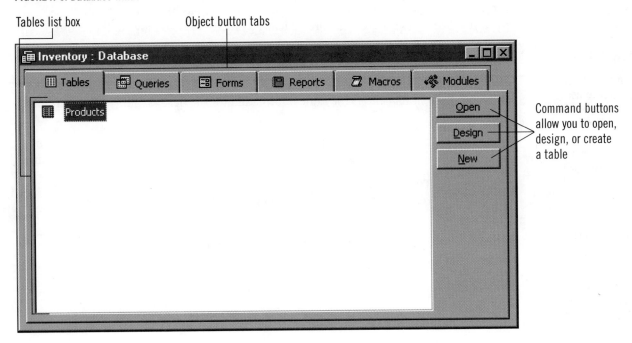

Entering and Editing Records

Data is entered in the datasheet. A **datasheet** is a grid which contains all the records in a table. Each record is contained in a row. Field names are listed as column headings. Careful data entry is vital to obtaining accurate reports from the database. If you enter data carelessly, the results of searches for particular information might be incorrect. You can change the contents of a field at any time. To edit a field, you first click in the field, select the information you want to change, then type the corrections. Table A-3 lists several keyboard shortcuts you can use when editing records. Michael is now ready to add a new record and edit existing records in the Products table. First, he will maximize the Datasheet window.

Steps

1. **Click the Maximize button in the Datasheet window title bar**
   The word "AutoNumber" appears below the last record in the Product ID field, as shown in Figure A-9. This is the primary key assigned by Access for this table. The **AutoNumber field** counts the number of records in the table. Access will increment this field by one to create the primary key data for your new record. The Product Num column contains identification numbers for Nomad's products. Now you are ready to enter the record shown in Figure A-10.

QuickTip

When you are entering data in a table, you can advance to the next field for that record by pressing either [Enter] or [Tab].

2. **Click the New Record button** ▶* **on the Database toolbar, press [Enter] to move to the Product Num field, type 11436, press [Enter], type Shimano Dirt Pirates, press [Enter], type 11, press [Enter], type 27, press [Enter], type 46483, press [Enter], type 24, press [Enter], type 10, press [Enter], type 71.25, press [Enter], type 25, press [Enter], type 15, press [Enter], type Each, then press [Enter]**
   Record number 18 for the product Shimano Dirt Pirates has been entered.
   Next, you'll correct an error in record 12 using a function key to move to the record.

3. **Double-click in the Units field for record 12**
   The contents of the Units field in record 12 is selected. This field should have the same contents as the field above it. You can either type the correct entry in the field, or use a keyboard shortcut that enters the same information for the field as in the previous record.

Trouble?

If you cannot see the column in the datasheet window, scroll to the right or left as needed to display the field you need. If you cannot see the row, scroll up or down to display the record you need.

4. **Press [Ctrl][']**
   The entry changes from 'Pair' to 'Each'. Next, you'll change the Reorder Level in the same record.

5. **Press [←] twice, then type 29**
   Compare your datasheet to Figure A-11. You save the changes made in the table.

QuickTip

When you switch views, from Datasheet to Design View, or when you close the table, any changes to the table are automatically saved.

6. **Click the Save button** 🖫
   When you modify the structure of a table or when you edit records, you need to save the table.

CLUES TO USE

Moving table columns

You can reorganize the columns in a table by moving them from one location to another. To move a column, click its field name so that the entire column is selected, then drag the pointer to the column's new location. As you drag, the mouse pointer changes to ⬚ . A heavy vertical line represents the new location. Release the mouse button when you have correctly positioned the column.

FIGURE A-9: Entering a record in a table

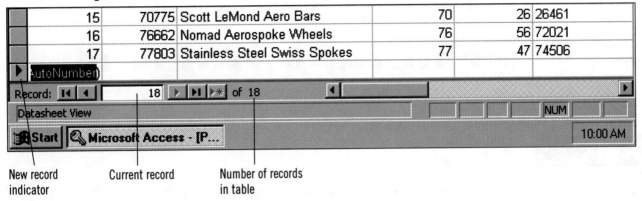

	15	70775	Scott LeMond Aero Bars	70	26	26461
	16	76662	Nomad Aerospoke Wheels	76	56	72021
	17	77803	Stainless Steel Swiss Spokes	77	47	74506
▶	AutoNumber					

Record: ◄◄ ◄ 18 ► ►◄ ►* of 18   ◄

Datasheet View   NUM

🔣 Start | 🔍 Microsoft Access - [P...   10:00 AM

New record   Current record   Number of records
indicator   in table

FIGURE A-10: Data in record 18

Product ID	Product Num	Product Name	Category ID	Supplier ID	Serial Number	Units in Stock	Units on Order	Unit Price	Reorder Level	Reorder Amount	Units	Disc. Status
18	11436	Shimano Dirt Pirates	11	27	46483	24	10	71.25	25	15	Each	No

TABLE A-3: Keyboard shortcuts in table

shortcut key	action
[F5]	Move to a specific record
[F6]	Move between window sections
[F7]	Open the Spelling dialog box
[Ctrl][']	Insert the value from the same field in the previous record
[Ctrl][;]	Insert the current date
[Ctrl][=]	Move to the first blank record
[Esc]	Undo changes in the current field or record
[Shift][Enter]	Save the current record

FIGURE A-11: Edited record

	15	0	$12.00	12	20	Pair	No
	13	12	$12.00	10	15	Pair	No
	25	0	$200.00	20	30	Each	No
	14	20	$72.00	17	20	Each	No
✎	27	30	$2.00	29	30	Each	No
	23	40	$2.00	50	40	Each	No
	27	40	$2.00	30	40	Each	No
	42	0	$32.00	40	30	Each	No
	30	0	$200.00	15	30	Each	No
	35	20	$2.25	40	20	Box	No
	24	10	$71.25	25	15	Each	No

Record: ◄◄ ◄ 12 ► ►◄ ►* of 18   ◄

Level of Product at which to Reorder   NUM

🔣 Start | 🔍 Microsoft Access - [P...   10:48 AM

Field modified to
match entry in
previous record

Edit record   Corrected field
indicator   entry

Previewing and Printing a Datasheet

After entering and editing the records in a table, you can print the datasheet to obtain a hard copy of the table data. Before printing, it's a good idea to preview the datasheet to see how it will look when printed and, if necessary, to make any adjustments to margins, page orientation, and so on. Michael is ready to preview and print the datasheet.

Steps

1. **Click the Print Preview button 🔍 on the Database toolbar**
   The datasheet appears on a miniature page in the Print Preview window, as shown in Figure A-12, and the Print Preview toolbar appears. You decide to use the Magnifier pointer to see how the datasheet looks when magnified.

2. **Click the Magnifier pointer ⊕ anywhere in the miniature datasheet**
   A magnified version of the datasheet appears. You notice that most of the fields seem to be cut off the page. You return the datasheet to its original appearance.

3. **Click ⊕ anywhere in the magnified datasheet**
   You decide to print in landscape mode in order to see more fields on each page.

4. **Click File on the menu bar, then click Page Setup**
   The Page Setup dialog box opens. This dialog box provides options for the way text looks on the page.

5. **Click the Page tab, click the Landscape radio button, as shown in Figure A-13, then click OK**
   Now you can see more of the fields for the table that will print on a page.

6. **Click File on the menu bar, then click Print**
   The Print dialog box as shown in Figure A-15 opens, giving you several options described in Table A-4. You do not have to make any changes to this dialog box.

7. **Click OK to print the datasheet, then click Close on the Print Preview toolbar to return to the datasheet**
   With the datasheet printed, you are ready to save the table.

8. **Click the Save button 💾 on the Standard toolbar**

> **QuickTip**
>
> Click the Print button 🖨 to print one copy of the entire datasheet using the default settings without making selections from the Print dialog box.

TABLE A-4: Print dialog box options

option	description
Printer	Displays the name of the selected printer and print connection
Print Range	Specifies all pages, certain pages, a range of pages to print, or selected records
Copies	Specifies the number of copies to print and whether to collate the copies
Print to File	Prints a document to an encapsulated PostScript file instead of a printer
Margins	Adjusts the left, right, top, and bottom margins (available through the Setup option)
Orientation	Specifies Portrait (the default) or Landscape paper (available through the Properties option)

FIGURE A-12: **Datasheet in Print Preview (portrait orientation)**

Close button   Magnifier pointer

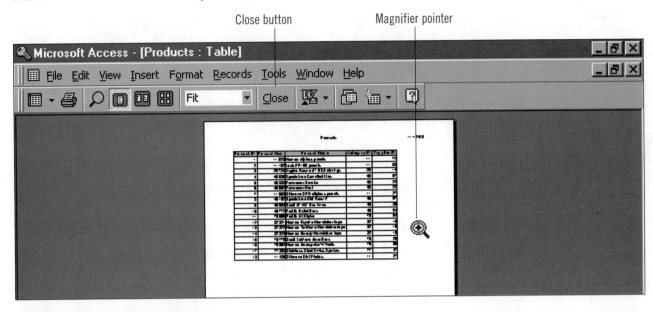

FIGURE A-13: **Page Setup dialog box**

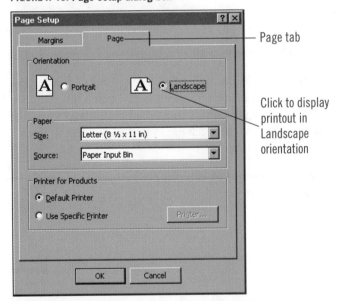

Page tab

Click to display
printout in
Landscape
orientation

FIGURE A-14: **Print dialog box**

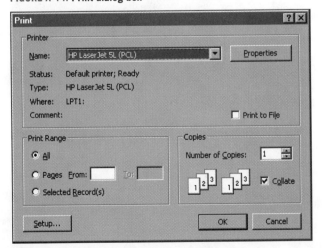

Getting Help

Access provides an extensive on-line Help system that gives you immediate access to definitions, explanations, and useful tips. The **Office Assistant** provides this information using a question and answer format. As you are working, the Office Assistant provides tips—indicated by a light bulb you can click—in response to your own working habits. Help appears in a separate window that you can resize and refer to as you work. You can press the [F1] key at any time to get immediate help. Michael wants to find information on moving through a database table, and he decides to use the Access Help Assistant to do so. Michael decides to use the animated Office Assistant to learn more about the database window.

1. **If the Office Assistant is not already displayed, click the Office Assistant button** **on the Standard toolbar**
   The Office Assistant lets you get information using a question and answer format.

2. **If the Office Assistant is displayed, click its window to activate the query box**
   You want information on how to navigate a datasheet.

3. **Type How do I move between records in a datasheet?**
   See Figure A-16. After you ask a question, the Office Assistant displays relevant topics from which you can choose.

4. **Click Search**
   The Office Assistant displays several topics related to your question, shown in Figure A-17.

5. **Click Moving between records using navigation buttons in Datasheet or Form view**
   The help window, shown in Figure A-18, can be printed by clicking the Options button, then clicking Print Topic. When you point to text that appears as a green underlined topic, the shape of the mouse pointer changes to 🖑. You can click green underlined text to open a dialog box to get more information about that topic.

QuickTip

You can close the Office Assistant at any time by clicking its Close button ☒.

6. **Click the Close button** ☒ **on the Help dialog box title bar**
   The Help window closes and you return to your worksheet.

CLUES TO USE

Changing the Office Assistant

The default Office Assistant is Clippit, but there are 8 others from which you can choose. To change the appearance of the Office Assistant, right-click the Office Assistant window, then select Choose Assistant. Click the Gallery tab, click the Back and Next buttons until you find an Assistant you want to use, then click OK. (You may need your Microsoft Office 97 CD to change Office Assistants.) Each Office Assistant makes its own unique sounds and can be animated by right-clicking its window and selecting Animate! See Figure A-15.

FIGURE A-15: Office Assistant dialog box

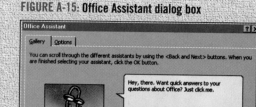

FIGURE A-16: Office Assistant

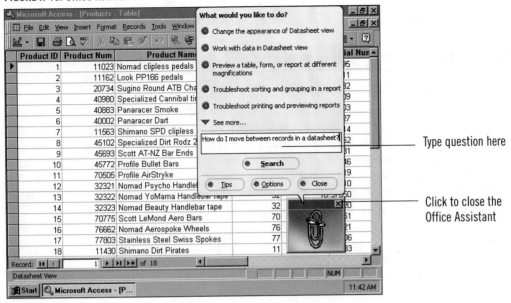

Type question here

Click to close the
Office Assistant

FIGURE A-17: Relevant Help Assistant Topics

Click a topic button

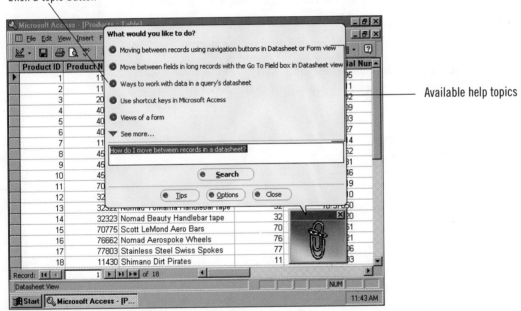

Available help topics

FIGURE A-18: Help window showing navigation buttons

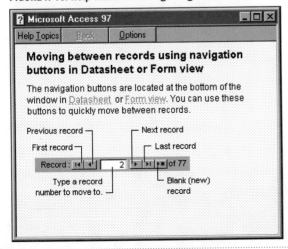

Access 97

Closing a Database and Exiting Access

When you have finished working in a database, you need to close the object you were working in, such as a table, and then close the database. Unlike other programs you might be familiar with, you don't have to save a table before you close it; Access updates your changes automatically. To close a table, or a database click Close on the File menu. When you have completed all your work in Access, you need to exit the program by clicking Exit on the File menu. Exiting closes all open objects. Table A-5 lists the different ways of exiting Access. ◀━━━ Michael has finished exploring Access for now. He needs to close the Products table and the Inventory database, then exit Access. Michael begins by closing the Products table.

Steps 1 2 3 4

1. **Click File on the menu bar, as shown in Figure A-19, then click Close**
Now you need to close the Inventory database.

2. **Click File on the menu bar**
The File menu opens and displays a list of commands. Notice that this Database File menu has different commands than the File menu in the Table window.

3. **Click Close**
Access closes the Database window and displays the startup window.

4. **Click File on the menu bar, then click Exit**
The Access program closes, and you return to the desktop.

QuickTip

Make sure you always properly end your Access session by using the steps in this unit. Improper exit procedures can result in corruption of your data files.

FIGURE A-19:

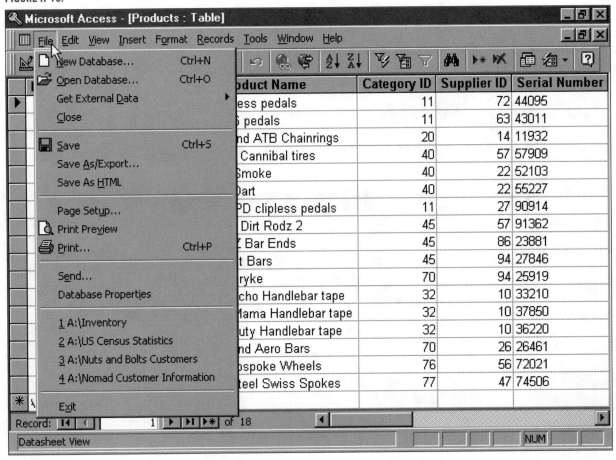

TABLE A-5: Ways to exit Access

method	key or command
Menu	Choose Exit from the File menu
Keyboard	Press [Alt][F4]
Mouse	Double-click the program control menu box

Practice

► Concepts Review

Label each of the elements of the Access window shown in Figure A-20.

FIGURE A-20

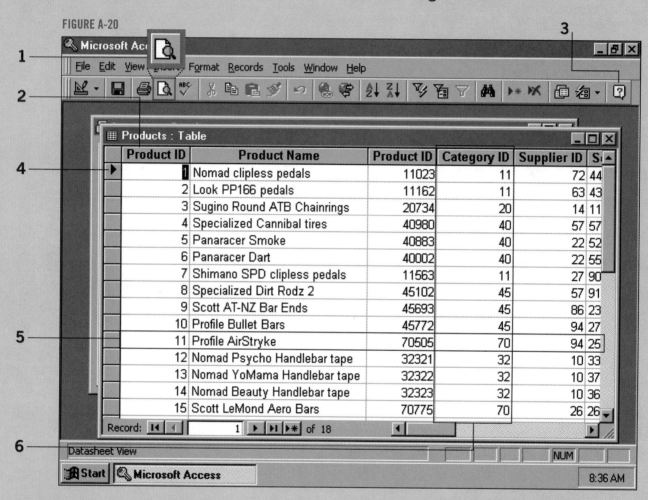

Match each of the following terms with the statement that describes its function.

7. Database window
8. Table
9. Database
10. Office Assistant
11. Shortcut keys

a. A collection of data related to a particular topic or purpose
b. Combination of keys resulting in the execution of a command
c. Area that contains all database objects
d. Stores related data in rows and columns
e. Provides information about Access

Select the best answer from the list of choices.

12. **An electronic database can perform all of the following tasks, *except*:**
    a. Displaying information visually
    b. Calculating data accurately
    c. Planning database objectives
    d. Recalculating updated information

13. **Which of the following is NOT a database?**
    a. Customer information
    b. Interoffice memo
    c. Telephone directory
    d. Dictionary

14. **Which button opens an existing database?**
    a. [button]   b. [button]   c. [button]   d. [button]

15. **Which button opens the Office Assistant?**
    a. [button]   b. [button]   c. [button]   d. [button]

16. **You can get Help in any of the following ways, *except*:**
    a. Clicking Help on the menu bar
    b. Pressing [F1]
    c. Clicking the Help button [button]
    d. Minimizing the Database window

▶ Skills Review

1. Start Access.
a. Make sure your computer is on and Windows is running.
b. Click the Start button, point to Programs, then click Microsoft Access.

2. View the Access Window.
a. Try to identify as many components of the Access window as you can without referring to the unit material.

3. Open a database table.
a. Make sure your Student Disk is in the appropriate disk drive.
b. Click the Open Database button on the Database toolbar.
c. Open the database named US Census Statistics from your Student Disk.
d. Click the object tabs in the Database window to see the contents of each object.
e. Open the Statistical Data table.

4. Enter and edit records.
a. Click the New Record button.
b. Enter the following record. State: Virginia, Region: South Atlantic, Year: 1991, Marriages: 68,771.
c. Change the year in record 6 to 1991.

5. Preview and print a datasheet.
a. Click the Print Preview button on the Database toolbar to display the datasheet in the Print Preview window.
b. After viewing the datasheet, click the Print button on the Print Preview toolbar.
c. After printing, return to the Database window.
d. Save the table.

6. Get Help.
a. Click the Office Assistant button on the Database toolbar.
b. Ask the Office Assistant the following question: "How can I view data?"
c. Click the topic "Ways to work with data in a table's datasheet."
d. Click the Options button, click Print Topic, then click OK.
e. Click the Close button on the Help window.
f. Click the Close button on the Office Assistant.

7. Close a database and exit Access.
a. Click File on the menu bar, then click Close to close the "Statistical Data" table.
b. Click File on the menu bar, then click Close to close the "US Census Statistics" database file.
c. Click File on the menu bar, then click Exit to exit Access.

▶ Independent Challenges

1. Ten examples of databases are given below. Using each of these examples, write down one sample record for each database and describe the fields you would expect to find in each.

- Telephone directory
- College course offerings
- Restaurant menu
- Cookbook
- Movie listing
- Encyclopedia
- Shopping catalog
- Corporate inventory
- Party guest list
- Members of the House of Representatives

2. Access provides online Help that explains procedures and gives you examples and demos. Help covers such elements as the Database window, the status bar, toolbar buttons, dialog boxes, and Access commands and options. Start Access then explore online Help by clicking the Office Assistant button. Ask the Office Assistant, "What is a database?" Find out about databases—what they are and how they work. Print out information you find on this topic.

FIGURE A-21

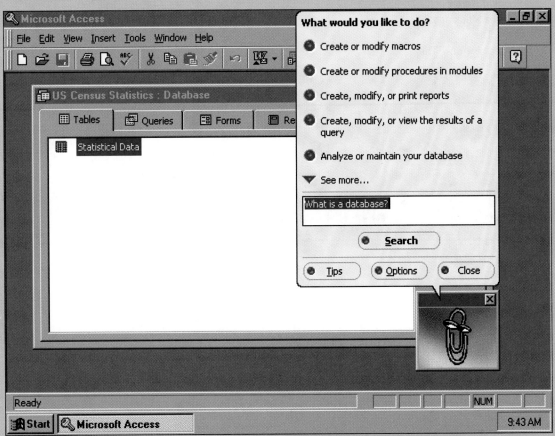

3. To become more accomplished at using databases, you've decided it would be fun to make a list of your favorite films. A database called Favorite Movies has been started. All you need to do is supply information about your favorite films.

To complete this independent challenge:

1. Open the database called Favorite Movies on your Student Disk.
2. Open the Film Favorites table.
3. Add at least ten entries. The table includes fields for up to 3 co-stars. If you don't know the year the film was released, leave the field blank, or estimate the year.
4. Preview the table, then print it in landscape mode. Submit your finished publication.

FIGURE A-22

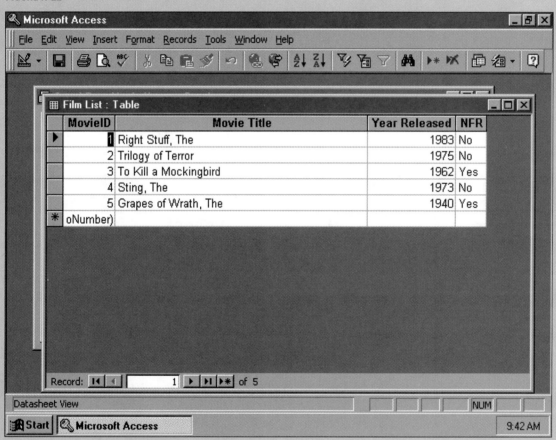

4. Databases on the World Wide Web can be used to retrieve current and historical information. You work for a prestigious socialite who is interested in film preservation. She has purchased The SpeakEasy move theater where she intends to hold many festivals featuring historically important films. Using the World Wide Web, find out about the National Film Registry, which is maintained by the Library of Congress, and begin compiling films for the first festival.

To complete this independent challenge:

1. Log on to the Internet and use your browser to go to http://www.course.com. From there, click the link Student On Line Companions, then click the Microsoft Office 97 Professional Edition—Illustrated: A First Course page, then click the Access link for Unit A.
2. Use the following site to compile your data, The National Film Registry [http://1cweb.loc.gov/film/].
3. Print the National Film Registry's fact sheet.
4. Find out its current membership.
5. Using the list of films, find all the films made in the 1950's.
6. Open the SpeakEasy Movie House database on your Student Disk.
7. Open the Film List table.
8. Enter these films in the Film List table.
9. Save the table.
10. Preview and print the datasheet.
11. Hand in a printout of your work.

► Visual Workshop

Modify the existing Customers table in the Corporate Customers database on your Student Disk, then print the datasheet.

FIGURE A-23

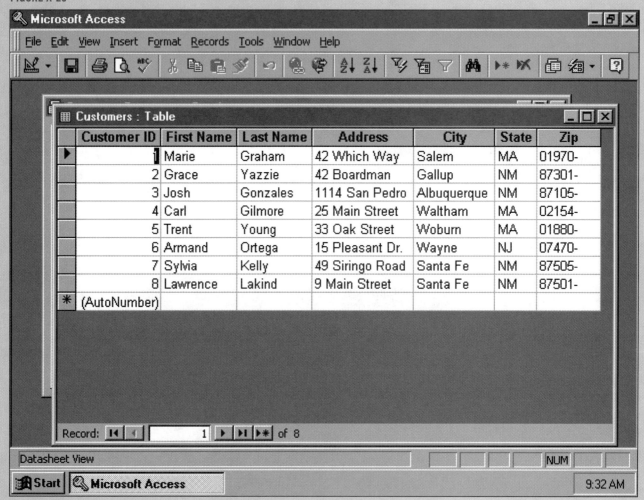

Creating
and Managing Data

Objectives

- ► **Plan a database**
- ► **Create a table**
- ► **Modify a table**
- ► **Find records**
- ► **Sort a table**
- ► **Filter a table**
- ► **Create a simple query**
- ► **Create a complex query**

Now that you are familiar with some of the basic Access features, you are ready to plan and build your own database. When you build a database, you create one or more tables containing the fields that hold the data. After you create a database, you can save, and manage the data within it. In this unit, you will learn how to find and organize data to display the results you want. You will also learn techniques for retrieving information from a table based on specified criteria. ━ Michael wants to build and maintain a database containing information about all Nomad customers who have booked tours since 1991. The information in the database will be useful when Michael budgets for the future, plans new tours, and prepares the company's Annual Report.

Access 97

Planning a Database

Before you start entering records in the database, you need to identify the goal of the database and plan how you want data stored in it. The planning stage is when you decide how many tables the database will include and what data will be stored in each table. Although you can modify a table at any time, adding a new field after records have been entered means additional work. It's impossible to plan for all potential uses of a database, but any up-front planning makes the process go more smoothly. Michael has done some preliminary planning on how the database can be used, but he knows from experience that other Nomad employees might have additional uses for the same customer information. Michael uses the following guidelines to plan his database:

CourseHelp

The camera icon indicates there is CourseHelp available with this lesson. Click the Start button, point to Programs, point to CourseHelp, then click Access 97 Illustrated. Choose the CourseHelp that corresponds to this lesson.

1. Determine the purpose of the database and give it a meaningful name

You need to store information on customers who have taken a Nomad tour. You name the database "Tour Customers," and name the table containing the customer data "Customers." You decide, for now, that the database will contain only one table because all the necessary customer information can be stored there.

2. Determine the results, called **output**, that you want to see, using the information stored in the database

You need to sort the information in a variety of ways: alphabetically by tour name, by tour date to gauge effective scheduling dates, and by postal code for promotional mailings. You will also need to create specialized lists of customers, such as customers who took a bike tour since 1991.

3. Collect all the information, called **input**, that will produce the results you want to see, talking to all the possible database users for additional ideas that might enhance the design

You think the current customer information form, shown in Figure B-1, is a good basis for your database table. The form provides most of the information Nomad wants to store in the database for each customer, making it a good starting point. After talking with the marketing director about targeting tours to specific age groups, you decide to add an Age field to your table.

4. Sketch the structure of the table, including each field's **data type**

Using all the information on the original customer information form, you plan each field, the type of data each field contains (such as whether the field contains text or values to be used in calculations), and a brief description of each field's purpose. Figure B-2 is a sketch of the Customers table, which has several new fields not included in the original customer information form.

QuickTip

Multiple database tables can be linked to one another; their information can be shared and queried.

FIGURE B-1: Original customer information form

Nomad Ltd

Customer Information Form

Customer Name:	Ginny Braithwaite
	3 Which Way, Apt. 2
	Salem, MA 01970
Tour:	Road Bike
Date:	June 15, 1998

FIGURE B-2: Plan for Customers table

Fields	Data type	Description
CustomerID	Unique number for each record	Identifies each record
FirstName	Text	Customer's first name (+ optional middle initial)
LastName	Text	Customer's last name
Address	Text	Customer's street address
City	Text	Customer's city
State	Text	Customer's state
PostalCode	Text	Customer's zip code
Tour	Text	Type of tour
Date	Date/Time	Starting date of tour
Age	Number	Customer's age

Creating a backup

The information in your database is very important. You should protect your investment of time spent planning the database and entering data in it by creating backup copies of the database file. The database file, which has the extension .MDB, should be copied to a disk or tape on a daily or weekly basis.

Creating a Table

After planning the structure of the database, the next step is to create the database file, which contains all the objects such as tables, forms, reports, and queries that will be used to enter and manipulate the data. When you create a database, you assign it a name. Once the file is created, you are ready to create the table (or tables) in the database. Access offers several methods for creating a table. It is easy to use the Access **Table Wizard**, which guides you through the process of creating a simple table, prompting you to choose the fields and options for your table. With his plan complete, Michael is ready to create the Tour Customers database file; he uses the Table Wizard to create his Customers table.

1. Start Access, click the **Blank Database option button** in the Create a New Database Using section of the dialog box, then click **OK**
   The File New Database dialog box opens.

QuickTip

If Access is already running, you can click the New Database button 🗋 on the Database toolbar to create a database.

2. Type **Tour Customers** in the File name text box, insert your Student Disk in the disk drive, click the **Save in list arrow**, click the appropriate drive, then click **Create**
   The Tour Customers database file is saved on your Student Disk. The Database window opens, displaying the new, empty database, as shown in Figure B-3.

3. In the Tour Customers: Database window, verify that the **Tables tab** is selected, then click **New**
   The New Table dialog box opens. You will use the Table Wizard to create the new table.

4. Click **Table Wizard**, then click **OK**
   The Table Wizard dialog box opens. The Table Wizard offers 25 business and 20 personal sample tables from which you can select sample fields. You will choose fields from the Customers sample table to include in your Customers table.

5. Make sure the **Business option button** is selected, click **Customers** in the Sample Tables list box, click **CustomerID** in the Sample Fields list box, then click the **Single Field button** ⟩
   The CustomerID field is included in the Fields in my new table box. You proceed to add all the necessary fields for the table.

6. Repeat Step 5 to enter the following fields in the new table: **ContactFirstName, ContactLastName, BillingAddress, City, StateOrProvince,** and **PostalCode**
   Compare your Table Wizard dialog box to Figure B-4. Because you will only be entering states (not provinces) you decide to rename that field.

Trouble?

If you inadvertently add the wrong sample field while in the first Table Wizard dialog box, select the field then click the Remove Field button ⟨ .

7. Click **StateOrProvince** in the Fields in my new table box, click **Rename Field**, type **State**, then click **OK**

8. Click **Next**
   The second Table Wizard dialog box opens. You intended to name the table "Customers," which Access suggests in this dialog box. You also want Access to set the **primary key**, a field that qualifies each record as unique. If you do not specify a primary key, Access will assign one for you.

9. Make sure the "Yes" option button is selected, click **Next**, click the **Modify the table design option button**, shown in Figure B-5, then click **Finish**
   The table opens in Design view, which allows you to add, delete, or modify the table's structure.

FIGURE B-3: Tour Customers database window

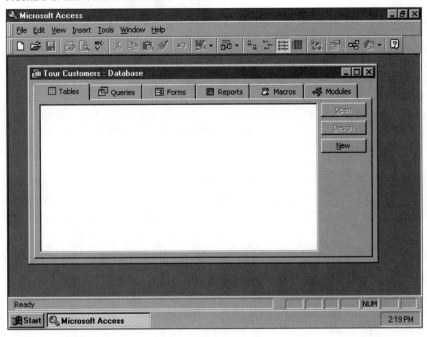

FIGURE B-4: Completed Fields in my new table list

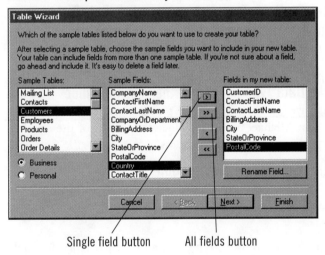

Single field button   All fields button

FIGURE B-5: Third Table Wizard dialog box

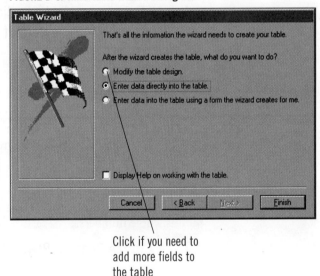

Click if you need to
add more fields to
the table

Creating a table manually

You can create a table manually, without using the Table Wizard, by clicking the New Table button in the New Table dialog box; you create the field names and their properties as you need them to store your specific data. Field names can contain up to 64 characters including letters, numbers, spaces, and some special characters. You might want to create a table manually if your application is unique or your fields are unusual.

Modifying a Table

After creating a table, you can modify it in **Design view**. Design view allows you to modify the structure of a table by adding and deleting fields, and adding **field descriptions** which clarify the purpose or function of a field and appear in the status bar when you enter data. You can also define other **field properties**, such as the number of decimal places in a number field.  Using the Table Wizard, Michael was able to add all but three of the fields in his table. Now, in Design view, he'll add the three remaining fields, add field descriptions, and modify certain field properties.

1. **Make sure the "Customers" table is open in Design view, as shown in Figure B-6**
Notice the row selectors at the left edge of the table. The selectors can contain **indicators**, such as the primary key indicator. You begin by adding a new field, "Tour," in the first available blank row. This field will identify the type of tour taken by each Nomad customer.

2. **Scroll the window until the first blank row is visible, click in the Field Name box in this row (under PostalCode), type Tour, then press [Enter]**
The Data Type field becomes highlighted and displays the word "Text." The Tour field will contain text information, so you accept the suggested data type and enter a description for the field. See Table B-1 for a description of the available data types.

3. **Press [Enter], type Type of tour in the Description column, then press [Enter]**
The next field Michael enters is a date field, which will contain the date the tour was taken. A date field has a data type of Date/Time.

4. **Type Date, press [Enter], click the Data Type list arrow, click Date/Time, press [Enter], type Starting date of tour in the Description column, then press [Enter]**
The last field you must enter is the Age field. This field will contain the age of the tour participant.

5. **Type Age, press [Enter], click the Data Type list arrow, then click Number**
By default, number fields are displayed with two decimal places. Because this is not an appropriate format for a person's age, Michael needs to change the format of the number. Use [F6] to move to the Field Properties section of the window.

6. **Press [F6] to switch panes to the Field Properties section**
Currently the Decimal Places box displays the option "Auto," which specifies the default two decimal places. You need to change the number of decimal places so that the ages will appear as whole numbers.

7. **Click in the Decimal Places box, click the list arrow, then click 0 to specify whole numbers**
Next you need to add a description for the Age field you just entered.

8. **Press [F6] to switch panes, press [Enter], then type Enter the Customer's age at the time of the tour in the Description column**
Next you add the descriptions for each of the remaining fields.

Time To
✔ Save
✔ Close

9. **Click in the CustomerID Description box, type Identification number, then click in each of the field name Description boxes and add a description for the six fields as shown in Figure B-7**

FIGURE B-6: Customers Table in Design view

Row selectors —
Primary key indicator —

Field Properties section —

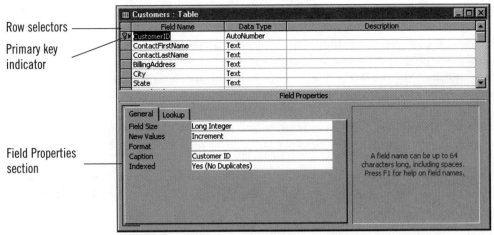

FIGURE B-7: Field descriptions for Customers Table

— Field descriptions

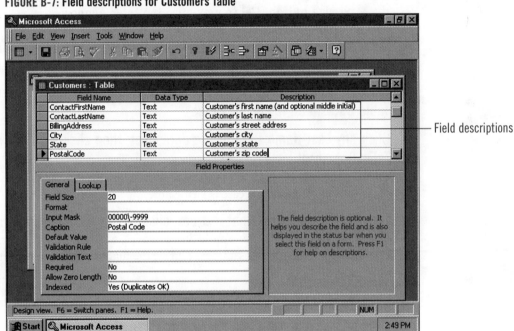

TABLE B-1: Available Data Types

data type	description	data type shortcuts
Text	Text or a combination of text and numbers that don't require calculations	T
Memo	Lengthy text or a combination of text and numbers	M
Number	Numeric data to be used in calculations	N
Date/Time	Date and time values	D
Currency	Currency values and numeric data used in calculations	C
Yes/No	Fields that can contain only one of two values	Y
OLE object	An object (such as a Word document) that is linked or embedded in an Access table	O
AutoNumber	Unique sequential number that Access assigns to each new record; can't be edited	A
Lookup Wizard	Creates a field that allows you to choose a value from another table or from a list of values	L

Finding Records

Finding records in a table is an important database task. Table B-2 lists a variety of keyboard shortcuts used to navigate a table. In addition, you can locate specific records using the datasheet. ~~Michael has been busy entering all his data into the Customers table in the database. He also renamed the field names to take up less room on the data sheet. He wants to locate the record for Carol Smith because her name was entered incorrectly; he needs to change the last name to "Smithers." Then he needs to enter a record for a new customer. Michael's work has been saved for you in the Tour Customer Data file on your Student Disk.

Steps

1. Click the **Open Database button** 📂 on the Database toolbar, click **Tour Customer Data** on your Student Disk, then click **Open**
   Next, open the Customers table and maximize it so it fills the screen.

2. Click the **Tables tab** in the Database window, click **Customers**, click **Open**, then click the **Maximize button** 🔲 to maximize the table window
   Access displays the Customers table, which contains 30 records, as shown in Figure B-8. You will use the Table Datasheet toolbar to change Carol Smith's last name to "Smithers." If the Table Datasheet toolbar is not displayed, continue to Step 3, otherwise skip to Step 4.

3. Click **View** on the menu bar, click **Toolbars** to display the Toolbars dialog box, click **Table Datasheet**, then click **Close**

4. Click any **Last Name field** in the datasheet, then click the **Find button** 🔍 on the Table Datasheet toolbar
   The Find in field dialog box opens, as shown in Figure B-9. By default Access searches the current field, which in this case is Last Name.

5. Type **Smith** in the Find What text box, click **Find Next**, then click **Close**
   Access highlights the name "Smith" in record 11, which is now the current record, for the customer Carol Smith. You can now replace the highlighted name with the correct name.

6. Type **Smithers**
   Next you want to see the last record in the table before you enter the new record.

7. Click **Edit** on the menu bar, click **Go To**, then click **Last**
   The last name of the customer in the last record is selected. Next, you must enter the new record.

Time To
✔ Save

8. Click the **New Record button** ▶* on the Table Datasheet toolbar, press **[Tab]**, then enter the following data in record 31
   Elizabeth Michaels, Mt. Bike, 6/20/98, 57 Beechwood Drive, Wayne, NJ, 07470, 39
   The new record has been added to the table.

TABLE B-2: Keystrokes for navigating a datasheet

keys	actions	keys	actions
[↑], [↓], [←], [→]	Move one field in the direction indicated	[Tab]	Move to next field in current record
[F5]	Move to Record number box on the horizontal scroll bar, then type number of record to go to	[Shift][Tab]	Move to previous field in current record
[Home]	Move to first field in current record	[Ctrl][Home]	Move to first field in first record
[End]	Move to last field in current record	[Ctrl][End]	Move to last field in last record
		[Ctrl][=]	Move to first blank record

FIGURE B-8: Customers table

Table Datasheet toolbar

Customer ID	First Name	Last Name	Tour	Date	Address	City	Sta
1	Ginny	Braithwaite	Road Bike	6/15/98	3 Which Way, Apt. 2	Salem	MA
2	Robin	Spencer	Mt. Bike	9/26/97	293 Serenity Drive	Concord	MA
3	Camilla	Dobbins	Road Bike	6/15/98	486 Intel Circuit	Rio Rancho	NM
4	Pip	Khalsa	Mt. Bike	6/20/98	1100 Vista Road	Santa Fe	NM
5	Kendra	Majors	Bungee	9/20/97	530 Spring Street	Lenox	MA
6	Tasha	Williams	Road Bike	6/15/98	530 Spring Street	Lenox	MA
7	Fred	Gonzales	Mt. Bike	6/15/98	Purgatory Ski Area	Durango	CO
8	John	Black	Road Bike	6/15/98	11 River Road	Brookfield	CT
9	Scott	Owen	Bungee	9/20/97	72 Yankee Way	Brookfield	CT
10	Virginia	Rodarmor	Bungee	9/20/97	123 Main Street	Andover	MA
11	Carol	Smithers	Bungee	9/20/97	123 Elm Street	Acton	MA
12	Crystal	Stevens	Road Bike	6/15/98	The Waterfront Apts.	Salem	MA
13	Luis	Lopez	Mt. Bike	6/20/98	1212 Agua Fria	Santa Fe	NM
14	Maria	Duran	Road Bike	6/15/98	Galvin Highway East	Chicago	IL
15	Salvatore	Wallace	Mt. Bike	6/20/98	100 Westside Ave	Chicago	IL
16	Michael	Nelson	Mt. Bike	9/26/97	229 Route 55	Durango	CO
17	Shawn	Kelly	Bungee	9/20/97	22 Kendall Square	Cambridge	MA
18	Tonia	Dickenson	Road Bike	6/15/98	92 Main Avenue	Durango	CO

Record: |◀ ◀ 1 ▶ ▶| ▶* of 30

Identification number

Navigation bar   Number of current record   Total number of records

Using wildcards in Find

Wildcards are symbols you can use as substitutes for characters in text to find any records matching your entry. Access uses three wildcards: the asterisk (*) represents any group of characters, the question mark (?) stands for any single character, and the pound sign (#) stands for a single number digit. For example, to find any word beginning with S, type "s*" in the Find What text box.

FIGURE B-9: Find in field dialog box

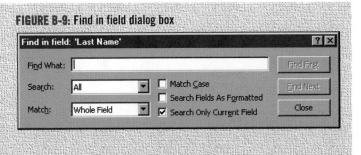

Sorting a Table

The ability to sort information in a table is one of the most powerful features of a database. **Sorting** is an easy way of organizing records according to the contents of a field. For example, you might want to see all records in alphabetical order by last name. You can sort records in **ascending order** (alphabetically from A to Z, numerically from 0 to 9), or in **descending order** (alphabetically from Z to A, numerically from 9 to 0). Michael sorts his table in a variety of ways, depending on the task he needs to perform. His most common tasks require a list sorted in ascending order by tour, and another list sorted in descending order by date.

Steps

1. Position the cursor on the **Tour field column head**, when the pointer looks like ...↓... , click the **Tour field name**
   The Tour column is selected. The table will be sorted by tour. In addition to clicking the Tour field name to select the field, you can also click any record's Tour field.

2. Click the **Sort Ascending button** 🔼 on the Table Datasheet toolbar
   The table is sorted alphabetically in ascending order by tour name, as shown in Figure B-10. You decide to print this sorted table for reference using the default settings.

3. Click the **Print button** 🖨 on the Table Datasheet toolbar
   The sorted datasheet prints. You want to return the table to its original order.

4. Click **Records** on the menu bar, then click **Remove Filter/Sort**
   The table returns to its original order in ascending order by Customer ID. You can also return a table with an AutoNumber field to its original order by sorting that field in ascending order. You decide to sort the records in descending order by the Date field to see the enrollment for each tour.

5. Click the **Date field name** to select the Date column

6. Click the **Sort Descending button** 🔽 on the Table Datasheet toolbar
   The records are sorted from most recent to least recent date, as shown in Figure B-11. The sorted list shows that the mid-June bike tour has a higher enrollment than the tour a week later. You want to print the sorted table.

7. Click the **Print button** 🖨 on the Table Datasheet toolbar
   Next you return the table to its original order.

8. Click **Records** on the menu bar, then click **Remove Filter/Sort**

FIGURE B-10: Table sorted in ascending order by Tour field

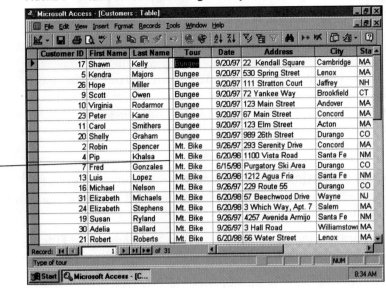

Records sorted by Tour

FIGURE B-11: Table sorted in descending order by Date field

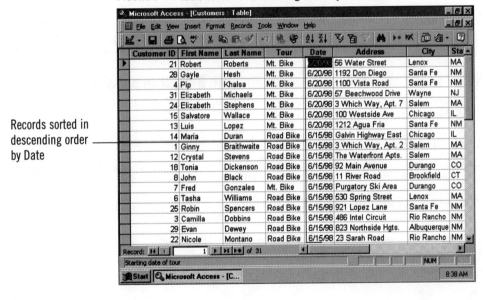

Records sorted in descending order by Date

CLUES TO USE

Using the menu bar to sort

In addition to using buttons on the Table Datasheet toolbar, you can also sort using the menu bar. After you select the field you want to sort, click Records on the menu bar, then click Sort. Click either Ascending or Descending on the Sort menu, shown in Figure B-12.

FIGURE B-12: Sort menu

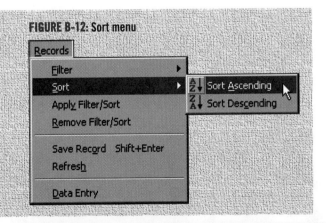

Filtering a Table

Sorting allows you to manipulate table records in a simple way and to display them in ascending or descending order. **Filtering** is a more complex method of organizing records, where you define the fields on which the table is sorted. A sort contains all the records in a table, whereas a filter shows only those records that qualify, based on your **criteria**. Qualifying records display in a temporary view that looks and acts like a table. Often, Michael needs a list of customers by a specific tour. He can filter the Customers table to obtain this list.

1. **Make sure the Customers table is open, with all records displayed**
   You want to narrow the number of records displayed so you can see only those records for customers who took a Mt. Bike tour.

Trouble?

If the grid is not cleared of any previous entries, your filter may get erroneous results.

2. **Click Records on the menu bar, click Filter, click Advanced Filter/Sort, then click the Clear Grid button ✕ from the Filter/Sort toolbar to clear the grid of any preexisting criteria**
   The Filter window opens, as shown in Figure B-13. The Filter window consists of two areas: the field list on top, containing all the fields in the table, and the filter grid on the bottom, where you specify the criteria for the filter. The toolbar displayed is the Filter/Sort toolbar. You want to create a filter to show a list of all the customers who took a Mt. Bike tour.

3. **Double-click Tour in the field list**
   Access places the Tour field in the first empty Field cell in the filter grid. Next, you define the criteria for the Tour field.

CourseHelp

If you have trouble with the concepts in this lesson, be sure to view the CourseHelp entitled Filtering a Records.

4. **Click the Criteria cell in the Tour column, type Mt. Bike, then press [Enter]**
   Access adds quotation marks around the entry to distinguish text from values. Your completed filter grid should look like Figure B-14.

5. **Click the Apply Filter button ▼ on the Filter/Sort toolbar**
   Only those records containing the Mt. Bike tour appear, as shown in Figure B-15. You can now remove the filter and return the table to its original order.

Time To

✓ Save

6. **Click the Remove Filter button ▼ on the Filter/Sort toolbar to include all the records in the table**

CLUES TO USE

When to use a filter

A filter is temporary and cannot be saved; however, you can print the results of a filter just as you print any datasheet. A filter is best used to narrow the focus of the records temporarily in the current table.

FIGURE B-13: Filter window for the Customers table

Field list   Table name   Field name goes here   Sort order goes here   Filter/Sort toolbar

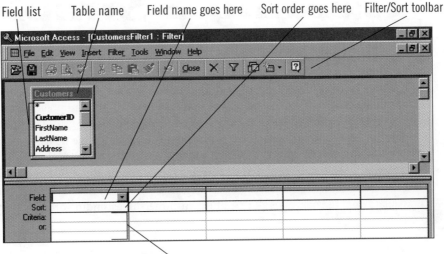

Criteria goes here

FIGURE B-14: Completed filter grid

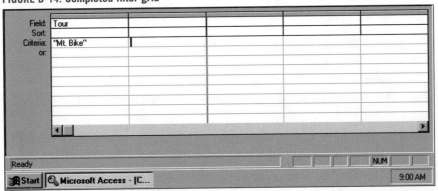

FIGURE B-15: Filtered table records

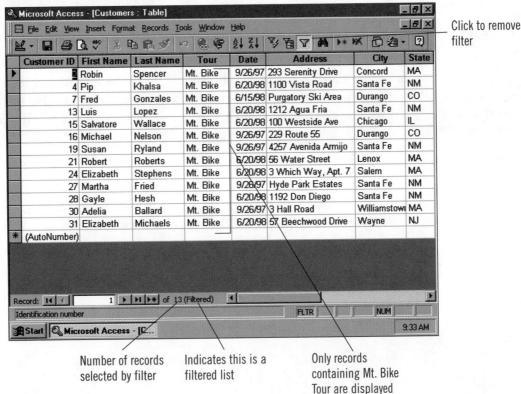

Click to remove filter

Number of records selected by filter

Indicates this is a filtered list

Only records containing Mt. Bike Tour are displayed

Creating a Simple Query

A **query** is a set of restrictions you place on a database table by specifying criteria to retrieve qualifying records. Unlike a filter, which only allows you to manipulate data temporarily, a query can be saved so that you do not have to recreate the fields in the grid. The query results also display only the fields you have specified, rather than showing all table fields. The most commonly used query is the **select query**, in which records are collected, viewed, and can be modified later.

The Nomad employee responsible for setting up Road Bike tours often asks Michael for a list of customers who have participated in these tours. Michael needs to create a query that displays only the names of all Road Bike customers in ascending order.

Steps

1. Click the **New Object button list arrow** on the Table Datasheet toolbar, then click **Query** on the pull-down palette
   The New Query dialog box opens and displays options for using the Query Wizard. You decide to use the Design View to create a new query.

2. Click **Design View**, then click **OK**
   The Select Query window opens, as shown in Figure B-16. The Query Design toolbar provides more buttons than does the Filter/Sort toolbar in the Filter window. You add the first field, sort, and criteria specifications to the Query Design grid. Scroll down the field list to display the **Tour field**.

Trouble?

If you enter a field in the query grid in error, select the field then press [Delete] to delete it.

3. Double-click **Tour** in the field list, then click the checked **Show box** in the grid to turn off the checkmark
   The Tour field name appears in the Field cell in the query grid, and the Table field displays the location of the field: the Customers table. The Show box indicates that the field will not be displayed in the query results. Next, specify the criteria for the query.

Trouble?

For a single table query, entries in the grid are not case sensitive: it doesn't matter if you use upper or lower case characters. Field criteria entered in the query grid for linked tables, however, are case sensitive.

4. Click the **Criteria cell** in the Tour column, type **Road Bike**, then press [Enter]
   You want the query results to show the last name, in ascending order, of each customer who participated in a Road Bike tour.

5. Double-click **LastName** in the field list, click the **Sort cell** in the LastName column, type **a** (for ascending), then make sure the Show box is selected for the LastName field
   Compare your grid to Figure B-17. You want to view the results of the query.

6. Click the **Datasheet View button** on the Query Design toolbar
   The results of the query are shown in Figure B-18. The results show the last names of the 10 customers that took Road Bike tours. You return to Design View.

7. Click the **Design View button** on the Query Datasheet toolbar
   The query grid is redisplayed. You want to save the query results.

8. Click the **Save button** on the Query Design toolbar, type **Road Bike customers** in the Query Name text box of the Save As dialog box, as shown in Figure B-19, then click **OK**
   The query is saved as part of the database file.

FIGURE B-16: Select Query window

Query Design toolbar

Tables used in query display here

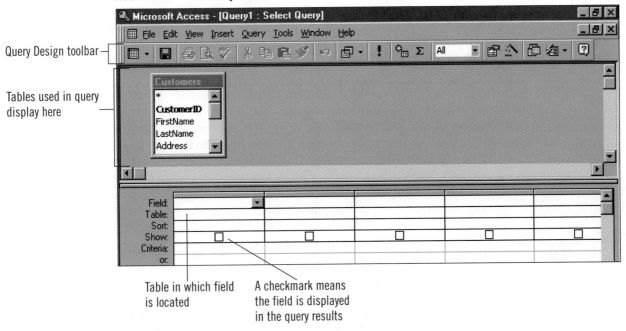

Table in which field is located

A checkmark means the field is displayed in the query results

FIGURE B-17: Sample query grid

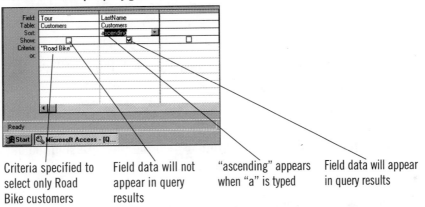

Criteria specified to select only Road Bike customers

Field data will not appear in query results

"ascending" appears when "a" is typed

Field data will appear in query results

FIGURE B-18: Results of simple query

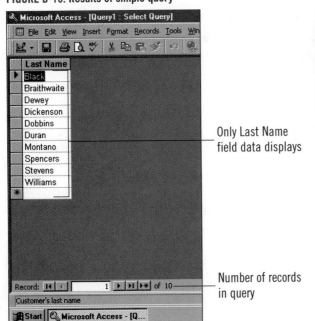

Only Last Name field data displays

Number of records in query

FIGURE B-19: Save As dialog box for query

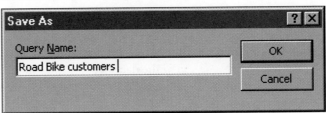

Creating a Complex Query

The criteria you specify for a query can be as simple as a list of all customer names, or as complex as a list of all customers over the age of 30, who live in New Mexico and took a tour in June. Using **expressions**, combinations of field names, constant values, and arithmetic operators, you can restrict the number of records returned by a query. The criteria **AND** and **OR** can also be used to broaden or narrow the number of selected records. For example, the result of a query of customers who took a Mt. Bike or Road Bike tour is different from the result of a query of customers who took a Mt. Bike or Road Bike tour and live in New Mexico. ▰▰▰▰ Each month, Michael wants to see a list of all customers, in descending order by last name, who took a Mt. Bike or Road Bike tour and who have a postal code greater than 50000. He decides to modify the previous query and save it as a new query.

Steps

1. **Click the Show box for the Tour field**
   You want to display the records of customers who took either a Mt. Bike or Road Bike tour, so you need to display the Tour field. You modify the current entry in the Criteria cell to include the second tour in the "or" field beneath the Criteria cell.

QuickTip

Arithmetic operators used in criteria when creating simple or complex queries are greater than (>), less than (<), equals (=), greater than or equal to (>=), less than or equal to (<=), and not equal to (<>).

2. **Click the Tour field or cell, type Mt. Bike, then press [Enter]**
   The entry "Mt. Bike" appears in the "or" cell. Next, you add the FirstName to the query grid and you want to sort the LastName field in descending order.

3. **Double-click FirstName in the field list, click the LastName field's Sort list arrow, then click Descending**
   The query design changes are specified as shown in Figure B-20. You decide to view the datasheet.

4. **Click the Datasheet View button ▦ on the Query Design toolbar**
   The results of the query are displayed in the datasheet. Notice that customers who took either a Mt. Bike or Road Bike tour are listed. The last names are sorted in descending order.

5. **Click the Design View button ▨ on the Query Datasheet toolbar**
   The query grid is redisplayed. You add the PostalCode field and its criteria to the query grid.

6. **Double-click PostalCode in the field list, click its Criteria cell, type >50000, press [↓] to enter the criteria in the "or" criteria cell, type >50000, then press [Enter]**
   If the Tour field scrolls out of view, scroll the window to view the completed query grid. You view the datasheet for the completed query.

7. **Click ▦**
   Because you wanted to view bike tour customers only with Postal codes above 50000, the query results are narrowed from 23 records to 14, and the query is being sorted by the LastName field, as shown in Figure B-21. Next, you save the modified query within the current database so you can view the results at any time.

QuickTip

You can save a filter as a query by choosing Save As Query from the File menu (while in the Filter window), then name the query and click [OK].

8. **Click File on the menu bar, click Save As/Export, type Bike Tours AND PostalCode >50000 in the New Name text box as shown in Figure B-22, then click OK**
   The new query is saved for future use. You close the query and the table and then exit Access.

9. **Close and exit Access.**

FIGURE B-20: "Or" specification in query grid

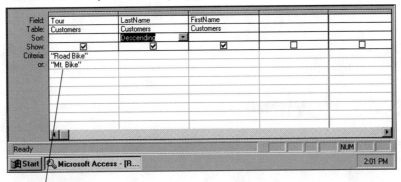

"Or" specification
used in criteria

FIGURE B-21: Results of complex query

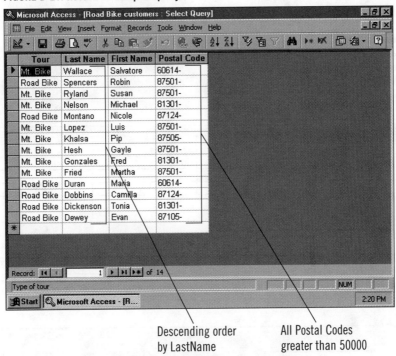

Descending order
by LastName

All Postal Codes
greater than 50000

FIGURE B-22: Save As/Export dialog box

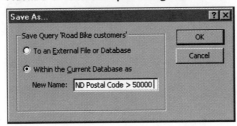

Using And and Or to affect query results

Using the Or criteria generally results in broader query results, as either of the criteria need to be true in order for a record to be selected. The And criteria demands that both criteria be true in order for a record to be selected.

Practice

▶ Concepts Review

Label each of the elements of the select Query window shown in Figure B-23.

FIGURE B-23

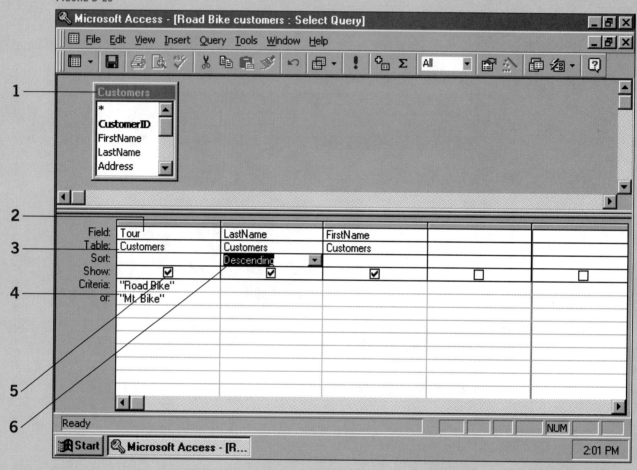

Match each button with its correct description.

7. ▶∗

8. ▦

9. 🗁

10. 🖨

11. 💾

12. 🔍

a. Open Database
b. Print
c. New Record
d. Find
e. Datasheet View
f. Save

Select the best answer from the list of choices.

13. Which button lets you create a new object?

a. ▦   b. ▦   c. ▦   d. ⚡

14. The button that sorts a table from A to Z is

a. 🗁   b. A↓   c. ▦   d. Z/A↓

15. The button used to add a new record to a table is

a. ≫   b. ▶❘   c. ▶∗   d. ❘◀

16. Each of the following is true about a filter, *except*:

a. It creates a temporary set of records that looks like a table
b. Its contents can be sorted
c. It includes all fields in the table
d. It can be saved for future use

17. Which button is used to clear the filter grid?

a. ▶∗   b. ✕   c. ▦   d. ▽

▶ Skills Review

1. Plan a database.

a. Plan a database that will contain the names and addresses of your business contacts.

b. Based on your own experience, decide which fields you need to include in the database.

c. Write down the necessary fields with names and descriptions for each field.

2. Create a table.

a. Start Access and insert your Student Disk in the disk drive.

b. Use the Blank Database option button to create a new database file.

c. Save the file as "Contacts" on your Student Disk.

d. Click the Tables object tab in the Database window, then click New.

e. Use the Table Wizard to create the new table.

f. In the Sample Tables list box, click Contacts. Make sure the Business option button is selected.

g. In the Sample Fields list box, choose each of the following fields for your table:
    ContactID
    FirstName
    LastName
    Address
    City
    StateOrProvince
    PostalCode
    Birthdate

h. Continue through the Table Wizard. Name the table "Business Contacts."

i. Click the Modify the table design option button in the third Table Wizard dialog box, then click Finish.

3. Modify a table.

a. In the first available blank row, add a new text field called "Other."

b. Click the ContactID field Description box.

c. Type "Unique number for Contact."

d. Add appropriate descriptions for the other fields.

4. Find records.

a. Open the database "Bicycle Parts" from your Student Disk. Open the "Products" table.

b. Use the Find button to locate all records in all fields that match any part of a field and contain the text "bar."

c. Make a note of how many occurrences there are?

5. Sort a table.

a. Sort the Products table in ascending order using the "Product Num field." Print the datasheet.

b. Return the datasheet to its original order.

c. Create and print a list of products in descending order by "UnitsInStock."

d. Return the datasheet to its original order.

e. Create and print a list of products in ascending order by "ProductName."

f. Return the datasheet to its original order.

g. Create and print a list of products in descending order by "SupplierID."

h. Return the datasheet to its original order.

6. Filter a table.

a. Create a filter that shows all products on order. A product on order has a value larger than 0 in the UnitsOnOrder field. (Hint: Set the criteria in the filter grid to ">0" for Units On Order.)

b. Print the datasheet.

c. Return the datasheet to its original order.

d. Create a filter for all non-discontinued items.

e. Print the resulting datasheet.

f. Return the datasheet to its original order.

7. Create a simple query.

a. Create a query for all the Products On Order that shows only the ProductNum field data and the product name for the items on order. Name this query "Products on Order."

b. Create a query for all non-discontinued items that shows the ProductName, SupplierID, UnitsInStock, and UnitPrice. Name this query "Non-discontinued Products."

c. Create another query that lists all products with a unit price greater than $50. Name this query "Products costing >$50." (*Hint:* Do not type the $ in the criteria.)

d. Use the "Non-discontinued Products" query to create a new query in which the ProductName, ProductNum, UnitsInStock, and UnitPrice field data display. Name this query "Available Products."

e. Modify the existing "Non-discontinued Products" query for discontinued products. Name this new query "Discontinued Products."

f. Print out the Discontinued Products query.

8. Create a complex query.

a. Create a query that shows the ProductName of all products with a DiscoStatus = Yes field AND that are sold by the pair (the Units field). Sort the query in ascending order by units. Name this query "Discoed, by Unit."

b. Print the datasheet for the query.

c. Save the Discoed, by Unit query as "Available, by Unit." Change the DiscoStatus = Yes field to DiscoStatus = No.

d. Print the datasheet for the query.

e. Modify the "Products on Order" query so that the results are sorted in ascending order by the SupplierID field. Make sure the SupplierID field data is displayed. Save the modified query. Print the query results.

f. Modify the "Products costing $50" query to include the following fields: ProductNum, ReorderLevel, and ReorderAmount. Save the modified query. Print the query results.

g. Modify the "Discoed, by Unit" query so that the results are sorted in descending order by units, and so that the data for the UnitPrice field is displayed. Save the modified query. Print the query results.

h. Close the file and exit Access.

▶ Independent Challenges

1. The Melodies Music Store has hired you as the customer service manager. You need to create queries in the store's music database, which is contained in the file "Melodies Music Store" on your Student Disk. The database includes one table, called Available titles.

To complete this independent challenge:

1. Start Access, open the database file "Melodies Music Store" on your Student Disk.
2. Using the Available titles table, find out how many records are in the Classic group. Should this classification be its own sub-group?
3. Sort the records by CategoryID, then by ProductName. Print the results.
4. Create a filter that examines records with a SerialNumber lower than 400000. Print this list.
5. Because musical categories overlap, group the eight classifications into three subgroups. You might, for example, group Alternative and Metal into a group called New Age; Classic, Pop, and Rock into a group called Rock N Roll; and World Music, Jazz, and Blues into a group called Easy Listening.
6. Create queries for each of the three subgroups. Each query must use an OR specification in the query grid. Name each query for its classification.
7. Query the Available titles table using each query, and print the results of each query.
8. Modify one of the subgroup queries to include a musical classification already included in another subgroup. For example, you could include Pop in Easy Listening as well as Rock N Roll. Print the results of the modified query and submit all printouts.

2. You work in the US Census Office for your city. Using the database "Census Bureau" from your Student Disk, create several queries that examine the data in the Statistical Data table. The records in the Statistical Data table contain marriage information by state.

To complete this independent challenge:

1. Add descriptions for each of the fields in the "Statistical Data" table.
2. Find the states in the same geographical area as your state. For example, if your state is Utah, other states in the Mountain Region are New Mexico, Colorado, Nevada, Montana, Arizona, Idaho, and Wyoming.
3. Create and save a query that selects records in your geographical area and sorts them in ascending order by state. Display the State and Marriages fields.
4. On paper, write down at least three additional queries that would extract meaningful data. Create and save each of these queries. Print a sample of each query's results and submit each of the samples with the hand-written work.

3. Your computer consulting firm has contracted to create a database for a special effects firm called Grand Illusions. Currently, Grand Illusions is working on five films, each having a minimum of three special effects they need to keep track of. Each special effect is created using some combination of computer imaging, prosthetics, multi-media, archived footage, and an in-house tool called Black Midnight.

To complete this independent challenge:

1. Create a database file on your Student Disk called Grand Illusions.
2. Create a table called Special Effects Register.
3. Create records for each special effect used in the five film projects. Each record should include the film name, special effect name, the Director's name, the tools used to create the effect, and the completion date of the effect.
4. Print the results of sorting the records in ascending order by film name.
5. Print the results of sorting the records in ascending order by completion date, then in ascending order by Director's name.
6. Create a query for each film which displays the completion date, Director's name, and the tools used.
7. Save the Query using the film name and Special Effects as the query name.
8. Print out each list and submit all printouts.

4. Proper use of search engines can help you find information about the elected officials in any state. The socialite for whom you work wants to be aware of who is elected to what post, and when their term is up. He has asked you to create a database based on the information you retrieve from the World Wide Web that contains this information.

1. Log on to the Internet and use your browser to go to http://www.course.com. From there click the link Student On Line Companions; then click the link to go to the Microsoft Office 97 Professional Edition—Illustrated: A First Course page, then click the Access link for Unit B.
2. Locate information about your state, and find out about your state's Federal elected officials.
3. Create a new database on your Student Disk called Elected Officials.
4. Include the following information in your table: the official's name, whether they are in the House or Senate, their official title, when their term began, when they're up for reelection, party affiliation, age, and number of years of elected service.
5. Save the table.
6. Create a query that finds Democrats, and one that finds Republicans.
7. Preview and print the datasheet.
8. Hand in a printout of your work.

Visual Workshop

Use the Customers table in the "Tour Customer Data" file on your Student Disk to create the following output using a fil-

FIGURE B-24

Customer ID	First Name	Last Name	Address	City	State	Postal Code	Tour	Date	Age
30	Adelia	Ballard	3 Hall Road	Williamstow	MA	02167-	Mt. Bike	9/26/95	42
13	Luis	Lopez	1212 Agua Fria	Santa Fe	NM	87501-	Mt. Bike	6/20/96	34
31	Elizabeth	Michaels	57 Beechwood Drive	Wayne	NJ	07470-	Mt. Bike	6/20/96	39
16	Michael	Nelson	229 Route 55	Durango	CO	81301-	Mt. Bike	9/26/95	40
2	Robin	Spencer	293 Serenity Drive	Concord	MA	01742-	Mt. Bike	9/26/95	32
24	Elizabeth	Stephens	3 Which Way, Apt. 7	Salem	MA	01970-	Mt. Bike	6/20/96	38

Creating
a Form

The Datasheet View gives you an overall look at the records in a table. Often, however, the fields you need to view in the table are not all visible unless you scroll left or right. Access allows you to easily create attractive screen forms that let you determine how you view each record's fields and the records in the database. You can design a screen form to match the design of a particular paper form to facilitate data entry. Because Nomad Ltd's Travel Division has been so successful with its bicycle tours, it keeps an inventory of supplies, which it then sells to tour customers. Michael wants to create a form to make it easier to enter inventory data.

Access 97

Creating a Form

You can create a form from scratch, or you can use the **Form Wizard**. The Form Wizard provides sample form layouts and gives you options for including specific fields in a form. Currently, the Travel Division fills out a paper form for each product in its bicycle inventory. Michael needs to create an Access form for the bicycle inventory data. He wants to design the form so that it looks similar to the original paper form, displays one record at a time, and displays all but one of the table's fields .

1. Start Access and insert your Student Disk in the appropriate drive

2. Click the **Open an Existing Database radio button**, then open the database **Bike Inventory** on your Student Disk
   This database file contains the bicycle inventory data. You want to create a new form for the Bicycle Products table.

3. Click the **Forms tab** in the Database window, then click **New**
   The New Form dialog box opens, as shown in Figure C-1. You need to identify the table on which the form will be based, then you can choose the Form Wizard option to create the form.

4. Click the **Choose the table or query where the object's data comes from: list arrow**, click **Bicycle Products**, click **Form Wizard**, then click **OK**
   A dialog box opens and lists all the fields in the table, as shown in Figure C-2. This dialog box allows you to select which fields you want to include in the form, and to determine the order in which they appear in the form. Instead of selecting each field individually, you decide to select all the fields at one time, and then exclude the one you don't want to appear.

5. Click the **All Fields button** [>>], use the scroll bar in the Selected Fields box to display the top of the list, click **ProductNum**, then click the **Remove Single Field button** [<]
   All the fields except ProductNum appear in the Selected Fields box. You are ready to choose a layout for your form. You decide to accept the default style: a Columnar layout.

6. Click [Next >], then click [Next >] to accept the Columnar layout
   Next, you choose a style for your form. You decide to use the Standard style.

7. Click **Standard**, then click [Next >]
   The final dialog box suggests the table name as the title for the form. You accept the title suggestion Bicycle Products and want to see the form with data in it.

8. Click **Finish**
   The Bicycle Products form opens in Form View, as shown in Figure C-3. The fields are listed in the form organized in columns, and the data for the first record in the table is displayed. The navigation buttons at the bottom of the form allow you to move from record to record. If you can't see all the fields, the vertical scroll bar allows you to move to areas of the form that currently are not visible.

QuickTip

The [< Back] button in the Form Wizard dialog boxes allows you to move to the previous dialog box and make changes, as necessary, before completing the form.

FIGURE C-1: New Form dialog box

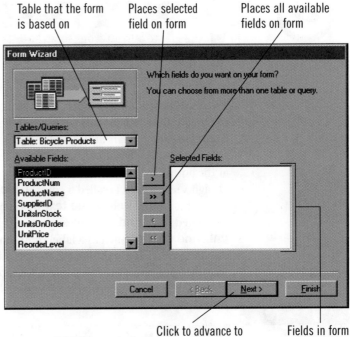

FIGURE C-2: Selecting fields in the Form Wizard dialog box

Table that the form is based on

Places selected field on form

Places all available fields on form

Click here to select the Form Wizard

Click to select a table or query on which to base the form

Click to advance to next dialog box

Fields in form appear here

FIGURE C-3: Bicycle Products form

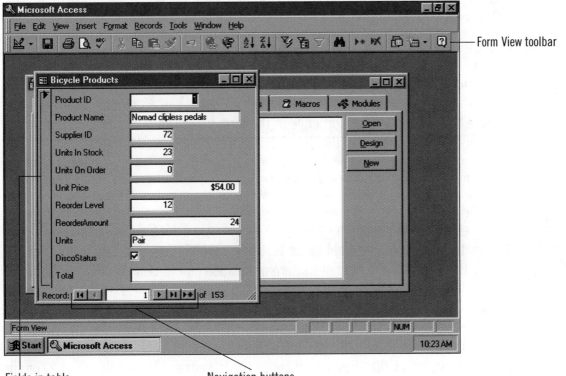

Form View toolbar

Fields in table

Navigation buttons

Using AutoForm

You can create a simple form by clicking the New Object button on the Database toolbar, then clicking AutoForm from the palette. AutoForm offers no prompts or dialog boxes; it instantly creates a columnar, tabular, or datasheet form that displays all the fields in the table or query.

Modifying a Form Layout

After you create a form, you can modify it easily by changing the locations of fields, adding or deleting fields, adding graphics, and changing the color of text and field data. You modify a form in Design View, which is divided into three sections: Form Header, Detail, and Form Footer. The **Form Header** appears at the beginning of each screen form and can contain an additional form title or logo. The **Detail** displays the fields and data for each record. The **Form Footer** appears at the bottom of each screen form and can contain totals, instructions, or command buttons. In Design View, a field is called a control. A **control** consists of the **field label** and the data it contains which is the **field value text box**. There are three types of controls: bound, unbound, and calculated. A **bound control**, such as a field, has a table or query as its information source; an **unbound control**, such as a label or graphic image, has its data source as something other than the database, and a **calculated control** uses an expression as its data source. 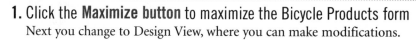 Michael wants to reposition the fields in the form to match the design of the paper form. This will make it easier to enter data from the paper-based forms into the screen form. Figure C-4 shows a completed paper form.

1. Click the **Maximize button** to maximize the Bicycle Products form
   Next you change to Design View, where you can make modifications.

2. Click the **Design View button** on the Form View toolbar
   The screen changes to Design View, as shown in Figure C-5. The form background changes to a grid, which helps keep fields aligned horizontally and vertically. The **Toolbox toolbar**, which might appear in a different area on your screen, contains buttons you can use to modify the form. The detail section contains the field labels that identify each field; and the field value text boxes, which represent where the actual data for each field will be displayed. Before moving any fields, you want to expand the size of the work area.

3. Place the pointer on the right edge of the form as shown in Figure C-5, the pointer changes to ↔, then drag the right edge to the 6" mark on the ruler
   You are ready to reposition fields on the form. To do this, you first need to **select** a field by clicking the control for the field. Black squares, called **handles**, appear around the perimeter of a selected control. If you click the field label control you only select the label. If you click the field value text box, you also select the field label. When you work with controls, the pointer assumes different shapes, which are described in Table C-1.

4. Click the **ProductName field value text box control**, then when the pointer is 🖐, drag the control to the right of its current location on the same position on the vertical ruler so the left edge of the label is at 2.5" on the horizontal ruler
   The Product Name label field is now in the middle of its original line, as shown in Figure C-6. You can select multiple controls simultaneously and modify them all together.

5. Click to deselect **ProductName**, press [Shift] and click each of the remaining controls *except* ProductID, then drag them so the left edge of the labels are at 2" on the horizontal ruler

6. Select the **DiscoStatus field value text box control** and drag it to the same vertical line as the ProductID control, with the left edge of its label at 2.5" on the horizontal ruler

7. Drag the **Total field value text box control** up so the bottom of the controls are at 2.5" on the vertical ruler
   Be sure your form's Design View matches the Design View displayed in Figure C-6. You might need to use the scroll bar to see the remaining controls.

FIGURE C-4: Bicycle Products paper form

Bicycle Products
Product ID:	1	DiscoStatus:	✔
Product Num:	11023	Product Name:	Nomad clipless pedals
Supplier ID:	72		
Units In Stock:	23		
Units On Order:	0		
Unit Price:	$54.00		
Reorder Level:	12		
Reorder Amount:	24		
Units:	Pair		
Total:	$1242.00		

FIGURE C-5: Bicycle Products form in Design View

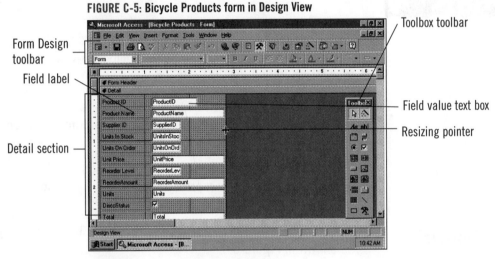

Toolbox toolbar

Form Design toolbar

Field label

Field value text box

Resizing pointer

Detail section

FIGURE C-6: Bicycle Products form with repositioned controls

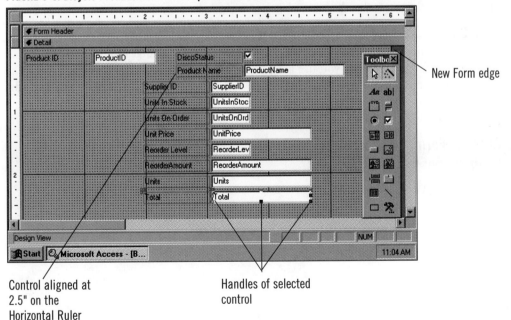

New Form edge

Control aligned at 2.5" on the Horizontal Ruler

Handles of selected control

TABLE C-1: Mouse pointer shapes

shape	action	shape	action
▷	Selects a control	👆	Moves the control where pointer is currently positioned
🖐	Moves all selected controls	↔	Changes a control's size

Access 97

Changing the Tab Order

Once the fields are moved to their new locations, you'll want to change the **tab order**, the order in which you advance from one field to the next when you press [Tab] to enter data in the form. The order of the fields in a table determines the default tab order. Even when controls are repositioned in a form, the tab order remains in the original order of the fields in the table. Michael wants the tab order to reflect the order in which the fields now appear on the form, which matches the paper form, to facilitate data entry from the paper form. He needs to modify the tab order for the form.

Steps

1. Click **View** on the menu bar, then click **Tab Order**

   The Tab Order dialog box opens. In this dialog box you can change the order of fields in any of the three sections on the form. Because fields are usually in the Detail section, this section is automatically selected. The Custom Order list box shows the current tab order, which still reflects the order of the fields in the table. You need to change the tab order so that the DiscoStatus field which indicates whether the product is currently offered or has been discontinued follows the ProductID field.

2. Click the **DiscoStatus row selector** in the Custom Order list box

   Now that the DiscoStatus control is selected, you can change its order by dragging its row to a new location.

   Trouble?

   If the pointer changes to an I you will rename the field rather than move it. Click outside the field and try again.

3. Drag the **DiscoStatus row** until it is below ProductID, then release the mouse button, as shown in Figure C-7

   You can also click the Auto Order button in the Tab Order dialog box to rearrange the tab order to left-to-right, top-to-bottom.

4. Click **OK**

   Although nothing visibly changes on the form, the tab order changes to reflect the order of the fields on the form. When you use the screen form to enter data from a paper form, the order in which you move from field to field by pressing [Tab] will match the order in the paper form.

   You save your work and view the form in Form View.

5. Click the **Form View button** 🔲 on the Form Design toolbar

   Compare your form to Figure C-8.

6. Save your work

FIGURE C-7: Tab Order dialog box

Indicates form section being displayed ———

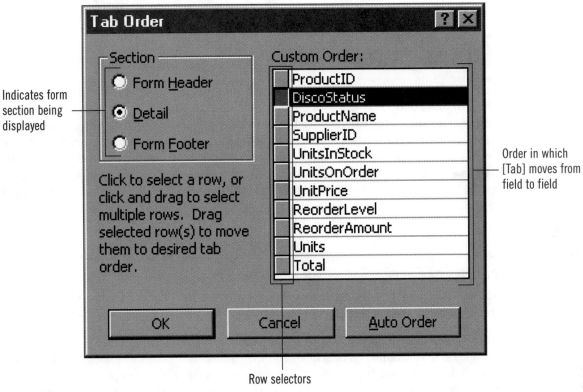

Order in which [Tab] moves from field to field

Row selectors

FIGURE C-8: Form displayed in Form View

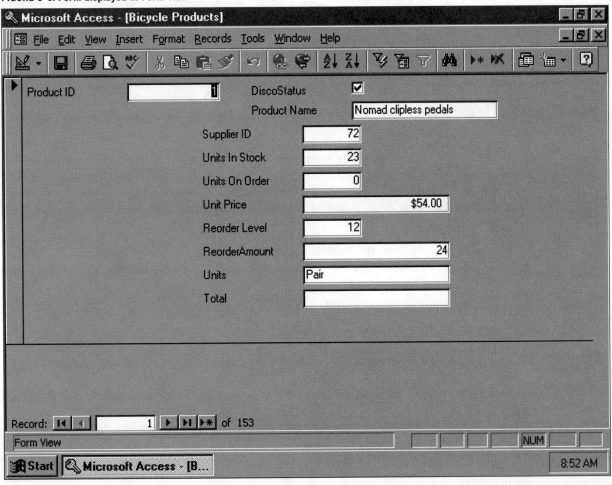

Using the Expression Builder

In addition to repositioning controls, you can also modify the **properties,** or characteristics, of a control to make data entry more efficient. A **calculated control** has a mathematical expression as its data source. The **Expression Builder** displays fields and mathematical symbols you can use to create an expression. By default, all controls occur as text boxes; however, you can create several types of controls, including toggle buttons and check boxes, using the Toolbox toolbar. 📎 Michael wants to create a calculated control that will display an in-stock value for each item in the inventory. To do this, he will use the Expression Builder to create an equation that multiplies the UnitsInStock field value by the UnitPrice field value. First, Michael returns to Design View.

Steps 1 2 3 4

1. Click the **Design View button** 🔽 on the Form View toolbar
You want the results of the expression to appear in the Total field. You must select the control for this field before creating the equation.

2. Click the **Total field value text box control**
Handles appear around the field label and the field value text box to indicate that the control is selected. Although you could type an expression directly into the text box, you choose to use the Expression Builder. You access the Expression Builder through the Properties Sheet.

3. Click the **Properties button** 📋 on the Form Design toolbar
The Properties Sheet opens for the Total control. The Properties Sheet shows the control's name and source, the field description, and other relevant information. Because you want to change the Total control to a calculated control, you need to modify the Control Source property.

4. Click the **Data tab** in the Total Control's Properties Sheet
The Expression Builder's Build button displays, as shown in Figure C-9.

5. Click the **Build button** ...
The Expression Builder dialog box opens, as shown in Figure C-10. This dialog box contains a section in which you build the expression, the buttons you use to build the expression, and the control fields and labels selected for the form. The word "Total" appears in the expression text box because that control was selected. Before building the expression, you must delete the word Total.

6. Double-click **Total** in the expression list box, then press **[Delete]**
You need to create an expression that will multiply the UnitsInStock field value by the UnitPrice field value.

Trouble?

If you enter the expression incorrectly, modify it using [Backspace], [Delete], and the arrow keys, then enter it again.

7. Click the **Equals button** =, double-click **UnitsInStock**, click the **Multiplication button** *, then double-click **UnitPrice**
The completed expression appears in the expression text box. See Figure C-11.

8. Click **OK** to return to the Properties Sheet for the Total control
Note that the Control Source property shows the expression as the source for the Total control.

FIGURE C-9: Properties Sheet for Total control

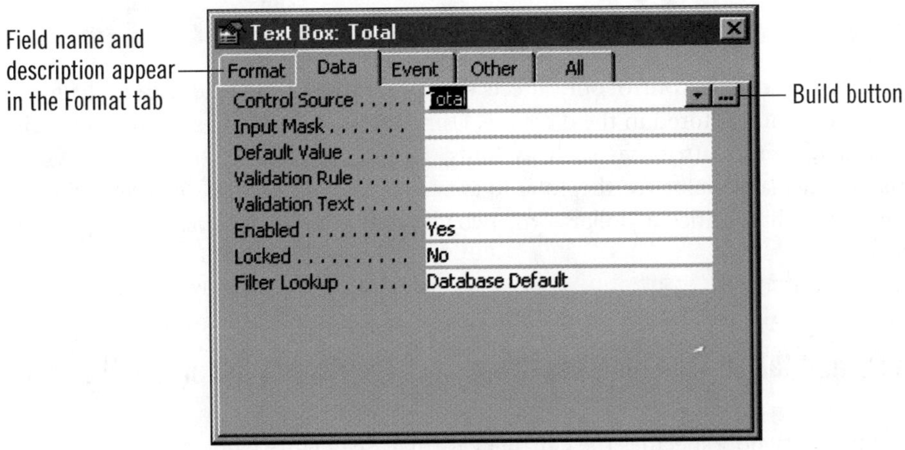

Field name and description appear in the Format tab

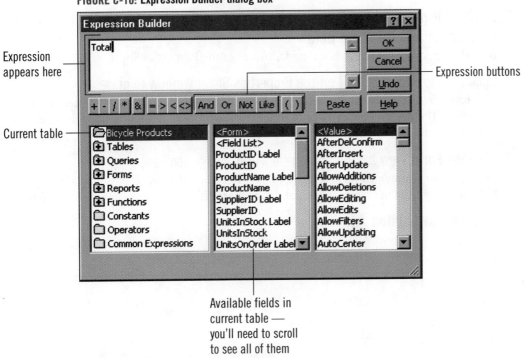

Build button

FIGURE C-10: Expression Builder dialog box

Expression appears here

Expression buttons

Current table

Available fields in current table — you'll need to scroll to see all of them

FIGURE C-11: Completed Expression Builder dialog box

Completed expression

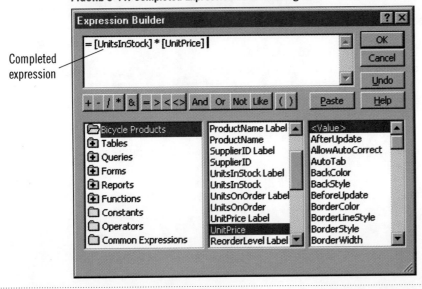

Access 97

Formatting Controls

Changing the format of a field's control only affects the appearance of the field data in the form; it does not affect how data is stored in the database. Using the Properties Sheet, you can modify numeric formatting, or text attributes such as fonts, font sizes, bolding, or italics. Michael wants the calculated value for the Total to appear extra bold and be displayed with the Currency format, which specifies a dollar sign, two decimal places, and commas separating thousands.

1. Click the **Format tab** on the Properties Sheet, click the **Format list arrow**, then click **Currency**
   The Format property now specifies the Currency format. See Figure C-12. Next, you change the format of this control to bold.

2. Scroll to display Font Weight, click the **Font Weight text box**, click the **Font Weight list arrow**, then click **Extra Bold**
   Now that these changes have been made, you close the Properties Sheet.

3. Click the **Close button** ☒ on the Properties Sheet window to close it
   The form is displayed in Design View. Note that the equation you created using the Expression Builder appears extra bold in the Total control. You want to view the completed form in Form View.

4. Click the **Form View button** 🗔 on the Form Design toolbar
   Compare your completed form to Figure C-13. The calculated result of the Total field for the first record appears in Currency format. Don't worry if your controls are spaced differently.

5. Click the **Save button** 🖫

QuickTip

You can bold, italicize, or underline a control by selecting it in Design View, then click the appropriate attribute button on the Form Design toolbar.

FIGURE C-12: **Completed Properties Sheet**

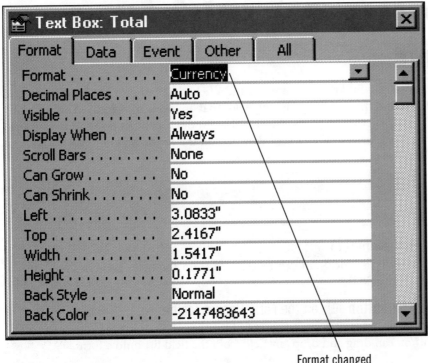

Format changed
to Currency

FIGURE C-13: **Completed form in Form View**

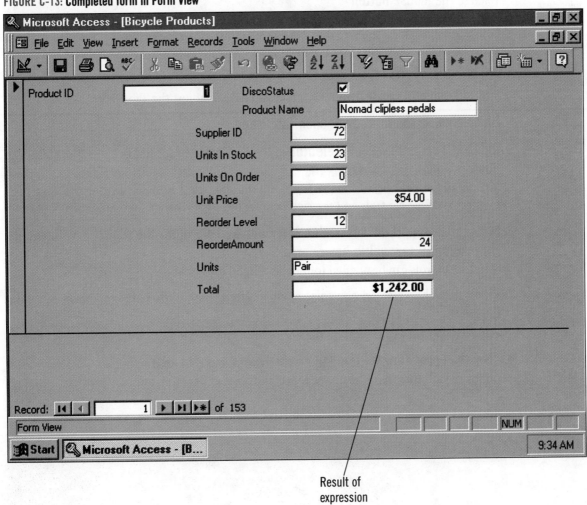

Result of
expression

Adding a Field to a Form

Once a form exists, you may find that you want to add a field that had previously been omitted. You can create a form, and then add any missing fields that are needed. After speaking with the data entry staff at Nomad, Michael learns that Product Number is an important field needed in the form. He returns to the Design View to add the ProductNum field that had not been included originally.

1. Click the **Design View button** 🔲
   The field to be added, ProductNum can be selected from the field list and placed on the form. You display the field list.

2. Click the **Field List button** 🗉 on the Form Design Toolbar
   The list of fields in the table display in Figure C-14, although your list may display in a different location. You can drag and drop any field from the field list onto a form.

3. Click the **ProductNum field**, drag it onto the form with the 🔲 pointer just beneath the currently positioned ProductID field as shown in Figure C-15, then release the mouse button
   The field displays directly underneath the existing ProductID field. If necessary, you can reposition the field by moving the control when the pointer looks like 🖑. Satisfied with the addition of this field, you close the Field List.

4. Click the **Field List button** 🗉
   The addition of this new field means that you have to adjust the Tab Order.

5. Right-click on the form, then click **Tab Order**

6. Click the **ProductNum row selector** in the Customer Order list box, drag it above the ProductName field, then click **OK**
   You decide to align the new field's label with the label directly above it using the [Shift] key to select multiple controls and the right-mouse button to change their alignment.

7. Click the **ProductNum text value box control**, hold down the **[Shift]** key, then click the **ProductID text value box control**
   Selected controls can be aligned to their left, right, top, and bottom edges.

8. Right-click the selected controls, point to **Align**, then click **Left**, as shown in Figure C-16
   You decide to view your work in the Form View.

Time To

✔ Save the form

9. Click the **Form View button** 🔲 on the Form Design toolbar
   Compare your form with its newly added and aligned field to Figure C-17.

FIGURE C-14: Field List displayed

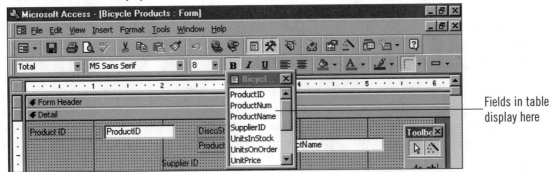

Fields in table display here

FIGURE C-15: Dragging a field to a form

Position of dragged field

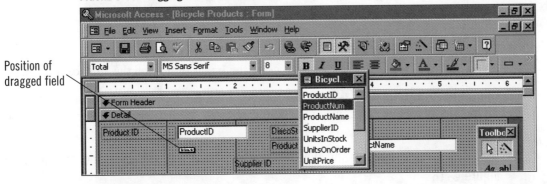

FIGURE C-16: Aligning controls

Selected controls

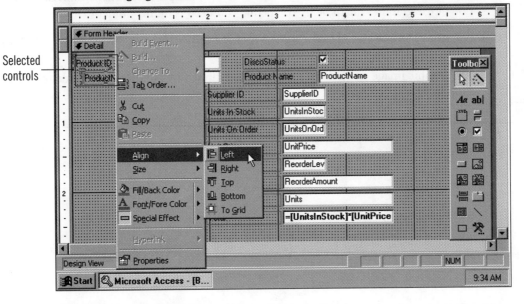

FIGURE C-17: Form with additional field

Adding a Graphic Image to a Form

Graphic images add style and a professional look to any form. Using graphic images purchased by your company, or designed by you using any art program can make a form look more appealing. ▬▬▬ Michael would like to include Nomad Ltd's logo on his form. He already has the logo in an electronic format and will insert the graphic image using the form's Design View.

Steps

QuickTip

You can lock down a toolbox button (so you don't have to keep clicking it for repeated use) by double-clicking it.

QuickTip

Most commonly available graphic image types can be used in a form. These types include .BMP, .PCX, .JPG, and .TIF.

1. **Click the Design View button 📐 on the Form View toolbar**
   A graphic image is inserted onto a form using the Image button on the Toolbox toolbar.

2. **Click the Image button 🖼 on the Toolbox toolbar**
   The pointer changes to ⁺🖼. You use this pointer to define the area where you want the image to be placed.

3. **Drag ⁺🖼 to the right 2" and down from the 1" mark to the 2" mark, as shown in Figure C-18**
   Once the area is defined, the Insert Picture dialog box opens. You supply the name and location of the graphics file to be used. The file you need is on the Student Disk.

4. **Click the Look in list arrow, select the 3½" Floppy (A:), click Nomad.tif, as shown in Figure C-19, then click OK**
   The graphic image displays on the form, surrounded by handles. You decide to look at the form in Form View.

5. **Click the Form View button 🔲 on the Design View toolbar**
   Compare your form to Figure C-20.

FIGURE C-18: Dragging an image's outline

Outline for new picture

Begin drawing here

End drawing here

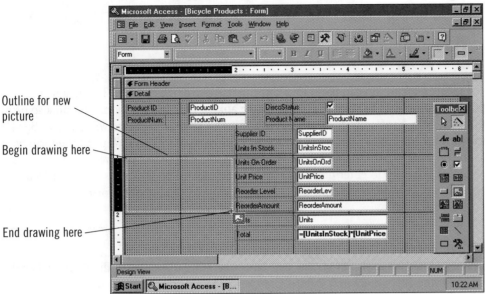

FIGURE C-19: Insert Picture dialog box

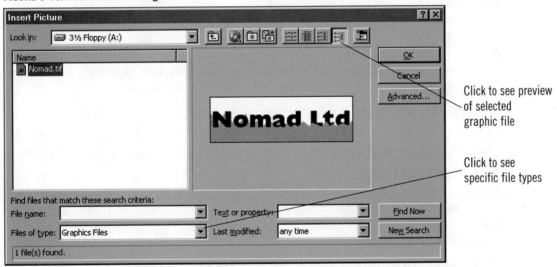

Click to see preview of selected graphic file

Click to see specific file types

FIGURE C-20: Picture embedded in form

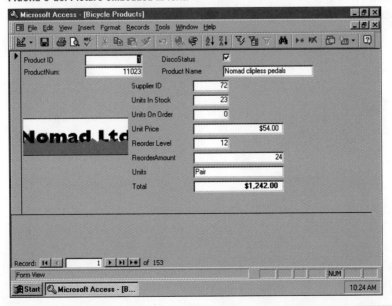

Using a Form to Add a Record

After you create a form, you can use it to add records to the database table. To add a record you press [Tab] to move from field to field, entering the appropriate information. You can also print a form to obtain a hard copy for sharing with others. ◄━━ Michael will use the Bicycle Products form to add a new record to the Bicycle Products table. Then he'll print the form with the data for the new record, and distribute the form to other Nomad employees so that they can see how to use the form to enter data. Because the Bicycle Products table is already selected in the Database window, Michael begins by adding a new record to the open form.

Steps

1. **Click the New Record button ▶✳ on the Form View toolbar**
   A new, blank record is displayed. The text "(AutoNumber)" appears in the ProductID field. Recall that the first ProductID field is the Counter field for the table. Record 154 of 154 appears in the status bar. See Figure C-21. You begin to enter the data for the new record.

2. **Press [Tab] to advance to the next field**
   The cursor moves to the DiscoStatus field. Remember that when you created the form, you changed the tab order so that DiscoStatus would be the second field moved to in the form. You will leave the DiscoStatus field blank to indicate that the product is currently offered (you would enter a checkmark in this field for a product that is discontinued). You continue to enter the data for the record, pressing [Tab] to move from field to field.

3. **Press [Tab] to advance to the ProductNum field, type 57129, press [Tab], type Nomad FinneganFast Tire, press [Tab], type 22, press [Tab], type 14, press [Tab], type 20, press [Tab], type 15.50, press [Tab], type 15, press [Tab], type 20, press [Tab], type Each, then press [Enter]**
   Compare your completed record to Figure C-22. Notice that the Total field shows the calculated result. The new record is stored in the Bicycle Products table. Next, you want to print the form containing the new record.
   You want to print only this page.

Time To

✔ Save
✔ Close the form
✔ Exit Access

4. **Click File on the menu bar, click Print, click the Selected Record(s) option button, then click OK**
   You close the form and return to the Database window.

FIGURE C-21: Blank form for new record

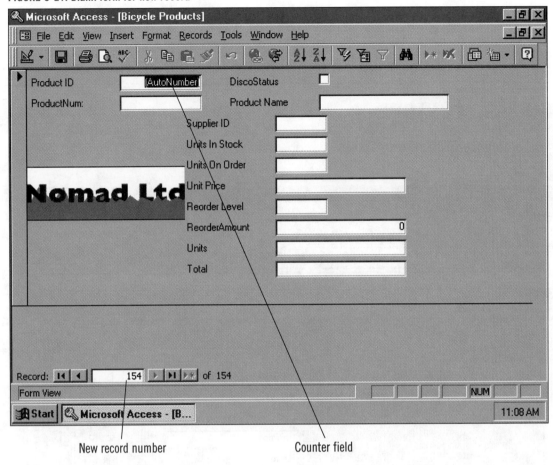

New record number   Counter field

FIGURE C-22: Completed record 154

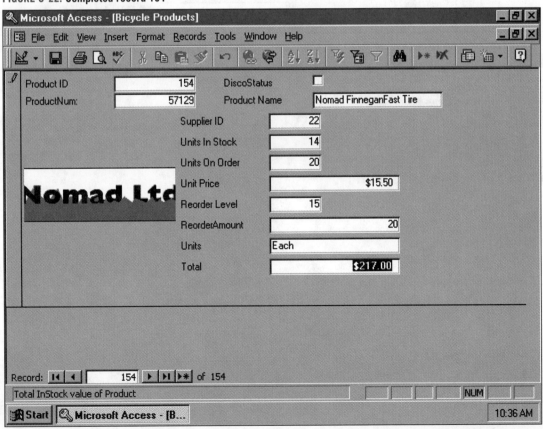

Practice

► Concepts Review

Label each of the elements of the Form Design window shown in Figure C-23.

FIGURE C-23

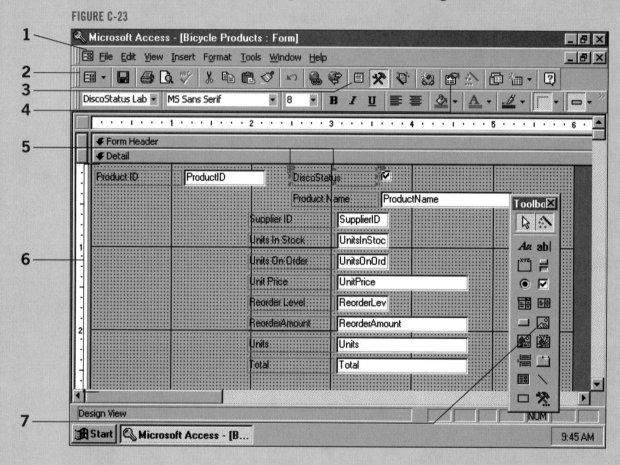

Match each button to its correct description.

8. `<<`
9. `...`
10. ![]
11. `>`
12. 🔍
13. ▦

a. Print Preview
b. Add a single field
c. Remove all fields
d. Form View
e. Design View
f. Build an expression

Select the best answer from the list of choices.

14. **Objects in a form or report are called**
    a. Properties
    b. Controls
    c. Pieces
    d. Handles

15. **The pointer used to resize a control is**
    a.
    b. ↔
    c. ⬉
    d. ✛

16. **A control is considered to be bound when**
    a. It is displayed in a form or report
    b. It is used to sort a table
    c. Its data source is found in a table
    d. Its data source is the result of an expression

17. **Which button is used to add an existing field to a form?**
    a. ▦
    b. ▣
    c. ▸∗
    d. ▣

18. **Which of the following is used to change the order used to advance from field to field?**
    a. Format tab in the Properties Sheet
    b. Data tab in the Properties Sheet
    c. Field List
    d. Tab Order

► Skills Review

1. **Create a form.**
   a. Start Access and make sure your Student Disk is in drive A. Open the file Bike Parts from your Student Disk.
   b. Create a new form for the Products table.
   c. Include all fields except CategoryID in the form.
   d. Use the Form Wizard to create a columnar form.
   e. Use the Stone style.
   f. Use the title Bicycle Parts Database for the form.
   g. Display the form with data.

2. **Modify a form layout.**
   a. Maximize the Form window and change the form's dimensions so that it is at least 6" wide.
   b. Select controls and position them so that all controls are displayed on the screen in an order you feel makes sense.

3. **Change the tab order.**
   a. Modify the tab order so that pressing [Tab] moves sequentially through the fields as you have arranged them.
   b. Write down your new tab order, and turn the list in.

4. Use the Expression Builder.

a. Click the text box button in the Toolbox, then create a calculated expression towards the bottom of the form.

b. Calculate the cost of any product reorder. (*Hint*: multiply ReorderAmount by the UnitPrice.)

c. Adjust the Tab Order for the new expression.

d. Save your changes.

5. Format controls.

a. Change the format of the UnitsOnOrder control so that it has one decimal place.

b. Change the number contained in the UnitsInStock field so that it appears in italics.

c. View the changes in Form View.

d. Save your changes.

6. Add a field to a form.

a. Display the Field List.

b. Add the CategoryID field to the form.

c. Modify the Tab Order for the insertion of the new field.

7. Add a graphic image to a form.

a. Use the Picture button on the Toolbox toolbar to define an area for a graphic image.

b. Insert the graphic file Nomad.tif, found on your Student Disk.

c. View the form using the Form View.

8. Use a form to add a record.

a. Open the Product Entry Form.

b. Enter the following new record: Product Num: 70701, Product Name: Nomad Honey Handlebar tape, Category ID: 32, Supplier ID: 10, Units In Stock: 52, Units On Order: 0, Unit Price: 2, Reorder Level: 30, Reorder Amount: 35, Units: Each, DiscoStatus: No.

c. Save the record.

d. Print the form containing the new record.

▶ Independent Challenges

1. As the Customer Service Manager of the Melodies Music Store, you must continue your work on the music database. Several of the store's employees will be using the database to enter data, and you need to design a form to facilitate this data entry. The employees will be entering data from a paper-based form, shown in Figure C-24. You also need to generate reports for output requests by management as well as customers.

To complete this independent challenge:

1. Open the file "Melodies Music Database" from your Student Disk.
2. Create a single-column form that includes all the fields in the table, then save it as Title Input.
3. The controls should be positioned so that they all fit on the screen. Make sure the tab order reflects any fields that you moved.
4. Use the newly created form to add three new records of your favorite artists.
5. Print the form containing one of the new records.
6. Add an expression that calculates a new field called OnHand that multiplies the UnitsInStock field value by the UnitPrice field value. (*Hint*: Use the text box button on the Toolbox to create a new control.)

FIGURE C-24

Product ID:	Category ID:
Artist:	
Product Name:	
	Serial Number:
Units in Stock:	
Unit Price:	

2. You work in the U.S. Census Office for your city. The records in the Statistical Data table, which is in the database file "US Census Statistics" on your Student Disk, contain marriage information by state. Each state is assigned a geographical area. Using the Statistical Data table, create a form to facilitate data entry, and create at least two reports showing different groupings of this information.

To complete this independent challenge:

1. Open the database "Census."
2. Create a single-column form containing all the fields in the table.
3. Modify the form by repositioning the controls, then adjusting the tab order.
4. Save the form using a name of your choice.
5. Preview the form after each of your modifications.
6. Create at least two forms based on information in the table. Save each form using a name of your choice.
7. In both forms, make sure the tab order reflects the order of your controls.
8. Use an expression in at least one form, and modify the formatting to include numeric formats and text attributes (bold, italics, or underlining) in both forms.

3. The medical consortium, Allied Surgeons and Physicians, are very satisfied with the database you've created, and would like you to create some customized forms for them.

Using the "Allied Surgeons and Physicians" database created by an employee of the medical group, create forms and reports that will make it easy for patient entries to be made.

To complete this independent challenge:

1. Open the database "Allied Surgeons and Physicians" on your Student Disk.
2. Create a form using the Patient Records table which displays all the fields in the table.
3. Arrange the fields in a way that seems efficient for data entry.
4. Make sure the tab order is updated to reflect the new order of fields.
5. Use the new form to add one new patient for each physician.
6. Print the form containing your new entries.
7. Add an expression that calculates each patient's current age.
8. Include formatting to make the form more attractive.
9. Obtain a graphic image—or create one yourself—and insert it on the form.
10. Submit all printouts.

4. You have been asked to maintain a database of stocks for electronic and other hi-technology firms. Use the World Wide Web to gather this information, then create an attractive form you can use to enter additional records.

To complete this independent challenge:

1. Log on to the Internet and use your browser to go to http://www.course.com. From there, click the link Student On Line Companions, then click the Microsoft Office 97 Professional Edition—Illustrated: A First Course page, then click the Access link for Unit C.
2. Find information for at least 10 hi-tech or electronic company stocks, including a minimum of the stock abbreviation, the name of the parent company, and the price per share. You can add any other fields you feel are necessary.
3. Create a new database file on your Student Disk called Hi-Tech stocks.
4. Use the Table Wizard to create a table.
5. Create a new form you'll use to enter the data into the table.
6. Enter the information you retrieved from the World Wide Web.
7. Preview and print the form.
8. Hand in a printout of your work.

► Visual Workshop

Use the Current Product List query in the Bike Inventory database on your Student Disk to create the following form using the skills you learned in this Unit.

FIGURE C-25

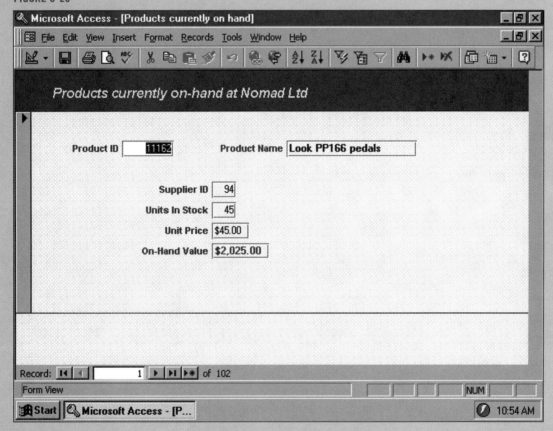

Creating
a report

Objectives

► **Create a report**
► **Group records in a report**
► **Align fields**
► **Resize a control**
► **Add an expression to a report**
► **Create a report from a query**
► **Save a form as a report**
► **Create labels**

Printed reports are an easy way of distributing information to others. Like information in a datasheet, reports can be based on a table or query, and can contain calculated expressions and sorted data. There are formatting options that let you design appealing reports that present information clearly. ◄— Michael wants to produce reports based on table data that he can distribute to other employees so they will know the status of products carried by Nomad stores.

Creating a Report

The ability to create thoughtful, concise reports enables you to share data with others in meaningful ways. The most significant data can lose its impact if it appears in an unprofessional or poorly laid out report. You can create reports in Access from scratch or you can use the Report Wizard. The **Report Wizard** provides sample report layouts and gives you options for including specific fields in the report. As with a form, the layout of a report includes sections for a Report Header, Detail, and Report Footer. Each report also includes a section for a Page Header and a Page Footer, so you can print information on each report page. ◄═══ Michael wants to create a report showing all but two fields in the Bicycle Products table. He plans on distributing this report to other Nomad employees and customers.

Steps

1. Start Access, open the **Product Inventory** database on your Student Disk, click the **New Object button list arrow** 🔳 ▾ on the Database toolbar, then click **Report**
   The New Report dialog box opens. You could also create a report by clicking the Reports tab in the Database window, then clicking New. You use the Bicycle Products table for this report, which you'll create using the Report Wizard.

2. Click the **Choose the table or query where the object's data comes from list arrow**, click **Bicycle Products**, click **Report Wizard**, then click **OK**
   The Report Wizard dialog box—which allows you to select which fields appear in the report—opens. You want all fields except the ProductID and Total fields to be included. Rather than individually select all but these two fields, you select all the fields and then remove the two fields you don't want.

3. Click the **All Fields button** ▸▸ in the Report Wizard dialog box
   All the fields move from the Available Fields list to the Selected Fields list. Now you can remove the fields you don't want included in the report.

4. Click **Total** in the Selected Fields list box, click the **Remove Field button** ◂ , click **ProductID** in the Selected Fields list box, then click ◂
   The Report Wizard dialog box on your screen should look like the one in Figure D-1.

5. Click 〔 **Next >** 〕 to display the next dialog box
   This dialog box, shown in Figure D-2, determines how the data in the report will be grouped.

FIGURE D-1: Completed Selected Fields list box

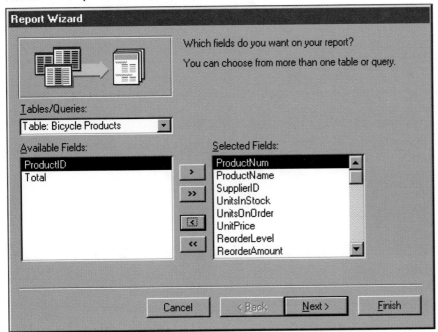

FIGURE D-2: Grouping dialog box

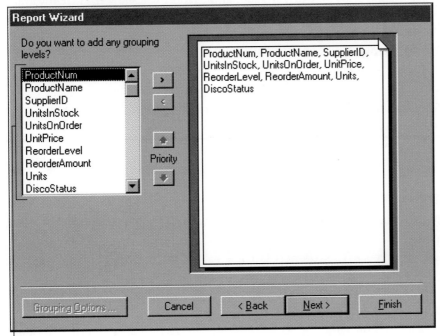

Choose how fields
are grouped using
available fields here

Using AutoReport

You can create a simple report quickly by clicking the New Object button 🗗 ▾ on the Database toolbar, then clicking AutoReport. AutoReport offers no prompts or dialog boxes; it instantly creates a single-column report that displays all fields in the table or query.

Grouping Records in a Report

The grouping of records is used to make a report easier for others to read. **Grouping** is a method of organizing records, just as sorting lets you choose the way records are displayed. For example, if you wanted to see records listed by the supplier from whom they were purchased, you would group the records by the SupplierID field. ⟶ Michael wants the report to display the inventory in groups by product name so that all of the data for the same products will be listed and totaled together.

QuickTip

The Sort Order button in this dialog box is a toggle; click to change from ascending to descending order.

1. Click **ProductName** in the **Do you want to add any grouping levels list box**, click the **Single Field button** `>`

   The ProductName field appears in blue and above the other fields. When printed, the records with all the same product names will be grouped together.

2. Click `Next >`

   This dialog box allows you to specify a sort order. You choose to sort by each record's DiscoStatus in ascending order (the default) so that the report will show all currently available items together and all discontinued items together.

3. Click the **first list arrow**, then click **DiscoStatus**

   Compare your dialog box to Figure D-3. Next, you choose which items will be totaled.

4. Click **Summary Options**, click to add a **checkmark** next to each item in the **Sum column**, as shown in Figure D-4, click **OK**, then click `Next >`

   The next two dialog boxes ask you to select a report style, paper orientation, and report title. You accept the default choices.

5. Click the **Landscape radio button**, click `Next >`, click `Next >` again, type **Products by DiscoStatus** in the What title do you want for your report text box, then click **Finish**

   Access compiles the report. The report is saved as part of the database file and the Print Preview window is opened. You need to decrease the Zoom factor to see the whole report.

6. Click the **Zoom button** 🔍 on the Print Preview toolbar

   The report appears, as shown in Figure D-5. Notice that the records are grouped by product name. You are satisfied with the report and need to preview and print your work.

Time To

✓ Save

7. Click the **Close button** on the Print Preview toolbar

   You return to Design View. You decide to print just the first page of the report to see how it looks.

8. Click **File** on the menu bar, click **Print**, type **1** in the From text box, type **1** in the To text box, then click **OK**

FIGURE D-3: Choosing the Sort order

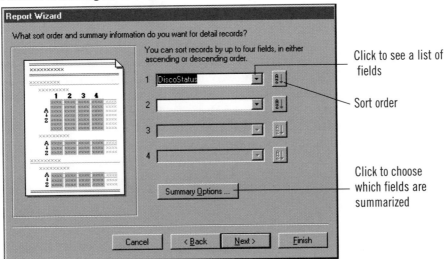

Click to see a list of fields

Sort order

Click to choose which fields are summarized

FIGURE D-4: Summary Options dialog box

Fields that can be summarized

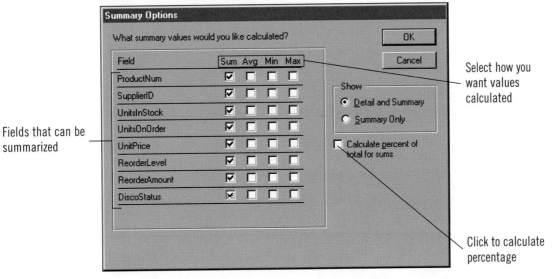

Select how you want values calculated

Click to calculate percentage

FIGURE D-5: Previewing the report

Records grouped by ProductName

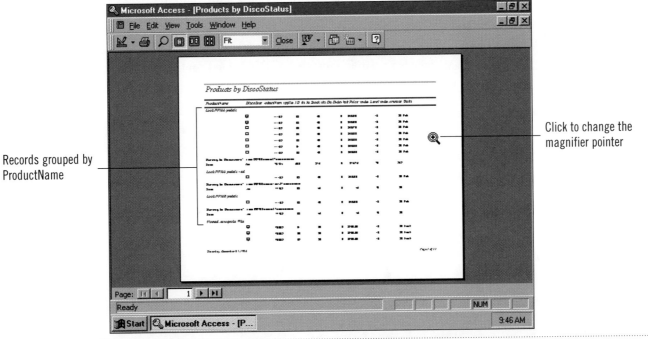

Click to change the magnifier pointer

Aligning Fields

You can make modifications to the format of a report, such as bolding column headings or changing the alignment of fields in a column. The Report Design window is divided into seven sections: the **Detail** section, which contains controls and the compiled data from the table, and a Header and Footer section for each of the following: Report, Page, and Group. The **Report Header** and **Report Footer** print only on the first and last page of the report; the **Page Header** and **Page Footer** print on every page. The **Group Header** references the field on which each group is based (in this case, the groups are based on ProductName). ◀▬ Although the Products by DiscoStatus report is adequate, Michael wants to give the report a more professional look. The field headings are not aligned with the data below them, as shown in Figure D-6. Because Michael's screen is already in Design View, he can easily align the field headings with their data to format the report.

Steps

1. **Press and hold [Shift], click each of the control headings in the Page Header section, *except* ProductName, then release [Shift]**
   You selected nine controls. You can scroll the window and move the Toolbox toolbar to select all the desired controls. Each selected control has handles surrounding it. First you center the selected controls and decrease the font size to make the text less crowded.

2. **Click the Center button ▤ on the Formatting toolbar, click the Font Size list arrow, then click 8**
   Access centers the headings for the selected controls in the Page Header section. See Figure D-7. You want to center align the controls in the Detail section of the report.

3. **Select the ProductNum control in the Detail section**
   Selecting this control without holding [Shift] deselects the previously selected controls. You continue to make multiple selections in the Detail section.

4. **Press and hold [Shift], click each of the controls in the Detail section, *except* the DiscoStatus control, release [Shift], then click ▤ on the Formatting toolbar**
   Access centers the selected controls in the Detail section. You decide that the current information in the ProductName Footer section is unnecessary and want to delete it, but first you deselect the controls in the Detail section.

5. **Click the first control in the ProductName Footer section to select it**

6. **Press and hold [Shift], click each of the controls in the ProductName Footer section, release [Shift], then press [Delete]**
   The report now has a gap in it created by the deleted controls. Later, you will add an expression in this section.

FIGURE D-6: Unedited Products by DiscoStatus report

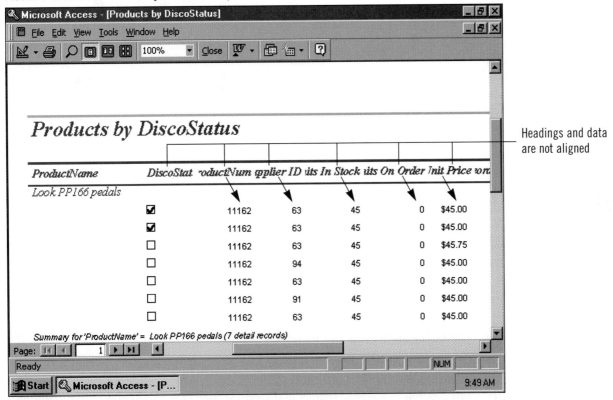

Headings and data are not aligned

FIGURE D-7: Centered controls in the report

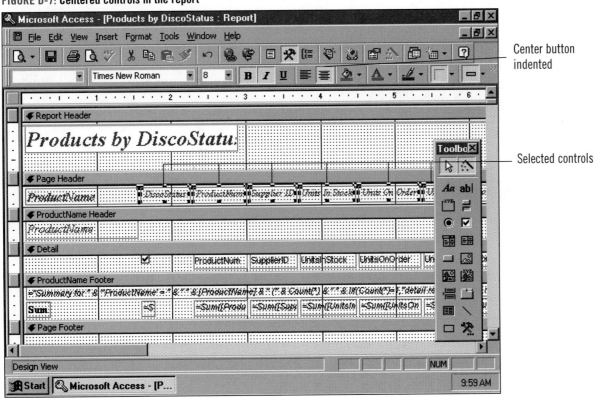

Center button indented

Selected controls

Resizing a Control

The position of controls, as well as their widths, can be changed individually or in groups. If you resize a group of controls it creates a neater, more unified look for your report. ✐━━ Next Michael decides to resize the width of the Units controls in the Detail and Page Header sections because they take up more space than the other controls. By resizing these controls, Michael will be able to tighten up the right side of the report.

Steps

1. Click the **Units control** in the Detail section, move the pointer to the right middle handle until the pointer changes to ↔, then drag the handle until it is aligned with 8.25" on the horizontal ruler, as shown in Figure D-8
   Repeat this procedure for the Units control in the Page Header section.

2. Click the **Units control** in the Page Header section, move the pointer to the right middle handle until the pointer changes to ↔, then drag the handle until it is aligned with 8.25" on the horizontal ruler
   The Units controls in the Page Header and Detail sections are now aligned and resized with each other. You want to preview the report and print a sample page.

3. Click the **Print Preview button** 🔍 on the Report Design toolbar
   The controls in the report are aligned, as shown in Figure D-9.

4. Click **File** on the menu bar, click **Print**, click **1** in the From text box, click **1** in the To text box, then click **OK**
   You close the Print Preview window and save the report.

5. Click the **Close button** on the Print Preview toolbar

6. Save your work

FIGURE D-8: Resizing a control

Line up the edge of
the control with the
horizontal ruler

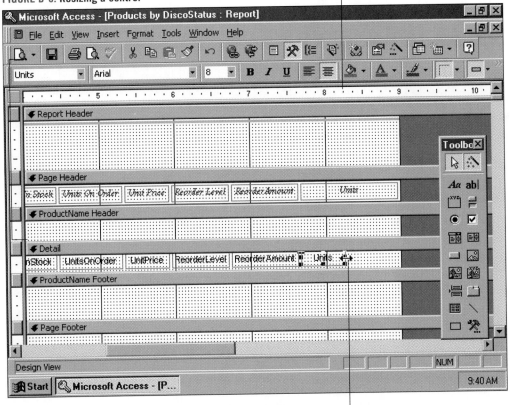

Resizing pointer

FIGURE D-9: Report in Print Preview

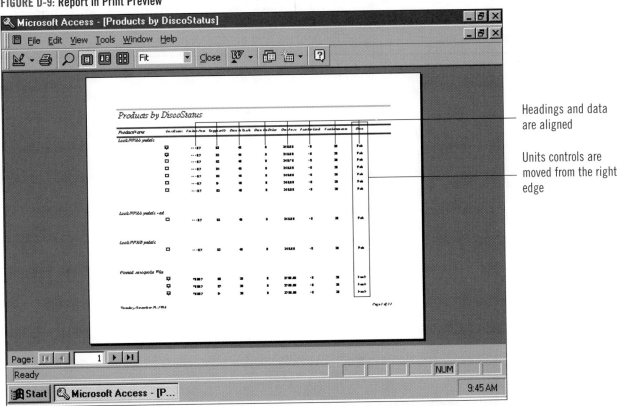

Headings and data
are aligned

Units controls are
moved from the right
edge

Adding an Expression to a Report

You have already seen how an expression can be incorporated in a form. You can also add an expression to a report to perform calculations. The expression can include field names, table names, and functions. A **function** is an easy-to-use preprogrammed mathematical equation. Michael wants to add an expression to the Products by DiscoStatus report. The expression will count the number of products in each group, by product identification number.

QuickTip

In addition to Count, Access provides many other functions for use in expressions. Ask the Office Assistant how you can use functions in expressions for more information.

1. **Click the Text box button** `abl` **on the Toolbox toolbar, then click in the ProductName Footer section directly under the ProductNum control at the 2¼" mark**
   This places an unbound control in the ProductName Footer section, where you will type the expression. The expression will include the Count function, which counts the number of occurrences of a specified field in a column.

2. **Click inside the unbound control, type =Count([ProductNum]), then press [Enter]**
   The expression appears in the control, as shown in Figure D-10, although some of its contents might be truncated, or cut off. You want to preview the report to see the results of the expression.

3. **Click the Print Preview button** `📷` **on the Report Design toolbar, click the Zoom button** `🔍` **if necessary**
   The number of records in each group has been counted, although the values need to be aligned with the values in the ProductNum column and it needs a descriptive label.

4. **Click the Close button on the Print Preview toolbar, then with the expression still selected, click the Align Left button** `▤` **on the Report Design toolbar**
   You decide to preview the report again to check the results of this modification.

5. **Click** `📷`**, view the results of the modified control, then click the Close button on the Print Preview toolbar**
   When viewing the report in Print Preview, you see the value in the expression is left-aligned in the ProductNum column. Next, add a label to describe what the values represent in the report.

6. **Click the unbound label text box control to the left of the expression, double-click the text in the box, type Items in Category, press [Enter], click the Font Size list arrow, click 9**
   The label is added to the report as shown in Figure D-11. You again preview the report.

7. **Click** `📷`
   Compare your previewed report with Figure D-12. Use Zoom as needed. You print the first page of the report, then close the Print Preview window and save the modifications.

Time To

✔ Save
✔ Close the report

8. **Click File on the menu bar, click Print, type 1 in the From text box, type 1 in the To text box, click OK, then click the Close button on the Print Preview toolbar**

Adding a field to a report

In addition to adding expressions, you can always add existing fields to a report. Any tables whose fields are available in the table can be dragged to areas within a report by clicking the Field List button `▤` on the Report Design toolbar, then dragging a field to an area of the report.

FIGURE D-10: **Truncated expression in control**

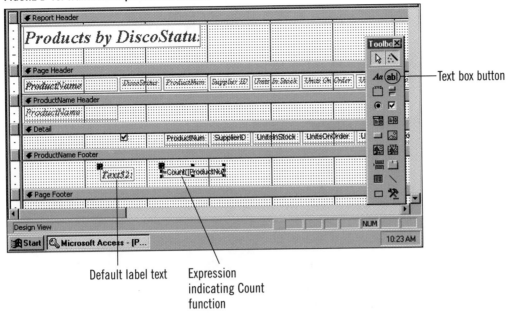

Text box button

Default label text

Expression indicating Count function

FIGURE D-11: **Descriptive label added to expression**

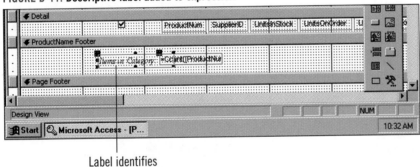

Label identifies results of expression

FIGURE D-12: **Completed report with expression and label**

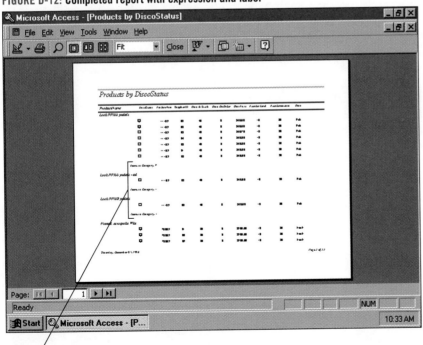

Labels and results of expression

Creating a Report from a Query

You've seen how to create a report based on the fields in a table. Many times, however, you will want to use a query as the basis for a report to save time since the query may already contain the information you want printed. ✎✎✎ Michael has created a query for the Bicycle Products table called Current Product List to display only current products. He wants to use this query as the basis for a new report. Again, he'll use the Report Wizard to create this report.

Steps

1. Click the **New Object button list arrow** 🖾 on the Database toolbar, then click **Report**, click the **Choose the table or query where the object's data comes from list box**, click the **Current Product List** then click **Report Wizard**
   Compare your New Report dialog box with Figure D-13.

2. Click **OK**
   The Report Wizard dialog box opens, as shown in Figure D-14. The Available Fields list box displays all the available fields in the query (not all the fields in the table). You want to include all these fields in the report.

3. Click the **All Fields button** >> , then click Next >
   You want the records grouped by ProductName.

4. Click **ProductName**, then click the **Single Field button** >
   The records will be grouped by the ProductName field, as shown in Figure D-15. You need to advance to the next dialog box which lets you determine the sort order. You decide that you don't need to sort by any other fields and accept the default.

5. Click Next >, click Next > again
   Next, you decide to accept the default layout and orientation, style, and report title.

6. Click Next >, click Next >, then click **Finish**
   Access creates the report and displays it in Print Preview.

7. Click the **Close button** on the Print Preview toolbar
   Satisfied with the report, you decide to print the first page as a sample.

8. Click **File** on the menu bar, click **Print**, type **1** in the From text box, type **1** in the To text box, then click **OK**

9. Save the report using the default report name **Current Product List**, then close it

QuickTip
When basing a report on a query, give the report the same name as the query name; this will remind you that the report and the query are related.

FIGURE D-13: New Report dialog box

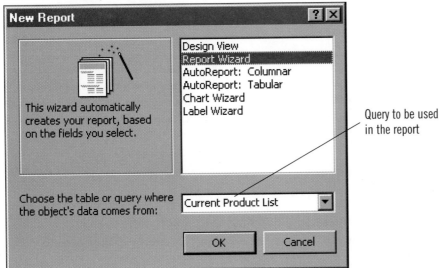

Query to be used in the report

FIGURE D-14: Report Wizard dialog box

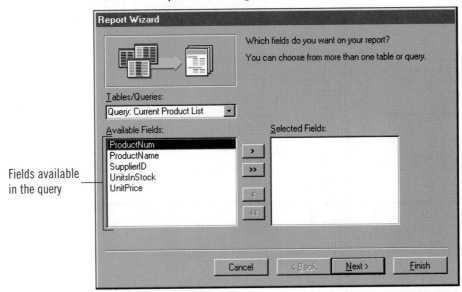

Fields available in the query

FIGURE D-15: Grouping records in the Report Wizard dialog box

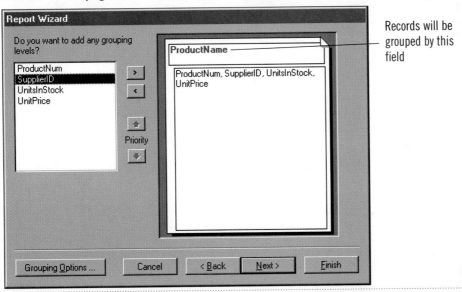

Records will be grouped by this field

Saving a Form as a Report

If you already have a form designed that meets your needs, you can work more efficiently by saving a form as a report. This can be an efficient way of creating a familiar-looking report, because your co-workers will already have seen the form. To save a form as a report, open the form in Design View, click File on the menu bar, click Save As Report, then supply a new name for the report. Michael creates a report from the Bicycle Products form.

Steps

1. **Click the Forms tab, then make sure the Bicycle Products form is selected**
   Once the form is selected, you can save it as a report using the context-sensitive pop-up menu.

2. **Right-click the Bicycle Products form**
   The pop-up menu appears, as shown in Figure D-16. You select the Save As Report command.

3. **Click Save As Report**
   You can keep the same name used in the form, but you choose to change the name for the report.

4. **Type Bicycle Products - from Form in the Report Name text box, as shown in Figure D-17, then click OK**
   You decide to preview the report created from the form.

5. **Click the Reports tab, click Bicycle Products - from Form report, then click the Print Preview button on the Database toolbar**

6. **If necessary, click the Maximize button and scroll to see all the records in the report**
   Compare your report to Figure D-18. Satisfied with the new report, you close the Preview window.

7. **Click the Close button on the Print Preview toolbar**

8. **Close the report**

FIGURE D-16: Pop-up menu

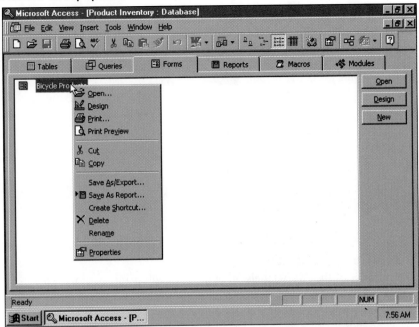

FIGURE D-17: Save Form As Report dialog box

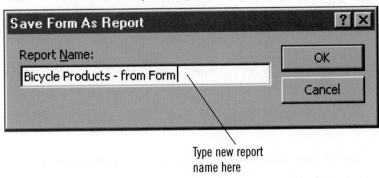

Type new report
name here

FIGURE D-18: Preview of report created from form

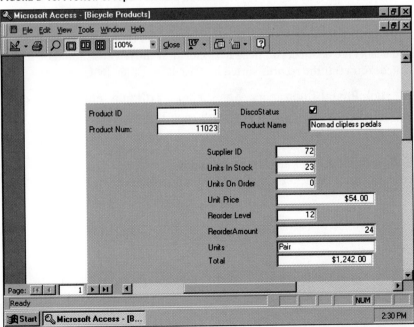

Creating Labels

Labels are a necessity in any office, and they are easy to create using the Access Label Wizard. If you use Avery labels, you'll be able to find the size and style label you currently use, making creating labels based on table or query records a snap. ◄ Michael needs to prepare labels for Nomad customers. He'll use the Label Wizard and the Customers table in the Bicycle Supplies database.

Steps 1 2 3 4

1. **Click the New button on the Reports tab**
   The New Report dialog box opens. You'll create your labels using the Customers table and the Label Wizard.

2. **Click Label Wizard, click the Choose the Table or query where the object's data comes from list arrow, click Customers, then click OK**
   Next, you select the number of the Avery labels on which you will print, as shown in Figure D-19. You decide to use Avery number 5160, that prints 3 labels across each sheet.

3. **Click 5160, then click** [Next >]
   The third dialog box allows you to change the font, font size, and other text attributes. You choose to accept the default values.

4. **Click** [Next >]
   In the next dialog box, you choose which fields you want to include in each label, as well as their placement. Each field is selected from the Available Fields list in the order you want them on the label. Any spaces, punctuation, or hard returns have to be entered using the keyboard.
   Enter the information for the first line in the label.

QuickTip

Double-click the field name in the Available Fields list to move it to the Prototype label text box.

5. **Click FirstName, click the Single Field button** [>]**, press the [Spacebar], click LastName, click** [>]**, then press [Enter]**
   Next, you'll enter the fields for the information containing the address, city, state, and postal code.

6. **Repeat step 5 entering the remaining fields using Figure D-20 as a guide**
   Once the fields in the label are defined, you need to decide how the records should be sorted when they are printed. You want the records sorted by PostalCode, then by LastName.

7. **Click** [Next >]**, click Postal Code, click** [>]**, click LastName, click** [>]**, click** [Next >]**, then click Finish to accept the default report name**
   The labels display in Print Preview.

Time To

✔ Close
✔ Exit

8. **Click the magnifier pointer 🔍 to see the whole page**
   Compare your screen to Figure D-21. You are pleased with the labels and will print them later.

FIGURE D-19: Second Label Wizard dialog box

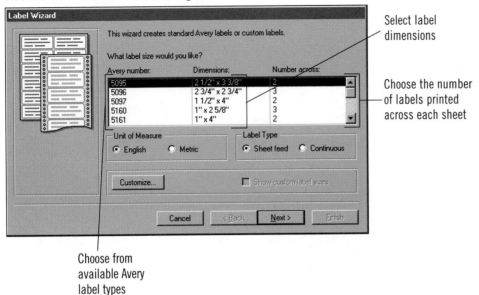

Select label
dimensions

Choose the number
of labels printed
across each sheet

Choose from
available Avery
label types

FIGURE D-20: Defining fields in a label

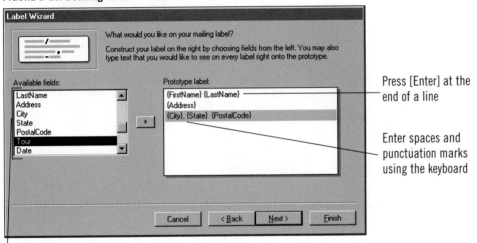

Press [Enter] at the
end of a line

Enter spaces and
punctuation marks
using the keyboard

Fields from the table
or query display here

FIGURE D-21: Completed labels

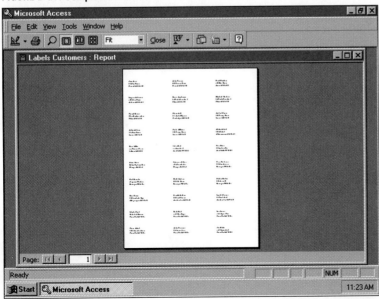

Practice

▶ Concepts Review

Label each of the elements of the Report Design window shown in Figure D-22.

FIGURE D-22

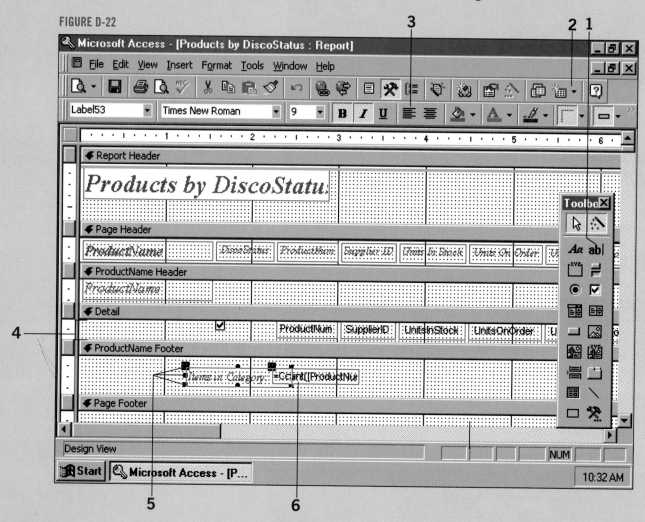

Match each button to its correct description.

7. 🗗 ▾   a. Print Preview
8. ab| b. Zoom
9. <   c. New Object
10. 🔎   d. Select field
11. 🔍   e. Remove field
12. >   f. Text box

Select the best answer from the list of choices.

13. Which key do you press to select multiple controls?
  a. [Ctrl]   **b.** [Alt]   **c.** [Shift]   **d.** [Tab]

14. The _____ section contains controls and compiles data.
  a. Detail   **b.** Report Header   **c.** Group Header   **d.** Report Footer

15. Which button is used to add an unbound control to a report?
  a. ⊟   **b.** 🖼   **c.** Aa   **d.** abl

16. Which of the following is true about report expressions?
  a. They can contain mathematical functions.
  b. In Design View, the contents may appear truncated.
  c. The label text can be customized.
  d. All of the above.

17. How can labels be created?
  a. Click 📋▾, then click Labels
  b. Click Reports from the menu bar, then click Label Wizard
  c. Click New from the Reports tab, then click Label Wizard
  d. Click 📇 from the Database toolbar

▶ Skills Review

1. Create a report.
   a. Open the Parts List database on your Student Disk.
   b. Create a Groups/Totals report based on the Products table using the Report Wizard.
   c. Include all the fields in the report.

2. Group records in a report.
   a. Group the report by UnitsinStock.
   b. Sort the report in ascending order by ProductName.
   c. Summarize three fields, get an average for unit price and a sum for the reorder amount and units on order fields.
   d. Accept the default report layout.
   e. Use the Formal style.
   f. Save the report as Products by Units in Stock.
   g. Preview the report with the data in it.
   h. Print the report.

3. Align fields.
   a. Align the fields so that the values are centered with the headings above them.
   b. Delete the reorder amount summary which detracts from the report.
   c. Preview and print the report.
   d. Save your changes.

4. Resize a control.
   a. Change the font size of the Page Header controls to 8.
   b. Move the ReorderAmount controls closer to the edge of the page.
   c. Resize the ReorderAmount control so it takes up only enough room to display its label.
   d. Save your modifications.
   e. Preview the report.

5. Add an expression to a report.
   a. Create an expression in the Detail section under ProductName that subtracts ReorderLevel from UnitsinStock. (*Hint*: Drag the section divider to make room for the new expression)
   b. Add the descriptive label "Reorder if Negative" to the left of the expression.
   c. Adjust the fonts sizes and control locations to create a professional-looking report.
   d. Preview and print the report.
   e. Save your changes.

6. Create a report from a query.

a. Use the Report Wizard and create a report using the Products sold as "Each" query.

b. Group the report by UnitsinStock.

c. Sort the report by ProductName.

d. Accept the default layout, style, and name for the report.

e. Preview the report with the data.

f. Move the controls and align the fields as necessary to create a professional-looking report.

g. Print the report.

7. Save a form as a report.

a. Save the Bicycle Parts Database form as a report. Name the new report: Parts List Database - from Form.

b. Print the first page of the new report.

8. Create labels.

a. Use the Label Wizard and the Products table to create stock room shelf labels using Avery 5160 labels.

b. The first line of the label should include the ProductNum and the ProductName.

c. The second line of the label should include the ReorderLevel and the ReorderAmount.

d. The third line of the label should include the UnitPrice.

e. Sort the labels by the ProductName.

f. Name this report "Shelf Labels."

g. Save your work.

h. Print the page of labels.

▶ Independent Challenges

1. You have been using the "Music Store" database for several weeks, and now need to design several reports that can be printed on a weekly basis. Four reports are needed: one that lists all the items in the Available titles table, and one for each of the existing queries.

To complete this independent challenge:

1. Open the file "Music Store" from your Student Disk.
2. Create a report using the Available titles table that displays all the table's fields, grouped by Artist and sorted in descending order by TitleName.
3. The UnitsInStock field should be summed, and the UnitPrice field should be averaged.
4. Use the Outline1 report layout and the Casual style.
5. Name this report Complete titles list.
6. Preview the report.
7. Modify the font size of the heading controls so all the column labels are visible.
8. Save your changes.
9. Preview and print the first page of the report.

▶ Independent Challenges

2. You have determined that shelf labels would make inventory control much more efficient at your music store. On a weekly basis, the inventory is checked against the cash register receipts and the shelves are restocked. Use the Available titles table in the "Music Store" database to design a shelf label.

To complete this independent challenge:

1. Open the file "Music Store" from your Student Disk.
2. Use the Label Wizard and the Available titles table to create shelf labels. Use Avery 5160 labels and red semi-bold, italics text.
3. The first line should say "Artist: ", then display the Artist name, the second line should display the TitleName, and the third line should display the SerialNumber, UnitsInStock, and UnitPrice.
4. Sort the labels by Artist, then by TitleName.
5. Name the report Available Titles Shelf Labels.
6. Save, preview and print report.

Independent Challenges

3. The database you created for the Allied Surgeons and Physicians is very successful. In fact, they would like you to create a report based on the "Patient Records" table.

To complete this independent challenge:

1. Open the file "ASP Database" from your Student Disk.
2. Create a report using the following fields in the Patient Records table: ID, FirstName, LastName, DateofBirth. Gender, Telephone, KnownAllergies, MostRecentVisit, and PhysicianLastName.
3. Group the records by PhysicianLastName.
4. Sort the records by LastName, then FirstName.
5. Use the Outline2 report layout and the Compact style.
6. Name this report All Patients list.
7. Preview the report.
8. Make sure all the column labels are visible.
9. Save your changes.
10. Preview and print the first page of the report.

 Independent Challenges

4. Use your knowledge and skills navigating the World Wide Web to create attractive reports of information about colleges and universities. Locate information about institutions that offer programs in computer use, create a database containing this information, then design reports that display this data.
To complete this independent challenge:

1. Create a new database called "Colleges" on your Student Disk. Include any fields you feel are important, but make sure you include the institution's name, state, and whether it is a 4 or 2-year school.
2. Log on to the Internet and use your browser to go to http://www.course.com. From there, click the link Student On Line Companions, then click the Microsoft Office 97 Professional Edition—Illustrated: A First Course page, then click the Access link for Unit D. Search the World Wide Web for schools that offer programs in computer science using any available search engines.
3. Compile a list of at least 15 institutions.
4. Enter the information in your database.
5. Create a report that includes all the fields in the table, and use the default grouping.
6. Sort the records by the state, then by the institution's name.
7. Save, preview and print the report.
8. Hand in a printout of your work.

▶ Visual Workshop

Use the Products table in the Parts List database to create these labels. Use the settings for Avery label 5161. Sort the labels by SupplierID, then by ProductName, and name the report "Warehouse Labels."

FIGURE D-23

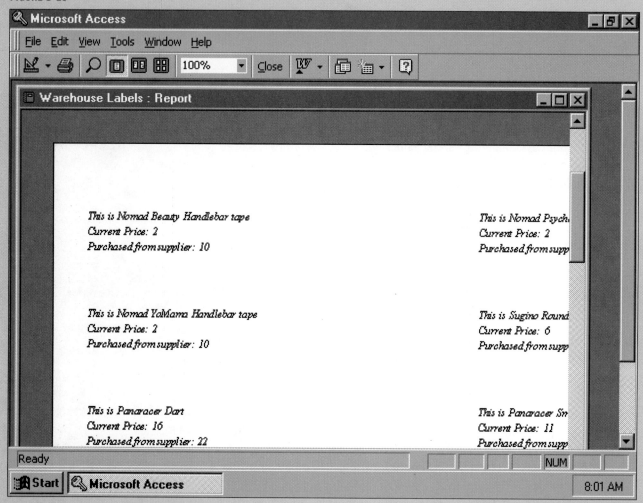

Modifying
a Database Structure

Objectives

- ► **Examine relational database requirements**
- ► **Plan a table**
- ► **Create new tables**
- ► **Create one-to-many relationships**
- ► **Delete fields**
- ► **Define field properties**
- ► **Define date/time field properties**
- ► **Define field validation properties**

In this unit, you will add new tables to an existing database and link them in one-to-many relationships to create a relational database. You will also modify several field **properties** such as field formatting and field validation to increase data entry accuracy. Michael Belmont has decided to expand the use of Access within Nomad to track customer, tour, and sales information. Because a single table database will not meet all of his needs, he will use multiple tables of data and link them together to create a relational database.

Examining Relational Database Requirements

A **relational database** is a collection of related tables that share information. The goals of a relational database are to satisfy dynamic information management needs and to eliminate duplicate data entry wherever possible. ◄══ After analyzing Nomad's sales transactions, Michael begins to see repeat customers. The Customers table shown in Figure E-1 allows Michael to sort and retrieve specific information on customers and tours very quickly, but does not have an easy way to track more than one sale to the same customer. The following list of database concepts will guide Michael's actions as he moves from a single table of data to the powerful relational database capabilities provided by Access.

A relational database is based on multiple tables of data. Each table should be based on only one subject.

Right now the Customers table in the Nomad database actually contains three subjects: Customers, Tours, and Sales. Michael knows that duplicate data across records of a table is a clue that a database needs to be redesigned into multiple tables. By breaking out each of these subjects into its own table, Michael will eliminate redundant data and increase the flexibility of his database.

Each record in a table should be uniquely identified with a key field or key field combination.

A **key field** is a field which contains unique information for each record. Typically, a customer table contains a Customer Identification (CustID) field to uniquely identify each customer. While using the customer's last name as the key field might accommodate a small database, it would be a poor choice and bad database design because it won't allow the user to enter two customers with the same last name.

Tables in the same database should be related, or linked, through a field common to each table in a one-to-many relationship.

To tie the information from the Customers table to the Sales table, the CustID field would need to be in both tables. Because the CustID field is a key field in the Customers table, this side of the relationship is the "one" side. Because the CustID field may be listed many times in the Sales table to record multiple sales to the same customer, this side of the relationship is the "many" side. Linking tables together with a common field in this manner is called creating a **one-to-many relationship** and is shown in Figure E-2.

FIGURE E-1: The datasheet of the Customers table

CustID	First	Last	Street	City	State	Zip	Tour	Date	Birth Date
1	Ginny	Braithwaite	3 Which Way	Salem	MA	01970	Road Bike	6/15/96	1/10/60
10	Virginia	Rodarmor	123 Main Street	Andover	MA	01810	Bungee	9/20/96	1/6/70
11	Kristen	Reis	4848 Ashley	Fontanelle	IA	50810	Big Sky	1/10/97	3/18/68
12	Tom	Reis	4848 Ashley	Fontanelle	IA	50810	Big Sky	1/10/97	7/3/65
13	Mark	Eagan	987 Lincoln	Schaumberg	IL	44433	Big Sky	1/10/97	1/29/60
14	Peg	Fox	125 Maple	Des Moines	IA	50625	Big Sky	1/10/97	4/10/59
15	Ron	Fox	125 Maple	Des Moines	IA	50625	Big Sky	1/10/97	8/28/87
16	Amanda	Fox	125 Maple	Des Moines	IA	50625	Big Sky	1/10/97	1/30/88
17	Rebecca	Gross	123 Oak	Bridgewater	KS	50837	Road Bike	6/15/96	9/20/62
2	Robin	Spencer	293 Serenity Dr.	Concord	MA	01742	Mt. Bike	9/26/96	1/30/52
3	Camilla	Dobbins	486 Intel Circuit	Rio Rancho	NM	87124	Road Bike	6/15/96	3/15/65
4	Pip	Khalsa	1100 Vista Road	Santa Fe	NM	87505	Mt. Bike	9/26/96	4/16/69
5	Kendra	Majors	530 Spring Street	Lenox	MA	02140	Bungee	9/20/96	5/4/70
6	Tasha	Williams	530 Spring Street	Lenox	MA	02140	Road Bike	6/15/96	5/8/71
7	Fred	Gonzales	Purgatory Ski Area	Durango	CO	81301	Mt. Bike	6/15/96	6/10/60
8	John	Black	11 River Road	Brookfield	CT	06830	Road Bike	6/15/96	7/15/65
9	Scott	Owen	72 Yankee Way	Brookfield	CT	06830	Bungee	9/20/96	3/15/65

Customers : Table

Record: 1 of 17

FIGURE E-2: A relational database with two tables

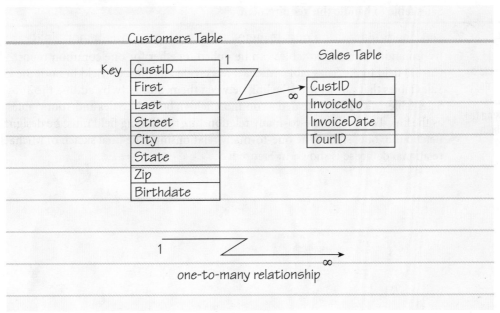

Planning a Table

Careful planning is crucial to successful relational database design and creation. Not only is duplicated data error-prone, but it limits the query and reporting capabilities of the overall database. Once you understand the concepts and goals of a relational database, you'll often need to redistribute the fields of the database into new tables. ◀━━ Michael realizes that the current single-table database provides no way to track additional sales to existing customers without duplicating all of the customer's demographic data such as name and address. Michael decides to get some advice on how to redesign his database from a database expert.

Details

List all of the fields of data that need to be tracked
Typically, these fields are already present in existing tables or paper reports. Still, it is a good idea to document each field on a single sheet of paper in order to examine all fields at the same time. This is the appropriate time to determine if there are additional fields of information that do not currently exist on any report, but that should be tracked for future purposes. Michael decides that in addition to the existing fields in the Customers table he would also like to start tracking tour cost, tour sales price, invoice date, tour handicap accessibility, and tour difficulty.

Group fields together in subject matter tables
The new Nomad database will track sales to customers, a common use for a relational database in business. It will contain three tables: Customers, Tours, and Sales.

Identify key fields that exist in tables
Each table should include a key field or key field combination in order to uniquely identify each record. Each customer, tour, and sale must be uniquely identified. Michael will use the CustID field in the Customers table, the TourID field in the Tours table, and the InvoiceNo field in the Sales table to handle this requirement.

QuickTip

The linking field should be the only field that is duplicated in two tables. For clarity, give the linking field the same name in both tables.

Link the tables with a one-to-many relationship via a common field
Information from linked tables can be pulled together for one common report. By adding the CustID field to the Sales table, Michael has created a common field in both the Customers and Sales tables that can serve as the link between them. Similarly, by adding the TourID field to the Sales table, Michael has created a common field in both the Sales and Tours tables that can serve as the link. For a valid one-to-many relationship, the linking field must be designated as the key field in the "one" side of the one-to-many relationship. The final sketch of Michael's redesigned relational database is shown in Figure E-3.

► AC E-4   **MODIFYING A DATABASE STRUCTURE**

FIGURE E-3: Final sketch of the redesigned relational database

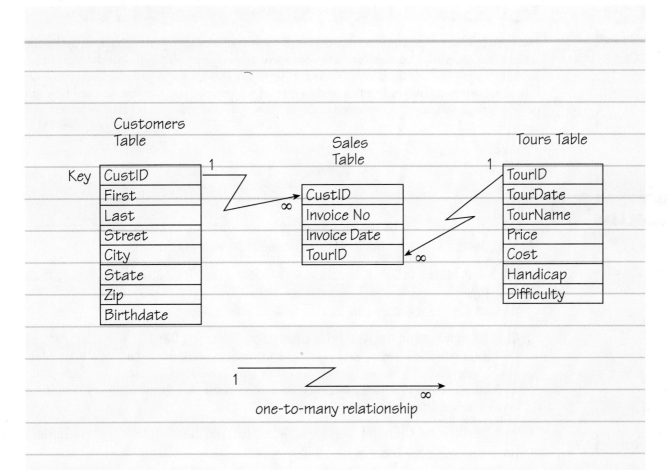

one-to-many relationship

Key field combinations

Identifying a single key field may be difficult in some tables. Examine, for instance, a table that records employee promotions over time that includes three fields: employee number, date, and pay rate. None of the fields individually could serve as a valid key field because none are restricted to unique data. The employee number and date together, however, could serve as a valid **key field combination** since the employee number and date together would uniquely identify the record.

Creating New Tables

Once you have developed a valid relational database design on paper, you are ready to define the tables in Access. All characteristics of a table including field names, data types, field descriptions, field properties, and key fields are designed in the table's **Design View**. In a relational database, it is important to define the length and data type of the linking field the same in both tables in order to create a successful link. ◀━━━ Using his new database design, Michael will create the Sales and Tours tables.

1. Start Access and open the **Nomad-E** database on your Student Disk

2. Click the **Tables tab** in the database window if it is not already selected, then click **New**
   You will enter the fields directly into the table's Design View.

3. Click **Design View** in the New Table dialog box, then click **OK**
   First define the field names, data types, and other field properties of the new Sales table. Field names should be as short as possible, but long enough to be descriptive because the field name entered in a table's Design View is used as the default name for the field in all later queries, forms, and reports.

QuickTip

You can press [Enter] or [Tab] to move to the next column in a table's Design View window.

4. Type **CustID**, press [Enter], press **t** to select the Text Data Type, and press [Enter] twice to bypass the Description column

5. Type the other fields and enter the data types as shown below:

Field Name	Data Type
InvoiceNo	**AutoNumber**
InvoiceDate	**Date/Time**
TourID	**Text**

6. Click **InvoiceNo** in the Field Name column, then click the **Primary Key button** 🔑 on the Table Design toolbar
   The completed table Design View for the Sales table is shown in Figure E-4. Next, name, save, and close the Sales table.

Trouble?

If you clicked the Access program window Close button rather than the table's Close button, you closed the entire Nomad-E database. To continue work, simply start Access, open Nomad-E, and resume work.

7. Click the **Save button** 💾 on the Table Design toolbar, type **Sales** in the Table Name text box in the Save As dialog box, click **OK**, then click the **Close button** in the Sales: Table Design View window
   Sales is now displayed in the Tables tab, and it is a table in the Nomad-E database.

8. Click **New**, click **Design View**, click **OK**, then design the **Tours** table using the field information for the Tours table shown in Figure E-5
   Now that you have entered all the field information for the Tours table, name and save the table.

9. Click 💾, type **Tours** in the Table Name text box in the Save As dialog box, click **OK**, then click the **Close button** in the Tours : Table Design View window
   Sales and Tours are now displayed in the Tables tab in the Nomad-E database.

FIGURE E-4: Design View for the Sales table

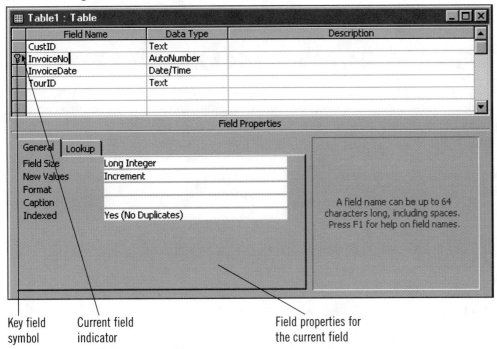

Key field
symbol

Current field
indicator

Field properties for
the current field

FIGURE E-5: Design View for the Tours table

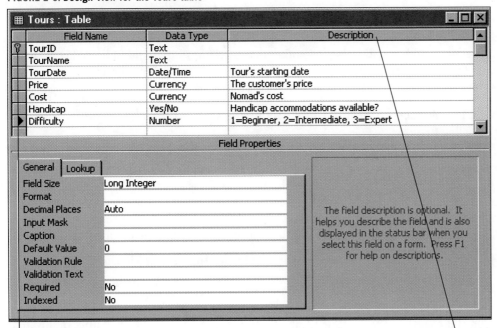

Assign Tour1D as
the Primary key
field

Field descriptions

Linked tables

A **linked table** is a table created in another database product, or another application such as Excel, that is stored in a file outside of the open database. You can add, delete, and edit records in a linked table from within Access but you can't change its structure. An **imported table** creates a copy of the information from the external file, and places it in a new Access table in your database.

Creating One-to-Many Relationships

Once the initial database design and table entry phase has been completed, you must identify which fields will link the tables in one-to-many relationships. Once the tables are linked, queries, reports, and forms can be designed with fields from multiple tables. 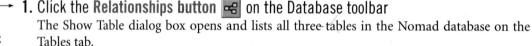 Michael's initial database sketch revealed that the CustID field will link the Customer table to the Sales table and that the TourID field will link the Tours table to the Sales table. Michael will now define the one-to-many relationships between the tables of the Nomad database.

Steps

Trouble?

If the Show Table dialog box is not open, click the Show Table button 📇 on the Relationships toolbar.

Trouble?

If all of a table's field names are not displayed in the Relationships window, drag the bottom border of the table window until the scroll bar disappears and all fields are visible.

QuickTip

To delete a table from the Relationships window, click the table and press [Delete].

QuickTip

To print a copy of the Relationships window, press [Print Screen] while viewing the window, start an empty word processing document, paste, then print the document.

1. Click the **Relationships button** 🔗 on the Database toolbar
   The Show Table dialog box opens and lists all three tables in the Nomad database on the Tables tab.

2. Click **Customers** on the **Tables tab** if it is not already selected, click **Add**, click **Sales**, click **Add**, click **Tours**, click **Add**, then click **Close**
   The field lists of all three tables have been added to the Relationships window with key fields in bold. Now Michael can create links between the tables.

3. Maximize the window, then drag the **CustID field** from the Customers table to the **CustID field** in the Sales table
   Dragging a field from one table to another in the Relationships window links the two tables with the chosen field and opens the Relationships dialog box shown in Figure E-6. **Referential integrity** between the tables helps insure data accuracy.

4. Click the **Enforce Referential Integrity check box** in the Relationships dialog box, then click **Create**
   The **one-to-many line** shows the linkage between the CustID field of the Customers table and the Sales table. The "one" side of the relationship is the unique CustID for each record in the Customers table. The "many" side of the relationship is identified by an infinity symbol pointing to the CustID field in the Sales table. This relationship allows repeat customer sales to be recorded in the Sales table without duplicating any of the static customer data in the Customers table. The only field that is duplicated is the data in the linking CustID field.

5. Drag the **TourID field** from the Tours table to the **TourID field** in the Sales table
   The TourID field will link the Sales table to additional information about each tour in the Tours table.

6. Click the **Enforce Referential Integrity check box** in the Relationships dialog box, then click **Create**
   The finished Relationships window with all of the field names displayed should look like Figure E-7. Close the Relationships window and save the layout changes.

7. Click the **Close button** in the Relationships window, then click **Yes**
   Michael is finished with the database today, so he'll close it.

8. Click the **Close button** in the Nomad-E : Database window

FIGURE E-6: Creating table relationships

Customers Table field list

Sales table field list

Tours table field list

The CustID field defines the one-to-many relationship between the customers and sales tables

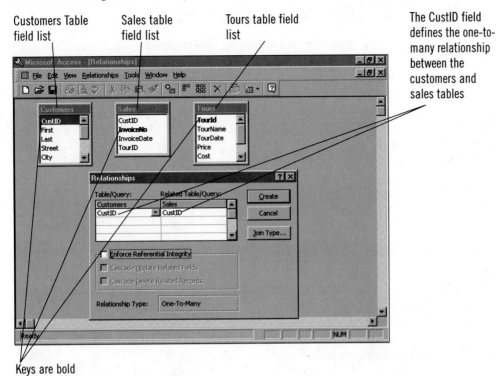

Keys are bold

FIGURE E-7: The final Relationships window

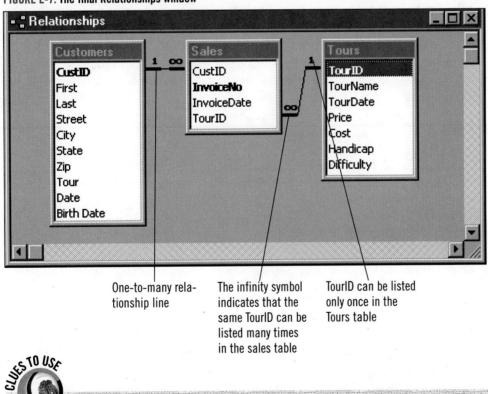

One-to-many relationship line

The infinity symbol indicates that the same TourID can be listed many times in the sales table

TourID can be listed only once in the Tours table

Why enforcing referential integrity is important

By using the Enforce Referential Integrity option, you are enforcing a set of rules to help maintain the accuracy of your database. In this case, referential integrity would not allow you to enter a CustID in the Sales table that had not already been entered in the

Customers table. Similarly, you could not enter a TourID in the Sales table that had not already been entered in the Tours table. That way, you cannot record a sale to an unidentified customer or nonexistent tour.

MODIFYING A DATABASE STRUCTURE

Deleting Fields

Once a database is redesigned to handle relational data, there can be quite a bit of "cleanup" work to do. Changes to a table such as adding new fields, deleting unnecessary fields, or changing field properties are done in a table's Design View. ◄■■■ When Michael redesigned his database, he moved the Tour information from the Customers table to the Tours table. In addition, he started tracking new fields that describe each tour such as Price, Cost, Handicap, and Difficulty. These changes created a considerable data entry project that Michael completed and saved as the database Nomad-E2.

1. Click the **Open Database button** 🖼 on the Database toolbar and open the **Nomad-E2** database

   The Nomad-E2 database contains the data Michael entered in the Tours and Sales tables. In order to verify his work, he printed the datasheets from the Tours table shown in Figure E-8 and the Sales table shown in Figure E-9. Now that the tour and sales information is saved in the appropriate tables of the Nomad-E2 relational database, you can eliminate the Tour and Date fields from the Customers table.

2. Click the **Tables tab** in the Nomad-E2 : Database window if it is not already chosen, click the **Customers table**, then click **Design**

3. Scroll down the field names, click the **Tour field selector**, then press **[Delete]**

   Access warns you that deleting this field will delete all of the data in the field. Since this information has been safely entered in the Tours table, you can delete the field from the Customers table.

4. Click **Yes**

5. Repeat steps 3 and 4 to delete the **Date field** from the Customers table

   The new Design View of the Customers table should look like Figure E-10. Save the changes to the table.

6. Click the **Save button** 🖫 on the toolbar

Trouble?

If the entire row isn't high-lighted, you selected the field name rather than the field selector button to the left of the field name.

Trouble?

If you delete the wrong field, you can undo the action by clicking the Undo button 🔙. You can only undo your last action, however, so you must act immediately once the mistake occurs.

FIGURE E-8: Datasheet for the Tours table

Current record indicator symbol →

Current record →

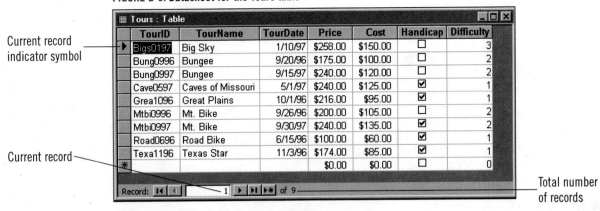

Total number of records →

FIGURE E-9: Datasheet for the Sales table

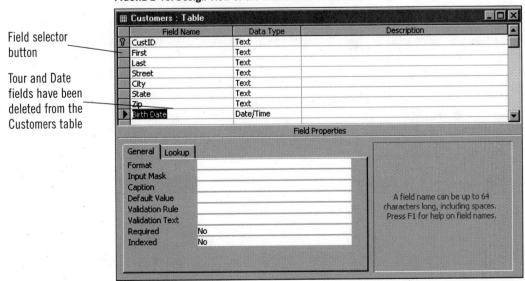

These sales represent repeat customers

FIGURE E-10: Design View of the final Customers table

Field selector button →

Tour and Date fields have been deleted from the Customers table →

Field Name	Data Type	Description
CustID	Text	
First	Text	
Last	Text	
Street	Text	
City	Text	
State	Text	
Zip	Text	
Birth Date	Date/Time	

Field Properties

General | Lookup

Format
Input Mask
Caption
Default Value
Validation Rule
Validation Text
Required   No
Indexed   No

A field name can be up to 64 characters long, including spaces. Press F1 for help on field names.

Access 97

Defining Field Properties

Field properties are the characteristics that apply to each field in a table, such as field size, default value, or field formats. Modifying these properties helps insure database accuracy and clarity. ◄ Michael decides to make three field property changes in the Customers table. He will alter the field size, format, and default value properties for the State field.

Steps

QuickTip

Most field properties are optional, but if they require an entry, Access provides a default value.

1. **Click each of the field names while viewing the Field Properties panel**
   The Field Properties panel of a table's Design View changes to display the properties of the selected field. For example, when a field with a Text data type is selected, the Field Size property is visible. When a field with a Date/Time data type is selected, Access controls the Field Size property and therefore doesn't display it for the user.

2. **Click the State field name**
   Shorten the length of the Field Size for the State field in the Customers table to two characters since every state will be identified by its two-letter abbreviation.

3. **Double-click 50 in the Field Size Field Property text box in the Field Properties panel, then type 2**
   Fifty is the default field size for a text field, but now the State field is limited to only two characters to prevent some keying errors. You will also force each entry in the State field to be uppercase letters, regardless of how the entry is typed.

QuickTip

The < (the less than sign) in the Format property forces all characters in the field to be lowercase letters.

4. **Click in the Format Field Property text box, then type > (the greater than sign)**
   The greater than sign forces all entries to be converted to uppercase characters. Since the majority of Nomad's new customers live in Iowa, designate IA as the default value for the State field.

5. **Click in the Default Value Field Property text box, then type IA**
   The Design View of the Customers table should now look like Figure E-11. Notice that the State field is chosen in the upper half of the window, and the Field Properties panel displays the properties that you have just changed.

6. **Click the Save button 🖫 on the Standard toolbar, then click Yes to continue when warned about losing data**
   Since none of the entries in the State field were longer than two characters, you won't actually lose any data. Display the Customers table datasheet to see the effect of his property changes.

7. **Click the Datasheet View button ▦ on the Table Design toolbar**
   Notice that IA is entered as the default property for the next new record as shown in Figure E-12.

FIGURE E-11: The State field property changes

Field size changed from 50 to 2

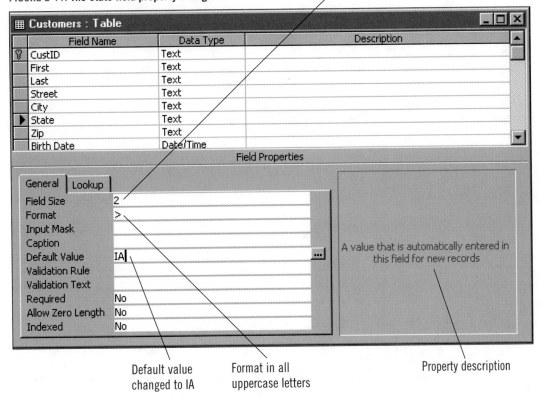

Default value changed to IA

Format in all uppercase letters

Property description

FIGURE E-12: The Customers table datasheet

CustID	First	Last	Street	City	State	Zip	Birth Date
1	Ginny	Braithwaite	3 Which Way	Salem	MA	01970	1/10/60
10	Virginia	Rodarmor	123 Main Street	Andover	MA	01810	1/6/70
11	Kristen	Reis	4848 Ashley	Fontanelle	IA	50810	3/18/68
12	Tom	Reis	4848 Ashley	Fontanelle	IA	50810	7/3/65
13	Mark	Eagan	987 Lincoln	Schaumberg	IL	44433	1/29/60
14	Peg	Fox	125 Maple	Des Moines	IA	50625	4/10/59
15	Ron	Fox	125 Maple	Des Moines	IA	50625	8/28/87
16	Amanda	Fox	125 Maple	Des Moines	IA	50625	1/30/88
17	Rebecca	Gross	123 Oak	Bridgewater	KS	50837	9/20/62
2	Robin	Spencer	293 Serenity Dr.	Concord	MA	01742	1/30/52
3	Camilla	Dobbins	486 Intel Circuit	Rio Rancho	NM	87124	3/15/65
4	Pip	Khalsa	1100 Vista Road	Santa Fe	NM	87505	4/16/69
5	Kendra	Majors	530 Spring Street	Lenox	MA	02140	5/4/70
6	Tasha	Williams	530 Spring Street	Lenox	MA	02140	5/8/71
7	Fred	Gonzales	Purgatory Ski Area	Durango	CO	81301	6/10/60
8	John	Black	11 River Road	Brookfield	CT	06830	7/15/65
9	Scott	Owen	72 Yankee Way	Brookfield	CT	06830	3/15/65
*					IA		

Record: 1 of 17

State default value

Defining Date/Time Field Properties

The Date/Time format property allows the user to use predefined date and time formats or use custom formats. Michael is concerned about dates past the year 1999. He wants the database to display all dates with four digits for the year so there is no confusion regarding which century is being displayed. Michael will first make this change to the Customers table.

QuickTip

Press [F6] to move between the upper and lower parts of a table's Design View window.

1. **Click the Design View button** on the Table Datasheet toolbar to return to the table's Design View

   You have to use a custom format for the Birth Date field because none of the predefined Date/Time formats match the format you want. For more information on predefined Date/Time formats, refer to Table E-1.

2. **Click the Birth Date field, then click the Format Field Property text box**

   The General Date format is the default. It is a combination of the predefined Short Date and Long Time settings. See Table E-1.

   To define a custom format, enter symbols that represent how you want the date to appear in the Format property text box.

3. **Type mm/dd/yyyy as shown in Figure E-13**

   Display the Customers table datasheet to see the effect of his property changes.

4. **Click the Datasheet View button** on the Table Design toolbar, then click **Yes** to save the changes

   Notice that all of the dates now display four digits as shown in Figure E-14.

5. **Click the Customers table datasheet Close button to close the window**

Planning for the 21st Century

The General Date format assumes that dates between 1/1/30 and 12/31/99 are twentieth century dates (1930–1999), and those between 1/1/00 and 12/31/29 are twenty-first century dates (2000–2029). If you wish to enter dates outside these ranges, you must enter all four digits of the date.

FIGURE E-13: The Birth Date field property change

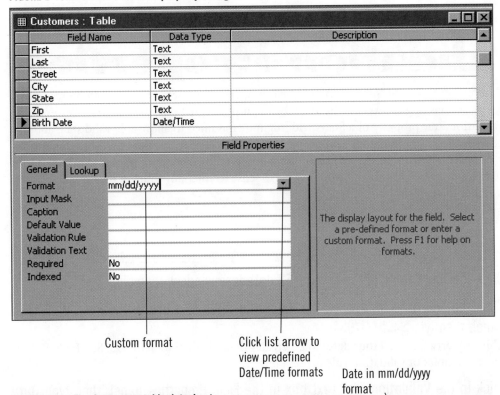

Custom format

Click list arrow to
view predefined
Date/Time formats

Date in mm/dd/yyyy
format

FIGURE E-14: The Customers table datasheet

CustID	First	Last	Street	City	State	Zip	Birth Date
1	Ginny	Braithwaite	3 Which Way	Salem	MA	01970	01/10/1960
10	Virginia	Rodarmor	123 Main Street	Andover	MA	01810	01/06/1970
11	Kristen	Reis	4848 Ashley	Fontanelle	IA	50810	03/18/1968
12	Tom	Reis	4848 Ashley	Fontanelle	IA	50810	07/03/1965
13	Mark	Eagan	987 Lincoln	Schaumberg	IL	44433	01/29/1960
14	Peg	Fox	125 Maple	Des Moines	IA	50625	04/10/1959
15	Ron	Fox	125 Maple	Des Moines	IA	50625	08/28/1987
16	Amanda	Fox	125 Maple	Des Moines	IA	50625	01/30/1988
17	Rebecca	Gross	123 Oak	Bridgewater	KS	50837	09/20/1962
2	Robin	Spencer	293 Serenity Dr.	Concord	MA	01742	01/30/1952
3	Camilla	Dobbins	486 Intel Circuit	Rio Rancho	NM	87124	03/15/1965
4	Pip	Khalsa	1100 Vista Road	Santa Fe	NM	87505	04/16/1969
5	Kendra	Majors	530 Spring Street	Lenox	MA	02140	05/04/1970
6	Tasha	Williams	530 Spring Street	Lenox	MA	02140	05/08/1971
7	Fred	Gonzales	Purgatory Ski Area	Durango	CO	81301	06/10/1960
8	John	Black	11 River Road	Brookfield	CT	06830	07/15/1965
9	Scott	Owen	72 Yankee Way	Brookfield	CT	06830	03/15/1965
*					IA		

Record: 1 of 17

TABLE E-1: Predefined Date/Time Formats

setting	examples	setting	examples
General Date (default)	4/3/97 5:34:00 PM	Long Time	5:34:23 PM
Long Date	Saturday, April 3, 1997	Medium Time	5:34 PM
Medium Date	3-Apr-97	Short Time	17:34
Short Date	4/3/97		

Access 97

Defining Field Validation Properties

The **Validation Rule** and **Validation Text** field properties can help you eliminate unreasonable entries by establishing criteria for the entry before it is accepted into the database. For example, the Validation Rule property of a State field might be modified to allow only valid state abbreviations as entries. The Validation Text property is used to display a message when a user tries to enter data that doesn't pass the Validation Rule property for that field. Michael started his business in 1995. Therefore, it wouldn't make sense to enter any tours in the Tours table with dates earlier than 1995.

Steps

QuickTip

You must use the # (pound sign) to identify date criteria and use the double quote character to identify text criteria in a Validation Rule expression.

1. Click the **Tours table** in the Nomad-E2 database window, then click **Design**

2. Click the **TourDate field**, click the **Validation Rule text box** in the Field Properties panel, then type **>=#1/1/95#**
   This property forces all tour dates to be greater than or equal to 1/1/1995. See Table E-2 for more examples of validation rule expressions.

3. Click in the **Validation Text text box** in the Field Properties panel, then type **Date must be later than 1/1/1995**
   The Validation Text property will appear on the screen when the field entry does not pass the criteria specified in the Validation Rule property. The Design View of the Tours table should now look like Figure E-15. Save the changes to the Tours table.

4. Click the **Save button** 🖫 on the Table Design toolbar, then click **Yes** when asked to test the existing data
   Since all dates in the TourDate field are more recent than 1/1/1995, there are no date errors in the current data and the table is saved. Michael will test the Validation Rule and Validation Text properties by trying to enter a pre-1995 date in the TourDate field of the Tours datasheet.

5. Click the **Datasheet View button** 📰 on the Table Design toolbar, press **[Tab]** twice to reach the **TourDate field**, type **1/1/94**, press **[Tab]**, then click **OK** to close the Validation Rule dialog box
   You know that the Validation Rule and Validation Text properties work properly, therefore close Access.

6. Press **[Esc]** to reject the invalid date entry, then click the **Close button** for the Access program window to close the database and program
   Since all changes to the objects and records within the database file are already saved, exiting the application does not open a Save dialog box.

FIGURE E-15: The TourDate field validation properties

TourDate field
is chosen

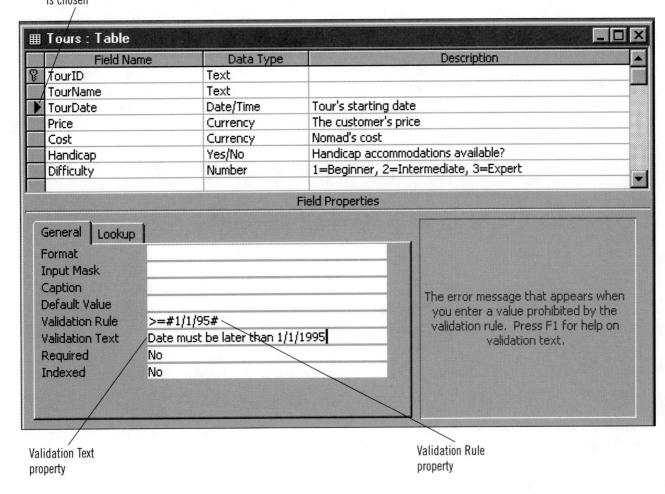

Validation Text
property

Validation Rule
property

TABLE E-2: Validation Rule Expressions

data type	validation rule expression	description
Number or Currency	>0	The number must be positive
Number or Currency	>10 And <100	The number must be between 10 and 100
Number or Currency	10 Or 20 Or 30	The number must be 10, 20, or 30
Text	"IA" Or "NE" Or "MO"	The entry must be IA, NE, or MO
Date/Time	>=#1/1/93#	The date must be on or after 1/1/1993
Date/Time	>#1/1/80# And <#1/1/90#	The date must be between 1/1/1980 and 1/1/1990

Validation property rules

The Validation Rule property and Validation Text properties go hand in hand. If you omit the Validation Rule, no data validation is performed and the Validation Text property is meaningless. If you set the Validation Rule property, but not the Validation Text property, Access displays a standard error message when the validation rule is violated.

Practice

► Concepts Review

Identify each element of a table's Design View shown in Figure E-16.

FIGURE E-16

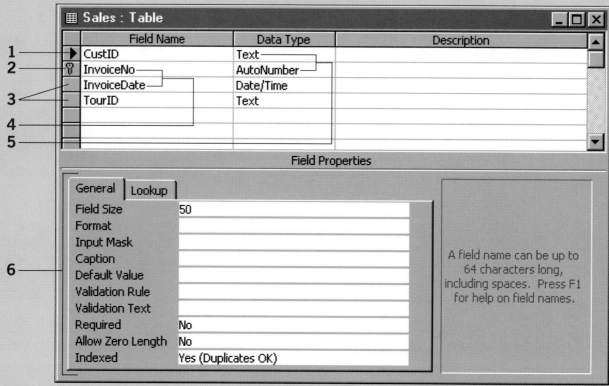

1
2
3
4
5
6

Match each term with the statement that describes its function.

7. Several tables linked together in one-to-many relationships
8. A field that holds unique information for each record in the table
9. Where all characteristics of a table including field names, data types, field descriptions, field properties, and key fields are defined
10. Characteristics that apply to each field of a table, such as field size, default values, or field formats
11. Helps you eliminate unreasonable entries by establishing criteria for the entry

a. Primary Key
b. Field Properties
c. Design View
d. Validation Rule and Validation Text
e. Relational database

Select the best answer from the list of choices.

12. **Which of the following steps would probably help eliminate fields of duplicate data in a table?**
    a. Redesign the database and add more tables.
    b. Redesign the database and add more fields.
    c. Change the formatting properties of the field in which the duplicate data existed.
    d. Change the validation properties of the field in which the duplicate data existed.

13. **Which of the following is NOT defined in the table's Design View?**
    a. Key fields
    b. Duplicate data
    c. Field lengths
    d. Data types

14. **Which of the following is NOT a common Data Type?**
    a. Text
    b. Alpha
    c. Number
    d. Date/Time

15. **Which feature helps the database designer make sure that one-to-many relationships are preserved?**
    a. Validation Text property
    b. Validation Rule property
    c. Field formatting
    d. Referential Integrity

16. **Which character is used to identify dates in a validation expression?**
    a. " (double quote)
    b. ' (single quote)
    c. # (pound sign)
    d. & (ampersand)

17. **Which Format Property Option displays all characters in the field as uppercase?**
    a. <
    b. >
    c. !
    d. @

▶ Skills Review

1. **Examine relational database requirements.**
   a. Examine your address book.
   b. Write down the fields you will need.
   c. Examine which fields contain duplicate entries.

2. Plan a table.

  a. Start Access.

  b. Use the Blank Database option button to create a new database file.

  c. Save the file as "Addresses-E" on your Student Disk.

  d. Click the Tables tab in the Database window, then click New.

3. Create new tables.

  a. Use Design View to create the new table with the following fields with the given data types.

First	Text
Last	Text
Street	Text
City	Text
State	Text
Zip	Text
Birthday	Date/Time

  b. Close the table, name, and save it as "Names".

  c. Do not define a primary key for Names.

  d. Reconsider what fields will contain duplicate data.

  e. Click the Tables tab in the Database window, then click New.

  f. Use Design View to create another new table with the following Text fields.

    Zip

    City

    State

  g. Identify Zip as the primary key.

  h. Close the table, then save it as "Zips".

4. Create one-to-many relationships.

  a. Click the Relationships button on the Database toolbar.

  b. Add both the Names and the Zips tables to the Relationships window.

  c. Drag the Zip field from the Zips table to the Zip field of the Names table to create a one-to-many relationship between these fields of the tables.

  d. Enforce referential integrity between the linking fields of the tables.

  e. Close the Relationships window, saving your layout changes.

5. Delete fields.

  a. Open the Names table in Design View.

  b. Click the City field selector button and delete the City field.

  c. Click the State field selector button and delete the State field.

  d. Close the Names table, saving the changes.

6. Define text field properties.

  a. Open the Zips table in Design View.

  b. Click the State field name and change the Field Size property to 2.

  c. Click the State field names Format property text box, then type > (greater than sign) to force all entries to uppercase letters.

  d. Close the Zips table, saving the changes.

7. **Define date/time field properties.**
   a. Open the Names table in Design View.
   b. Click the Birthday field names Format property text box, then type MM/DD/YYYY to display all dates with four-digit years.
   c. Close the Names table, saving the changes.

8. **Define field validation properties.**
   a. Note that this address listing will contain contacts from only three states: IA, KS, and MO.
   b. Open the Zips table in Design View.
   c. Click the State field name, click the Validation Rule property text box, then type ="IA" OR "KS" OR "MO".
   d. Note that this validation rule could be extended to accept more valid entries for all 50 states.
   e. Click the Validation Text text box, then type "State must be IA, KS, or MO".
   f. Close the Zips table, saving the changes.
   g. Print a copy of each table's datasheet in the Addresses-E database.

▶ Independent Challenges

1. As the president of a civic organization, you have decided to launch a recycling campaign. Various clubs will gather recyclable trash and make deposits at recycling centers. You need to develop a relational database that tracks how much material has been taken to each of the centers, as well as the club that is responsible for the deposit. The following fields will be tracked in this database:

Club Information:
Name, Street, City, State, Zip, Phone, Club Number (a unique number to identify each club)
Deposit Information:
Date, Weight, Deposit Number (a sequential number for each drop off)
Recycle Center Information:
Name, Street, City, State, Zip, Phone, Center Number (a unique number to identify each recycling center)

To complete this independent challenge:

1. Plan the database.
   a. Sketch how the fields will be organized into three tables: Clubs, Deposits, and Recycling Centers.
   b. Determine if there are key fields in the tables.
   c. Determine how the tables should be linked using one-to-many relationships. This may involve adding a linking field to a table to establish the connection.
2. Create and save a database called "Cleanup-E".
3. Create the three tables in the Cleanup-E database using appropriate field names, data types, and key fields.
4. Create one-to-many relationships to link the tables. Be sure to enforce referential integrity as appropriate.
5. Print the Relationships window of the database using the [Print Screen] technique. Be sure that all fields of each table are visible.
6. Add a Validation Rule property to the Date field that only allows dates of 1/1/97 or later to be entered into the database. The property entry is >=#1/1/97#.
7. Add a Validation Text property to the Date field that states "Dates must be later than 1/1/1997".

2. You want to document the books you've read in a relational database. The following fields will be tracked:
Book Information:
Title, Category (such as Biography, Mystery, or Science Fiction), Rating (a numeric value from 1–10 that indicates how satisfied you were with the book), Date Read
Author Information (Note: If a book has more than one author, enter the name of the author listed first.):
First Name, Last Name, Author Number (a unique number to identify each author)

To complete this independent challenge:

1. Plan the database.
   a. Sketch how the fields will be organized into two tables: Books and Authors.
   b. Determine if there are key fields in the tables.
   c. Determine how the tables should be linked using one-to-many relationships. This may involve adding a linking field to a table to establish the connection.
2. Create and save a database called "Readings-E".
3. Create the three tables in the Readings-E database using appropriate field names, data types, and key fields.
4. Create the one-to-many relationship to link the tables. Be sure to enforce referential integrity as appropriate.
5. Print the Relationships window of the database using the [Print Screen] technique discussed in the Quick Tip of the "Creating one-to-many relationships" lesson. Be sure that all fields of each table are visible.
6. Change the field size of the author's First Name field and Last Name field to 25.

3. You work for a large medical clinic and wish to track the time physicians are spending on civic activities such as the Rural Outreach Program and the Low Income Health Screening Program. The database should track the date and number of hours each physician has logged with each program. The following fields will be tracked in this database:
Physician Information:
First Name, Last Name, Physician Number (a unique number to identify each physician)
Activity Information:
Date, Hours
Program Information:
Name, Program Number (a unique number to identify each program)

To complete this independent challenge:

1. Plan the database.
   a. Sketch how the fields will be organized into three tables: Physicians, Activities, and Programs
   b. Determine if there are key fields in the tables (*Hint*: The Activities table does not have a Key field.)
   c. Determine how the tables should be linked using one-to-many relationships. This may involve adding a linking field to a table to establish the connection.
2. Create and save a database called "Doctors-E".
3. Create the three tables in the Doctors-E database using appropriate field names, data types, and key fields.
4. Create one-to-many relationships to link the tables. Be sure to enforce referential integrity as appropriate.
5. Print the Relationships window of the database using the [Print Screen] technique discussed in the Quick Tip of the "Creating one-to-many relationships" lesson. Be sure that all fields of each table are visible.

WEB WORK

4. You wish to find and document nine-digit ZIP codes for several addresses in a database. You know that nine-digit ZIP codes make the mail service more efficient because the nine digits specify the specific street address in addition to the city and state of the addressee.

To complete this independent challenge:

1. Log on to the Internet and use your browser to go to http://www.course.com. From there, click Student Online Companions, click Microsoft Office 97 Professional Edition – Illustrated: A Second Course, click the Access link for Unit E, then click the link for the United States Postal Service.
2. Read the homepage and click hypertext links to find the interactive ZIP+4 lookup service. (*Hint*: Finding the interactive ZIP+4 lookup service should take about two hypertext links.)
3. Use the Zip+4 Code Lookup page to find the ZIP+4 code for at least four addresses of friends or acquaintances and jot them down.
4. Plan a database to handle address information with ZIP+4 ZIP codes.
    a. Sketch how the fields will be organized into two tables: Names and Zips.
    b. Determine if there are key fields in the tables.
    c. Determine how the tables should be linked using one-to-many relationships. This may involve adding a linking field to a table to establish the connection.
5. Create and save a database called "Addresses9-E".
6. Create the two tables in the Addresses9-E database using appropriate field names, data types, and key fields. Recognize that this relational database is extremely similar to the one you created in the Skills Review with one exception: a ZIP code extension field needs to be added to the Names table.
7. Create the one-to-many relationship to link the tables. Be sure to enforce referential integrity as appropriate.
8. Print the Relationships window of the database using the [Print Screen] technique discussed in the Quick Tip of the "Creating one-to-many relationships" lesson. Be sure that all fields of each table are visible.
9. Open the Zips table in Datasheet View and enter the four ZIP codes, cities, and states that you researched on the Internet.
10. Print the Zips datasheet.
11. Open the Names table in Datasheet View and enter the four addresses that you researched on the Internet.
12. Print the Names datasheet.

Access 97

Visual Workshop

Create a new database that includes the two tables, Alumni and Donations, shown in Figures E-17 and E-18. Give each of the fields a text Data Type, except for Value (use Currency) and Date (use Date/Time). Make sure that the Social Security Number is the key field in the Alumni table and links the Alumni table with the Donations table in a one-to-many relationship. Enforce referential integrity for the linking Social Security Number field between the tables. (*Hint:* The Donations table does not have a Key field.) Enter the records for both tables, then save and name the database "VW-E" on your Student Disk. Print the datasheets of both tables.

FIGURE E-17

	First	Last	Street	City	State	Zip	Phone	SSN
	Doug	Allen	888 Maple	Ames	IA	50010	515-555-8888	444-44-4444
	Lisa	Eagan	777 Oak	Johnston	IA	50015	515-777-9999	111-11-1111
	Kelsey	Wambold	555 Elm	Fontanelle	IA	50846	515-888-1111	222-22-2222
▶	Aaron	Washington	222 Apple	Bridgewater	IA	50837	515-222-4444	333-33-3333

Alumni : Table

Record: 4 of 4

FIGURE E-18

Donations : Table

	Value	Date	Type	SSN
	$100.00	5/1/97	Art	111-11-1111
	$200.00	5/1/97	Cash	222-22-2222
	$500.00	5/2/97	Stock	333-33-3333
	$50.00	6/2/97	Cash	111-11-1111
	$1,000.00	6/2/97	Cash	444-44-4444
	$500.00	6/2/97	Stock	333-33-3333
	$500.00	7/1/97	Cash	444-44-4444
	$500.00	7/1/97	Cash	333-33-3333
*	$0.00			

Record: 8 of 8

Creating
Multiple Table Queries

Objectives

- ► Create select queries
- ► Sort a query on multiple fields
- ► Develop AND queries
- ► Develop OR queries
- ► Develop calculated fields
- ► Add calculations on groups of records
- ► Develop crosstab queries
- ► Create update queries

In this unit, you will create **queries**, database objects that answer questions about the data by pulling fields and records that match specific criteria into a single datasheet. A **select query** retrieves data from one or more linked tables and displays the results in a datasheet. Queries can also be used to sort records, develop new calculated fields from existing fields, or develop summary calculations such as the sum or average of the values in a field. **Crosstab queries** present information in a cross tabular report, and **update queries** quickly change existing data in a table. Michael Belmont redesigned the Nomad database into multiple tables to eliminate redundant data entry. Michael will create select, crosstab, and update queries to display and change the data in his database.

Creating Select Queries

Queries are developed by using the Query Wizard or by directly specifying requested fields and query criteria in **Query Design View**. The resulting query datasheet is not a duplication of the data that resides in the original table's datasheet, but rather, a logical view of the data. If you change or enter data in a query's datasheet, the data in the underlying table (and any other logical view) is updated automatically. Queries are often used to present and sort a subset of fields from multiple tables for data entry or update purposes. ◢◣◤ Michael creates a query to answer the question, "Who is buying what?" He pulls fields from several tables into a single query object which displays a single datasheet.

Steps

1. Start Access and open the **Nomad-F** database

2. Click the **Queries tab** in the Nomad-F: Database window, click **New**, click **Design View** in the New Query window, then click **OK**
   Use the Show Table dialog box to add the Tours table and the Customers table to the Query Design View. You also need to include the Sales table because it contains the linking fields that match specific customers to the specific tours they have purchased.

Trouble?

Click the Show Table button 🔲 on the Query Design toolbar to add table field lists to Query Design View. To delete a field list click the list and press [Delete].

3. Click **Customers**, click **Add**, click **Sales**, click **Add**, click **Tours**, click **Add**, then click **Close**
   The Query Design View displays **field lists** for the three tables. Each table's name is in its field list title bar. Key fields are bold, and often serve as the "one" side of the one-to-many relationship between two tables. Relationships are displayed with **one-to-many join lines** between the linking fields as shown in Figure F-1. View the customer's last name in the query datasheet.

4. Drag the **Last field** in the Customers table field list to the Field cell in the first column of the Query design grid
   The order in which the fields are placed in the **Query design grid** will be their order in the datasheet. Select the First field from the Customers table, then add the TourName and TourDate fields from the Tours table.

QuickTip

Double-click the table's title bar to select all fields then drag them as a group to the grid if you want all fields in the resulting datasheet.

5. Drag the **First field** from the Customers table to the Field cell in the second column, drag the **TourName field** from the Tours table to the Field cell in the third column, then drag the **TourDate field** from the Tours table to the Field cell in the fourth column
   You sort the datasheet by TourDate.

6. Click the **Sort cell** of the **TourDate field** in the Query design grid, click the **Sort list arrow**, then click **Ascending**
   The resulting Query design grid should look like Figure F-2.

7. Click the **Datasheet View button** 🔲 on the Query Design toolbar
   The records of the datasheet are now listed in chronological order by TourDate as shown in Figure F-3. You scroll through the datasheet and notice that Mark Egan purchased two tours, and that his name has been incorrectly entered in the database. Change "Eagan" to the correct spelling "Egan" directly within the query datasheet.

8. Scroll and click before the **first letter A** of either **Eagan** in the Last column in the datasheet, press **[Delete]**, then click any other record in the datasheet
   The update shows that you are using a properly defined relational database and that any change to the data is automatically applied to all other occurrences of the customer's name.

9. Click the **Query datasheet Close button**, click **Yes** when prompted to save the changes, type **Customer Purchases** in the Query Name text box, then click **OK**
   The query is now saved and listed on the Queries tab in the Nomad-F: Database window.

FIGURE F-1: Query Design View

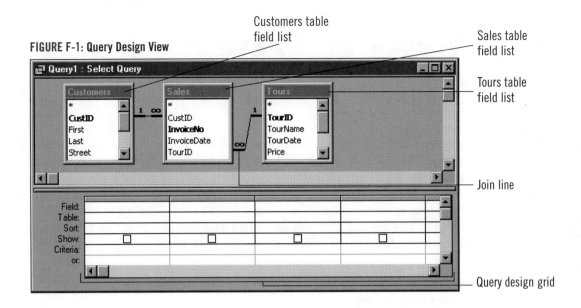

Customers table field list

Sales table field list

Tours table field list

Join line

Query design grid

FIGURE F-2: Completed Query design grid

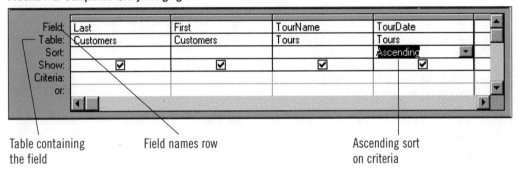

Table containing the field

Field names row

Ascending sort on criteria

FIGURE F-3: Datasheet sorted in ascending order by TourDate

Last	First	TourName	TourDate
Braithwait	Ginny	Road Bike	6/15/96
Owen	Scott	Bungee	9/20/96
Dobbins	Camilla	Bungee	9/20/96
Majors	Kendra	Bungee	9/20/96
Williams	Tasha	Bungee	9/20/96
Gonzales	Fred	Mt. Bike	9/26/96
Khalsa	Pip	Mt. Bike	9/26/96
Spencer	Robin	Mt. Bike	9/26/96
Black	John	Mt. Bike	9/26/96
Rodarmor	Virginia	Mt. Bike	9/26/96
Reis	Kristen	Big Sky	1/10/97
Fox	Amanda	Big Sky	1/10/97
Fox	Ron	Big Sky	1/10/97
Fox	Peg	Big Sky	1/10/97
Eagan	Mark	Big Sky	1/10/97
Reis	Tom	Big Sky	1/10/97
Eagan	Mark	Bungee	9/15/96

Record: 1 of 20

CLUES TO USE

The difference between queries and filters

Use a filter to temporarily view or edit a subset of records when viewing a datasheet. Use a query to view the subset of records without first opening a specific table, to choose fields from multiple tables for the query, to control which fields from the subset of records appear in the results, or to perform calculations on values in fields.

Sorting a Query on Multiple Fields

Sorting, or placing the records of a datasheet in either ascending or descending order, is a common task and can be specified in the Query design grid. Multiple sort fields determine the order in which records are displayed when two records contain the same data in the primary sort field. Michael wants to sort the Customer Purchases query on multiple fields to more clearly identify those customers who have purchased more than one tour. He needs an alphabetical listing of his tour sales by customers. Customers who have the same last name will be sorted by first name within last, and for those customers who have purchased more than one tour, the records need to be listed in chronological order by TourDate.

1. Click the **Queries tab** in the Nomad-F : Database window if necessary, click **Customer Purchases**, then click **Design**

The Query Design window of the Customer Purchases - Select Query opens. You want to show the First field in the first column, but make the Last field the primary sort field. Since Access sorts the fields in order from left to right, add the First field to the query grid twice. The first occurrence of the First field is used for display purposes. The second occurrence of the First field is used for sorting purposes.

2. Drag the **First field** from the Customer's field list to the first column of the Query design grid

The Query design grid now has the fields First, Last, First. Use the Show checkboxes to specify this sorting.

3. Click the **First field Show checkbox** in the third column to deselect it

Now that the grid includes all the fields needed to accommodate this datasheet, add the sort criteria.

4. Click the **Sort cell** of the **Last field** in the second column, click the **Sort list arrow**, click **Ascending**, then click the **Sort list arrow** for the **First field** in the third column, then click **Ascending**

The new Query design grid is shown in Figure F-4. By setting up the Query design grid in this way, you specify the Last field as the primary sort field, the First field as the secondary sort field, and the TourDate field as the third sort field.

5. Click the **Datasheet View button** 🖽 on the Query Design toolbar

The resulting datasheet is shown in Figure F-5. Michael wants to use this information in an upcoming sales meeting, so print a copy of the datasheet.

6. Click the **Print button** 🖨 on the Query Datasheet toolbar

You review the printout, and verify that it has the information you need. Now you can save the Customer Purchases query.

7. Click the **Save button** 🖫 on the Query Datasheet toolbar

Trouble?

If you drag a field from a Field list to the wrong column of the Query design grid, click the column selector and drag the column to its new location. Existing fields shift to make room for the inserted column.

FIGURE F-4: Query design grid for a sort order that doesn't follow the order of the fields on the datasheet

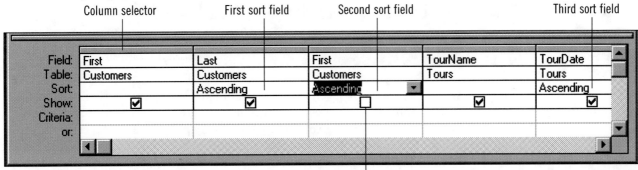

Column selector   First sort field   Second sort field   Third sort field

Field:	First	Last	First	TourName	TourDate
Table:	Customers	Customers	Customers	Tours	Tours
Sort:		Ascending	Ascending		Ascending
Show:	☑	☑	☐	☑	☑
Criteria:					
or:					

This column will not be displayed but is still used for sorting purposes

FIGURE F-5: Customer Purchases query with three sort fields

Secondary sort   Primary sort   Third sort field

Customer Purchases : Select Query

First	Last	TourName	TourDate
John	Black	Mt. Bike	9/26/96
Ginny	Braithwaite	Road Bike	6/15/96
Camilla	Dobbins	Bungee	9/20/96
Mark	Egan	Big Sky	1/10/97
Mark	Egan	Bungee	9/15/97
Amanda	Fox	Big Sky	1/10/97
Peg	Fox	Big Sky	1/10/97
Peg	Fox	Mt. Bike	9/30/97
Ron	Fox	Big Sky	1/10/97
Ron	Fox	Mt. Bike	9/30/97
Fred	Gonzales	Mt. Bike	9/26/96
Pip	Khalsa	Mt. Bike	9/26/96
Kendra	Majors	Bungee	9/20/96
Scott	Owen	Bungee	9/20/96
Kristen	Reis	Big Sky	1/10/97
Kristen	Reis	Bungee	9/15/97
Tom	Reis	Big Sky	1/10/97
Virginia	Rodarmor	Mt. Bike	9/26/96

Record: ◀◀ ◀ [1] ▶ ▶◀ ▶✱ of 20

Example of when the Second sort field is used

Example of when the Third sort field is used

Developing AND Queries

Using Access you can query for specific records that match two or more criteria, or limiting conditions. **Criteria** are tests for which the record must be true to be selected for a datasheet. To create an **AND query** in which two or more criteria are present, enter the criteria for the fields on the same Criteria row of the Query design grid. If two AND criteria are entered for the same field, the AND operator separates the criteria in the Criteria cell for that field. ➤ Michael wants to send a special mailing to a subset of his customers who have recently purchased tours in Massachusetts. He creates an AND query because the State field must equal Massachusetts and the TourDate field must be greater than 09/01/96.

Steps 1 2 3 4

1. **Click the Design View button** ![button] **on the Query Datasheet toolbar**
   Instead of creating a query from scratch, modify the Customer Purchases query. The only additional field you have to add to the query is the State field.

2. **Scroll and click the State field in the Customers table, then drag the State field to the fourth column in the Query design grid after the First field**
   The TourName and TourDate fields move to the right to accommodate the new field in the grid. Next, enter the state criterion.

3. **Click the Criteria cell of the State field, type MA, then click the Datasheet View button** ![button] **on the Query Design toolbar**
   The resulting datasheet in Figure F-6 shows five customers from Massachusetts. Return to the Query design window to complete the second part of this query which involves selecting only those tour dates that are after 9/1/96. See Table F-1 for more information on using special comparison operators.

QuickTip

To resize a column in the Query design grid, click the right boundary of the column selector then drag it left or right.

4. **Click** ![button] **on the Query Datasheet toolbar, scroll in the grid to view the TourDate field, click the Criteria cell of the TourDate field, then type >9/1/96**
   The resulting Query design grid is shown in Figure F-7. Notice that Access entered double quotes automatically around the text criterion in the State field. Access enters # (pound signs) around date criteria. Numeric criteria aren't surrounded by any special character.

5. **Click** ![button] **on the Query Design toolbar**
   Multiple criteria added to the same line of the Query design grid (AND criteria) must *each* be true for the record to be displayed in the resulting datasheet, therefore causing the resulting datasheet to display fewer records. In this case, the date criterion eliminated one record in the datasheet. Save this query with a different name.

6. **Click File on the menu bar, click Save As/Export to save this query with a new name, type MA after 9/1/96 in the New Name: text box, then click OK**

FIGURE F-6: Datasheet for MA query

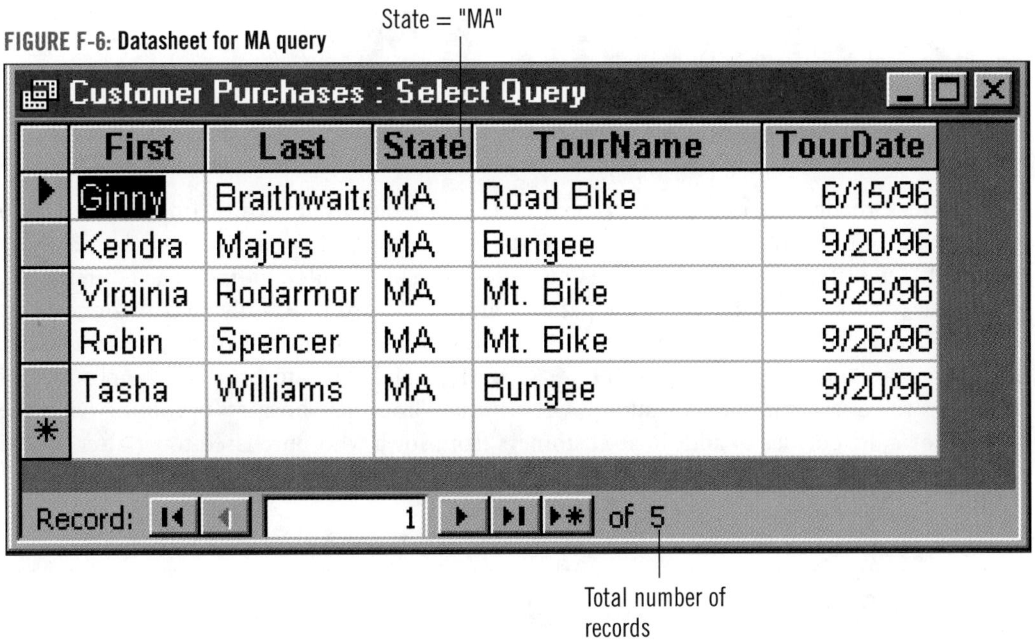

State = "MA"

	First	Last	State	TourName	TourDate
▶	Ginny	Braithwaite	MA	Road Bike	6/15/96
	Kendra	Majors	MA	Bungee	9/20/96
	Virginia	Rodarmor	MA	Mt. Bike	9/26/96
	Robin	Spencer	MA	Mt. Bike	9/26/96
	Tasha	Williams	MA	Bungee	9/20/96
*					

Customer Purchases : Select Query

Record: I◀ ◀ 1 ▶ ▶I ▶* of 5

Total number of records

FIGURE F-7: Query design grid for AND query

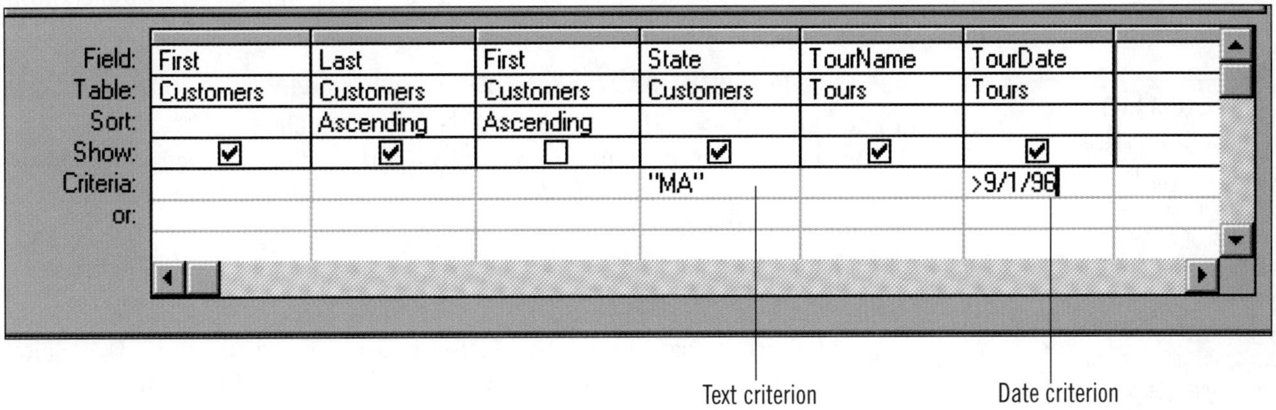

Field:	First	Last	First	State	TourName	TourDate	
Table:	Customers	Customers	Customers	Customers	Tours	Tours	
Sort:		Ascending	Ascending				
Show:	☑	☑	☐	☑	☑	☑	
Criteria:				"MA"		>9/1/96	
or:							

Text criterion

Date criterion

TABLE F-1: Comparison operators for the Criteria row of the Query design grid

operator	description	example	result
>	greater than	>50	Value exceeds 50
>=	greater than or equal to	>=50	Value is 50 or greater
<	less than	<50	Value is less than 50
<=	less than or equal to	<=50	Value is 50 or less than 50
<>	not equal to	<>50	Value is any number other than 50
Between...And	finds values between two numbers or dates	Between #2/2/95# And #2/2/98#	Dates between 2/2/95 and 2/2/98
In	finds a value that is one of a list	In(IA,KS,NE)	Value equals IA or KS or NE
Null	finds records which are blank	Null	No value has been entered
Is Not Null	finds records which are not blank	Is Not Null	Any value has been entered
Like	finds records that match the criteria	Like "A"	Value equals A
Not	finds records that do not match the criteria	Not "2"	Numbers other than 2

Developing OR Queries

OR queries broaden the number of records that will be displayed because only one criterion joined by an OR operator needs to be true for the record to be displayed on the resulting datasheet. OR criteria are entered in the Query design grid on different lines. Each criteria line of the Query design grid is evaluated separately and the record must only be true for one row in order to be displayed in the datasheet. If two OR criteria are specified for the same field, they are separated by the **OR operator**. ◀━━ Michael decides to broaden the number of records in the query datasheet by adding OR criteria. Since new business is coming from the state of Iowa, he decides to add those customers from Iowa who purchased tours after 9/1/96 to his existing query.

Steps

1. **Click the Query Design View button** 🔲 **on the Datasheet toolbar**
   To add OR criteria, enter criteria in the 'or' row of the Query design grid.

2. **Click the or State criteria cell below the MA entry, then type IA**
   If you don't put the date criteria into this row, the datasheet will pull all customers from Iowa, regardless of when their tour date occurred.

3. **Click then drag to select >#9/1/96#, right-click, click Copy, click the TourDate or criteria cell below the >#9/1/96# entry, right-click, then click Paste**
   The >#9/1/96 entry is copied to the or row in the TourDate field. If the record matches *either* row of the criteria grid, it is included in the query's datasheet. Figure F-8 shows the OR criteria in the Query design grid.

4. **Click the Datasheet View button** 🔲 **on the Query Design toolbar**
   The resulting datasheet is shown in Figure F-9. All of the records contain State data of either MA or IA, and TourDate data after 9/1/96. Also, notice that the sort order (Last, First, TourDate) is still in effect. Save this query as a separate database object as well.

5. **Click File on the menu bar, click Save As/Export, type MA and IA after 9/1/96, then click OK**
   You have completed this query. Close the datasheet.

6. **Click the MA and IA after 9/1/96 datasheet Close button**
   The Nomad-F database Queries tab displays the new queries that you created.

> **QuickTip**
>
> If the criterion expression becomes too long to completely fit in a cell of the Query design grid, right-click the cell then click Zoom on the shortcut menu. The Zoom dialog box provides space to enter lengthy criteria expressions.

Field:	First	Last	First	State	TourName	TourDate	
Table:	Customers	Customers	Customers	Customers	Tours	Tours	
Sort:		Ascending	Ascending				
Show:	☑	☑	☐	☑	☑	☑	
Criteria:				"MA"		>#9/1/96#	
or:				"IA"		>#9/1/96#	

FIGURE F-9: Datasheet for OR query

Customer Purchases : Select Query

First	Last	State	TourName	TourDate
Amanda	Fox	IA	Big Sky	1/10/97
Peg	Fox	IA	Mt. Bike	9/30/97
Peg	Fox	IA	Big Sky	1/10/97
Ron	Fox	IA	Mt. Bike	9/30/97
Ron	Fox	IA	Big Sky	1/10/97
Kendra	Majors	MA	Bungee	9/20/96
Kristen	Reis	IA	Bungee	9/15/97
Kristen	Reis	IA	Big Sky	1/10/97
Tom	Reis	IA	Big Sky	1/10/97
Virginia	Rodarmor	MA	Mt. Bike	9/26/96
Robin	Spencer	MA	Mt. Bike	9/26/96
Tasha	Williams	MA	Bungee	9/20/96

Record: |◄ ◄ 1 ► ►| ►* of 12

Access 97

Using wildcard characters in query criteria

To search for a pattern, use a ? (question mark) to search for any single character and an * (asterisk) to search for any number of characters. Wildcard characters are often used with the Like operator. For example, the criterion

Like "10/*/97" would find all dates in October of 1997 and the criterion Like "F*" would find all values that start with the letter F.

Developing Calculated Fields

Arithmetic operators such as the ones shown in Table F-2 are used to create mathematical calculations in a query. Often these operators are used to develop a completely new field of information in a query. If you can calculate a new field of information based on existing fields in a database, never define it as a separate field in the table's Design View. The query method of creating the data ensures that the new field contains accurate, up-to-date information. ◄▬▬▬ Michael has decided to track profit (the difference between his cost and his price) per tour. To accomplish this, he creates a query that tells him how much profit he has realized for each tour booked.

Steps 1234

1. Click the **Queries tab**, if necessary, click **New**, click **Design View**, then click **OK**
   You need the InvoiceNo, TourName, TourDate, Price, and Cost fields from the Sales and Tours tables to develop this query.

2. Click **Sales**, click **Add**, click **Tours**, click **Add**, then click **Close**

3. Drag the **InvoiceNo field** from the Sales table to the **first Field column** of the Query design grid, drag the **TourName field** from the Tours table to the **second Field column**, then drag the **TourDate field** from the Tours table to the **third Field column**
   A **calculated field** is created by entering a field name followed by a colon in the Field cell of the Query design grid followed by an expression. An **expression** is a combination of operators such as + (plus), - (minus), * (multiply), or / (divide), raw values (such as numbers or dates), functions, and fields that produce a result. Field names used in an expression are surrounded by square brackets.

4. Click the blank **Field cell** of the fourth column, then type **Profit:[Price]-[Cost]**
   The Query design grid should now look like Figure F-10. You further decide to sort the records from the most profitable sales transaction to the least profitable.

5. Click the **Sort cell** of the **Profit field**, click the **Sort list arrow**, then click **Descending**
   View this query to see the results of your work.

QuickTip

Double-click the thin black vertical line separating field names in the Query design grid or datasheet to make the column width automatically adjust to the widest entry in the column.

6. Click the **Datasheet View button** 🔲 on the Query design toolbar
   The query's datasheet appears with the calculated field, Profit. The records are sorted from the highest to the lowest profit as shown in Figure F-11. You cannot enter information directly into the datasheet of a calculated field. The data shown in the Profit field is totally dependent upon the underlying fields of Price and Cost which are not displayed in this datasheet. To use this query at a meeting, print the resulting datasheet.

7. Click the **Print button** 🖨 on the Query Datasheet toolbar
   You are done with this query. Close the datasheet.

8. Click the **Datasheet Close button**, then click **Yes** when prompted to save changes

9. Type **Profit by Sale** as the query name, then click **OK**

CLUES TO USE

Functions in calculated expressions

Functions can be used in expressions. You can develop a function to calculate information based on data in a record, or use a "built-in" function available within Access. The **Date** built-in function, for example, returns today's date and can be used in an expression or custom function to determine the number of days between today and another date.

FIGURE F-10: A calculated field

Calculated field

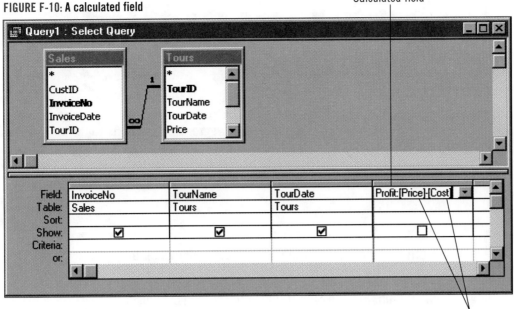

Existing field
names used in the
expression

FIGURE F-11: Datasheet sorted in descending order by Profit

Double-click line to
adjust column
width automatically

Descending sort
order

InvoiceNo	TourName	TourDate	Profit
17	Bungee	9/15/97	$120.00
18	Bungee	9/15/97	$120.00
12	Big Sky	1/10/97	$108.00
13	Big Sky	1/10/97	$108.00
11	Big Sky	1/10/97	$108.00
14	Big Sky	1/10/97	$108.00
15	Big Sky	1/10/97	$108.00
16	Big Sky	1/10/97	$108.00
20	Mt. Bike	9/30/97	$105.00
19	Mt. Bike	9/30/97	$105.00
10	Mt. Bike	9/26/96	$95.00
8	Mt. Bike	9/26/96	$95.00
7	Mt. Bike	9/26/96	$95.00
4	Mt. Bike	9/26/96	$95.00
2	Mt. Bike	9/26/96	$95.00

Record: 1 of 20

TABLE F-2: Arithmetic operators

operator	description
+	Addition
-	Subtraction
*	Multiplication
/	Division
^	Exponentiation

CREATING MULTIPLE TABLE QUERIES AC F-11 ◄

Adding Calculations on Groups of Records

As your database grows, you probably will be less interested in individual records and more interested in information about groups of records. A query can be used to calculate information about a group of records by adding appropriate **aggregate functions** to the Total row of the Query design grid. Aggregate functions are summarized in Table F-3. ◀━━ Michael decides that he would like to have a total profit figure for each tour he has offered. This query first groups the records for each individual tour, and then calculates a total on the Profit field.

1. **Click the Profit by Sale query on the Queries tab, then click Design**
   Instead of creating this query from scratch, modify the existing Profit by Sale query.

2. **Drag the TourID field from the Sales table to the second column of the Query design grid**
   The fields move to the right to accommodate the move. The records will be grouped by TourID and summarized by Profit. The InvoiceNo field is not required for this query.

3. **Click the InvoiceNo field column selector, then press [Delete]**
   Deleting the field from the Query design grid does not affect the data in the underlying table. Next, add the Total row to the Query design grid.

4. **Click the Totals button [Σ] on the Query Design toolbar**
   By default, the entry for each field of the new Total row is Group By. To get a total profit for each TourID, change the Group By function to Sum for the Profit column.

5. **Click the Total cell of the Profit field, click the Group By list arrow, then click Sum**
   The Query design grid now looks like Figure F-12.

6. **Click the Datasheet View button [⊞] on the Query Design toolbar**
   As you can see from the resulting datasheet, Michael netted $648 from the 1/10/97 Big Sky tour. It was the most profitable tour when summarized across the database. Add a Count function to determine how many individual sales transactions are included in each summarized profit figure.

7. **Click the Design View button [⊠] on the Query Datasheet toolbar, click the Total cell of the TourID field, click the Group By list arrow, click Count, then click [⊞]**
   The resulting datasheet is shown in Figure F-13 and shows that six Big Sky tours were sold. Print the query.

8. **Click the Print button [🖶] on the Query Datasheet toolbar**
   You add this datasheet to your Nomad file of printouts. Close and save the Profit by Sale query.

9. **Click the Profit By Sale Close button, then click Yes to save the changes**

> **QuickTip**
> Click the list arrow of the Top Values button on the Query design toolbar to quickly narrow the number of records in the resulting datasheet to the top 5, 25, 100, 5%, or 25% of the total records.

FIGURE F-12: Query design grid with Total row

Totals button   Top Values box

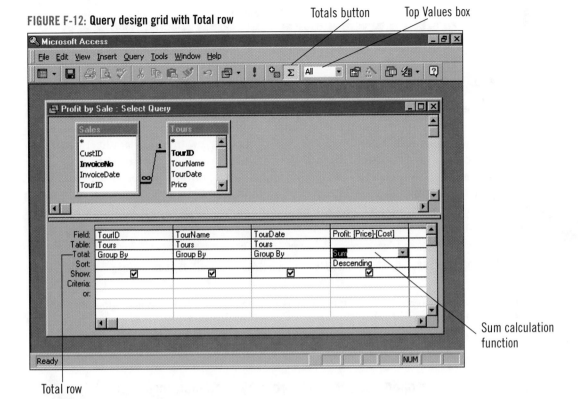

Total row

FIGURE F-13: Datasheet with Count and Sum functions

Count function   Sum function

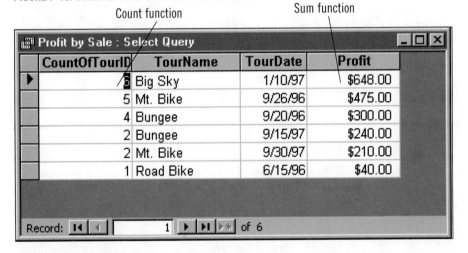

TABLE F-3: Aggregate functions

aggregate function	used to find the
Sum	total of values in a field
Avg	average of values in a field
Min	minimum value in the field
Max	maximum value in the field
Count	number of values in a field (not counting null values)
StDev	standard deviation of values in a field
Var	variance of values in a field
First	field value from the first record in a table or query
Last	field value from the last record in a table or query

Developing Crosstab Queries

Crosstab queries provide another method to summarize data by creating a datasheet in which one or more fields are chosen for the row headings, another field is chosen for the column headings, and a third field, usually a numeric field, is summarized within the datasheet itself. You can create a crosstab query directly from a Query Design window or use the Crosstab Query Wizard. Michael needs to analyze his company's profit from a customer perspective. He creates a query that summarizes profit not only by TourID, but also by Customer so that he can develop marketing plans around his high-profit customers. Michael sketched the design for a final report in Figure F-14. Michael uses the Crosstab Query Wizard to guide his actions.

Steps 1 2 3 4

QuickTip

You can make any query into a crosstab query by choosing the Crosstab option from the Query type button on the Query toolbar.

Trouble?

If the Crosstab Wizard has been recently used, you may see different default options in each dialog box. Be sure to check each option as you move through the dialog boxes. Click the Back button to review previous dialog boxes. Be sure to double-check the query name and modify the default option if necessary.

1. **Click the Queries tab if necessary, click New, click Crosstab Query Wizard, then click OK**
   The first step to creating a crosstab query is to assemble the fields in a single query object. The Profit by Customer query will be used as the basis for the crosstab query. It contains the needed fields of CustID, Last, TourID, and Profit.

2. **Click the Queries option button, click Profit by Customer, then click** Next >
   Identify the CustID and Last fields as row headings.

3. **Click the CustID field, click the Add Selected Field button** > **, click the Last field, click** > **, then click** Next >
   The sample pane displays the results of your choices as you build the query. Next Michael identify the column heading field.

4. **Click the TourID field, then click** Next >
   Finally, identify the field which will be crosstabulated, and the aggregate function shown in Figure F-15.

5. **Click Profit, click Sum in the Functions column, then click** Next >
   Accept the default name Profit by Customer_Crosstab and view the crosstab query

6. **Click** Finish **, then click the datasheet Maximize button if necessary**
   The resulting datasheet for the Crosstab query is shown in Figure F-16. You could switch to Query Design View and sort this query by Profit or enter limiting criteria as with any other query. In this case though, just print a copy of the crosstab datasheet for a future meeting.

7. **Click the Print button** 🖨 **on the Query Datasheet toolbar, click the Crosstab query datasheet Close button**

Types of Query Wizards

The Simple Query Wizard is another way to create a select query rather than use the Query Design View. The Find Duplicates Query Wizard is used to determine whether a table contains duplicate values in one or more fields. The Find Unmatched Query Wizard is used to find records in one table that don't have related records in another table.

FIGURE F-14: Sketch of a crosstab query

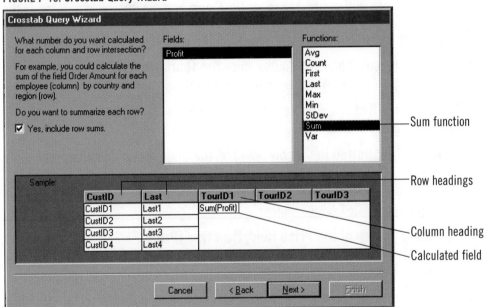

Row headings

Column heading

Total Profit

Total Profit per customer

Profit per customer per tour

FIGURE F-15: Crosstab Query Wizard

Crosstab Query Wizard

What number do you want calculated for each column and row intersection?

For example, you could calculate the sum of the field Order Amount for each employee (column) by country and region (row).

Do you want to summarize each row?

☑ Yes, include row sums.

Fields:

Profit

Functions:

Avg
Count
First
Last
Max
Min
StDev
Sum
Var

— Sum function

Sample:

— Row headings

CustID	Last	TourID1	TourID2	TourID3
CustID1	Last1	Sum(Profit)		
CustID2	Last2			
CustID3	Last3			
CustID4	Last4			

— Column heading

— Calculated field

Cancel   < Back   Next >   Finish

FIGURE F-16: Crosstab query datasheet

Total profit per customer

CustID	Last	Total Of Profit	Bigs0197	Bung0996	Bung0997	Mtbi0996	Mtbi0997
1	Braithwaite	$40.00					
10	Rodarmor	$95.00				$95.00	
11	Reis	$228.00	$108.00		$120.00		
12	Reis	$108.00	$108.00				
13	Egan	$228.00	$108.00		$120.00		
14	Fox	$213.00	$108.00				$105.00
15	Fox	$213.00	$108.00				$105.00
16	Fox	$108.00	$108.00				
2	Spencer	$95.00				$95.00	
3	Dobbins	$75.00		$75.00			
4	Khalsa	$95.00				$95.00	
5	Majors	$75.00		$75.00			
6	Williams	$75.00		$75.00			
7	Gonzales	$95.00				$95.00	
8	Black	$95.00				$95.00	
9	Owen	$75.00		$75.00			

— Column headings

— Row headings

Record: 14 ◀ 1 ▶ ▶I ▶* of 16

Datasheet View

NUM

Creating Update Queries

Update queries allow you to select a group of records then update all of them with one action. For example, you may wish to delete a group of records with a **Delete** query, change the value of a field with a basic Update query, or add several records to an existing table with an **Append** query. An update query starts as a select query with an Update to row added to the Query design grid. Table F-4 shows examples of update formulas. Michael wants to increase the prices of all 1997 tours by 20%.

1. Click the **Queries tab**, click **New**, click **Design View**, then click **OK**
The only table you need for this update query is the Tours table.

2. Click **Tours**, click **Add**, then click **Close**
You need the TourDate field in order to select 1997 tours and the Price field to increase the data in that field by 20%. You have to insert the Price field in the first column in the Query design grid, and the TourDate field in the second column in the Query design grid.

3. Double-click the **Price field**, then double-click the **TourDate field**
Specify that only those tours with dates on or after 1/1/97 are chosen.

4. Click the **Criteria cell** of the **TourDate field**, then type **>=1/1/97**
Change the select query into an update query.

5. Click the **Query Type button list arrow** on the Query Design toolbar, then click **Update Query**
The Sort and Show rows of the Query design grid changes to an Update To row where the formula for the new updated value is entered.

6. Click the **Update To cell** of the **Price field**, then type **[Price]*1.2**
This formula will update the current prices of all tours selected by 20%. The Query Design grid now looks like Figure F-17.

7. Click the **Run button** on the Query Design toolbar to update the database, click **Yes** when asked if you want to update 4 rows, click the **Datasheet View button** on the Query Design toolbar, click the **Restore Window button**.
The resulting datasheet of the update query is shown in Figure F-18. Since you don't want to inadvertently run the query again and increase prices a second time, do not save the query.

8. Click the **Access Close button**, click **No** when prompted to save the changes to the query, close the database, then close Access
Michael can use this information to project higher profit margins for Nomad.

Trouble?
Don't click the Run button twice or you will update the Price field of the chosen records by 20% a second time.

FIGURE F-17: Query Design View of an update query

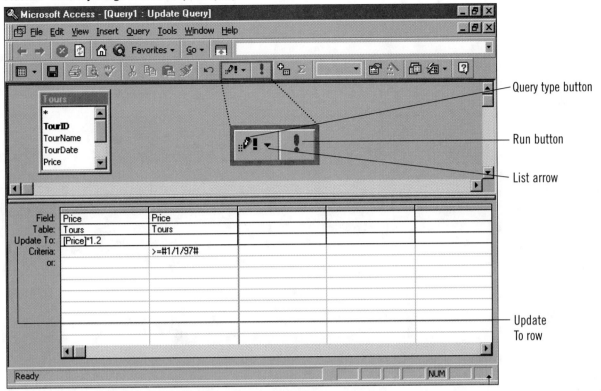

Query type button

Run button

List arrow

Update To row

FIGURE F-18: Datasheet of an update query after running the update

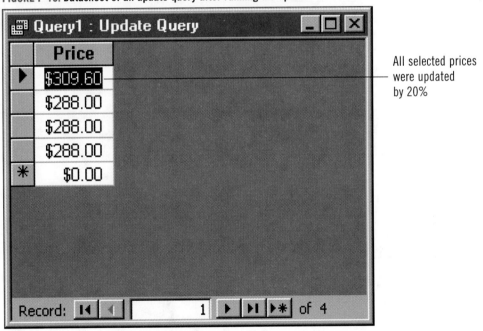

All selected prices were updated by 20%

TABLE F-4: Update query formulas and results

update formula	result
"Vice President"	Changes the values of the chosen field to the text Vice President
#1/1/98#	Changes the values of the chosen field to the date 1/1/98
7	Changes the values of the chosen field to 7
[Cost]*1.05	Updates the values of the chosen field to five percent more than the current value of the Cost field

Practice

▶ Concepts Review

Identify each element of a table's Design View shown in Figure F-19.

FIGURE F-19

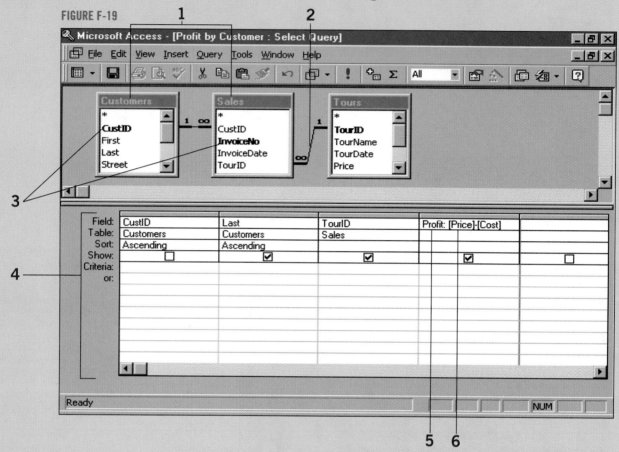

Match each term with the statement that describes its function.

7. Placing the records of a datasheet in a certain order
8. Used to create mathematical calculations in a query
9. A database object that answers questions about the data
10. Conditions that select only certain records
11. Operator used to combine two expressions

a. Query
b. Arithmetic operators
c. And
d. Sorting
e. Criteria

Select the best answer from the list of choices.

12. The query datasheet can best be described as:
   a. A duplication of the data in the underlying table's datasheet.
   b. A logical view of the selected data from an underlying table's datasheet.
   c. A separate file of data.
   d. A second copy of the data in the underlying tables.

13. Queries are often used to:
   a. Create copies of database files.
   b. Eliminate the need to build multiple tables.
   c. Create option boxes and list boxes from which to choose field values.
   d. Present a subset of fields from multiple tables.

14. When you update data in a table that is displayed in a query:
   a. You must also update the query.
   b. You must relink the query to the table.
   c. The data is automatically updated in the query.
   d. You have the choice whether you want to update the data in the query or not.

15. To assemble several fields from different tables, use a(n):
   a. Select Query.
   b. Update Query.
   c. Delete Query.
   d. Append Query.

16. The order in which records are sorted is determined by:
   a. The order in which the fields are listed in the underlying table.
   b. The alphabetic order of the field names.
   c. The left-to-right position of the fields in the Query grid.
   d. Ascending fields are sorted first in the Query grid. Descending fields are sorted second.

17. Crosstab queries are used to:
   a. Summarize information based on fields in the column and row headings of the report.
   b. Update several records at the same time.
   c. Select fields for a datasheet from multiple tables.
   d. Calculate price increases on numeric fields.

Skills Review

1. Create select queries using multiple tables
a. Start Access and open the database Addresses-F.
b. Create a new select query using Design View using both the Names and Zips tables.
c. Add the following fields to the Query design grid in this order:
First, Last, Street, and Zip from the Names table
City and State from the Zips table
d. Save the query as "Basic Address List", view the datasheet, print the datasheet, then close the query.

2. Sort a query on multiple fields
a. Think about how you would modify the "Basic Address List" query so that it is sorted in ascending order by Last, then by First, but do not change the order of the fields in the resulting datasheet.
b. Add another First field to the right of the Last field in the Query design grid to make the first three fields in the Query design grid First, Last, and First.
c. Add the ascending sort criteria to the second column and third column fields, and uncheck the Show checkbox in the third column.
d. Save the query as "Sorted Address List", view the datasheet, print the datasheet, then close the query.

3. Develop AND queries
a. Think about how you would modify the "Basic Address List" query so that only those people from IA with a last name that starts with "F" are chosen.
b. Enter F* (the asterisk is a wildcard) as the criterion for the Last field to choose all people whose last name starts with F. Enter IA as the criterion for the State field.
c. Be sure to enter the criteria on the same line in the Query design grid to make the query an AND query.
d. Save the query as "Iowa F Names", view the datasheet, print the datasheet, and close the query.

4. Develop OR queries
a. Modify the "Iowa F Names" query so that only those people from IA with a last name that starts with "F" or "B" are chosen.
b. Enter the OR criterion B* on the or row for the Last field in the Query design grid. Access will assist you with the syntax for this type of criterion and enters "Like B*" in the cell when you click elsewhere in the grid.
c. Be sure to reenter the IA criterion on the or row for the State field in the Query design grid to make sure that your query doesn't display all names that start with B, but only those who live in Iowa.
d. Save the query as "Iowa B or F Names", view the datasheet, print the datasheet, then close the query.

5. Develop calculated fields
a. Plan how you might create a new select query using Design View using just the Names table to determine the number of days old each person is based on the information in the Birthday field.
b. Add the following fields from the Names table to the Query design grid in this order:
First, Last, Birthday
c. Create a calculated field called "Days Old" in the fourth column of the Query design grid with the expression Days Old:Date()-[Birthday]
(Note: Date() is an Access function that always represents today's date.)
d. Save the query as "Days Old", view the datasheet, print the datasheet, then close the query.

6. Add calculations on groups of records
a. Create a new select query using Design View, then add the Names and Zips tables.
b. Add the following fields:
Zip from the Names table
City and State from the Zips table
c. Add the Total row to the Query design grid and change the function from Group By to Count for the Zip field
d. Save the query as "Count Zip", view the datasheet, print the datasheet, then close the query.

7. Develop crosstab queries
a. Use the Crosstab Query Wizard to create a new crosstab query that counts the number of people who live in each City and State.
b. Use the Basic Address List query as the basis for the new crosstab query.
c. Select City as the row heading and State as the column heading.
d. Count the First field for the calculation within the crosstab datasheet.
e. Name the query "Crosstab of Cities and States".
f. View, Save, print, then close the datasheet.

8. Create update queries
a. Think about how you would create a new select query using Design View to update the city "Overland Park" to the correct post office designation of "Shawnee Mission."
b. Use Design View to design a new query.
c. Add just the Zips table to the Query design grid.
d. Add the City field from the Zip table to the query.
e. Click Query on the menu bar, then click Update Query.
f. In the Criteria cell, enter "Overland Park".
g. In the Update To cell, enter "Shawnee Mission".
h. Run the query to update the record that contains the Overland Park entry in the City field.
i. Save the query as "Shawnee Mission".
j. Close the database, then exit Access.

► Independent Challenges

1. As the president of a civic organization, you have developed a database that tracks donations of recyclable material called Cleanup-F. Now that several deposits have been made and recorded, you wish to query the database for several different listings that are needed for the next meeting.

To complete this independent challenge:

1. Start Access and open the database Cleanup-F.
2. Create a query that pulls the following fields into a datasheet and print the datasheet.
Name (of Clubs), Deposit Date, Weight, Name (of Recycle Centers)
Call the query "Deposits by Club".
3. Modify Deposits by Club so that it is sorted ascending by club Name, and then ascending by Deposit Date. Print the datasheet and save the query as "Deposits Sorted by Club then Date".
4. Modify Deposits Sorted by Club then Date to eliminate both the deposit Date and Name (of Center) fields. Then, group the records by club Name and total the Weight. Print the datasheet and save the query as "Total Weight by Club".

5. Modify Total Weight by Club so that the records are sorted from the highest total deposit weight to the lowest. Print the datasheet and save the query as "Sorted Total Weight by Club".

6. Create a new query that pulls the following fields with the given criteria into a datasheet.
Fields: Name (of Center), deposit Date, Weight
Criteria: Recycle Center Name = East Side
Sorting: Sort ascending by deposit Date

7. Save the query with the name "East Side Deposits", view, then print the datasheet.

8. Close the database and exit Access.

2. Now that you've developed a relational database that documents the books you've read called Readings-F, your friends are starting to ask for recommended reading lists. You wish to query your book database to satisfy the requests of your friends.

To complete this independent challenge:

1. Start Access and open the database Readings-F.

2. Create a query that pulls the following fields into a datasheet:
Title, Category, Rating, and Last Name
Print the datasheet, save, and name the query "Books I've Read".

3. Modify Books I've Read so that it is sorted in a descending order on Rating and then in an ascending order by Last Name. Print the datasheet and name the query "Books I've Read Sorted by Rating and Author".

4. Use the Crosstab Query Wizard and the Books I've Read query to find out how many books you've read within each category by each author. Use Last Name as the row heading field, Category as the column heading field, and count the Title field within the body of the Crosstab report. Print the datasheet and name the query "Crosstab of Authors and Categories".

5. Modify the Books I've Read Sorted by Rating and Author query so that only fiction books with a rating of 7 or above are displayed.

6. Save the query as "Top Fiction Books", then print the datasheet.

7. Close the database and exit Access.

3. You have recently helped the medical director of a large internal medicine clinic put together and update a database called Doctors-F that tracks extra-curricular activities. You wish to query the database for specific listings of information to present to the committee responsible for philanthropic activities.

To complete this independent challenge:

1. Start Access and open the database Doctors-F.

2. Create a query that pulls the following fields into a datasheet:
First Name, Last Name, Date, Hours, and Name (of Program)
Save the query as "Physician Activities", then print the datasheet.

3. Modify Physician Activities so that it is sorted ascending by Last Name and then ascending by Date. Print the datasheet and name the query "Physician Activities Sorted by Name and Date".

4. Modify the Physician Activities Sorted by Name and Date query to eliminate the Date and Name fields. Then, group the records by Last Name and First Name and subtotal them by Hours. Print the datasheet and save the query as "Total Physician Hours".

5. Modify Total Physician Hours so that the records are listed from the physician who has volunteered the most time to the least. Print the datasheet and save the query as "Total Physician Hours Sorted from High to Low".

6. Create a new query that pulls the following fields with the given criteria into a datasheet:
   Fields: Name (of program), Last Name, Date, Hours
   Criteria: Hours are greater than 2 and Program equals "Heart Healthy" or Hours are greater than 2 and
   Program equals "Diabetes Campaign"
   Sorting: Sort ascending by Name then Last Name

7. Save the query as "Heart and Diabetes", then print the datasheet.

8. Create a new query that pulls the Program Name field from the Programs table and updates any occurrences of
   "Elderly Outreach" to "Senior Outreach".

9. Save the query as "Elderly to Senior".

10. Create a new query that pulls the First Name field and Last Name field from the Physicians table. Make the First
    Name field the first column and the Last Name field the second column. Sort by Last Name, then by First Name.

11. Add the Hours field to the third column of the grid of the new query.

12. Add a calculated field to the fourth column of the grid that calculates the total time spent by the staff during
    the activity. The total time is calculated as three times the hours spent by the physician to account for the
    hours spent by the physician, the nurse, and the aide. The entry in the fourth column should be as follows:
    Total Staff:[Hours]*3

13. Save the query as "Total Time."

14. Close the database and exit Access.

4. You are interested in finding out about technical jobs currently available at IBM. Using information
about job openings posted at IBM's Web site, you have started an Access database that you can query for
the opportunities that most interest you.
To complete this independent challenge:

1. Log on to the Internet and use your browser to go to http://www.course.com. From there, click
   Student Online Companions, click the link for this textbook, then click the Access link for Unit F.

2. Use the IBM Employment site to find out what jobs are posted on the web page, and print at least two pages of
   the web site.

3. Open the IBM-F database.

4. Using the information you printed from IBM's site, enter two new records into the Job Listing Query.

5. Create a new query that first displays the Category field from the Category table, second displays the Job Title
   from the Job Titles table, and third shows the Job Reference # field from the Job Titles table.

6. Having recently read an article about job prospects for developers, you decide to determine how many of the job
   postings in the database match this title. Modify the query by entering "Developers" in the Criteria cell of the
   Job Title field.

7. Sort the records ascending by the Category field.

8. Resize the columns of the resulting datasheet so that all the information in each column is displayed.

9. Save the query as "Developers Query", print the datasheet, close the datasheet and database, then exit Access.

► Visual Workshop

Open the VW-F database and create a new query as shown in Figure F-20. Notice that the records are sorted alphabetically by last name and the total value of their donations is summarized in the SumOfValue field. Save the query as "Summarized Donations" then print the datasheet.

FIGURE F-20

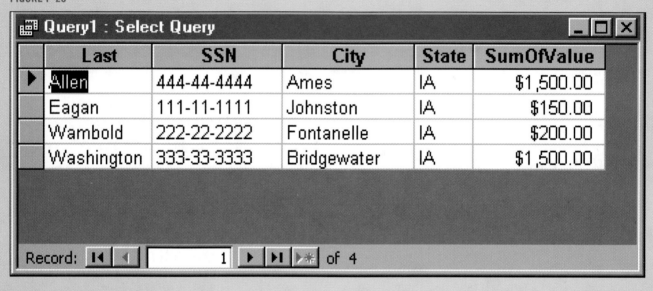

Last	SSN	City	State	SumOfValue
Allen	444-44-4444	Ames	IA	$1,500.00
Eagan	111-11-1111	Johnston	IA	$150.00
Wambold	222-22-2222	Fontanelle	IA	$200.00
Washington	333-33-3333	Bridgewater	IA	$1,500.00

Record: 1 of 4

Developing
Forms with Subforms

Objectives

- ► **Create a form from multiple tables**
- ► **Move and resize controls**
- ► **Add labels and format controls**
- ► **Sort records within a form**
- ► **Find records within a form**
- ► **Filter records within a form**
- ► **Change the default value of a form control**
- ► **Add list boxes**

Adding new records or modifying existing data in a database must be easy and straightforward. A datasheet is often too cumbersome or complex for extensive data entry purposes. A **form** overcomes these obstacles by allowing you to present fields in any logical or useful screen arrangement. Also, forms allow you to add **controls** such as field labels, field text boxes, list boxes, and option buttons to help identify the data on the form. ◄▬▬ Michael wants to develop forms that match Nomad's source documents, the paper documents on which data is initially recorded. Entering data through well-designed forms will encourage fast, accurate data entry and will shield the data entry person from the complexity of tables, queries, and datasheets.

Creating a Form from Multiple Tables

A form displays the fields of a table or query in an arrangement that you design, and can be based on one of five general layouts: Columnar, Tabular, Datasheet, Chart, and PivotTable. See Table G-1 for more information on the different form layouts. Once the form is created, the design can be changed. ✎ Michael will develop a sales transaction form that Nomad employees can use to record additional tour sales including customer and invoice information at the time of the sale. The form requires fields from both the Customers and Sales tables in the Nomad database.

Steps ₁₂₃₄

1. **Start Access and open the Nomad-G database**

2. **Click the Forms tab in the Nomad-G : Database window, click New, click Form Wizard in the New Form dialog box, then click OK**
   The **Form Wizard**, as shown in Figure G-1, prompts you to select the fields, layout, and style of the form. You use the Form Wizard to select all the fields from both the Customers and Sales tables which are not currently gathered in any single query object.

3. **Click the Select all fields button** [>>] **to select all fields from the Customers table, click the Tables/Queries list arrow, click Table: Sales, click the Select all fields button** [>>]**, then click** [Next >]
   Next, you must decide how to view the data. Arranging the form by Customers places the customer information at the top of the form, and places invoice and tour information in a subform. A **subform** links multiple records from one table (Sales) to a single record of another table (Customers). It is especially effective when you want to show data from tables with a one-to-many relationship.

4. **If necessary, click by Customers, click the Form with subform(s) option button, then click** [Next >]
   Next, choose a tabular form layout then choose a Standard style in the following dialog box.

5. **Click the Tabular option button, click** [Next >]**, click Standard, then click** [Next >]
   Form names appear on the Forms tab and should be descriptive so you can identify the forms at a later time. Change the default form name and accept the default subform name.

6. **Type Customer Form in the Form: text box, click** [Finish]**, then click the Customer Form Maximize button**
   The form is shown in Figure G-2. By placing the customer information in the main form and the sales information in the subform, you can show multiple sales transactions for the same customer on the same form.

Using AutoForm

The **AutoForm** option creates the specified type of form for the chosen table or query. To quickly create a columnar form, click the table or query object with the fields you wish the form to contain, click the New Object button on the Database toolbar, then click AutoForm.

FIGURE G-1: Form Wizard

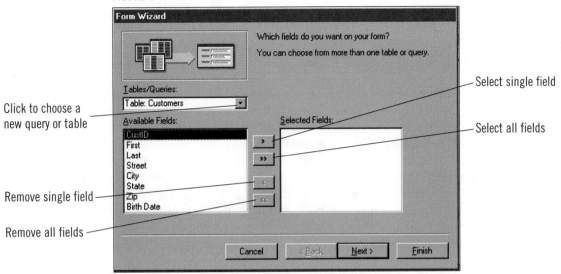

Click to choose a new query or table

Remove single field

Remove all fields

Select single field

Select all fields

FIGURE G-2: Customer Form

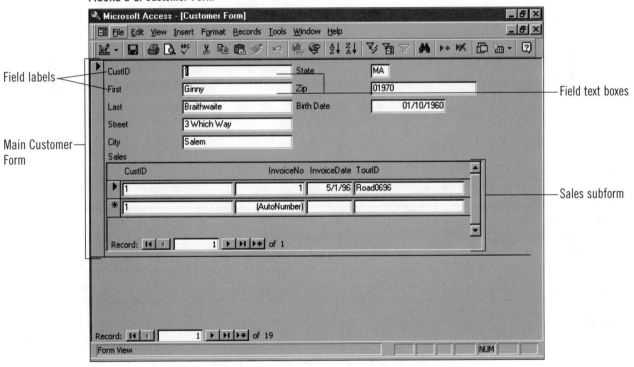

Field labels

Main Customer Form

Field text boxes

Sales subform

TABLE G-1: Form layouts

layout	description
Columnar	Each field appears on a separate line with a label to its left, one record for each screen
Tabular	Each field appears as a column heading and each record as a row; displays multiple records just like a datasheet, but provides more design control and flexibility; for example, you could change elements such as colors, fonts, headers, or footers
Datasheet	Each field appears as a column heading and each record as a row; the datasheet layout displays multiple records, but formatting options, except for resizing columns, are limited
Chart	Numeric fields are present in a chart (graph) format
PivotTable	Fields are chosen for column and for row headings, and a field is summarized in the intersection of the appropriate column and row in a cross-tabular format

Access 97

Moving and Resizing Controls

Even though the Form Wizard sets up a workable form, some rearrangement and resizing of the fields is often necessary for the form to best meet your needs. Form elements are called **controls** and can be bound or unbound. An **unbound control** is not linked to the data of any table; it exists only within the form itself. Field labels are the most common unbound control, but other types include clipart, lines, and instructional labels. **Bound controls** are linked to data in underlying tables. The most common bound control is a field text box. Check boxes, list boxes, and option buttons can also be bound controls. When you add a field to a form, Access automatically adds both an unbound control (the descriptive field label) and a bound control (a field text box). ◄═══ Michael rearranges and modifies the controls on the form to better suit his data entry needs.

Steps

1. **Click the Design View button** 📐 **on the Form View toolbar**
   Use Design View to move, delete, or add any elements to the form. The fields from the Customer table appear in the upper half of the form, and a large control to designate the size and position of the Sales Subform appears in the lower half. Delete the unnecessary labels from the form.

Trouble?

If the Toolbox covers the form, drag the Toolbox title bar to the right edge of the window so the entire form is visible.

Trouble?

If you select the wrong label, click it again while holding [Shift] to deselect it and retain the other selections.

QuickTip

The Object list box on the left edge of the Formatting (Form/Report) toolbar always displays which control is currently selected on the form. In addition, you can select a control by clicking the Object list arrow, then clicking the desired control from the list.

QuickTip

You can press and hold [Ctrl] while pressing an arrow key to move objects very small distances (less than a grid mark).

Time To

✔ Save
✔ Close

2. **Click the First label, press and hold [Shift], click the Last label, click the Street label, click the City label, click the State label, click the Zip label, then release [Shift]**
   Pressing [Shift] while clicking the second and subsequent controls allows you to select multiple controls at the same time as shown in Figure G-3.

3. **Press [Delete]**
   Deleting the labels does not affect the data displayed on the form in the field text boxes.

4. **Click the First text box, move the mouse pointer to the top edge of the text box until it changes to** ✋, **drag the First text box to the left under the CustID label, click the Last text box, move the mouse pointer to the top edge of the text box until it changes to** ✋, **then drag the Last text box up and to the right of the First text box**
   See Table G-2 for more information on mouse pointer shapes used in Form Design View. Next, move the address text boxes so they are all on the same line. You have to move the Birth Date field out of the way to make room for the address fields. You will then move the Birth Date field to its correct location.

5. **Move the Birth Date text box down and to the right to an empty space on the form, then move the Street, City, State, and Zip to the positions shown in Figure G-4**
   You want the Birth Date field label and text box next to the CustID field.

6. **Click the Birth Date text box, move the mouse pointer to the top edge of the text box until it changes to** ✋, **then drag the Birth Date text box to the right of the CustID field**
   The CustID and Zip text boxes are wider than necessary.

7. **Click the CustID text box, press and hold [Shift], click the Zip text box, move the mouse pointer to the middle resize handle on the right side of the Zip text box; drag to the left to the 4.5" mark on the ruler**
   The new form design organizes the information logically, without the unnecessary labels.

8. **Click the Form View button** 🗒 **on the Form Design toolbar**
   Compare your screen to the form shown in Figure G-5. Now you can save and close the new form.

FIGURE G-3: Form Design View

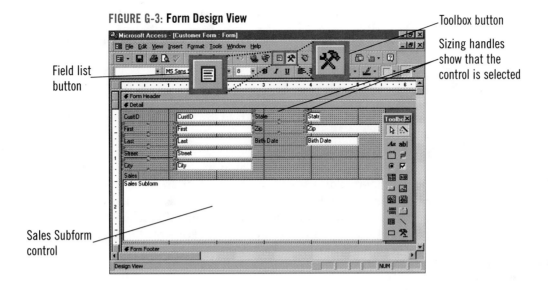

Field list button

Toolbox button

Sizing handles show that the control is selected

Sales Subform control

FIGURE G-4: Customer Form after fields are moved

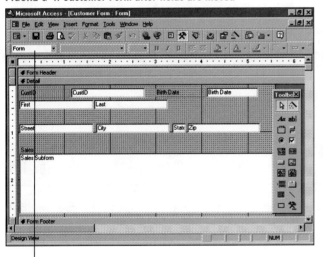

Object list box

FIGURE G-5: Final Customer Form

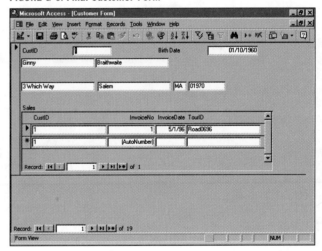

TABLE G-2: Mouse pointer shapes used in Form Design View

pointer	used to
⬚	Select controls
✋	Move multiple controls
I	Move one control
↔	Resize a control horizontally
↕	Resize a control vertically
⤢ and ⤡	Resize a control diagonally (horizontally and vertically at the same time)
✛	Resize sections of a form

Adding Labels and Formatting Controls

Even though unbound controls such as field labels and lines help identify and organize related information on a form, sometimes more descriptive labels are necessary. Formatting, enhancing the appearance of controls, can also improve a form's readability. The **Formatting** (Form/Report Design) toolbar provides the most popular formatting options for changing a label's border, font name, font size, or color. Formatting options that are not available on the toolbar must be changed through the control's property sheet. ✎ Michael decides to add a label to the Detail section of the form. See Table G-3 for more information on form sections. He will also change the label alignment so labels are positioned closer to the field text boxes they describe. His first step will be to add a label to identify the address information, then he'll realign the labels closer to their corresponding text boxes.

1. Click **Customer Form** on the Forms tab if necessary, click **Design**, click the **Label tool** 🔠 in the Toolbox, click above the **address text fields at 5/8" on the ruler**, then type **Address Information:**

   Select both the CustID and Birth Date labels so that you can change the alignment property on both labels at the same time.

2. Click the **CustID label**, press and hold [Shift], click the **Birth Date label**, then release [Shift]

   You want to right-align these labels. Since the Formatting toolbar doesn't contain a right-alignment button, make the change on the property sheet for these controls.

3. Click the **Properties button** 🖳 on the Form Design toolbar, click the **Format tab**, scroll to display the **Text Align property**, click the **Text Align text box**, click the **Text Align list arrow**, then click **Right**

   The title bar of the property sheet displays the selected control's name. In this case, multiple controls are selected. The Customer Form should look like Figure G-6. Close the property sheet and view this form.

4. Click the **Properties button** 🖳 on the Formatting toolbar, then click the **Form View button** 🖳 on the Formatting toolbar

   The CustID and Birth Date labels are right aligned on the form.

5. Click the **Save button** 🖫 on the Form View toolbar

   The final Customer Form should look like Figure G-7.

QuickTip
Click the Properties button 🖳 to toggle the form property sheet on or off.

Trouble?
If you move, resize, or change a property of the wrong control, click the Undo button 🔙 to undo your last action.

TABLE G-3: **Form sections**

section	description
Detail	Appears once for every individual record
Form Header	Appears at the top of the form and often contains a label with the form's title
Form Footer	Appears at the bottom of the form and often contains a label with instructions on how to use the form
Page Header	Appears at the top of a printed form with information such as page numbers or dates. The Page Header and Page Footer sections can be added to the form by clicking View on the menu bar, then clicking Page Header/Footer
Page Footer	Appears at the bottom of a printed form with information such as page numbers or dates

FIGURE G-6: Customer Form with label and alignment changes

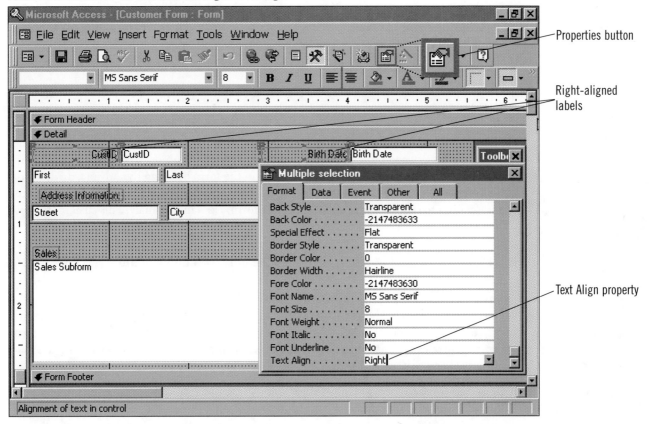

Properties button

Right-aligned labels

Text Align property

FIGURE G-7: Customer Form

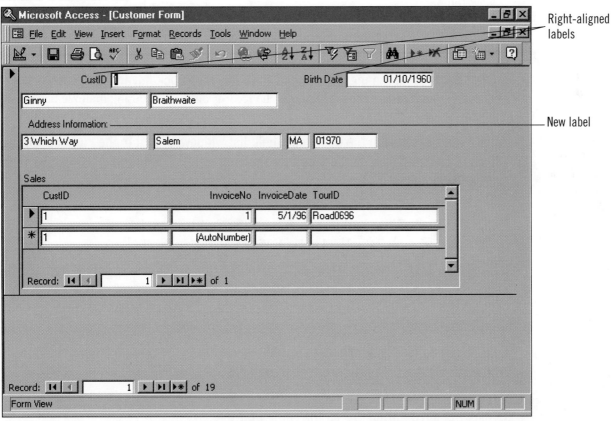

Right-aligned labels

New label

Sorting Records within a Form

Once a form is created, you can **sort** the records the same way that you sort within a datasheet. This is helpful to the user who entered data using a form, but needs to order the records in a certain way to make sure that the same customer is not being added to the database. If the form is based on a query that has already specified a sort order, the records will appear in that order when the form is opened but can be resorted at any time. Advanced sorts using more than one field in the sort order can be applied directly within the form by using the Advanced Filter/Sort option. Now that Michael has developed the Customer Form to record sales, he will use the Sort features to reorder the records within the form. He wants to analyze his customers based on their age, so he decides to sort the customers on the Birth Date field.

1. Click the Birth Date text box, then click the Sort Descending button ⤵ on the Form View toolbar
   Amanda Fox is displayed as the record with the highest birth date (she is the youngest in the database) as shown in Figure G-8. Notice that two sets of record navigation buttons are displayed, one for the form, and one for the subform. The navigation buttons for the subform control the sales records for each customer. Use the main form record navigation buttons to move between customer records.

2. Click the Next record button ▶ in the Customer form navigation buttons
   Ron Fox, the next customer's record, should be displayed in the Customer Form. Ron Fox has two sales records in the Sales subform. Sort the records by name.

3. Click the Last text box (Fox), then click the Sort Ascending button ⤴ on the Form View toolbar
   John Black is displayed as the first record. You can further sort the records using both the First and Last fields. Since the buttons on the toolbar only accommodate a single-field sort, use the Advanced Filter/Sort option to sort on two fields.

4. Click Records on the menu bar, point to Filter, then click Advanced Filter/Sort
   The filter window opens so you can sort the records on the form using multiple fields. The filter window is very similar to the Query design grid and already shows the Last sort criterion.

QuickTip
Double-click a field in the field list to move it to the next available column in the grid.

5. Click the First field in the Customers field list window, drag it to the Field cell of the second column, click the Sort cell for the First field, click the Sort list arrow, then click Ascending
   The finished filter window should look like Figure G-9.

6. Click the Apply Filter button ▽ on the Filter/Sort toolbar
   The Customer form is displayed in Form View with the sort applied.

QuickTip
Type a record number in the record indicator box and press [Enter] to quickly move to that record in the database.

7. Click the Next record button ▶ in the Customer Form navigation buttons six times to move to record 7 for Ron Fox
   When two customers have the same last name, the First field determines which record is sorted first. Use the form to enter another sale for Ron Fox.

8. Click in the first blank InvoiceDate field in the Sales subform (in a new record row), type 7/1/98, press [Tab], then type Bung0998
   The forms work well for entering new sales for existing customers.

9. Click the Save button 🖬 on the Form View toolbar

FIGURE G-8: Form sorted descending by Birth Date

Sort Ascending button

Sort Descending button

Sales Subform Navigation buttons

Main Customer Form Navigation buttons

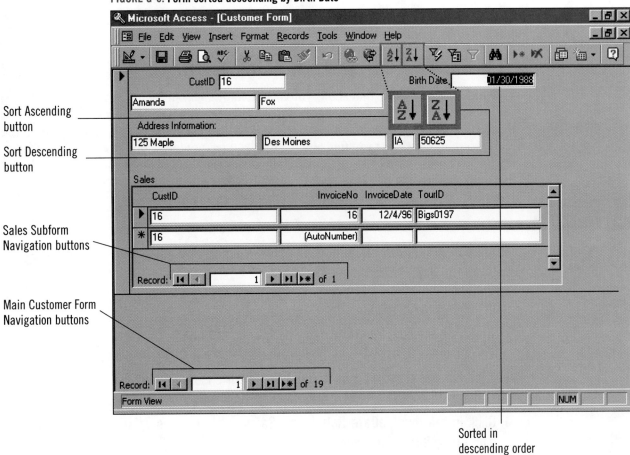

Sorted in descending order

FIGURE G-9: Filter window

Apply Filter button

Sort row

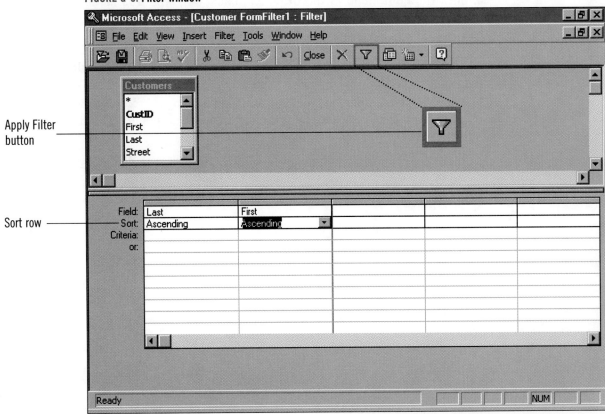

Access 97

Finding Records within a Form

Access has a **Find** feature that allows you to search for a text string in any field. With the Find dialog box, you can locate specific records or find certain values within fields. You can navigate through records as Access finds each occurrence of the item you're looking for. If you want to replace certain values that you find, use the **Replace** feature found on the Edit menu. Michael will use the Find feature to answer questions about his customers and sales. Michael is making a presentation in Des Moines, Iowa, and wants to find all customers from that state.

Steps 1234

1. Click **IA** in the **State field** in the Customer Form, then click the **Find button** 🔍 on the Form View toolbar
   The Find in field dialog box opens as shown in Figure G-10. The options in the Find dialog box allow you to customize the search.

2. Type **IA** in the Find What text box, then click **Find First**
   The Amanda Fox record is the first one that matches the find criteria.

3. Click **Find Next** three times to find Fritz Friedrichsen's record, then click **Close**
   Fritz Friedrichsen just booked a tour, so record the sale to Fritz in the subform.

4. Click in the **InvoiceDate field** in the Sales subform, type **7/1/98**, press **[Tab]**, then type **Bung0998** in the TourID text box
   The sale is recorded as shown in Figure G-11. Next, find all customers who live in Des Moines.

5. Click the **Fontanelle** in the City field, click 🔍, type **Des Moines**, then click **Find First** in the Find dialog box
   Amanda Fox is the first customer in the database who lives in Des Moines.

6. Click **Find Next**, then view each found record until you have reached the end of the records
   A dialog box indicating that you have finished searching the records appears when you have found all of the records that match the find criteria. You should have found three customers who live in Des Moines.

7. Click **OK** in the Search item not found warning message dialog box
   You found what you needed, so close the Find in field dialog box.

8. Click **Close**

FIGURE G-10: Find dialog box

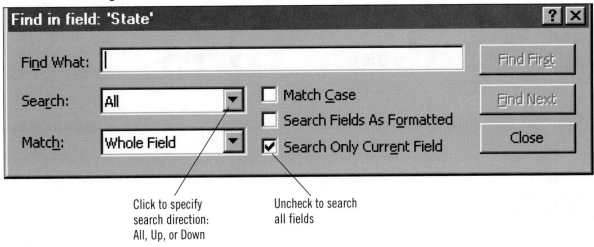

Find in field: 'State'

Find What: [   ]

Search: [All ▼]   ☐ Match Case   Find First

Match: [Whole Field ▼]   ☐ Search Fields As Formatted   Find Next
                         ☑ Search Only Current Field   Close

Click to specify
search direction:
All, Up, or Down

Uncheck to search
all fields

FIGURE G-11: Adding a sale using the Customer Form

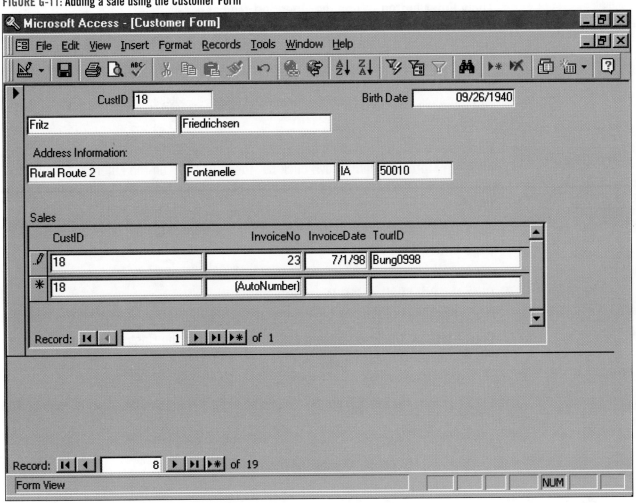

Filtering Records within a Form

Filtering is another way to locate the records that match certain criteria, but filtering is more powerful than using the Find button. Filtering presents ALL of the records that meet the specified criteria instead of just the first or next record that meets the criteria. ![] Michael wants to filter for all customers from Massachusetts because he knows that several new exciting tours will be offered in the New England area from the fall of 1998 through the winter of 1999.

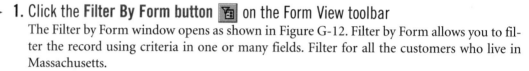

QuickTip

Click the Filter by Selection button ![] to apply a filter that finds the records based on the information in the current field.

1. Click the **Filter By Form button** ![] on the Form View toolbar
   The Filter by Form window opens as shown in Figure G-12. Filter by Form allows you to filter the record using criteria in one or many fields. Filter for all the customers who live in Massachusetts.

2. Click the blank **State field**, click the **State field list arrow**, click **MA**, then click the **Apply Filter button** ![] on the Filter/Sort toolbar
   The navigation buttons indicate that five customers match this filter criterion. The next question is to find all customers over 30 years of age that live in Massachusetts or Connecticut.

3. Click ![] on the Form View toolbar, click the **Birth Date field**, then type **<1/1/67**
   This entry will find all Massachusetts customers who turned 30 before 1/1/97. To find the customers who live in Connecticut, you must enter this "OR" criterion on another part of the filter screen.

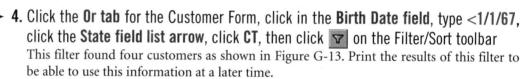

Trouble?

If this filter does not show four customers, return to the Filter by Form window to see if a criterion has been entered into the wrong field. Be sure to check each Or tab as well.

4. Click the **Or tab** for the Customer Form, click in the **Birth Date field**, type **<1/1/67**, click the **State field list arrow**, click **CT**, then click ![] on the Filter/Sort toolbar
   This filter found four customers as shown in Figure G-13. Print the results of this filter to be able to use this information at a later time.

5. Click the **Print Preview button** ![] on the Form View toolbar, then click the **Next page button** ![]
   You view the four forms on the screen, and they look just fine.

6. Click the **Print button** ![] to print the records
   Now, close the Print Preview window and remove the filter.

7. Click **Close** on the Print Preview toolbar to return to the Customer Form, then click the **Remove Filter button** ![] on the Form View toolbar
   Now you can save then close the form.

8. Click the **Save button** ![] on the toolbar, then click the **Customer Form Close button**

FIGURE G-12: Filter by Form

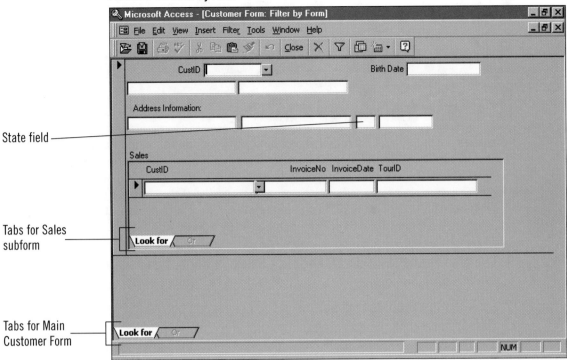

State field

Tabs for Sales
subform

Tabs for Main
Customer Form

FIGURE G-13: Filtered Customer Form

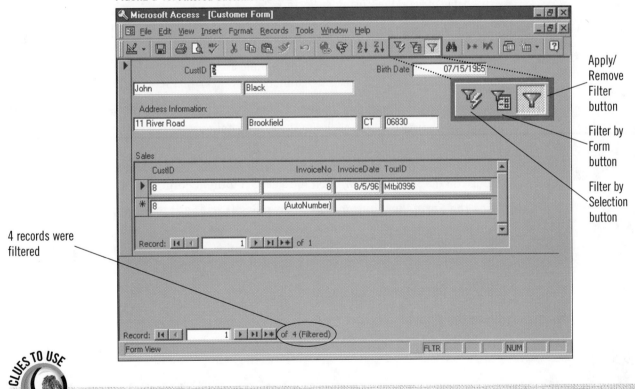

Apply/
Remove
Filter
button

Filter by
Form
button

Filter by
Selection
button

4 records were
filtered

Filtering with complex criteria expressions

When criteria are entered in more than one field of the Filter by Form window, both criteria must be true for the record to be displayed. These are called AND criteria. To enter OR criteria, in which only one or another set of criteria must be true for a record to be displayed, use the Or tab at the bottom of the Filter

by Form window. You can use wildcard characters such as the asterisk * for multiple characters and the question mark ? for single characters with either AND or OR criteria. These criteria evaluation rules are exactly the same as those used to evaluate criteria in the Query design grid.

Changing the Default Value of a Form Control

Properties are simply the characteristics of the controls on the Form. You change the properties of a control in Form Design View. Properties can be as basic as the control's color, text alignment, or default value, or as complex as branching to a different form when the control is clicked. The control's property sheet is a comprehensive list of the control's properties. Michael wants to make the current date the default value of the InvoiceDate field on the Sales subform. He'll open the Sales Subform in Design View to make this change.

Steps

1. Click the **Forms tab** if necessary, click **Sales Subform**, then click **Design**
   The Sales Subform opens in Design View as shown in Figure G-14.

2. Click the **InvoiceDate text box**, click the **Properties button** on the Form Design toolbar, then click the **Data tab** on the property sheet
   The Data tab of the InvoiceDate properties sheet shows properties that have to do with the source, validation, and default value of the data that can be entered in the InvoiceDate text box. Change the default value of this text box to display today's date. This will eliminate extra data entry on the Customer Form.

3. Click in the **Default Value text box**, then click the **Expression Builder button**
   The Expression Builder dialog box opens as shown in Figure G-15. Use the Expression Builder dialog box to guide your actions to build an expression that results in a single value. In this case, the expression is a single function, =Date(), that returns today's date.

4. Double-click the **Functions folder** in the first list box, click the **Built-In Functions folder** in the first list box, click the **Date/Time** category in the second list box, double-click **Date** in the third list box, then click **OK**
   The =Date() expression is added as the value for the Default Value property. To see the change on the Sales Subform, open the Sales Subform in Form View.

5. Click the **Form View button**, then press **[Ctrl][End]** to move to the last field of the last record
   The default InvoiceDate is today's date confirming that the changes to the form were successful.

6. Click the **Save button** on the toolbar

7. Close the subform

Inherited properties

If you change a control's property setting on a form, the change doesn't affect the underlying query or table. Likewise, if you change the property setting for a field in a table or query after you've created a form that uses the field, the property setting for the control on the form isn't updated; you must do this manually.

There are exceptions to the last rule, however. If you change the Default Value, Validation Rule, or Validation Text properties in a table's Design View, these changes will be enforced in any controls based on these fields later.

FIGURE G-14: Sales subform in Form Design View

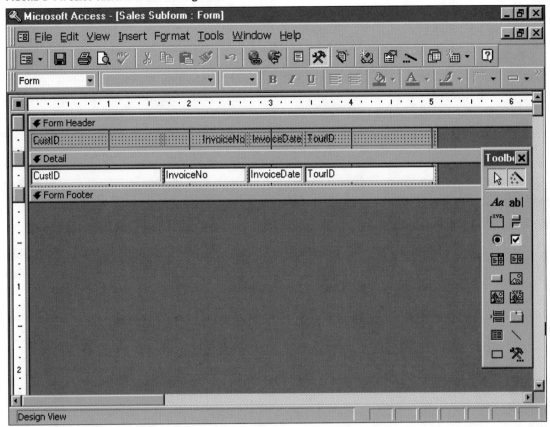

FIGURE G-15: Expression Builder dialog box

Expression text box

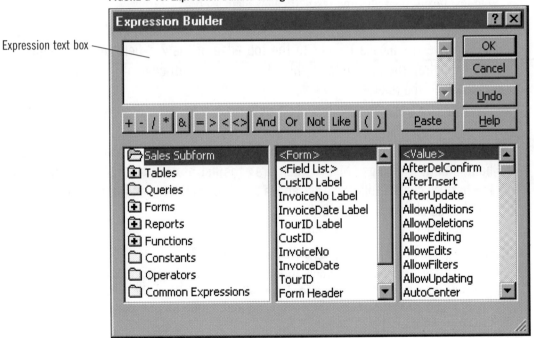

Adding List Boxes

By default, fields are added to a form as bound text boxes, but sometimes other controls such as list boxes, combo boxes, or options buttons would handle the data entry process easier or faster for a particular field. Both the **list box** and **combo box** controls provide a list of values from which the user can choose an entry. A combo box also allows the user to make an entry from the keyboard, so it is really a list box plus a text box combined. ➤ Michael realizes that it would be easier to choose an appropriate entry from the State field from a list. He has added a States table to the database. The States table has two fields: the two-letter state abbreviation and state description. He also developed a query that sorts the states alphabetically called "States sorted ascending." Michael will change the State field on the Customer Form to a list box bound to the state query.

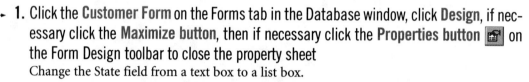

QuickTip

Double-click a control to access its property sheet.

1. Click the **Customer Form** on the Forms tab in the Database window, click **Design**, if necessary click the **Maximize button**, then if necessary click the **Properties button** 🔳 on the Form Design toolbar to close the property sheet
Change the State field from a text box to a list box.

2. Right-click the **State field text box**, point to **Change To**, then click **List Box**
When you create a list box that looks up values, you need to decide where the data for the list will come from. Change the Row Source property for the list box to handle this requirement.

Trouble?

Be sure to change the Row Source property instead of the Control Source property. The Control Source property controls what underlying field in a table or query is updated. The Row Source property controls what items are displayed in the list box.

3. Click the **Properties button** 🔳 on the Form Design toolbar, click the **Data tab** if necessary, click the **Row Source text box**, click the **list arrow**, then choose **States sorted ascending** as shown in Figure G-16
List boxes need more width to display the information than text boxes. Therefore move the Zip text box to the right, and resize the new State list box.

4. Click the **Properties button** 🔳 to close the property sheet, click the **Zip text box field**, move the mouse pointer to the top edge of the Zip field until it changes to 🖐, then drag the field to the right side so that the left edge of the field rests at the **4" mark** on the ruler
With the Zip field moved to the right, you have room to make the State list box wider and shorter so that it doesn't overlap with the Sales Subform control.

5. Click the **State list box**, position the mouse pointer on the lower-right corner resize handle until it changes to ↗, then drag the **list box control** up and right so that the list box control fills the area above the Sales Subform and to the left of the Zip text box as shown in Figure G-17
View the changed Customer Form.

Trouble?

If the text box is not wide enough, click the Design View button and resize the control.

6. Click the **Form View button** 🔳 on the toolbar
The final Customer Form is shown in Figure G-18. The first customer lives in Salem, MA. To change the state data for any record, you can simply scroll to the appropriate entry in the list box and click the state abbreviation desired. Done for the day, save then close the Customer Form, then exit Access.

7. Click the **Save button** 🔳, click the Customer Form **Close button**, then click the **Access Close button**

FIGURE G-16: Property sheet for State list box

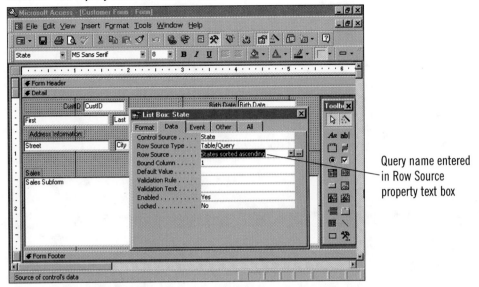

Query name entered in Row Source property text box

FIGURE G-17: Resized State list box

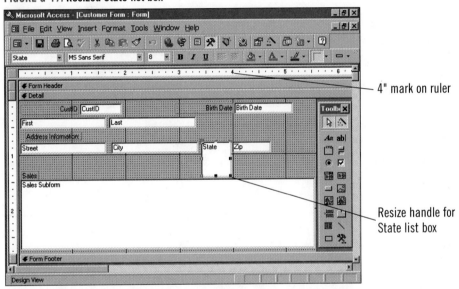

4" mark on ruler

Resize handle for State list box

FIGURE G-18: Customer Form with State list box

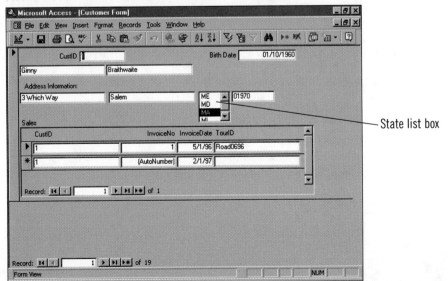

State list box

Practice

► Concepts Review

Identify each element of a form's Design View shown in Figure G-19.

FIGURE G-19

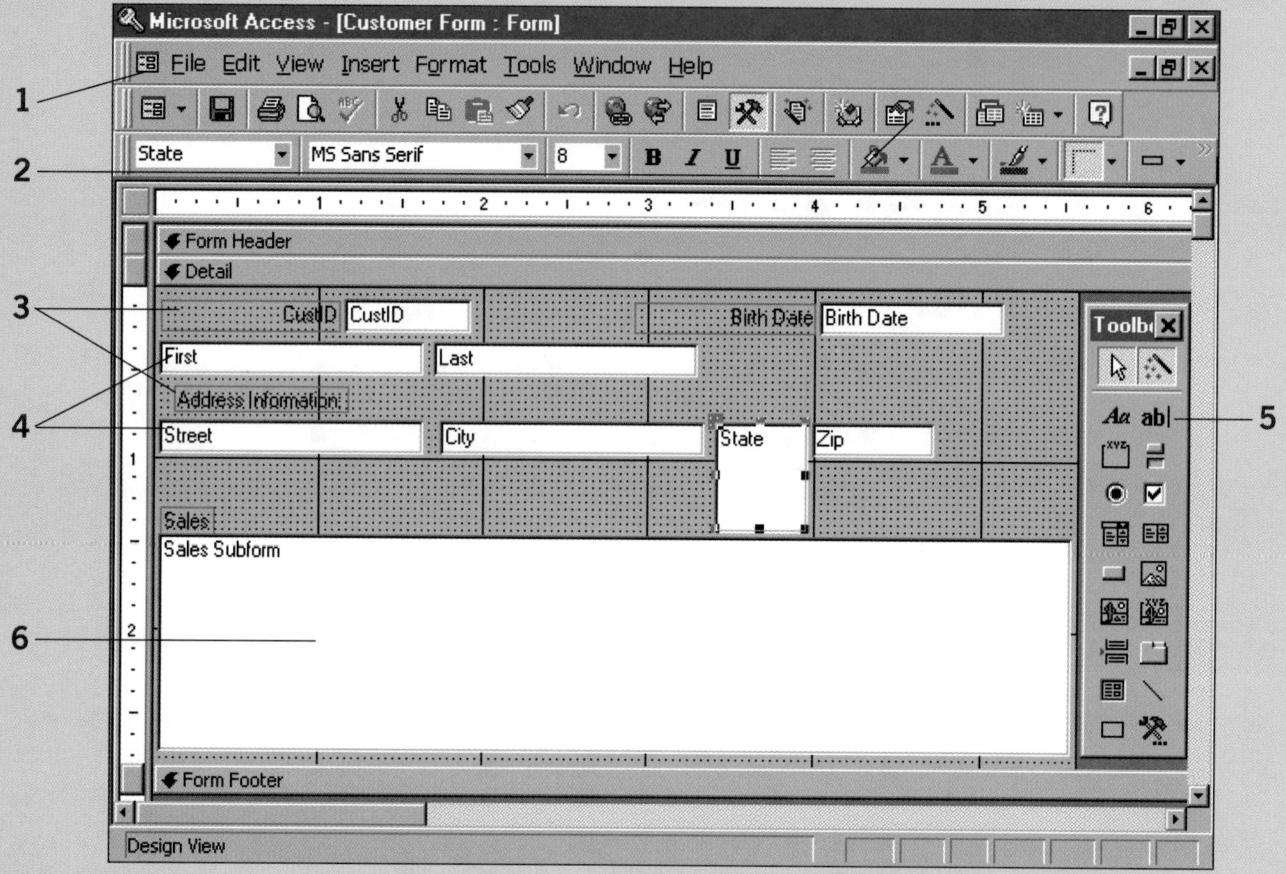

Match each term with the statement that describes its function.

7. Elements you add to a form such as labels, text boxes, and list boxes
8. An Access object that allows you to present the fields of one record in almost any screen arrangement you desire
9. The ability to locate specific subsets of records
10. Form elements that are linked to data in underlying tables and therefore change when the form switches from record to record
11. An element on a form that is not linked to the data of any table or query

a. Bound control
b. Controls
c. Filter
d. Form
e. Unbound control

Select the best answer from the list of choices.

12. **To select records based on criteria, you should use which feature?**
    a. Filter
    b. Find
    c. Form Wizard
    d. Sort

13. **Which of the following is the most common type of bound control?**
    a. Option group
    b. List box
    c. Text box
    d. Label

14. **Which of the following is the most common type of unbound control?**
    a. Check box
    b. Field label
    c. List box
    d. Combo box

15. **To quickly access a new blank record to enter new data, use which buttons?**
    a. Toolbox
    b. Form Design View toolbar
    c. Record Navigation
    d. Formatting toolbar

16. **To view multiple linked records of one table simultaneously with a single record of another table in a form use a:**
    a. Subform
    b. List box
    c. Design template
    d. Link control

Skills Review

1. Create a form from multiple tables.

a. Start Access and open the database Addresses-G.

b. Create a new form using the Form Wizard.

c. Add all the fields from both the Names and the Zips tables. By choosing all of the fields from both tables, you'll be adding the linking Zip field from both tables. When the Form Wizard is complete, you'll notice the Zip field from the Zips table in the main form and the Zip field in the Names table in the subform.

d. View the data with the Form with subform option by Zips.

e. Choose a Tabular layout and a Colorful 1 style.

f. Title the Form "Names within Zips" and the subform "Names Subform".

g. View the form, then close the form.

2. Move and resize controls.

a. Open the Names Subform in Design View.

b. In the Detail section, select the first four field text boxes: First, Last, Street, and Zip and narrow them to about half of their current width. Repeat this process in the Form Header section for the first four labels: First, Last, Street, and Zip.

c. In the Detail section, individually move the Last, Street, Zip, and Birthday text boxes left. All of the five text box controls in the Detail section should fit between the 0" and 5" marks on the ruler. Repeat this process in the Form Header section for the labels.

d. Save and close the Names Subform.

e. Open the Names within Zips form to view the changes to the Names Subform within the main form. You should be able to see all five fields of the subform clearly.

3. Add labels and formatting controls.

a. Open the Names within Zips form in Design View.

b. Add a label in the upper-right corner of the form with the text, "This form is used to enter new zip codes and contact information."

c. Select all of the labels (Zip, City, and State) on the form, and right align the text within the control by changing the Text Align property to Right in the property sheet.

d. Close the property sheet.

e. View the form.

4. Sort records within a form.

a. Open the Names within Zips form in Form View.

b. Sort the records in ascending order by City. Print the first record using the Selected Records option on the Print dialog box. Click File on the menu bar, click Print to open the Print dialog box, click Selected Records, then click OK.

c. Sort the records in ascending order by State. Print the first record.

d. Using the Advanced Filter/Sort option from the Filter option of the Records menu, further refine the sort to first sort ascending by State and then ascending by Zip. Print the first two records.

5. **Find records within a form.**
   a. Click the State text box then click the Find button on the toolbar.
   b. Enter MO in the Find What text box, then click Find First to find the first record with the State equal to MO.
   c. Print the record.
   d. Close the Find dialog box.

6. **Filter records within a form.**
   a. Use the Filter by Form button to filter for records where the Zip equals 50837. Apply the filter.
   b. Print the record.
   c. Use the Filter by Form button to filter for all contacts where the birth dates are before 1/1/55 (less than 1/1/55).
   d. Print the first record.

7. **Change the default value of a form control.**
   a. Open the Names within Zips form in Design View.
   b. Open the property sheet for the State text box and change the Default Value property to IA.
   c. Open the Names within Zips form in Form View, click the New Record button to move to a blank record at the end of the datasheet, enter 50846 in the Zip text box, then enter Fontanelle in the City text box.
   d. Print the record. It should show the default IA entry in the State field even though you didn't directly enter this data on the form.

8. **Add list boxes.**
   a. Open the Names within Zips form in Design View.
   b. Right-click the State text box, then click Change to change the State text box to a list box.
   c. Change the Row Source property of the State list box to the States table. (The States table was added to the Addresses-G database for this exercise.)
   d. Widen and shorten the State list box so that you can clearly see the entries in Form View and so that the list box doesn't overlap the Names subform.
   e. Save the changes to the form.
   f. Print the first record.
   g. Close the database and exit Access.

► Independent Challenges

1. As the president of a civic organization, you have developed a database that tracks donations of recyclable material called Cleanup-G. Now that several deposits have been made and recorded, you wish to develop a form to record the deposits.

To complete this independent challenge:

1. Start Access and open the database Cleanup-G.
2. Using the Form Wizard, create a form/subform based on the Deposits By Club query.
3. Use all four fields in the form, and view the form by Clubs.
4. Use a datasheet layout, and a Colorful2 style.
5. Name the form "Deposits By Clubs Form" and the subform "Deposits Subform".
6. Filter the form so that only those deposits of 50 pounds or greater are displayed.
7. Sort the resulting records in descending order on club name and print the first record.
8. Close the database and exit Access.

2. Now that you've developed a relational database that documents the books you've read called Readings-G, you'd like to develop a form to quickly enter new records.

To complete this independent challenge:

1. Start Access and open the database Readings-G.
2. Using the Form Wizard, create a form/subform using all the fields of both the Books and Authors tables.
3. View the data by Authors.
4. Use a datasheet layout, and an Evergreen style.
5. Name the form "Books within Authors" and the subform "Books Subform".
6. Open the Books Subform in Design View, then narrow the Category and Author Number text boxes in the Detail section and the Category and Author Number labels in the Form Header section to about half of their current size.
7. Move the text boxes in the Detail section and the labels in the Form Header section so that they all fit within the first five inches of the form.
8. Save and close the subform.
9. Return to the Books within Authors form and filter the form so that only Non-Fiction books are displayed.
10. Print the first record.
11. Close and save the form.
12. Close the database and exit Access.

3. You have recently helped the medical director of a large internal medical clinic put together and update a database called Doctors-G that tracks extra-curricular activities. You wish to develop a form to use as a data entry mechanism for the database.

To complete this independent challenge:

1. Start Access and open the database Doctors-G.
2. Using the Form Wizard, create a form/subform using all the fields from the Physicians and Activities tables, and only the Program Name field from the Programs table.
3. View the data by Physicians.
4. Use a datasheet layout, and a Stones style.
5. Name the form "Activities by Physician" and the subform "Activities Subform".
6. Open the Activities Subform in Design View, then delete the Physician Number and Program Number text boxes in the Detail section. Also, delete the Physician Number and Program Number labels in the Form Header section.
7. Move the Name label and Name text box next to the Hours label and text box so that all of the remaining controls in the Activities Subform fit within the first three inches of the form.
8. Save and close the subform.
9. Return to the Activities by Physician form and sort it in ascending order by First Name within Last Name.
10. Print the first record.
11. Close and save the form, then close the database and exit Access.

4. Your dance club is making a trip to the famous Alberto's Nightclub, and has asked you to develop a small Access database to track the special events that Alberto's Nightclub offers. You've called the database Alberto-G. Now you'll go to the Alberto's Nightclub web site to find out what events are offered for this week and will add the information into the database using a form you've already developed. Then you will sort, filter, and query the information for various requests from dance club members.

To complete this independent challenge:

1. Log on to the Internet and use your browser to go to http://www.course.com. From there, click Student Online Companions, click the link for this text, then click the Access link for Unit G.
2. Use the Alberto's Nightclub site to find out what events are being offered for the week, and print the web page.
3. Start Access, then open the Alberto-G database.
4. Enter the week's event information into the Days of the Week form. The Days of the Week form is a form that contains a subform of events linked to the main form by the day of the week. The first event for Monday has already been entered. Leave this event in the database as an example of how to enter the event information and simply add the rest of the current week's events that you found on the web site.
5. Print the Monday record from the Days of the Week form.
6. Sort the records alphabetically on the Theme field and print the first record.
7. Filter the records so that only the Salsa themes are showing. Print the Salsa records.
8. Find the records who have a teacher named "DJ Polo." Print the DJ Polo records.
9. Create a query that sorts the Theme Name field in the Themes table in an ascending order and call it "Sorted Themes".
10. Delete the Theme text box in the Days of the Week form. Add the Theme field back to the form as a list box that uses the Sorted Themes query as the source of the information.
11. Resize the Theme list box so that it doesn't overlap with the Events Subform.
12. Close and save the form.
13. Close the database and exit Access.

Visual Workshop

Open the VW-G database and create a new form/subform as shown in Figure G-20. Use all of the fields in both the Alumni and Donations tables. Notice that the labels in the main form have been right aligned.

FIGURE G-20

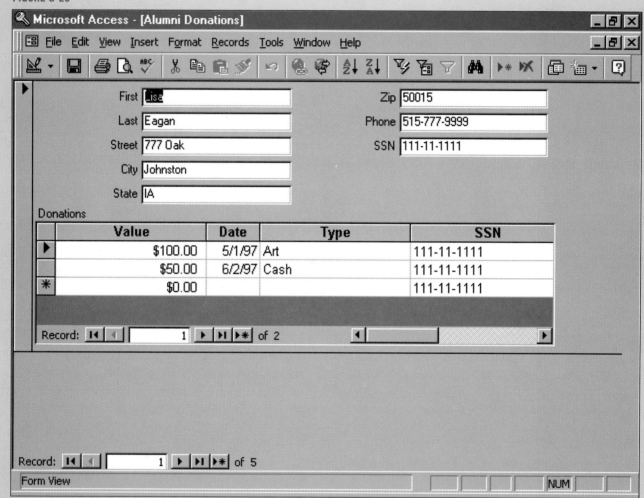

Creating
Complex Reports

Objectives

- ► Create a report from a query
- ► Use report sections
- ► Use group headers
- ► Add calculations to group footers
- ► Modify control alignment
- ► Add graphics to reports
- ► Use color
- ► Add special effects

Although you can print data in forms and datasheets, **reports** give you more control over how data is displayed and greater flexibility in presenting summary information such as subtotals on groups of records. Reports are often used to distribute information in formal presentations or meetings. Since a report definition (the report object) can be saved, it can be developed once but used many times to produce a paper report. Printed reports always reflect the most up-to-date data in a consistent format each time they are printed. As with form designs, report designs allow you to add bound controls such as text boxes and unbound controls such as lines, graphics, or labels. Michael's datasheet and form printouts have been very valuable; however, he wants to create more professional documents that include subtotals on groups of records to share with potential investors. In addition, he wants the reports to contain clip art images, various colors, and advanced formatting enhancements.

Creating a Report from a Query

The **Report Wizard** provides an interactive way to select fields from multiple tables or queries for a report. It also asks questions regarding how you want the records of the report to be grouped and formatted. **Grouping** provides a way to sort records so that summary statistics can be applied to a group of records that meet certain criteria. Grouping is not allowed within a form object. Another way to differentiate between a form and report object is to think about the primary purpose of the object. Forms are used for effective data entry. Reports provide effective printed output. ◆ A potential investor has asked for a report showing sales and profit information for each tour. Michael will use the Report Wizard to create the report.

1. Start Access and open the **Nomad-H** database, click the **Reports tab** in the Nomad-H : Database window, then click **New**

   The options in the New Report dialog box are very similar to those used to develop a form. Design View allows you to manually add controls to the report. AutoReport creates reports based on the chosen object with predefined settings.

2. Click **Report Wizard** in the New Report dialog box, then click **OK**

3. Click the **Tables/Queries**: list arrow, then click **Query: Profits**

   The Profits query has the four fields needed for this report as shown in Figure H-1.

4. Click the **Select all fields button** >> , then click Next >

   The next wizard dialog box determines how the records are displayed.

5. Click **by Tours**, then click Next >

   Since the records are already grouped by individual tour, you don't need to establish further grouping levels.

6. Click Next >

   The next wizard dialog box determines how the records within the detail section of the report are sorted. Choose to sort the invoices in ascending order.

7. Click the **first list arrow**, click **InvoiceNo**, then click Next >

   Finally, choose the layout, orientation, style, and title for the report.

8. Click the **Block Layout option button**, verify that the **Portrait Orientation option button** is selected, click Next > , click the **Corporate** style, click Next > , type **Profit by Tour Report** as the report title, click Finish , then **Maximize** the report window

   Print Preview of the Profit by Tour Report is shown in Figure H-2. Print Preview won't allow you to make any changes to the report, but does allow you to see exactly how your report will print. Refer to Table H-1 for more information on the buttons on the Print Preview toolbar.

QuickTip

If you can't see the entire report, scroll to see all the records and fields. Click ⊖ on the report to reduce the printout to show an entire printed page on the screen. To magnify a portion of the report on the screen, click ⊕ on the part of the report you wish to magnify.

FIGURE H-1: Report Wizard

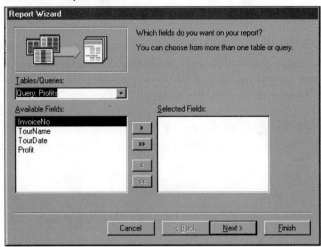

FIGURE H-2: Print Preview

Report Header section

Page Header section

Detail section

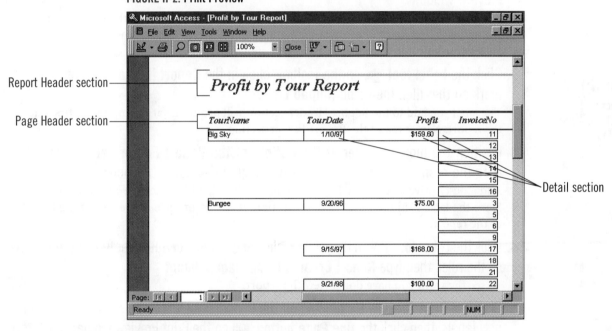

TABLE H-1: Buttons on the Print Preview toolbar

name	button	description
Print		Send a copy of the report to the default printer
Zoom		Toggles the print preview screen between 100% zoom and fit one page zoom
One page		Adjusts the zoom (magnification) level to fit one page of the report on the screen
Two pages		Adjusts the zoom level to fit two pages of the report on the screen
Multiple Pages		Displays multiple full pages in a matrix (2 rows by 3 columns, for example)
Zoom control	Fit	Adjusts the zoom level by clicking the list arrow and choosing the desired percentage
Close window	Close	Closes the print preview screen and displays the report's Design View
OfficeLinks		Sends the report to Word or Excel by clicking the list arrow and clicking Word or Excel
Database Window		Displays the database window which lists all objects in the database
New Object		Creates a new database object
Office Assistant		Provides Help topics or tips to help you complete a task

Using Report Sections

Just as Form Design View is used to modify forms, Report Design View is used to modify reports. Report Design View consists of **sections** (designated areas of the report design) in which controls and formatting specifications are placed. Because reports allow more sophisticated analysis of groups of records, the sections become very important design elements. See Table H-2 for a description of the different sections of a report. ➤➤ Michael wants to add the company name, "Nomad Ltd," to the top of the first page of the report. He'll switch to Report Design View to add the label to the appropriate section of the report's Design View.

Steps 1234

Trouble?

If the Toolbox isn't displayed, click the Toolbox button 🛠 to display it.

1. Click the **Design View button** 🗠 on the Print Preview toolbar to close the Print Preview window
   The Profit by Tour Report Design View is shown in Figure H-3. Each report consists of several sections that determine how the final report will print. Because the underlying records are grouped by TourName, this report also contains a group header section.

2. Click the **Label tool** 🗛 on the Toolbox, click in the **Report Header section** at the 4" mark on the ruler, then type **Nomad Ltd**
   The label you add to the Report Header section will print only at the top of the first page of the report. Next, expand the Report Footer section.

3. Position the mouse pointer at the **bottom of the Report Footer** section bar, then drag the **resize pointer** ✛ as shown in Figure H-4 down 1/2 inch
   Add a descriptive label to the Report Footer section that identifies the author of the report. Since the label is in the Report Footer section, it will print once at the end of the last page of the report.

4. Click the **Label tool** 🗛 on the Toolbox, click in the **Report Footer section** at the 1" mark on the ruler, then type **Report Created by Michael Belmont**
   To see the work you have done, view the report.

5. Click the **Print Preview button** 🔍 on the Report Design toolbar, scroll to observe the new labels, then click the **One Page button** 🗔 on the Print Preview toolbar
   The entire page of the report is now in the Print Preview window as shown in Figure H-5. Close the Print Preview window.

6. Click 🗠 to return to Design View

7. Click the **Save button** 💾 on the toolbar to save the report

TABLE H-2: Report sections

section	description
Report header	Appears only at the top of the first page of the report and usually contains the report name or company logo
Page header	Appears at the top of every page (but below the report header on the first page) and usually contains field labels
Group header	Appears at the beginning of a group of records ("Group" is replaced by the field name)
Detail	Appears once for every record in the underlying datasheet and usually contains bound field text boxes
Group footer	Appears at the end of each group of records ("Group" is replaced by the field name)
Page footer	Appears at the bottom of each page and usually contains the current date and page number
Report footer	Appears at the end of the last page of the report, before the page footer

FIGURE H-3: Report Design View

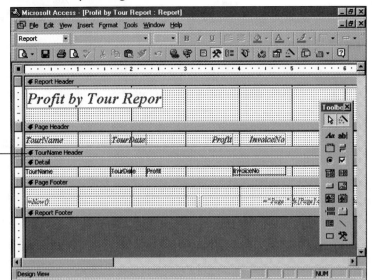

Group Header section (grouped by TourName)

FIGURE H-4: Resizing report sections

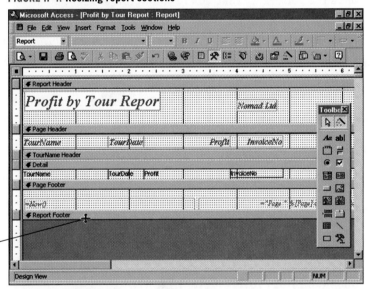

Drag the Resize pointer down

FIGURE H-5: Print Preview at One Page Magnification

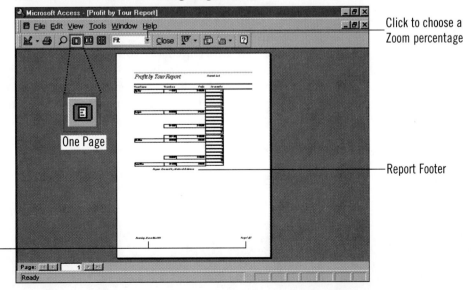

Click to choose a Zoom percentage

Report Footer

Date and page number added by Report Wizard

Access 97

Using Group Headers

A **group header** appears on its own line on a report just before the Detail section of a new group of records. Use the group header to display information that applies to the group of records. For example, you can include a field text box control that displays the name of the field by which the records are grouped. After reviewing the Profit by Tour Report, Michael decides to expand the report to make it easier to read. Michael will move the TourName text box to the TourName group header section rather than have this print on the same line as the TourDate, Profit, and InvoiceNo fields in the Detail section. He will also reformat the TourName text box control to make each new tour group more prominent on the report.

Steps

1. Position the mouse pointer on the **section divider bar** between the TourName Header section and the Detail section, then drag ✛ down to the top of the Page Footer section
   Now that the TourName Header section is opened, you can move the TourName control from the Detail section to the TourName Header section.

2. Click the **TourName text box** in the Detail section, position the mouse pointer at the top edge of the control when it changes to 🖑, then drag the **TourName text box** straight up into the TourName Header section as shown in Figure H-6
   With the TourName text box still selected, you will reformat the control to enhance the TourName section and make the report easier to read.

3. Click the **Line/Border Color list arrow** 🖉▾ on the Formatting (Form/Report) toolbar, click **Transparent**, click the **Font Size list arrow** 8 ▾ on the Formatting (Form/Report) toolbar, then click **10**
   In addition to removing the border and increasing the font size, change the text color and attributes.

4. Click the **Font/Fore Color button** 🄰▾ on the Formatting (Form/Report) toolbar, click the **Bold button** **B**, then click the **Italic button** *I*
   View the report to verify that you have increased the visibility of the TourName field by formatting it as red, bold, italic text in the TourName header section.

5. Click the **Print Preview button** 🔍
   Adjust the view to see the report in the window at 100% view.

6. Click the **Zoom list arrow** on the Print Preview toolbar, click **100% View**, then scroll to observe the new labels
   The final report is shown in Figure H-7. Notice that the TourDate and Profit text box controls don't appear for each record in the Detail section even though the controls appear in the Detail section. The Hide Duplicates property has been set to "Yes" for the TourDate and Profit text box controls in this report, and therefore this field prints only once for the group of records that have duplicate values in these fields.

7. Click **Close** on the Print Preview toolbar

8. Click the **Save button** 💾 on the toolbar to save the report

FIGURE H-6: Moving report controls

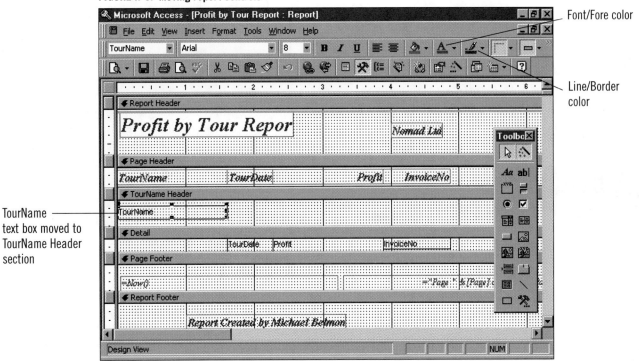

Font/Fore color

Line/Border color

TourName text box moved to TourName Header section

FIGURE H-7: Print Preview of a report with a group header section

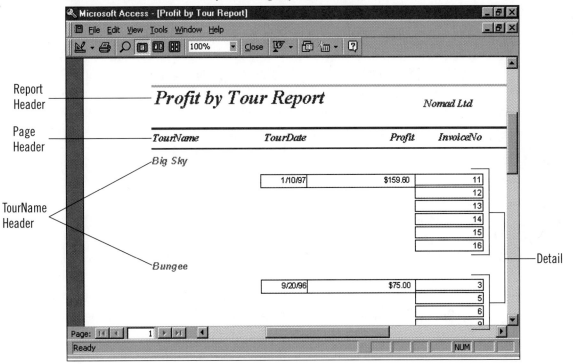

Report Header

Page Header

TourName Header

Detail

Hide Duplicates property

The Hide Duplicates property hides multiple occurrences of the same data for the fields in the Detail section of the report. To view or change the Hide Duplicates property, click the field in Report Design View, click the Properties button 🖼 on the toolbar, then click the Format tab.

Adding Calculations to Group Footers

A **group footer** appears on its own line on a report just below the Detail section of a group of records. **Calculated expressions**, bound report controls that total groups of records, are often added to the group footer to total or count the records within the group. Michael decides to add a total profit figure and count the number of tours sold after each unique group of records. Michael will place these two calculated expressions in the TourDate group footer.

1. **Click the Sorting and Grouping button** [icon] **on the Report Design toolbar, verify that the TourName field is selected, click the Group Footer text box, click the Group Footer property list arrow, then click Yes**
   The Sorting and Grouping dialog box shown in Figure H-8 controls how the records are sorted as well as whether or not the group header and footer sections appear for each sort field. Now that a TourName Footer section has been opened on the report, you will add a text box to the section to hold the calculated expression that totals the profits.

Trouble?

Be sure to click the Text Box button [abl], NOT the Label button [Aa] to insert a text box.

2. **Click** [icon] **to close the Sorting and Grouping dialog box, click the Text Box button** [abl] **on the Toolbox, then click in the TourName Footer section just below the Profit text box in the Detail section**
   With the unbound text box in place, access the Control Source property for the new text box and enter the appropriate expression that will calculate the total profit.

3. **Click the Properties button** [icon] **on the Report Design toolbar, verify that the Data tab is selected, click the Control Source property text box, then type =Sum([Profit])**
   The expression is shown in Figure H-9. Next, close the property sheet and delete the unnecessary label control that was automatically added to the left of the text box control.

Trouble?

The label control on your screen may or may not be labeled Text 16. It won't affect your work if it is a different number.

4. **Click** [icon] **to close the property sheet, click the new label control, then press [Delete]**
   In addition to adding up the profits per tour, you can count the number of sales that contributed to that profit figure. Rather than type a new expression, copy the existing text box control in the TourName footer, paste it in the section, then edit the Control Source property so that it counts the InvoiceNo field rather than sums the Profit field.

5. **Click the =Sum([Profit]) text box, right-click, click Copy, click at the 1" mark on the ruler in the TourName Footer, right-click, then click Paste**
   Now that the text box with the calculated expression has been duplicated, edit the expression to count the number of invoices, and position the control under the InvoiceNo field.

QuickTip

Clicking inside a text box control and editing the expression accomplishes the same task as changing the expression in the Control Source property of the property sheet.

6. **Click and drag to select =Sum([Profit]) inside the new control, then type =Count([InvoiceNo]), click outside the control, click to select the new control, position the mouse pointer at the top edge of the control until it changes to** [icon] **, then drag the =Count control to the right of the =Sum control so that it is directly below the InvoiceNo field**
   View the report to see the changes you made.

7. **Click the Print Preview button** [icon] **, then scroll to view the total profit and number of invoices**
   The updated report is shown in Figure H-10. Close the Print Preview window.

8. **Click Close on the Print Preview toolbar**
   Now you can save the report.

9. **Click the Save button** [icon] **on the toolbar to save the report**

FIGURE H-8: Sorting and Grouping dialog box

TourName is first sort and is also grouped

InvoiceNo is second sort

Group Footer property

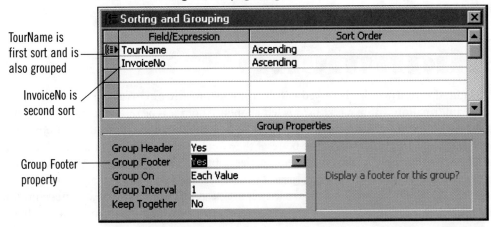

FIGURE H-9: Entering a calculated expression

Sorting and Grouping button

Properties button

Data tab

Calculated expression

Extra label control

New text box control is selected

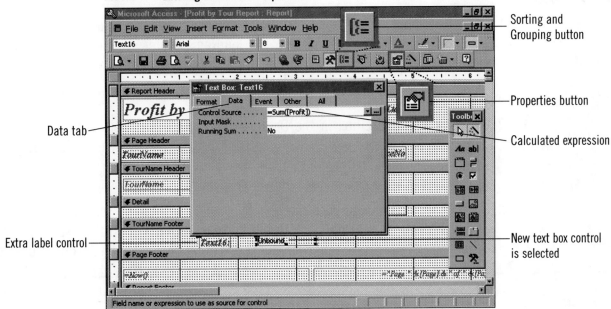

FIGURE H-10: Print Preview of a report with calculated expressions in the group footer

Group footer

Count of invoices

Sum of Profit (6 tours @ $159.60 each)

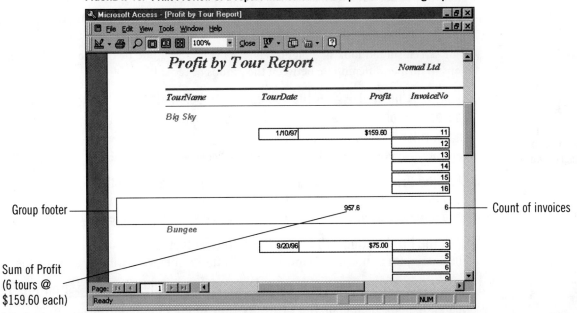

Access 97

Modifying Control Alignment

By default, the information displayed within a single numeric or currency field is right aligned and the information within a text field is left aligned. Another type of alignment involves aligning the edges of multiple controls with respect to each other. For example, the text boxes in the TourName Footer section would look better if they were precisely aligned underneath the information they summarize in the Detail section. See Table H-3 for more information on aligning controls with respect to each other. ✎ Michael wants to format and align the new text boxes in the TourName Footer section to make the report clearer. He aligns the new expressions under their respective columns and also modifies the summarized Profit text box to appear with a currency format.

Steps 1 2 3 4

1. Click the **InvoiceNo text box** in the Detail section, press and hold **[Shift]**, click the **=Count([InvoiceNo]) expression** in the TourName Footer section, release **[Shift]**, click **Format** on the menu bar, point to **Align**, then click **Right**
Now that the InvoiceNo fields are right aligned with respect to each other, align the Profit fields.

2. Click the **Profit text box** in the Detail section, press and hold **[Shift]**, click the **=Sum([Profit]) expression** in the TourName Footer section, release **[Shift]**, click **Format** on the menu bar, point to **Align**, then click **Right**
In addition to aligning the controls, format the =Sum([Profit]) expression as currency.

3. Click in the TourName Footer section to cancel the current selection, click the **=Sum([Profit]) expression**, click the **Properties button** 🖼 on the Report Design toolbar, click the **Format tab**, click the **Format text box**, click the **Format property list arrow**, scroll and click **Currency**, then click the 🖼 to close the property sheet
Add a descriptive label in the TourName Footer section so that the reader can clearly understand that this part of the report shows summary statistics.

4. Click the **Label tool** 🄰 on the Toolbox, click near the top at the left edge in the **TourName Footer section**, type **Summarized profit and count statistics:**, then click outside the control
Your screen should look like Figure H-11. Finally, add a line below the calculated expressions to further differentiate between the groups of records.

5. Click the **Line tool** ╲ in the Toolbox, click below the new label in the **TourName Footer section** at the left edge of the report, then drag **+** to the right to the 5" mark on the ruler
Look at the report in Print Preview to see the work you have done.

6. Click the **Print Preview button** 🔍 on the Report Design toolbar
The horizontal lines add definition to the different sections of the report. They make it easier to understand which records are summarized in the TourName footer.

7. Click the **Print button** 🖨 on the Print Preview toolbar
The final report is shown in Figure H-12. Close the Print Preview window and save the report.

8. Click **Close** on the Print Preview toolbar, click the **Save button** 💾 on the Report Design toolbar, then click the **Profit by Tour Report Close button**

FIGURE H-11: Modifying controls in Report Design View

New label control

Line tool

Controls are right-aligned with respect to each other

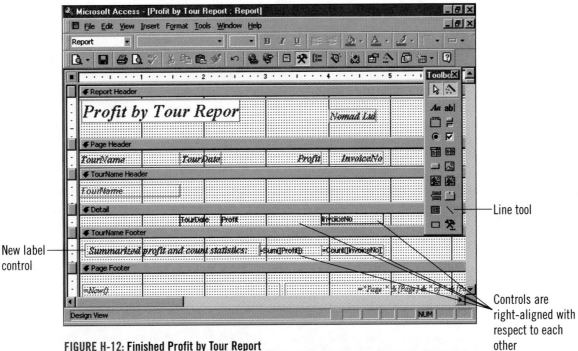

FIGURE H-12: Finished Profit by Tour Report

Line added to the TourName footer

Controls are right-aligned with respect to each other

Summarized profit has a currency format

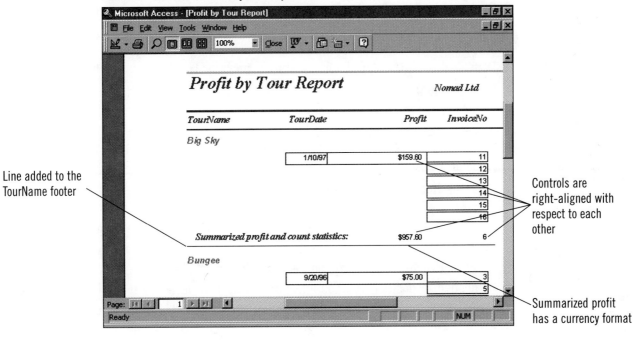

TABLE H-3: Aligning controls with respect to each other

menu option	description
Format|Align|Left	Aligns the left edges of the selected controls with the left edge of the leftmost control in the selection
Format|Align|Right	Aligns the right edges of the selected controls with the right edge of the rightmost control in the selection
Format|Align|Top	Aligns the top edges of the selected controls with the top edge of the topmost control in the selection
Format|Align|Bottom	Aligns the bottom edges of the selected controls with the bottom edge of the bottommost control in the selection
Format|Align|Grid	Aligns the upper-left corner of each selected control to the nearest point on the grid

Adding Graphics to Reports

Graphics refers to any non-text or non-numeric element such as lines, clipart, or boxes placed in the report. Lines and boxes are usually added to increase the report's clarity and professionalism. Clipart is usually added to create visual interest in a report that might otherwise be dull with just numbers and text. When you use the AutoReports or Reports Wizard, Access automatically adds lines to certain sections of the Report Design View to differentiate the sections and make it easier to read. ◀══ Michael wants to create an attractive Tours Report listing all of Nomad's past and present tours as a customer handout. Michael will use the AutoReport: Tabular option and then add a clipart image to the Report Header section.

1. Click the **Reports tab** if necessary, click **New**, click **AutoReport: Tabular**, click the **Choose the table or query where the object's data comes from list arrow**, click **Tours**, then click **OK**
   The **AutoReport: Tabular** option automatically creates a tabular report as shown in Figure H-13 with all the fields of the Tours table and opens in Print Preview mode. After scrolling through the report, you decide to delete the Cost field (you don't want the customer to see this field!)

2. Click the **Design View button** 🗒 on the Print Preview toolbar, scroll to the right, click the **Cost label** in the Page Header section, press and hold **[Shift]**, click the **Cost text box** in the Detail section, release **[Shift]**, then press **[Delete]**
   With the Cost information eliminated, you can move the Handicap label to the left.

3. Click the **Handicap label** in the Page Header section, point to the edge so the mouse pointer changes to ✋, then drag to the left so that the Handicap label is centered over the checkmark in the Detail section
   The realigned label is shown in Figure H-14. Now you can add a clipart image to enhance the Report Header section.

4. Click the **Image button** 🖼 on the Toolbox, then click at the 6" mark in the **Report Header**
   The Insert Picture dialog box opens, allowing you to select the clipart image you wish to add to the report.

5. Click the **Preview button** 🖳 on the Insert Picture dialog box toolbar, click the folders as needed to position the Look in: box to the drive letter with the MS Office folder, double-click the **MS Office folder**, double-click the **clipart folder**, scroll, then click the **Buttrfly.wmf** file as shown in Figure H-15, then click **OK**
   The butterfly clipart image was added to the report view; print the report.

6. Click the **Print Preview button** 🔍 then click the **Print button** 🖨 on the Print Preview toolbar
   The final report is shown in Figure H-16. The butterfly adds an interesting visual touch to an otherwise basic report. After looking over all your enhancements, close the Print Preview window.

7. Click **Close** on the Print Preview toolbar
   Save the report, naming it Tours Report.

8. Click the **Save button** 💾 on the Report Design toolbar, then type **Tours Report** in the Name text box, then click **OK**
   Now you can close the report.

Trouble?

If the Handicap field appears on the report as a textbox displaying "Yes" or "No" instead of a checkbox, change it to a checkbox in Design View. Delete the Handicap textbox in the report's Detail section, click 🗒, drag the Handicap field from the field list back to the same location. The new Handicap field appears as a checkbox. Delete the attached new "Handicap" label.

Time To

✓ Close the report

FIGURE H-13: AutoReport created from the Tours table

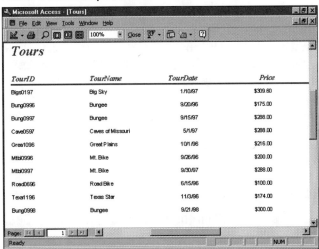

FIGURE H-14: Moving controls

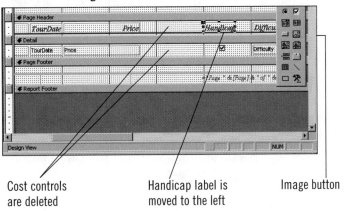

Cost controls   Handicap label is   Image button
are deleted   moved to the left

FIGURE H-15: Insert Picture dialog box

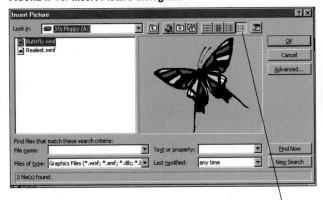

Preview button

FIGURE H-16: Final report with clipart

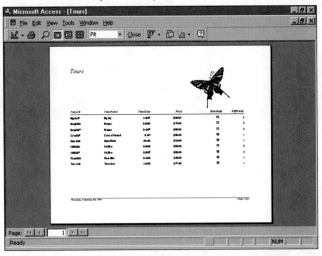

Graphic image files supported by Access

You can insert many popular graphic file formats into a form or report. You don't need a separate graphic filter to insert the following graphic file formats: Enhanced Metafile (.emf), Windows Bitmap (.bmp, .rle, .dib), Windows Metafile (.wmf) and Icon (.ico) graphics. Metafiles scale better than bitmaps because they're made up of lines rather than patterns of individual dots.

Using Color

Discriminate use of color can enhance any report. Access allows you to change several colors of a report including the borders, text, and backgrounds by using the buttons on the Formatting (Form/Report) toolbar. Michael just purchased a new color laser printer for Nomad and has decided to add color to the Tours Report. Specifically, he'll change text, background, and border colors to highlight the most important information on the report.

Steps

1. Click **Tours Report** on the Reports tab, then click **Design**

2. Click the **Tours label** in the Report Header section, press and hold **[Shift]**, click the **TourName label** in the Page Header section, click the **TourName text box** in the Detail section, release **[Shift]**, then click the **Font/Fore Color button** ⬛ on the Report Design toolbar

   The text color changes to bright red. Now that you have accented the most important words of the report with red text, add a background color to the TourDate information.

3. Click the **TourDate label** in the Page Header section, press and hold **[Shift]**, click the **TourDate text box** in the Detail section, release **[Shift]**, click the **Fill/Back Color list arrow** ⬛ on the Report Design toolbar, then click the **light gray color box** (the last color box in the fourth row)

   The Report Design View now looks like Figure H-17. Next, add one more accent color to the report. Border the Difficulty field with the same dark blue color displayed in many of the labels.

4. Scroll and click the **Difficulty text box** in the Detail section, click the **Line/Border list arrow** ⬛ on the Report Design toolbar, then click the **dark blue box** (the sixth color box in the first row)

   Review the changes, then preview and print the report.

5. Click the **Print Preview button** ⬛, then click the **Print button** ⬛ on the Print Preview toolbar

   The final report is shown in Figure H-18.

6. Close the Print Preview window, then save the report

How to create custom colors

If you change a control's property setting on a report, the change doesn't affect the underlying query or table. Likewise, if you change the property setting for a field in a table or query after you've created a report that uses the field, the property setting for the control on the report isn't updated; you must do this manually. There are exceptions to the last rule, however. If you change the Default Value, Validation Rule, or Validation Text properties in a table's Design View, these changes will be enforced in any controls based on these fields later.

FIGURE H-17: Changing control colors

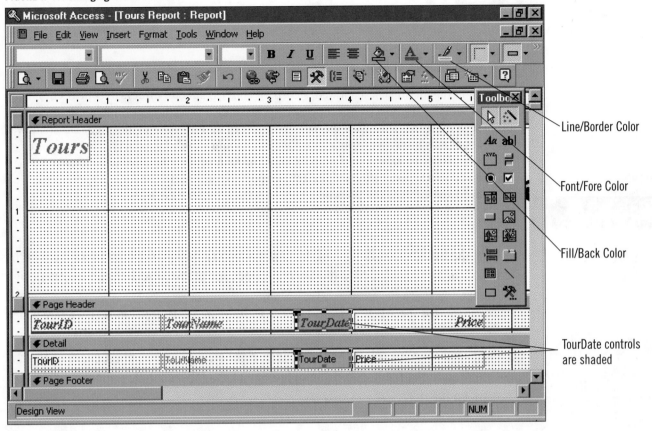

FIGURE H-18: Finished report with color accents

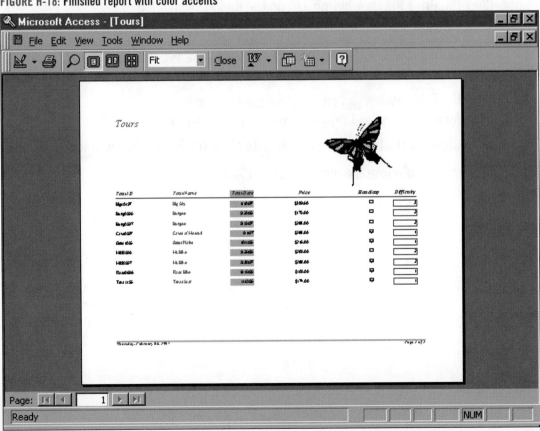

Adding Special Effects

You can add raised, sunken, shadowed, etched, or chiseled **special effects** to controls by changing the settings of the Special Effect property. The sunken special effect is often used to make a button look indented. The raised special effect makes a button look not indented. The shadowed effect is especially attractive for titles, and the etched and chiseled special effects create interesting borders. Refer to Table H-4 for an example of each of the special effects. ✒️ Michael wants to add some special effects to the Tours report to continue to enhance its appearance. He'll add a shadowed effect to the title and a chiseled effect to the Price fields.

Steps

1. Click the **Design View button** 📐 to view the report's design, click the **Tours label** in the Report Header section, click the **Special Effect list arrow** ▭▾ on the Report Design toolbar, then click the **Special Effect: Shadowed button** ▭
   The shadowed special effect requires more width than a default flat look. Therefore widen the Tours label to make sure it has enough room to look proper on the report.

2. Position the mouse pointer on the **middle, right sizing handle** until it changes to ↔ , then drag to the right so that the right edge of the label control is aligned with the 1" mark on the ruler
   Now add a chiseled effect to the Price text box.

3. Click the **Price text box** in the Detail section, click the **Special Effect list arrow** ▭▾ then click the **Special Effect: Chiseled button** ▭

4. Click the **Print Preview button** 🔍 on the Report Design toolbar
   The final report is shown in Figure H-19. The shadowed effect on the title really draws attention to that area of the report. The chiseled effect helps keep the information in the TourDate column aligned with the information in the Price column. Satisfied with the changes, print a hard copy of the report.

5. Click the **Print button** 🖨 on the Print Preview toolbar
   Done for the day, save and close the report, then exit Access.

6. Click **Close** on the Print Preview toolbar to close the Print Preview window

7. Save the report, close the report, then exit Access

FIGURE H-19: Tours Report with special effects

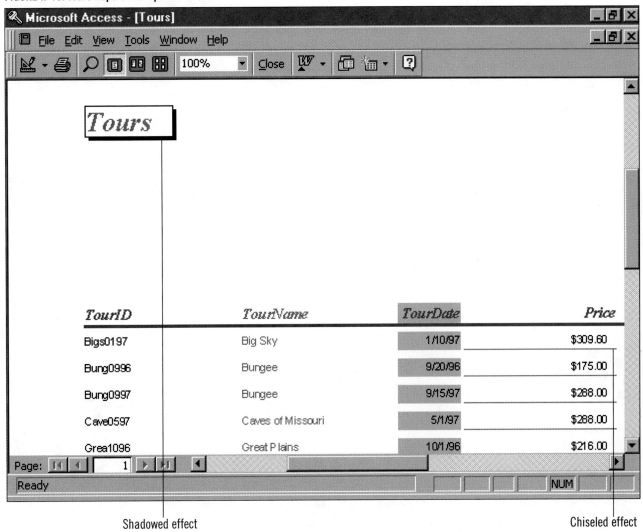

Shadowed effect

Chiseled effect

TABLE H-4: Special effects

special effect	sample
Flat	Alaska
Raised	Alaska
Sunken	Alaska
Etched	Alaska
Shadowed	Alaska
Chiseled	Alaska

Practice

► Concepts Review

Identify each element of a form's Design View shown in Figure H-20.

Match each term with the statement that describes its function.

10. An entry in an unbound text box that returns a value such as the sum or count of a field

11. Automatically creates a columnar or tabular report

12. The database objects most likely used to distribute information in formal presentations or meetings

13. Sorting records in a certain order, and distinguishing them with an identifying header and/or footer in the body of the report

14. Sunken, etched, or chiseled "looks" added to a report control

15. A report section that appears just before the Detail section

16. A report section that appears just after the Detail section

17. A report section that appears once for every record

18. An element such as a line or clipart placed on the report

a. Group header
b. Group footer
c. Calculated expressions
d. Reports
e. Grouping
f. Detail section
g. Special effects
h. Graphic
i. AutoReport

Select the best answer from the list of choices.

19. **Which of the following is a benefit of reports over forms?**
    a. Reports allow you to add calculations on groups of records.
    b. Reports allow you to add bound or unbound controls.
    c. Reports allow you to sort records.
    d. Reports allow you to add graphic images such as lines and clipart.

20. **Which of the following is NOT a valid report section?**
    a. Report Header
    b. Group Header
    c. Detail
    d. Summary

21. **Which of the following report sections would you probably use to add group calculations?**
    a. Page Header
    b. Detail
    c. Group Footer
    d. Summary

22. **Which of the following calculated expressions displays the correct syntax to return the total of the values in the Cost field?**
    a. =Total((Cost))
    b. =Sum(Cost)
    c. =Total([Cost])
    d. =Sum([Cost])

23. **Which of the following is NOT a valid color property?**
    a. Interior Color
    b. Fill/Back Color
    c. Font/Fore Color
    d. Line/Border Color

Skills Review

1. **Create a report from a query.**
   a. Start Access and open the database Addresses-H.
   b. Begin to create a Report using the Report Wizard based on the Basic Address List query.
   c. Add all the fields from the Basic Address List query.
   d. View the data within the report by Zips but do not include any additional grouping levels.
   e. Sort the records in ascending order by Last within the groups.
   f. Choose an Outline 1 layout, a Landscape orientation, and a Soft Gray Style.
   g. Title the Report "Address Report by City".
   h. Print the Address Report by City.

2. **Use report sections.**
   a. Open the Address Report by City report in Design View.
   b. Expand the Page Header section about one half inch.
   c. Add the descriptive label "Report is sorted by City, then by Last" to the left edge of the Page Header section.
   d. Save the report.

3. **Use group headers.**
   a. View the Address Report by City report in Design View.
   b. In the City Header section, move the State text box to the right of the City text box.
   c. Delete the State label.
   d. In the City Header section, move the City label, City text box, and State text box down so that the bottom edge of the three controls rests slightly above the Last, First, and Street labels.
   e. Save the report.

4. **Add calculations to group footers.**
   a. View the Address Report by City report in Design View.
   b. Use the Sorting and Grouping button to access the properties for the City group, and display the group footer for this section.
   c. In the City Footer section, use the label tool to add the label "Count of addresses in this city:" to the left edge of the section.
   d. In the City Footer section, use the text box tool to add an unbound text box at the 3" mark.
   e. Modify the Control Source property of the new text box to the following expression: =Count([Last]) to count the number of entries in the Detail section for each city.
   f. In the City Footer section, delete the extra label.
   g. Move and resize the controls as necessary.
   h. Save and print the report.

5. Modify control alignment.

  a. Open the Address Report by City report in Design View.

  b. Resize the City label in the City Header so that the right edge ends at the 0.75" mark on the ruler.

  c. In the City Header, move the City text box to the left by dragging the upper left corner of the control so that the left edge is even with the Last label beneath it.

  d. In the City Header, make sure that the City text box and the Last label are left aligned with respect to each other. Several horizontal lines surround the Last, First, and Street labels in the City Header section. Don't forget about the Undo button if your alignment commands go awry.

  e. In the City Header, resize the City text box so that the right edge is even with the Last label beneath it.

  f. In the City Header, move the State text box so that the left edge is even with the First label beneath it.

  g. In the City Header, make sure that the State text box and the First label are left aligned with respect to each other.

  h. Save the report and print it.

6. Add report graphics.

  a. View the Address Report by City report in Design View.

  b. In the Report Header section, add an appropriate image control to the 5" mark.

  c. Insert the Realest.wmf picture in the image control. It should be found in the C:\MSOFFICE\CLIPART folder. If you can't find this image, insert another one of your choice.

  d. Save and print the report.

7. Use color.

  a. View the Address Report by City report in Design View.

  b. In the City Header section, select the City label, City text box, and State text box and apply a red text color to the controls.

  c. In the Detail section, select the Last, First, and Street text boxes and apply a bright blue border to the controls.

  d. In the Detail section, select the Last text box and apply a light gray fill color to the control.

  e. Save and print the report.

8. Add special effects.

  a. View the Address Report by City report in Design View.

  b. In the Report Header section, select the Address Report by City label and apply a raised special effect.

  c. In the City Header section, select the City label and apply an etched special effect.

  d. Save, print, and close the report.

  e. Close the database and exit Access.

▶ Independent Challenges

1. As the president of a civic organization, you have developed a database that tracks donations of recyclable material called Cleanup-H. Now that several deposits have been made and recorded, you wish to create several reports.

To complete this independent challenge:

1. Start Access and open the Cleanup-H database.
2. Use the Reports Wizard to develop a report from the Deposits by Club query.
3. Use all the fields in the query and view the information by Recycle Centers.
4. Do not add any additional grouping levels, sort the records in ascending order by Date, use an Outline 1 layout, use a portrait orientation, and specify a Casual style.
5. Name the report "Recycle Center Deposits".
6. Modify the Recycle Centers.Name label in the Recycle Centers.Name Header section so that the label only displays "Recycle Centers".
7. Using the Reports Wizard, develop another report on the Deposits by Club query with the same choices except for the following: view the information by Clubs and name the report "Club Deposits".
8. Modify the Clubs.Name label in the Clubs.Name Header section so that the label only displays "Clubs."
9. Print both reports and note the differences in the way the records are grouped.
10. Close the database and exit Access.

2. Now that you've developed a relational database that documents the books you've read called Readings-H, you'd like to develop a couple of reports to professionally display the information.

To complete this independent challenge:

1. Start Access and open the Cleanup-H database.
2. Use the Reports Wizard to develop a report from the Books I've Read query.
3. Use all the fields in the query, view the data by Authors, don't add further grouping levels, sort the records by Title, use a Block layout, use a portrait orientation, and apply a Bold style.
4. Title the report "Books I've Read Report".
5. Change the text color of the label in the Report Header section to black.
6. Change the Line/Border color of all of the lines in the Report Header and Page Header section to red.
7. Apply bold formatting to the Last Name text box in the Detail section.
8. Apply a shadowed special effect to the label in the Report Header section. Be sure to widen the label to accommodate for the special effect.
9. Print and save the report.
10. Close the database and exit Access.

3. You have recently helped the medical director of a large internal medical clinic put together and update a database that tracks extra-curricular activities called Doctors-H. You wish to develop a report of activities in the database.

To complete this independent challenge:

1. Start Access and open the Cleanup-H database.
2. Use the Reports Wizard to develop a report from the Physician Activities query.
3. Use all the fields in the query, view the data by Physicians, do not add any more grouping levels, sort the fields by date, use a Stepped Layout, use a portrait orientation, and apply a Formal style.

4. Title the report "Physician Activities Report".

5. Open the First Name Footer section and add an unbound text box to the section.

6. Modify the Control Source property of the text box to be the expression =Sum([Hours]).

7. Modify the label in the First Name Footer section to read "Total Number of Hours Volunteered", and make sure it is positioned just to the left of the new expression text box.

8. Make sure the new label and text box in the First Name Footer section are top aligned with respect to each other.

9. Make sure the Hours label in the Page Header, the Hours text box in the Detail section, and the new expression text box in the First Name Footer are all right aligned as well as right aligned with respect to each other.

10. Add a line control at the bottom of the First Name Footer section that stretches from the 0" to the 6" mark on the ruler.

11. Save and print the report.

12. Close the database and exit Access.

4. You are considering attending Keller Graduate School of Management to obtain an MBA after you finish your undergraduate degree. You'd like to analyze the courses Keller offers by discipline (information systems, marketing, management, and so on) to determine if they have the depth and breadth of electives you desire. You have started an Access database called MBA-H to record Keller's courses. Now you need to return to Keller's home page to find the current listing of information systems courses and add them to your database before you can build a report that analyzes the courses by discipline.

To complete this independent challenge:

1. Log on to the Internet and use your browser to go to http://www.course.com. From there, click Student Online Companions, click the link for this textbook, then click the Access link for Unit H.

2. Print the pages (about five) describing the MBA courses available from Keller Graduate School of Management.

3. Log off the Internet and open the MBA-H database.

4. Add the five elective Information Systems courses to the courses table.

5. Use the Report Wizard and create a report using all the fields from the Courses Sorted Alphabetically within Discipline query, group the records by Disciplines Name, sort ascending on Course Number, use a Stepped layout, use a portrait orientation, apply the Formal style, and name the report "KGSM Courses Report".

6. Add a Discipline Name group footer then add a control that counts the number of offerings within each discipline within the footer. Align the counting control under the Course Number column and make sure that a descriptive label clarifies the expression.

7. Add a horizontal line at the bottom of the Discipline Name Footer to help separate the groups of records.

8. Add a shadow effect to the label in the Report Header.

9. Preview the report and make sure that all labels print clearly. (*Hint:* You may have to adjust the labels in the various headers.)

10. Save and print the report.

11. Close the database and exit Access.

▶ Visual Workshop

Open the VW-H database and create a new report as shown in Figure H-21. The report is based on the Donations Query, viewed by Alumni, further sorted by Value, given a Stepped layout, a portrait orientation, and a Corporate style. Also, notice that the Value field is summarized for each donor and a horizontal line separates the donors.

FIGURE H-21

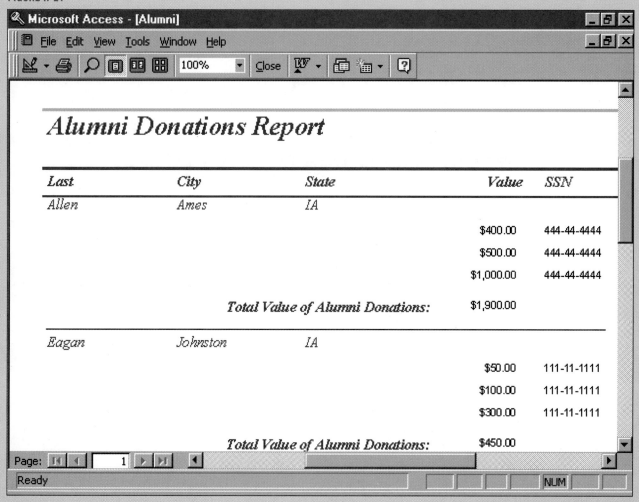

Sharing
Access Information with Other Office Programs

Objectives

- ▶ Import records from an Excel spreadsheet
- ▶ Link information from an external source
- ▶ Export records to an Excel spreadsheet
- ▶ Analyze records with Excel
- ▶ Copy records to a Word table
- ▶ Mail merge records with a Word document
- ▶ Create hyperlinks across Office documents
- ▶ Create a field to store hyperlinks

The Microsoft Office suite provides compatible tools that you can combine to solve business problems. Choosing the right tool for each task is important because you often need features from one program and data from another. For example, you can create an attractive document form in Word, link data through hyperlinks to an Access database, then publish the document as a customer order form to the Internet. Customers can place orders based on data in your Access file, and the information supplied by customers can be updated in your customer files in Access. ◀━━ Now that Michael Belmont has developed a fairly extensive database tracking Nomad's customers, tours, and sales, colleagues have requested information from his database. To maximize the potential of the Nomad information system, Michael's information manager, Rachel Best, will use several information-sharing techniques to extract information from and add information to the existing Nomad database.

Importing Records from an Excel Spreadsheet

External data sources can include other Access databases, Excel spreadsheets, or other databases such as FoxPro, Paradox, or dBASE. Access provides two choices for sharing data from an **external source**: you can either **import** or **link** the information. Importing creates a duplicate copy of the information within the **destination program**, which in this case is a current Access database. Linking creates only a path to the external source. Regardless of whether you have imported or linked to the external source, you can read, use, and in most cases update the data. Refer to Table I-1 for more information.

Rachel's first task is to determine the best way to incorporate the information from an Excel spreadsheet called Reps that lists information on Nomad's sales representatives. She decides to import the records into the Nomad database.

1. **Start Access, open the Nomad-I database on your Student Disk, then click the Tables tab if necessary**
   You want to add a Reps table to this database. Import the external data from the Excel spreadsheet.

2. **Click File on the menu bar, point to Get External Data, then click Import**
   You use the Import dialog box to find the Reps spreadsheet on your Student Disk. Therefore, the Look in: text box must specify the drive and folder that contains your student files and you must change the Files of type: text box to display Excel spreadsheet files.

3. **If the proper drive and folder are not already selected, click the Look in: list arrow, click the drive and/or folder(s) that contain your student files, click the Files of type: list arrow, then click Microsoft Excel (*.xls)**
   You should see the Reps.xls file listed as shown in Figure I-1.

4. **Click Reps.xls, then click Import**
   The Import Spreadsheet Wizard dialog box opens, prompting you for answers about how to import the data into the Access database. First, you determine the worksheets and ranges to include in the table. Accept the default options Show Worksheets and Sheet1.

5. **Click** `Next >` **, click the First Row Contains Column Headings option box, then click** `Next >`
   The Import Wizard walks you through the importing steps, and displays a sample of the table at the bottom of the dialog box as shown in Figure I-2. The next two questions ask whether you want to add the data to a new or existing table as well as whether you want all of the columns of data. This spreadsheet information is added to a new table, and each of the fields (columns) is imported as is. Therefore, accept the default options on the next two wizard dialog boxes.

6. **Click** `Next >` **, then click** `Next >`
   The next question asks about primary keys. The RepID field works well for this purpose, so override the default by choosing the RepID field as the primary key.

7. **Click the Choose my own Primary Key option button, click the list arrow, click RepID, then click** `Next >`
   In the last wizard dialog box, you name the new table.

8. **Type Reps, click Finish, then click OK**
   The import process is finished. Reps is now a table in the Nomad-I database. To be sure that the information imported successfully, view the Reps datasheet.

9. **Double-click Reps to view the new datasheet shown in Figure I-3**

Time To
✔ Close the datasheet

FIGURE I-1: Import dialog box

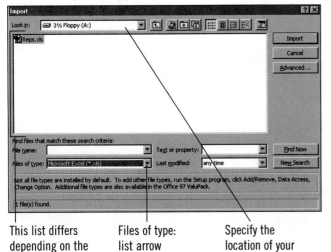

This list differs depending on the files on your student disk

Files of type: list arrow

Specify the location of your student files

FIGURE I-3: Reps datasheet

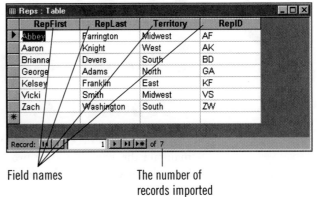

Field names

The number of records imported

FIGURE I-2: Import Spreadsheet Wizard

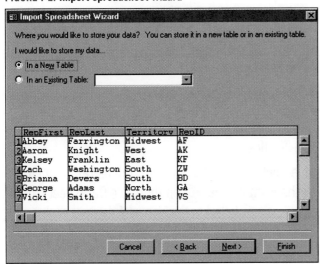

TABLE I-1: Importing versus linking

issue	importing	linking
Number of copies of data	Two copies of the data exist: one in the original external source and one in the Access database	The original external source contains the only copy of the data
Data update capabilities	Once the data is imported, the user can alter it in the same way as any other data in the Access database	The user can add, delete, or edit the data but usually cannot change the data's format or other field properties
Data changes in Access	Changes to the data made in Access exist only within Access	Changes to the data made in either the external source or in the destination program (the Access database) are reflected in the other
Technical difficulty	Importing data is an automated method of copying data, and usually is as easy as copying and pasting	Linking involves more planning and thought, requiring that both the source and destination programs have this linking capability

Linking Information from an External Source

Linking becomes necessary when you wish to preserve only one copy of the data, and must maintain the external source program. This might happen when you have two separate databases that need to share data and cannot be merged for security reasons, or if you have a working budget in a spreadsheet and need just the total in an Access database. ➤ Nomad's marketing group keeps a separate Access database in which they plan future tours. Rachel wants to use the data in her Nomad database but determines that it is better to link the information instead of importing it. That way, each group can operate their databases independently but Rachel's database remains up-to-date with any future tours that the marketing group enters.

1. **Click File on the menu bar, point to Get External Data, then click Link Tables**
   You use the Link dialog box to find the Marketing Access database on your Student Disk. Therefore, the Look in: text box must specify the drive and folder that contains your student files.

2. **If necessary, click the Look in: list arrow, then click the drive and/or folder(s) that contain your student files**
   You should see the Marketing.mdb file in the Link dialog box.

3. **Click Marketing.mdb, then click Link**
   You specify that the Future Tours table from the Marketing database should be linked to the Nomad database in the Link Tables dialog box.

QuickTip

Linked objects are identified by a special icon, ♦▥, on the tab in the database window.

4. **Click Future Tours, click OK, double-click Future Tours on the Tables tab to open the table in Datasheet View, then click the Print button 🖨 on the Table Datasheet toolbar**
   The Future Tours table with seven records is now linked to the Nomad-I database as shown in Figure I-4. To prove that changes in the Marketing database are dynamically updated in the Future Tours table of the Nomad-I database, close the Future Tours table in the Nomad-I database, open the Marketing database, add a record, then observe the change in the Nomad-I database.

Trouble?

Depending on how Access is installed on your system, you may need to follow a different path to start the program. Unlike other Microsoft programs that enable you to work simultaneously with multiple files if you need to work with more than one database at a time, Access requires that you start it once for each database you wish to open.

5. **Click the Future Tours table's Close button, click Start on the taskbar, point to Programs, click Microsoft Access to start Access a second time, open the Marketing database, then open the Future Tours table in Datasheet View**
   A second Access button appears in the Taskbar indicating that you have started the program twice.

6. **Press [Ctrl][End] to move to the last field of the last record, press [Tab] to move to the TourID cell of the first blank record, then enter the following tour information:**

TourID	TourName	TourDate	Price	Cost	Handicap	Difficulty
Dirt1299	Dirt Bike Special	12/1/99	$500.00	$300.00	No	3

   Close the Marketing database and open the Future Tours table in the Nomad-I database to see the additional record that was dynamically updated in the Nomad-I database.

7. **Click File on the menu bar, then click Exit**
   The Access window that contains the Nomad-I database opens.

8. **Double-click the Future Tours table to open its datasheet**
   The linked Future Tours table is shown in Figure I-5. Since TourID is a key field, the new Dirt Bike Special record has already been reordered within the datasheet.

9. **Click the Future Tours table's Close button**
   The Nomad-I database window should be on your screen.

FIGURE I-4: Linked Future Tours table

TourID	TourName	TourDate	Price	Cost	Handicap	Difficulty
▶ Bigs0199	Big Sky	1/12/99	$450.00	$200.00	☐	3
Bung0999	Bungee	9/22/99	$350.00	$250.00	☐	2
Cave0599	Caves of Missouri	5/3/99	$350.00	$180.00	☑	1
Great1099	Great Plains	10/3/99	$220.00	$120.00	☐	2
Mtbi0999	Mt. Bike	9/1/99	$350.00	$190.00	☑	2
Road0699	Road Bike	6/17/99	$170.00	$90.00	☑	1
Texa1199	Texas Star	11/2/99	$200.00	$100.00	☐	1
*			$0.00	$0.00	☐	0

Future Tours : Table

Record: 1 of 7

Seven records

FIGURE I-5: Linked Future Tours table with the new record

TourID	TourName	TourDate	Price	Cost	Handicap	Difficulty
▶ Bigs0199	Big Sky	1/12/99	$450.00	$200.00	☐	3
Bung0999	Bungee	9/22/99	$350.00	$250.00	☐	2
Cave0599	Caves of Missouri	5/3/99	$350.00	$180.00	☑	1
Dirt1299	Dirt Bike Special	12/1/99	$500.00	$300.00	☐	3
Great1099	Great Plains	10/3/99	$220.00	$120.00	☐	2
Mtbi0999	Mt. Bike	9/1/99	$350.00	$190.00	☑	2
Road0699	Road Bike	6/17/99	$170.00	$90.00	☑	1
Texa1199	Texas Star	11/2/99	$200.00	$100.00	☐	1
*			$0.00	$0.00	☐	0

Future Tours : Table

Record: 1 of 8

New record was
dynamically linked
from Marketing to
Nomad-I

Control Tips

Pointing to a button in the Taskbar causes a pop-up **ControlTip** to appear when the button cannot display the entire contents of the program's title bar. The ControlTip displays whatever text is in the title bar of the respective window. If all windows are maximized within Access, the ControlTip displays both the program *and* the object name, thus making it easier to determine which Access button refers to which open database.

Exporting Records to an Excel Spreadsheet

An Excel spreadsheet is very similar to an Access datasheet, with one important exception. You can enter text **labels** and numeric **values** in an Excel spreadsheet, but you can also enter **formulas** directly into the spreadsheet grid, a feature not available in Access. Excel formulas automatically update when any of the values in the formula change. If you are building an Excel spreadsheet and most of the text and numbers you wish to analyze already exist in an Access database, use the Access **export** feature to copy the information from any Access datasheet automatically to an Excel spreadsheet. Refer to Table I-2 to learn more about using the best tool for a specific task. The accounting department asked Rachel to prepare an Excel file that contains sales transaction information from the Nomad-I database. The accountants will use this historical data, assumptions provided by upper management, and the capabilities of Excel to project tour sales and expenses into the future. Rachel pulled the information together in a query called Profit Detail.

1. **Click the Nomad-I database Queries tab, then double-click the Profit Detail query to view the datasheet**
   The Profit Detail Select Query datasheet shown in Figure I-6 lists the details on each sales transaction requested by the accounting department. Next, you export the data to an Excel file.

2. **Click File on the menu bar, click Save As/Export, click the To an External File or Database option button, then click OK**
   The Save Query 'Profit Detail' In dialog box opens, requesting that you specify a location, file name, and file type for the file. Therefore, the Save in: text box must specify the drive and folder that contains your student files and the Save as type: text box should specify Microsoft Excel 97 (*.xls).

QuickTip

If the Save in text box specifies the path to your student files, just change the specification for the file type in this step.

3. **Click the Save in: list arrow, click the drive and/or folder(s) that contain your student files, click the Save as Type: list arrow, then click Microsoft Excel 97 (*.xls)**
   The Save Query dialog box should look like Figure I-7.

4. **Click Export**
   Access takes the data from the Profit Detail query and creates an Excel spreadsheet file. This process may take a few seconds.

Trouble?

Depending on your system, you may need to follow a different path to start Excel or change the folder to find the file.

5. **Click Start on the taskbar, point to Programs, start Microsoft Excel, click the Open button 📂 on the Standard toolbar, then open the Profit Detail spreadsheet**
   Notice that the field names are placed in the first row. Use Excel to create two formulas.

6. **Click cell F1, type 10%, then press [Enter]**
   The accounting department is considering raising the price of all tours by 10 percent, so enter a formula in cell F2 to determine this answer.

QuickTip

Formulas in Excel must start with an equal sign, =. A formula with dollar signs designates an absolute cell reference.

7. **Click cell F2, type =D2*F1+D2, then press [Enter]**
   Now enter a descriptive label in cell G1 and a formula in cell G2 to calculate the potential profit at the higher price.

8. **Click cell G1, type Profit, press [Enter], type =F2-E2, then press [Enter]**
   Your spreadsheet should look like Figure I-8. Your Excel expert will copy the formula to the other cells to complete this spreadsheet. For now, just save, print, and close the spreadsheet.

9. **Click the Save button 🖫, click the Print button 🖨, then click the Profit Detail Close button to close the spreadsheet**

FIGURE I-6: Profit Detail datasheet

FIGURE I-7: Save Query dialog box

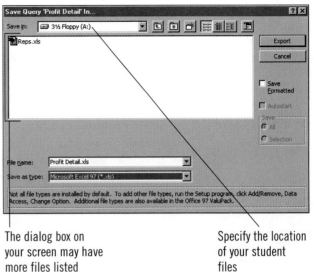

The dialog box on your screen may have more files listed

Specify the location of your student files

FIGURE I-8: Profit Detail spreadsheet with formulas

Field names

Cell F1

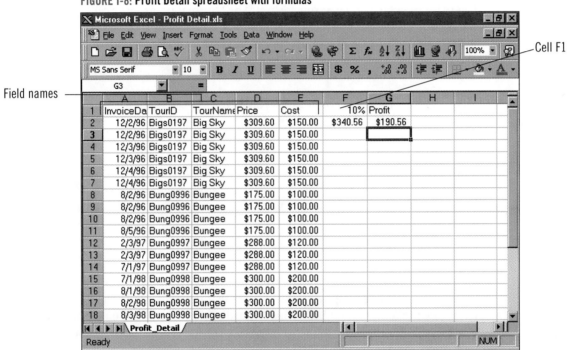

TABLE I-2: Using the best tool for the job

task	best tool	why
Doing repetitive "what-if" analysis or number crunching	Excel	Automatic recalculation in Excel allows you to quickly view changes to assumptions, save various "scenarios," and easily graph the results
Entering, editing, and formatting large amounts of text	Word	Word's automatic word wrap and text insertion let you easily manage large blocks of text; advanced word-processing features such as automatic table of contents, automatic footnotes, and grammar checking are available only in Word
Entering or editing large amounts of data	Access	Access manages relational data in linked tables, reducing data redundancy and increasing the accuracy of the information as well as the flexibility of the reporting of that data; Access has powerful form-creation tools and extensive reporting tools; multiple users can share and update Access files simultaneously, whereas Word and Excel files can be edited only by one user at a time

Analyzing Records with Excel

Although Access reports are capable of calculating statistics on groups of records, the best tool for repetitive "what-if" analysis is Excel. **What-if analysis** allows the user to apply assumptions interactively to a set of numbers and watch the resulting calculated formulas update instantly. A popular what-if analysis is projecting future revenues and expenses to project future profits. In this case, you might apply different growth percentages to both the revenue and expense areas to see the resulting effect on profits. The accounting department worked on the Profit Detail spreadsheet within Excel to create a true what-if analysis. This involved finishing the formulas, formatting the spreadsheet, inserting descriptive text in row 1, and adding a column to calculate increases in expenses. The department will use the spreadsheet to do what-if analysis on revenues and expenses, thereby projecting profits.

1. **Click the Open button** 📂 **on the Excel Standard toolbar, then open the What-if spreadsheet from your Student Disk**
   Figure I-9 shows the updated spreadsheet. The information in white cells is the original data exported from the Access query. The information in yellow cells represents the additions made to the spreadsheet by the accounting department. The formulas in columns F, G, and H are further explained in Table I-3. The cells in blue show the user where to make entries to perform the what-if analysis. Increase both revenue and expenses by 20 percent.

2. **Click cell F2, type 20%, then press [Enter]**
   The percentage entered in cell F2 is used to calculate individual projected revenue figures for each tour in column F. Because 25 tours were exported into this spreadsheet, 25 cells (F3 through F27) contain formulas that update automatically if a new growth percentage is entered in cell F2. Also, profit formulas have been entered in column H to subtract that row's expense from that row's revenue. When all 25 formulas in column G update, all 25 formulas in column H that are dependent upon the cells of column G also update. View the totals at the bottom of the spreadsheet.

3. **Press [Page Down] to view the total revenue, expense, and profit figures in row 28**
   The total profit for this set of assumptions (20 percent increase in revenue and a 10 percent increase in expenses) should be $3,910.62 as displayed in cell H28. After reviewing these assumptions, upper management determined that it would be unrealistic to charge 20 percent more per tour without increasing Nomad's costs. To charge 20 percent more per tour, Nomad will probably have to increase the value of the tour package by about 20 percent as well. Apply this assumption to the spreadsheet.

4. **Press [Ctrl][Home], click cell G2, type 20%, press [Enter], then press [Ctrl][End]**
   View the new total profit figure as shown in Figure I-10. The total profit for the new set of assumptions should be $3,579.12. The percentage entered in cell G2 is used to calculate individual projected expense figures for each tour in column G. Cells G3 through G27 automatically update each time a new entry is placed in cell G2. The profit calculations in cells H3 through H27 are dependent upon the expenses in column G.

5. **Click the Save button** 💾 **on the Standard toolbar**
   You are done with the analysis and can exit Excel.

6. **Click File on the menu bar, then click Exit**

FIGURE I-9: **What-if spreadsheet**

Original data
exported from Access

Cells for What-if
analysis

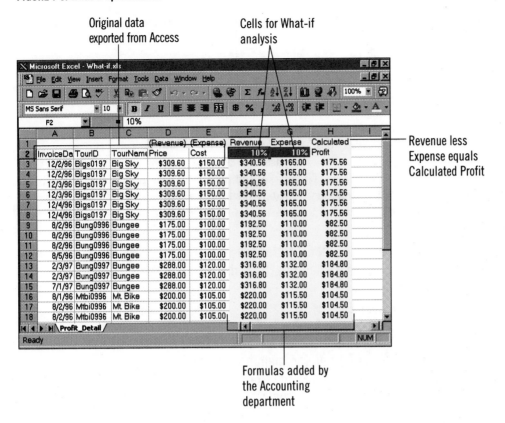

Revenue less
Expense equals
Calculated Profit

Formulas added by
the Accounting
department

FIGURE I-10: **What-if spreadsheet with new assumptions**

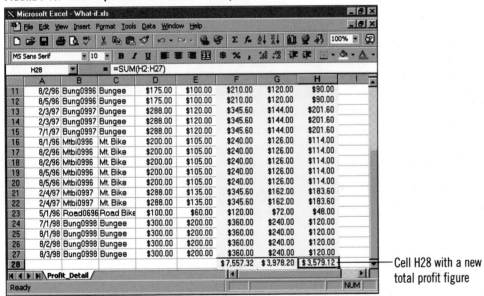

Cell H28 with a new
total profit figure

TABLE I-3: **Formulas used in the What-if spreadsheet**

cell	formula	explanation
F3	=D3*F2+D3	Multiply the entry in cell D3 by the percentage in cell F2, then add the result to the value in cell D3; if you copy the formula, the reference to cell F2 is fixed and the other references change
G3	=E3*G2+E3	Multiply the entry in cell E3 by the percentage in cell G2, then add the result to the value in cell E3
H3	=F3-G3	Subtract the value in G3 from the value in F3

SHARING ACCESS INFORMATION WITH OTHER OFFICE PROGRAMS

Copying Records to a Word Table

Sometimes you need to share information from an Access database with a user who needs to include the information as part of a document. Since Word is probably the most commonly used program within the Microsoft Office Suite, it's nice to know that records within an Access database can easily be transferred to a Word document using simple copy and paste commands. When records copied in Access are pasted to a Word document, they are formatted within the document as a Word table. This makes the pasted records easy to edit, delete, and sort. ◢ The president's secretary asked Rachel to provide a list of customers and addresses from the Nomad-I database in the form of a Word document.

1. Start **Access** and open the **Nomad-I** database if necessary, close the **Profit Detail** query if necessary, click the **Tables** tab, then double-click the **Customers** table to open the Datasheet View
   Select all the records in the table.

QuickTip

[Ctrl][A] is a keystroke shortcut to select all records of a datasheet.

2. Click the **select-all button** on the datasheet to select all the records in the table as shown in Figure I-11, click **Edit** on the menubar, then click **Copy**
   The Copy command copies all the selected records to the Windows Clipboard. Start Word and paste the copied records to a new document.

Trouble?

Depending on your system, you may need to follow a different path to start Word.

3. Click **Start** on the taskbar, point to **Programs**, click **Microsoft Word**, click the **Paste button** 📋 on the Word Standard toolbar, then press **[Ctrl][Home]** to view the beginning of the document
   The Word document is shown in Figure I-12. The records are pasted into the document as rows in a Word table. The first row of the Word table displays the field names. To use these names effectively, the secretary needs an ordered list. Sort the records alphabetically by last name before printing the document.

4. Click **Table** on the menu bar, then click **Sort**
   The Sort dialog box opens. You can specify up to three fields to consider in the sort order when sorting rows of a Word table. In this case, you sort the records by last name, and if two customers have the same last name, you further sort the records by first name.

5. Click the **Sort by list arrow**, click **Last**, click the first **Then by list arrow**, then click **First**
   The Sort dialog box should look like Figure I-13.

6. Click **OK**, then click the document to deselect the text
   When satisfied with the new Word document, you save it.

7. Click the **Save button** 💾 on the Standard toolbar, click the **Save in: list box**, specify the drive and/or folder(s) that contain your student files, then click **Save**
   You have saved the Word document with the default name CustID.doc. Print the document.

Time To

✔ Exit Word

8. Click the **Print button** 🖨 on the Standard toolbar

FIGURE I-11: All records of the Customers table are selected

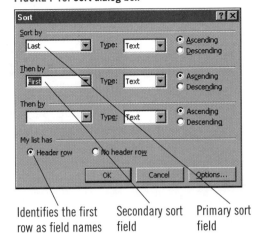

FIGURE I-13: Sort dialog box

CustID	First	Last	Street	City	State	Zip	Birth Date
1	Ginny	Braithwaite	3 Which Way	Salem	MA	01970	01/10/1960
10	Virginia	Rodarmor	123 Main Street	Andover	MA	01810	01/06/1970
11	Kristen	Reis	4848 Ashley	Fontanelle	IA	50810	03/18/1968
12	Tom	Reis	4848 Ashley	Fontanelle	IA	50810	07/03/1965
13	Mark	Egan	987 Lincoln	Schaumberg	IL	44433	01/29/1960
14	Peg	Fox	125 Maple	Des Moines	IA	50625	04/10/1959
15	Ron	Fox	125 Maple	Des Moines	IA	50625	08/28/1987
16	Amanda	Fox	125 Maple	Des Moines	IA	50625	01/30/1988
17	Rebecca	Gross	123 Oak	Bridgewater	KS	50837	09/20/1962
18	Fritz	Friedrichsen	Rural Route 2	Fontanelle	IA	50010	09/26/1940
19	George	Gershwin	922 Ivory Lane	Clive	IA	50644	09/01/1940
2	Robin	Spencer	293 Serenity Dr.	Concord	MA	01742	01/30/1952
20	Hannah	Hanover	55 Switzer	Greenfield	IA	50849	05/01/1961
21	Ivan	Italy	500 Pisa Tower	Lenexa	KS	66222	09/06/1960
3	Camilla	Dobbins	486 Intel Circuit	Rio Rancho	NM	87124	03/15/1965
4	Pip	Khalsa	1100 Vista Road	Sante Fe	NM	87505	04/16/1969
5	Kendra	Majors	530 Spring Street	Lenox	MA	02140	05/04/1970
6	Tasha	Williams	530 Spring Street	Lenox	MA	02140	05/08/1971

Record: 1 of 21

Select all button

Identifies the first row as field names

Secondary sort field

Primary sort field

FIGURE I-12: Customer table records pasted into a Word document

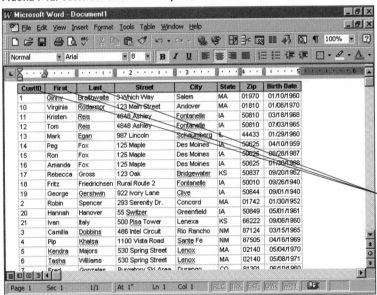

Access field names

Access 97

Drag and drop database objects

In addition to copying records from an Access datasheet and then pasting them to an open Word document, you can use a more direct technique—but you must have excellent mouse skills. Click any table or query name in the Access Database window, then drag the object to a visible edge of an open Word window or to the Word button displayed in the taskbar. A table is created in the active document of the Word window that contains the datasheet of records that were dropped there. You can also drag and drop datasheet objects (tables and queries) from one Access database to another, from Access to Excel, and from Excel to Access.

Mail Merging Records to a Word Document

Although you can easily copy records from an Access datasheet to a Word table, this extra step is not necessary when the goal is to complete a mail merge. It is possible to create the **main document**—the form letter in Word—yet leave the **data source**—the document or object that contains the variable information, such as addresses and names—in an Access datasheet. 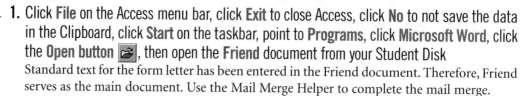 Rachel will merge address information from Access with a sales promotion letter created in Word. She'll use the Mail Merge Helper within Word to guide her steps.

 Steps

1. Click **File** on the Access menu bar, click **Exit** to close Access, click **No** to not save the data in the Clipboard, click **Start** on the taskbar, point to **Programs**, click **Microsoft Word**, click the **Open button** 📂, then open the **Friend** document from your Student Disk
Standard text for the form letter has been entered in the Friend document. Therefore, Friend serves as the main document. Use the Mail Merge Helper to complete the mail merge.

 Trouble?

It isn't necessary that you close Access at this time, but the remaining steps will be clearer if you do. This is because you use the Mail Merge Helper to open Access again when you use an Access object as the data source.

2. Click **Tools** on the menu bar, click **Mail Merge**, click **Create**, click **Form Letters**, then click **Active Window**
The Mail Merge Helper dialog box opens as shown in Figure I-14, identifying the three major steps of completing a mail merge: identifying the main document, identifying the data source, and merging the two together. The active window (friend.doc) is the main document. Next, specify the data source.

3. Click **Get Data**, click **Open Data Source**, click the **Look in: list arrow** if necessary, click the drive and/or folder(s) that contain your student files, click the **Files of type: list arrow**, click **MS Access Databases (*.mdb)**, click **Nomad-I.mdb**, then click **Open**
The computer loads the Access file and presents a dialog box of choices for the data source. You can choose records from either a table or query datasheet. Rachel prepared a query that sorts the records according to the Zip field. Use this object as the data source.

4. Click the **Queries tab**, click **Customers sorted by Zip** if necessary, then click **OK**
The Mail Merge Helper determines that there are no merge fields in the main document, so it cannot determine how to merge the main document and data source fields. Therefore, you need to edit the main document to specifically place the merge fields.

5. Click **Edit Main Document**
The main document, friend.doc, appears again with the Mail Merge toolbar at the top.

6. Double-click the date, click **Insert** on the menu bar, click **Date and Time**, click the date in the same format as in the form letter, click **OK**, then press **[Enter]** twice
Enter the inside address fields.

 Trouble?

Click the Undo button 🔄 if you insert the wrong merge field or if you forget to enter the proper punctuation between merge fields.

7. Click **Insert Merge Field** on the Mail Merge toolbar, click **First**, press **[Spacebar]**, click **Insert Merge Field**, click **Last**, press **[Enter]**, click **Insert Merge Field**, click **Street**, press **[Enter]**, click **Insert Merge Field**, click **City**, type **,** (comma), press **[Spacebar]**, click **Insert Merge Field**, click **State**, press **[Spacebar]** twice, click **Insert Merge Field**, click **Zip**, click after Dear, click **Insert Merge Field**, click **First**, then type **,** (comma)
Compare your document to Figure I-15.

8. Click the **Merge to New Document button** 📑 on the Mail Merge toolbar
Twenty-one records should be merged with the main document, which will result in 21 letters, each to a different person. The first letter is shown in Figure I-16.

QuickTip

As long as the main document and data source are saved, it isn't necessary to save the merged result.

9. Click **File** on the menu bar, click **Print**, print the first two pages of the merged document, click the **Form Letters1 document Close button**, click **No** so you don't save the document, click the **Save button** 💾 to save friend.doc, click **File** on the menu bar, then click **Exit** to exit Word

FIGURE I-14: **Mail Merge Helper**

Helpful text ———

Specifies the final
merged document
(form letters, cata-
logs, envelopes, or
labels)

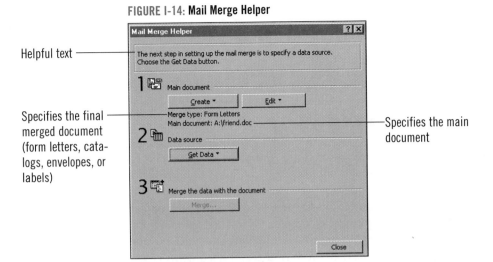

Specifies the main
document

FIGURE I-15: **Main document with merge fields**

Insert Merge Field
button

Merge fields
Inside address

Salutation

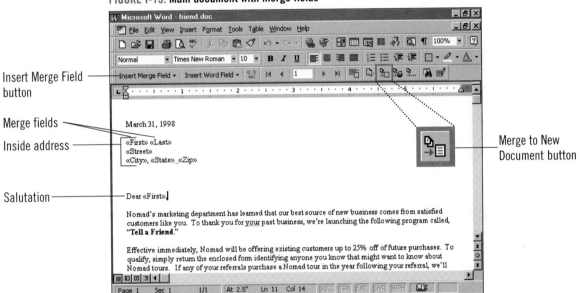

Merge to New
Document button

FIGURE I-16: **First page of the merged document**

Address fields
pulled from
Access database

21 records were
merged

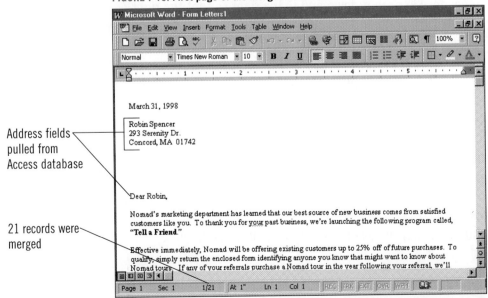

Creating Hyperlinks Across Office Documents

Access allows you to build **hyperlinks** on forms or datasheets. When clicked, hyperlinks dynamically open documents created with different applications such as Word, Excel, or PowerPoint. Hyperlinks can also open documents on the global **Internet** or on a local **intranet** if you and your computer have proper connections to these networks. Hyperlinks can be either textual or graphical. A **hypertext** link appears as colored or underlined text. Graphical hyperlinks can be intricate pieces of clip art or simple arrows or lines. ◄═══ Rachel wants to make it easy for other Nomad users to move quickly between Access and documents created in other products. In particular, she will create hyperlinks from the main Customer Form to two separate Word documents that contain additional information that might be needed when entering new sales.

Steps 1 2 3 4

1. Start Access if necessary, open **Nomad-I** from your Student Disk, click the **Forms tab**, double-click **Customer Form** to open it in Form View, then click the **Maximize button** 🔲
   This form is used to add new customers as well as sales. Depending on the customer's questions while booking the sale, however, you may want to access dynamically a Word document that the marketing department has developed to give additional details on each of the company's current tours. Add a text hyperlink to the form's Design View.

2. Click the **Design View button** 📝, click the **Insert Hyperlink button** 🔗 on the Form Design toolbar
   The Insert Hyperlink dialog box opens. In the Link to file or URL: text box, enter the path and filename of the document, Descriptions.doc, to which you wish to link.

QuickTip

If you know the entire path to the Descriptions.doc file, you can type it in the Link to file or URL: text box directly.

3. Click the **Link to file or URL Browse button**, click the **Look in: list arrow**, click the drive and/or folder(s) that contain your Student Disk, then double-click **Descriptions.doc**
   The Insert Hyperlink dialog box should look like Figure I-17. Add the link to the form.

4. Click **OK**
   The blue link is added as an object to the upper-left corner of the Detail section of the form. Move the control between the Birth Date and Zip text boxes, then change the text of the hyperlink.

Trouble?

Your hyperlink may look different than the one in Figure I-19 if the path to your student files is different than A:\.

5. Move the mouse pointer to the edge of the **blue link object**; when the mouse pointer changes to 👆, drag it down and to the right so that the right edge of the link rests at the 5" mark on the ruler between the Birth Date and Zip text boxes
   The form looks like Figure I-18. To change the hyperlink's text, change its caption property.

6. Click the **Properties button** 📋 on the Form Design toolbar, click the **Format tab**, select the text in the Caption property text box if necessary, type **Click for tour info**, then click 📋 to close the property sheet
   View and test the results of the hyperlink in Form View.

7. Click the **Form View button** 📧 on the Form Design toolbar, position the mouse pointer on the new **hypertext link** so that the hypertext 👆 mouse pointer appears, then click the **Click for tour info hypertext link**
   Your screen should look like Figure I-19. The link started Word and opened the document.

QuickTip

The Access form also displays the Web toolbar to make navigation across Web pages easier.

8. Click **File** on the menu bar, click **Exit** to exit Word, click the **Save button** 💾 on the Standard toolbar to save the form, then close the form

FIGURE I-17: Insert Hyperlink dialog box

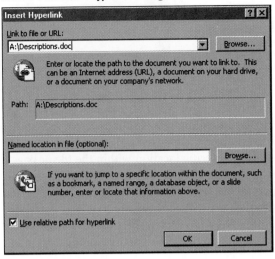

FIGURE I-18: Hyperlink added to form

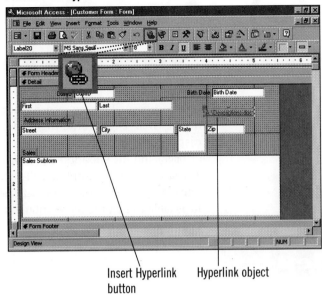

Insert Hyperlink button · · · · Hyperlink object

FIGURE I-19: Word document opened through the hyperlink

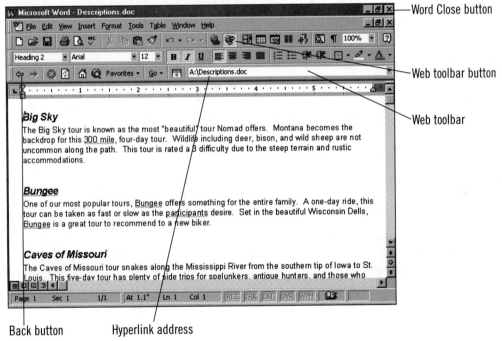

Word Close button

Web toolbar button

Web toolbar

Back button · · · · Hyperlink address

Using Access to create a World Wide Web application

You can use Microsoft Access 97 to create a World Wide Web application such as a corporate home page, an online magazine or newsletter, a registration system for a trade show, or an online product catalog from which customers can order products. To create a Web application from an Access object, use the Save as HTML option on the File menu to invoke the Publish to the Web Wizard that prompts you for information to complete the process.

Creating a Field to Store Hyperlinks

A **hyperlink field** is created with a hyperlink data type. A hyperlink field is used to store **hyperlink addresses** for each record that points to local, intranet, or Internet resources such as documents, Web pages, or e-mail addresses. The hyperlink address contains three parts: the **displaytext** (the text that appears in the field), the **path** to the file (the **URL** or **UNC** for the file or page) and the **subaddress** (a tag that identifies the specific location within the file or page). The last two parts are optional. The three parts of the hyperlink address are separated by pound signs (#) when entered in the datasheet. ◢ Rachel decides to add a hyperlink field to the Reps table to link the representatives' resumes to their individual records in the Reps datasheet. First, she adds a hyperlink field called Resume to the Reps table, then she enters Datasheet View to add a hyperlink address in the Resume field of the first record to make sure that the links work.

1. **Click the Tables tab, click the Reps table, then click Design**
   Add the Resume field with a hyperlink data type in the Reps table Design View.

2. **Click the first blank Field Name cell, type Resume, press [Tab], type h (for Hyperlink), then press [Tab]**
   The Reps table Design View should look like Figure I-20. Now that the field is added, enter Datasheet View and add a hyperlink address for the first record. The UNC for Abbey Farrington's resume document is #a:\abbeyf.doc#.

3. **Click the Datasheet View button [⊞] on the Table Design toolbar, click Yes to save the table, click the Resume field in the Abbey Farrington record, type #a:\abbeyf.doc#**
   The datasheet should look like Figure I-21. Test the hyperlink address.

4. **Press [Enter], then click #a:\abbeyf.doc#**
   The resume for Abbey Farrington opens in Word as shown in Figure I-23. When you are satisfied that the hyperlink works, print the resume.

5. **Click the Print button [🖨] on the Standard toolbar**

6. **Click File on the menu bar, then click Exit**
   Closing a program places you back at the previous Access window with the Reps datasheet displayed. Notice that Access modified the hyperlink address to eliminate the unnecessary pound signs since the first and third parts of the address were not specified. Also note that the hyperlink now appears purple instead of blue, indicating that it has been recently clicked. Print the datasheet.

7. **Click the Print button [🖨] on the Standard toolbar**
   Since you're finished for the day, exit Access.

8. **Click File on the menu bar, then click Exit**

Trouble?

The hyperlink address must describe the actual location of the file. If the student files have been copied to a different drive or folder, be sure to include that information in the hyperlink address.

FIGURE I-20: Reps table with Resume hyperlink field

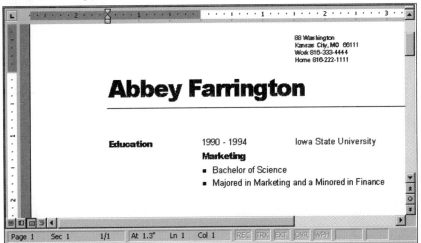

Resume field   Hyperlink data type

FIGURE I-21: Hyperlink address in a datasheet

RepFirst	RepLast	Territory	RepID	Resume
Abbey	Farrington	Midwest	AF	#a:abbeyf.doc#
Aaron	Knight	West	AK	
Brianna	Devers	South	BD	
George	Adams	North	GA	
Kelsey	Franklin	East	KF	
Vicki	Smith	Midwest	VS	
Zach	Washington	South	ZW	

Record: 1 of 7

Hyperlink address

FIGURE I-22: Abbeyf.doc document

Abbey Farrington

88 Washington
Kansas City, MO 66111
Work 816-333-4444
Home 816-222-1111

Education   1990 - 1994   Iowa State University
Marketing
- Bachelor of Science
- Majored in Marketing and a Minored in Finance

Page 1   Sec 1   1/1   At 1.3"   Ln 1   Col 1

URLs and UNCs

URL (Uniform Resource Locator) is an address to a resource on the Internet such as a Web page, newsgroup, or e-mail address. A URL expresses the protocol to be accessed as well as where the resource is located. Web page URLs start with http such as the following: http://www.ibm.com. The http stands for Hypertext Transfer Protocol, which is a set of rules for moving hypertext files (Web pages) across the Internet.

UNC (Universal Naming Convention) is the standard format for paths that include a local area network file server. The protocol for a UNC is \\server\share\path\ filename. Local area networks, or LANs, connect local resources—those that can be connected by a direct cable. LANs do not cross a public thoroughfare such as a street because of distance and legal restrictions on how far and where cables can be pulled. Connecting computer resources across public thoroughfares usually requires connecting with existing public communications networks through telecommunications hardware and software. The connection of a LAN to a telecommunications network creates a WAN, a wide area network.

Practice

► Concepts Review

Identify each element shown in Figure I-23.

FIGURE I-23

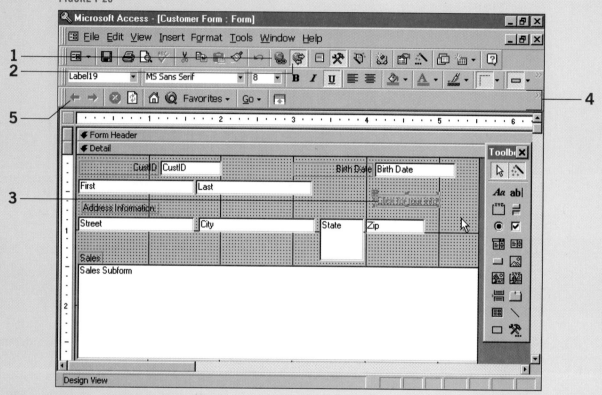

Match each term with the statement that describes its function.

6. Creates a duplicate copy of the information from the external source in an Access database.

7. The ability of a formula to update automatically when one of the raw numbers that feeds the formula changes.

8. Creates a path to the information in an external source for use in an Access database.

9. Allows the user to apply assumptions interactively to a set of numbers and watch the resulting calculated formulas update instantly.

10. The form letter with standard text letter used in a Word mail merge.

11. The document or object that contains the actual address information used in a Word mail merge.

a. Importing
b. Linking
c. Main document
d. Data source
e. "What-if" analysis
f. Automatic recalculation

Select the best answer from the list of choices.

12. Which of the following is *not* true about importing data into an Access database?
   a. The original external source contains the only copy of the data.
   b. Once the data is imported, it can be altered in the same way as any other data in the Access database.
   c. Changes to the data made in Access exist only to the copy of the data within Access.
   d. Importing data is an automated method of copying data. Importing is usually as easy as copying and pasting.

13. Which of the following is *not* true about linking data to an Access database?
   a. The original external source contains the only copy of the data.
   b. The user can add, delete, or edit the data but usually cannot change the data's format or other field properties.
   c. Excel and dBASE are two examples of external sources of information that can be linked to an Access database.
   d. Linking is usually as easy as importing.

14. The best tool for repetitive "what-if" analysis is
   a. Access
   b. Excel
   c. PowerPoint
   d. Word

15. When records copied in Access are pasted to a Word document, they are formatted within the document as
   a. an Access form object
   b. an Excel spreadsheet
   c. a Word table
   d. an ASCII file

16. In a mail merge, the document or object that contains the variable information, such as addresses and names, is called the
   a. datasheet
   b. database
   c. relational database
   d. data source

17. Hyperlinks can be
   a. words
   b. arrows
   c. clip art
   d. all of the above

18. To create a hyperlink field, you must
   a. create the field with a hyperlink data type in Table Design View
   b. put the Web address in the data source property of the field on a form
   c. use the HTML editor
   d. use the hypertext markup language editor

▶ **Skills Review**

1. Import records from an Excel spreadsheet.

   a. Start Access and open the database Addresses-I.

   b. Click File on the menu bar, point to Get External Data, then click Import to import records from the New Addresses spreadsheet on your Student Disk.

   c. Make sure that the first row is identified as column headings, and that the data is imported into the existing Names table.

   d. Open the datasheet of the Names table and print it.

   e. Close the datasheet of the Names table.

2. Link information from an external source.

   a. Point to the Get External Data option on the Access File menu, then click Link Tables to link the records of the Family table in the Relatives database to the open Addresses-I database.

   b. Start building a new select query in Query Design View using the linked Family table and the Zips table.

   c. Add all the fields from the Family table, and the City and State fields from the Zips table to the select query.

   d. Open the new query in Datasheet View and print it.

   e. Save the query as Family Query.

3. Export records to an Excel spreadsheet.

   a. Use the Save As/Export option on the File menu to export the datasheet of the Family Query to an external file.

   b. Specify the filename as Family Analysis.xls. Be sure that the Save as Type option displays Microsoft Excel 97 (*.xls), then export the information.

   c. Open the Family Analysis.xls spreadsheet in Excel.

   d. Click cell A8 and type your first name. Click cell B8 and type your last name.

   e. Save and print the Family Analysis.xls spreadsheet.

   f. Close the Family Analysis.xls. spreadsheet.

   g. Return to the Addresses-I database, then close the Family Query datasheet.

4. Analyze records with Excel.

   a. Open the Family Calculations.xls file in Excel. The white cells represent the information you exported from Access. The yellow cells represent additional Excel entries.

   b. Click cell I2 and type the date of the next birthday for that person based on the birth date in column E (6/1/97, 6/1/98, or 6/1/99, depending on today's date).

   c. Finish entering the date of the next birthday for each person in cells I3 through I7.

   d. Notice that column J reflects the number of days until that person's next birthday and is automatically recalculated when a valid date entry is made in the appropriate cell of column I.

   e. Save and print the spreadsheet.

   f. Close the Family Calculations.xls spreadsheet, then exit Excel.

5. Copy records to a Word table.

   a. Open the Basic Address List query in Datasheet View.

   b. Select all the records and click the Copy button on the Query Datasheet toolbar.

   c. Start Word, then click the Paste button.

   d. Save the document as People.doc, then print it.

   e. Close the document People.doc.

   f. Use the taskbar to return to Access, then exit Access. Don't save the data on the Clipboard.

6. **Mail merge Access records to a Word main document.**
    a. Open the Ames.doc document in Word.
    b. Click Tools on the menu bar, then click Mail Merge to open the Mail Merge Helper dialog box.
    c. Complete the Main document information in the Mail Merge Helper dialog box by specifying form letters and the active document as the main document.
    d. Complete the Data source information in the Mail Merge Helper dialog box by opening a data source, the Addresses-I.mdb database on your Student Disk.
    e. Choose the Basic Address List query as the source of the data, then edit the main document.
    f. Edit the date as the current date.
    g. Complete the inside address and salutation with merge fields using the Insert Merge Field button on the Mail Merge toolbar between the date and the salutation of the letter as in the following example:
    (Date)

    «First» «Last»
    «Street»
    «City», «State» «Zip»

    Dear «First»,
    h. Click the Merge to New Document button to complete the merge.
    i. Print the first page of the resulting merged document.
    j. Close and do not save the resulting merged document.
    k. Save and close the Ames document, then exit Word.

7. **Create hyperlinks across Office documents.**
    a. Start Access. If necessary, open the Addresses-I.mdb database.
    b. Click the Forms tab, then create an Autoform:Tabular form based on the Basic Address List query.
    c. Open Design View for the new form, then add a hyperlink to the right of the State text box using the Insert Hyperlink button on the Form Design toolbar. In the Link to file or URL text box, enter the path to the Faculty.doc document on your Student Disk.
    d. Save the form with the name Address List Form, open it in Form View, then print one record in Form View.
    e. Click the hypertext link, then print the Faculty.doc document.
    f. Close the Faculty.doc document and exit Word.
    g. Return to the Address List Form and close it.

8. **Create a field to store hyperlinks.**
    a. Open the Names table in Design View and add a field called Favorite Web Page with a hyperlink data type to the bottom of the list of fields.
    b. Save the table, then open it in Datasheet View.
    c. Enter #http://www.microsoft.com# in the Favorite Web Page field of the Jeff Baker record.
    d. If both you and your PC have Internet connection capability, click the hyperlink entry in Jeff Baker's record to connect to the Microsoft home page. Print the first page of the Microsoft Web site. If you do not have Internet connection capability, skip to Step e.
    e. Return to the Names datasheet and print it.
    f. Close the Names datasheet and close the Addresses-I.mdb database.
    g. Exit Access.

► Independent Challenges

If you complete all of the exercises in this unit, you may run out of space on your Student Disk. To make sure you have enough disk space, please copy the following files onto a new disk: Cleanup-I.mdb, Toxic.xls, Deposit Analysis.xls, Readings-I.mdb, Review.doc, Doctors-I.mdb, Policy.doc, Peds.doc, Careers.mdb, and VW-I.mdb. Use the new disk to complete the rest of the exercises in this unit.

1. As the president of a civic organization, you have developed a database, Cleanup-I, that tracks donations of recyclable material. You wish to use this information with Excel spreadsheets to add more information to your database quickly, as well as analyze the existing information further.

To complete this independent challenge:

1. Start Access, then open the database Cleanup-I.
2. Import the information from the Toxic.xls spreadsheet to the Cleanup-I database. The first row of the spreadsheet contains the column headings, and the information should be stored in a new table. Do not make any changes to the fields and do not specify a primary key.
3. Name the table Substances.
4. Export the information from the Deposits by Club query to an Excel spreadsheet called Deposit Analysis.xls.
5. Open Deposit Analysis.xls, then enter the following two formulas:
   a. Click cell C17, type =Sum(C2:C16), then press [Enter] to add up the values in column C that represent the deposit weights. (*Hint*: You can also use the AutoSum button if you are familiar with this Excel feature.)
   b. Click cell C18, if necessary, type =Average(C2:C16), then press [Enter] to determine the average of the deposit weights.
6. Save Deposit Analysis.xls, then print the spreadsheet.
7. Close Deposit Analysis.xls and Cleanup-I.mdb.
8. Exit Access and exit Excel.

2. Now that you've developed a relational database, Readings-I, that documents the books you've read, you want to copy some of the information to Word as well as merge the information to a Word document.

To complete this independent challenge:

1. Start Access, then open the Readings-I.mdb database.
2. Open the Books I've Read query in Datasheet View.
3. Copy all the records in the Books I've Read query.
4. Start Word.
5. Enter your name at the top of a blank document, then paste the records below your name.
6. Click after the table and write a paragraph on the book that you enjoyed the most, and why you enjoyed it. (Notice that *Jurassic Park* got the highest rating and therefore is the book that you will describe.)
7. Save the document as Books.doc, print the document, then close the document.
8. Open the Review.doc document from your Student Disk.
9. Use the Mail Merge option from the Tools menu and specify Form Letters and the active document (Review.doc) as the main document.
10. Specify the Books I've Read query from the Readings-I.mdb database as the data source for the merge.
11. Edit the main document by adding three merge fields as follows:
    Book: <<Title>>
    Rating: <<Rating>>
    Author: <<Last_Name>>
12. Save Review.doc, then click the Merge to New Document button to complete the merge.
13. Save the merged document as Book Review Merge.doc, then print the first two pages.
14. Exit Word, saving any open documents as necessary, then close Readings-I.mdb and exit Access.

3. You have recently helped the Medical Director of a large internal medicine clinic put together and update a database, Doctors-I, that tracks extracurricular activities. You need to add a hyperlink to a form in the database as well as add a hyperlink field to the Physicians table.

To complete this independent challenge:

1. Start Access, then open the Doctors-I.mdb database.
2. Create an AutoForm: Columnar form based on the Physician Activities query.
3. Add a hyperlink to the right of the Name fields that points to the Policy.doc document on the Student Disk, then open the form in Form View.
4. Click the hyperlink. It should open the Policy.doc document in Word describing the clinic's position on public health care.
5. Print the Policy.doc document, then exit Word.
6. Return to Access, save the open form, then close it.
7. Open the Physicians table in Design View, then add a new field called Specialty with a hyperlink data type.
8. Save the Physicians table, then open it in Datasheet View.
9. Add a hyperlink address to the Aaron Douglas record that points to the Pediatrician document, Peds.doc, on the Student Disk.
10. Click the hyperlink address. It should open the Peds.doc document in Word that describes the Pediatric department in the clinic.
11. Print the Peds.doc document, then close Word.
12. Save the Physicians table, then close Doctors-I.mdb and exit Access.

4. You are interested in summer jobs in the Kansas City area and have decided to use the Internet to research employment opportunities there. Search for the information on the World Wide Web, add the data to a small Access database of potential job opportunities, then merge the data with a Word document that inquires about summer employment opportunities.

To complete this independent challenge:

1. Log on to the Internet and use your browser to go to http://www.course.com. From there, click Student Online Companions, click the link for the book you are using, then click the Access link for Unit I.
2. Locate two interesting companies in the Kansas City area (other than DHS, Informix, and the *Kansas City Star*, because they are already in the database), then print those Web pages. Make sure that you print the address for the company.
3. Open the Careers.mdb database, then add to the Companies table the information from the two companies that you found.
4. Open Word and create a cover letter for a resume. For this example, address the letter to the "Director of Personnel" (in real life, you should address all employment letters to a specific individual within a company if you hope to make a positive impact), include a few sentences stating that you have included your resume describing your background, and inquire about summer employment opportunities. Your instructor may wish to have you research cover letters for this part of the exercise.
5. Save the document as Cover.doc.
6. Use the Mail Merge option on the Tools menu to create form letters using Cover.doc as the main document. Use the Companies table from the Careers.mdb as the data source.
7. Perform the merge and print the first two pages of the merged document.
8. Close the merged document without saving it.
9. Save and close Cover.doc.
10. Save and close the Companies table within Careers.mdb.
11. Close Careers.mdb and exit Access.

▶ Visual Workshop

Open the VW-I database and create the form shown in Figure I-25 using the AutoForm: Columnar option and the Donations Query as the source of the information. Save the form and add the hyperlink to the ISU.doc document on your Student Disk as shown. If necessary, modify the path to the ISU.doc document in the hyperlink control to the specific location of your student files.

FIGURE I-24

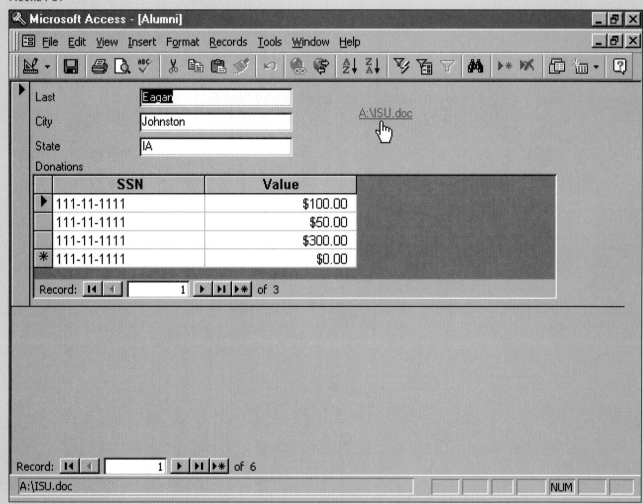

Creating
Advanced Queries

Objectives

► **Query for top values**
► **Format data in datasheets**
► **Create a parameter query**
► **Create an AutoLookup query**
► **Create a make-table query**
► **Create an append query**
► **Create a delete query**
► **Create a union query**

Queries are database objects that answer questions about the data. The most common query is the **select query**, which pulls fields and records that match specific criteria into a single datasheet. Other types of queries—such as parameter, action, and SQL queries—are powerful tools for displaying, analyzing, and updating data. In addition to exploring some of the sophisticated features of select queries, this unit defines these new types of queries, provides an example of a situation in which each would be appropriate, and gives you a chance to practice using each.

Rachel Best, the database administrator for the Nomad database, has become very familiar with the capabilities of Access. Users come to Rachel with extensive data-analysis and data-update requests, confident that she can provide the information they need. Rachel uses powerful query features and new query types to handle these requirements.

Querying for Top Values

Once a large number of records are entered into a table of a database, it is less common to build a query to list all of the records and more common to list only the most significant records by choosing a subset of the highest or lowest values from a sorted query. The **Top Values** feature within the Query Design View allows you to respond to these types of requests. ◄━━━ Customers and sales in the Nomad database have grown. Top management needs Rachel to print a datasheet listing the names of the top five customers, sorted by profit per customer. She creates a select query, then uses the Top Values feature to satisfy this request.

Steps

1. Start Access, open the **Nomad-J** database, then click the **Queries tab**
   You build a new select query in Query Design View to gather the fields necessary for the query.
2. Click **New**, click **Design View**, then click **OK**
   To complete this query, you need fields from three tables: Customers, Sales, and Tours.
3. Click **Customers**, click **Add**, click **Sales**, click **Add**, click **Tours**, click **Add**, then click **Close**
   Query Design View now displays with the three linked tables in the upper portion of the screen. Add the fields to the query design grid that answer the profitability question for upper management.
4. Click and drag **First** from the Customers table to the first column of the query design grid, then click and drag **Last** from the Customers table to the second column of the query design grid
   Now you need to add a field to calculate the profit. The Price field in the Tours table contains the price per tour charged to the customer. The Cost field in the Tours table contains Nomad's cost per tour. The difference between these two fields is the profit for each tour sold.
5. Click the third **Field cell** of the query design grid, type **Profit: [Price]-[Cost]**, then press **[Enter]**
   As currently designed, the query results display one record for every sale, including the first and last names of the customer to whom each sale was made and the profit on that sale. To list each customer only once and summarize the total profit on multiple sales for each customer, add the Totals row to the query design grid and summarize the Profit field.
6. Click the **Totals button** ∑ on the Query Design toolbar, click the **Group By Total cell** for the **Profit field**, click the **list arrow**, then click **Sum**
   Your screen should look like Figure J-1. Management's request isn't just to show the profits for each customer, but to show only the top five customers. To accomplish this, sort the records in descending order by profits, then use the Top Values feature to display the top five records. See Table J-1 for more information on how to use the Top Values feature.
7. Click the **Sort cell** of the Profit field, click the **list arrow**, click **Descending**, click the **Top Values list arrow** on the Query Design toolbar, then click **5**
   Now that you've added the appropriate advanced features to the select query, you're ready to view the resulting datasheet.
8. Click the **Datasheet View button** 🏢 on the Query Design toolbar
   The resulting datasheet, shown in Figure J-2, summarizes profits by customer. Profits are sorted in descending order. Interestingly, six records are displayed instead of five because there is a tie for fifth place. Two customers show summarized profits of $159.60! Save and name the query, then print the list for management.
9. Click the **Save button** 💾 on the toolbar, type **Top "5" Customers** in the Query Name text box, click **OK**, then click the **Print button** 🖨

FIGURE J-1: **Totals row added to the query grid**

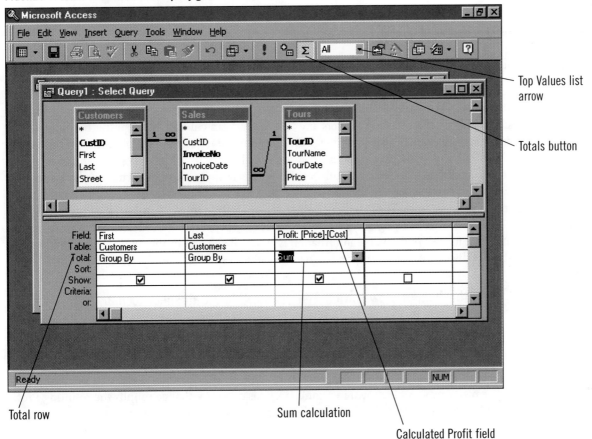

Top Values list arrow

Totals button

Total row

Sum calculation

Calculated Profit field

FIGURE J-2: **Top 5 datasheet**

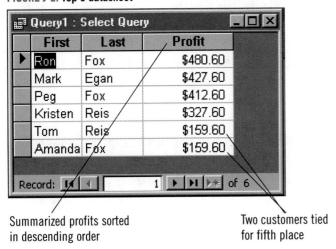

Summarized profits sorted in descending order

Two customers tied for fifth place

TABLE J-1: **Ways to use the Top Values feature**

action	to display
Click 5, or 25, or 100 from the Top Values list	The top 5, or 25, or 100 records
Enter a number such as 10 in the Top Values text box	The top 10 (in this case) records
Click 5% or 25% from the Top Values list	The top 5 or 25 percent of records
Enter a percentage, such as 10%, in the Top Values text box	The top 10 percent (in this case) of records
Click All from the Top Values list	All of the records

Access 97

Formatting Data in Datasheets

The **datasheet** of a query shows the resulting records in a column (field) and row (record) layout. Although Access datasheets, unlike Access reports, do not support sophisticated reporting features such as report, page, or group headers and footers, you can enhance the appearance of the data in a datasheet. For example, you can change the font face and font size and apply character formatting such as bold, italics, underlining, and color. You can also modify the gridlines style and background color. To make the data easier to understand, you can apply numeric formatting to values in a datasheet. After viewing the datasheet printout for the top five customers, Rachel decides to improve its appearance. The first thing Rachel changes is the numeric format of the Profit field. Since this is a summarized management report rather than a specific account of sales transactions, Rachel knows that for this purpose, the information is clearer if she rounds the values to the nearest dollar instead of displaying dollars and cents. Then she enhances the datasheet's font style.

1. Click the **Design View button** on the Query Datasheet toolbar, right-click the **Profit field** in the query design grid, then click **Properties**
   The Field Properties window opens in which you can modify certain characteristics of the Profit field.

2. Click the **Decimal Places** text box, then type **0**
   The property sheet is shown in Figure J-3. This property change rounds the resulting Profit field to the nearest dollar. To view the changes, remove the property sheet, then return to Datasheet View.

QuickTip

Click any entry in the Profit column to display the actual profit figure, rounded to the nearest penny.

3. Click the **Properties button** on the Query Design toolbar, then click the **Datasheet View button** on the Query Design toolbar
   The Profit field is now rounded to the nearest dollar, making the figures easier to read. To enhance the datasheet further, change the font face, font color, and font size.

4. Click the **Selector button** to select the entire datasheet, click **Format** on the menu bar, then click **Font**
   The Font dialog box opens as shown in Figure J-4. It displays the default font characteristics: Arial, Regular, 10 points, and black.

5. Scroll the **Font list**, click **Comic Sans MS**, click **20** in the **Size list**, click the **Color list arrow**, scroll and click **Blue**, then click **OK**
   The three font changes are applied to the entire datasheet. You want to get a good view of the changes.

6. Click the **Maximize button** on the datasheet, then click **Ron** in the first record to deselect the datasheet
   Increasing the font size of the data increases its clarity, but now you must widen the First column because it isn't wide enough to display the entire entry for each record.

7. Position the mouse pointer on the **right boundary** of the First field selector to change your mouse pointer to a ↔, then double-click to widen the First column to display the widest entry in the column
   Your datasheet should look like Figure J-5. Print the datasheet, then save and close the Top "5" Customers query.

8. Click the **Print button**, then click the **Save button**

Time To
✔ Close the datasheet

FIGURE J-3: Profit field properties

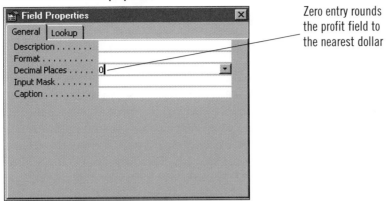

Zero entry rounds the profit field to the nearest dollar

FIGURE J-4: Font dialog box

Selector button

Font face

Font color

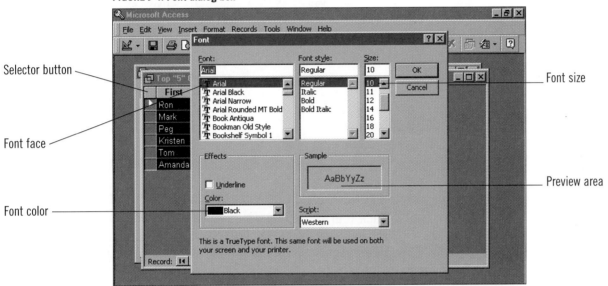

Font size

Preview area

FIGURE J-5: Formatted datasheet

Field selectors

Resize column mouse pointer

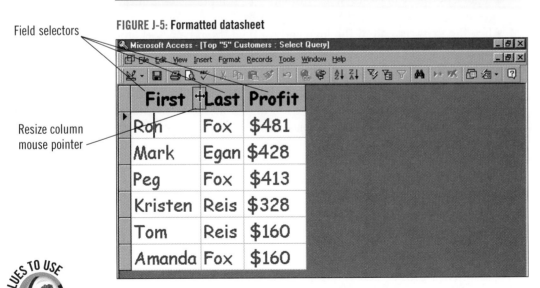

Formatting the gridline style and background color of a datasheet

To format the gridline style and the background color of the current datasheet displayed in Datasheet View, click Format on the menu bar, then click Cells to open the Cells Effects dialog box. Then click the options for which gridlines to display (vertical or horizontal), the cell effect (flat, raised, or sunken), the gridline color, and the background color you wish to apply.

Creating a Parameter Query

A **parameter query** displays a dialog box prompting you for information to enter as criteria for retrieving records. This dialog box displays each time the parameter query runs. For example, you could use a parameter query to prompt you for a specific customer name to show only sales to the customer. You can also use a parameter query as the basis of a form or report. In this case, each time the form or report is displayed, the parameter query's dialog box prompts the user for criteria to determine which records to display in the form or report. ✎ When planning future tours, the Nomad marketing department often comes to Rachel requesting sales information for a specific time period. Rachel designs a parameter query that prompts the user for two dates. The resulting datasheet displays all the sales that were made between those two dates.

1. Click the **Queries tab** if necessary, click **New**, click **Design View**, then click **OK**
   The parameter query starts as a select query. The only three fields you wish to display in this query are the InvoiceDate, TourName, and TourDate, which are found in the Sales and Tours tables. You use the double-click method to add each table name in the Show Table dialog box to the query design window.

2. Double-click **Sales**, double-click **Tours**, then click **Close**
   The tables are in place, and the Show Table dialog box is closed. Double-clicking places the field names, in order, into the next available column in the query design grid.

3. Double-click **InvoiceDate** in the Sales table, double-click **TourName** in the Tours table, then double-click **TourDate** in the Tours table
   With the fields in place, add the parameter query criteria to the appropriate criteria cells in the query design grid. **Parameter criteria** consist of a comparison operator such as = (equal to), < (less than), >= (greater than or equal to), Like, or Between, and then a prompt surrounded by square brackets. Access displays the prompt when the query is run. The response determines the criteria for the resulting datasheet.

4. Click the **Criteria cell** of the InvoiceDate field, then type **>=[Type the start date:]**
   The resulting query design grid is shown in Figure J-6. Test the parameter query.

5. Click the **Datasheet View button** 🔲 to open the Enter Parameter Value dialog box, type **1/1/97** in the Type the start date: text box, then press **[Enter]**
   While this parameter query works well to display all the tours sold on or after a specified date, you wish to modify it to display all tours sold within two dates. Return to Query Design View and modify the parameter query.

6. Click the **Design View button** 🔲 on the Query Datasheet toolbar, right-click the **Criteria cell** of the InvoiceDate field, then click **Zoom**
   The Zoom dialog box opens, providing you a bigger area to enter long criteria. Use the Between And operator to specify two dates for the InvoiceDate field.

7. Type **Between [Type start date:] And [Type end date:]** in the Zoom dialog box as shown in Figure J-7, then click **OK**
   Test the new parameter query that prompts for two dates.

8. Click 🔲, type **1/1/97** in response to the first prompt, press **[Enter]**, type **1/1/98** in response to the second prompt, then press **[Enter]**
   Only five sales were recorded between these two dates, as shown in Figure J-8. Save this query with the name Sales Between Two Dates, then close the datasheet.

9. Click the **Save button** 🔲, type **Sales Between Two Dates**, then click **OK**

Time To

✔ Close the datasheet

FIGURE J-6: Parameter query

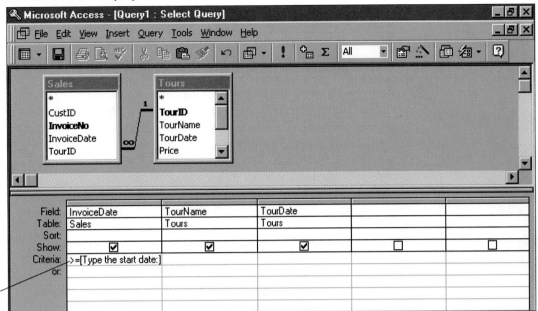

Parameter criteria

FIGURE J-7: Zoom dialog box

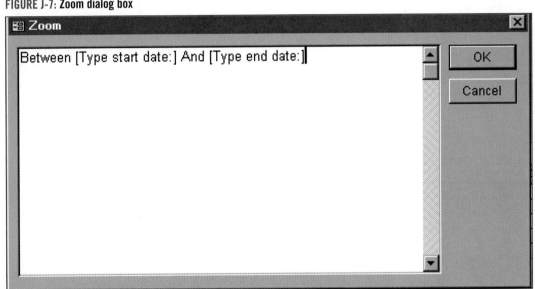

FIGURE J-8: Sales between 1/1/97 and 1/1/98

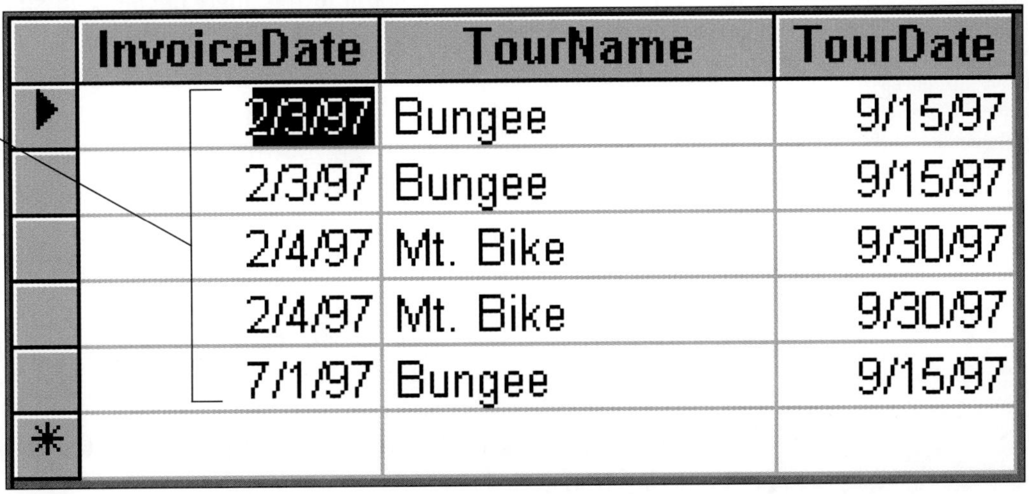

InvoiceDate is between 1/1/97 and 1/1/98

InvoiceDate	TourName	TourDate
2/3/97	Bungee	9/15/97
2/3/97	Bungee	9/15/97
2/4/97	Mt. Bike	9/30/97
2/4/97	Mt. Bike	9/30/97
7/1/97	Bungee	9/15/97

Access 97

Creating an AutoLookup Query

An **AutoLookup query** is a multiple-table query that automatically fills in certain field values for a new record. When you enter a value in the join field in an AutoLookup query datasheet, Access looks up and fills in existing information in other fields related to that value. You use the **join field** to link the two tables in the query together in a one-to-many relationship. The "one" side of the one-to-many relationship is usually a **primary key** field. The "many" side of the relationship is called the **foreign key.** The marketing department asked Rachel if there is a way to display the entire state's name in this datasheet in addition to the two-letter abbreviation. Since the state's name is already recorded in the States table, Rachel links the Customers and States tables together with a one-to-many relationship, then uses an AutoLookup query to look up the state name information automatically from the States table in the query's resulting datasheet.

1. Click the **Relationships button** on the Database toolbar, click the **Show Table button** on the Relationships toolbar, double-click **States**, click **Close**, then click the **Maximize button** if necessary
   The States table is added to the Relationships window. Rearrange the tables in the Relationships window to place the soon-to-be linked fields closer together.

2. Click the **States table title bar**, then drag it below the Sales table as shown in Figure J-9
   Next, build the relationship between the States and Customers tables.

3. Click and drag the **State field** in the States table to the State field of the Customers table
   The Relationships window opens, providing an opportunity to define the relationship further.

4. Click the **Enforce Referential Integrity check box**
   The Enforce Referential Integrity option specifies that you can't enter a two-letter state abbreviation in the State field of the Customers table that isn't first recorded in the State field of the States table. See Figure J-10.

5. Click **Create** to finalize the link, click the **Relationships window Close button**, then click **Yes** when prompted to save the changes to the layout
   You need fields from both the Customers and States tables for this AutoLookup query.

6. Click the **Queries tab** if necessary, click **New**, click **Design View**, click **OK**, double-click **Customers**, double-click **States**, then click **Close**
   Add all fields from the Customers table, and the StateName field from the States table.

7. Double-click the **Customers table title bar**, drag all the **highlighted Customers fields** to the query design grid, scroll in the query design grid so that the State field is visible, then drag the **StateName field** to the Zip column
   The StateName field is inserted between the State field and the Zip field. Test your AutoLookup query by opening it in Datasheet View and adding two records.

8. Click the **Datasheet View button** on the Query Design toolbar, click the **New Record button** on the Query Datasheet toolbar, then type the following two new records pressing **[Enter]** or **[Tab]** to move from field to field

CustID	First	Last	Street	City	State	StateName	Zip	Birth Date
27	Joe	Jackson	33 Elm St.	Clive	IA (default)	[Tab]	50644	7/1/1970
28	Jane	Joslin	44 Redbud	Lenox	MA	[Tab]	02140	8/1/1975

   Your screen should look like Figure J-11. The StateName information was automatically looked up from the State table.

9. Click the **Save button**, type **Customers & States** in the Query Name text box, click **OK**, then close the datasheet

QuickTip

Double-click a linking line in the Relationships window to view the Relationships dialog box defining that relationship. Single-click a linking line in the Relationships window and press [Delete] to delete an existing relationship.

Trouble?

For the AutoLookup query to work as intended, the linking field *must* be pulled from the "many" side of the linking relationship. In this case, the State field *must* be pulled from the Customers table.

FIGURE J-9: **Relationships window with the States table**

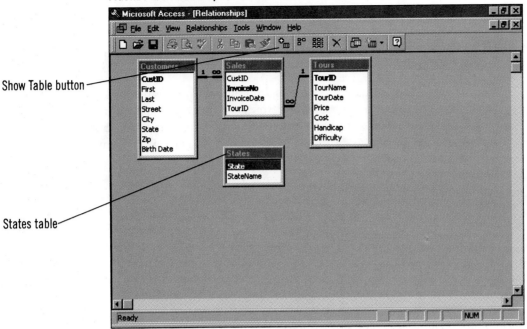

Show Table button

States table

FIGURE J-10: **Relationships dialog box**

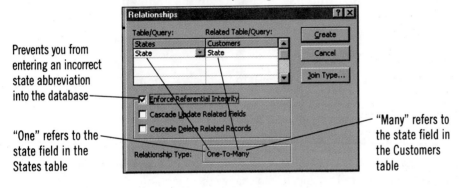

Prevents you from entering an incorrect state abbreviation into the database

"One" refers to the state field in the States table

"Many" refers to the state field in the Customers table

FIGURE J-11: **Customers & States AutoLookup query**

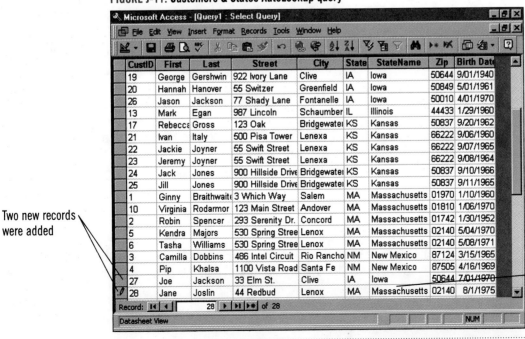

Two new records were added

StateName field is automatically looked up

Creating a Make-table Query

Make-table queries are one of four types of **action queries**, queries that makes changes to many records in just one operation. A **make-table** query creates a new table from all or part of the data in one or more tables. Make-table queries are useful for many data-sharing, backup, and database-performance reasons. See Table J-2 for more information on the make-table query as well as other action queries. ✎ The Nomad-J database contains sales records from 1996 through the present. Rachel decides to make a separate table of the 1996 sales records so that she can quickly make a backup of this data.

Steps 1234

1. **Click the Queries tab if necessary, click New, click Design View, then click OK**
   A make-table query starts like a select query. You must add the appropriate tables to Query Design View and add the appropriate fields to the query design grid. In this case, you need only one table, Sales.

2. **Double-click Sales, then click Close**
   Add all of the fields of the Sales table to the query design grid.

3. **Double-click the Sales table title bar, then drag all the highlighted Sales fields to the query design grid**
   Add the criteria in the InvoiceDate field to select only those transactions that occurred in 1996. Since the entry is somewhat long, use the Zoom dialog box.

Trouble?

Be sure to enter a space before and after "and" so that Access makes the correct assumptions about where the date criteria start and end.

4. **Right-click the Criteria cell of the InvoiceDate field, click Zoom, then type >=1/1/96 and <1/1/97**
   The Zoom dialog box is shown in Figure J-12

5. **Click OK, then click the Datasheet View button [▦] on the Query Design toolbar**
   The resulting datasheet is shown in Figure J-13. Notice that all of the InvoiceDate fields have 1996 entries. Return to Query Design View to change the query into a make-table query.

6. **Click the Design View button [▨] on the Query Datasheet toolbar, click the Query Type button list arrow [▦▾] on the Query Design toolbar, then click Make-Table Query**
   The Make Table dialog box opens, prompting you for the name of the new table as well as the database on which to place the new table. You place the new table, 1996 Sales, in the current database.

7. **Type 1996 Sales, then press [Enter]**
   Now run the query and create the new table.

8. **Click the Run button [❗] on the Query Design toolbar, then click Yes when prompted about pasting sixteen rows into a new table**
   Since you need to run this query only once, it isn't necessary to save it. Close the make-table query, then view the new table's datasheet to make sure the 1996 Sales table contains the 1996 records.

Time To

✔ Close the datasheet

9. **Click the Make Table Query Close button, click No when prompted to save the changes, click the Tables tab, then double-click the 1996 Sales table to view the records**
   The sixteen 1996 sales records have been duplicated in the 1996 Sales table.

FIGURE J-12: Zoom dialog box

Query Type button

InvoiceDate criteria

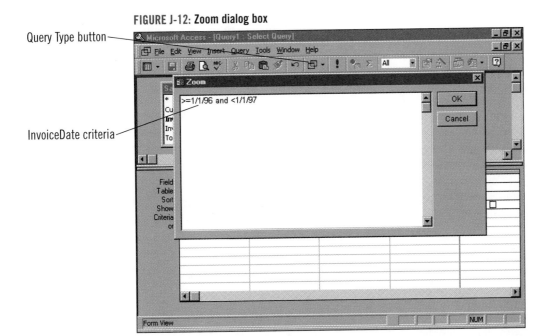

FIGURE J-13: 1996 sales records

All InvoiceDate fields are in 1996

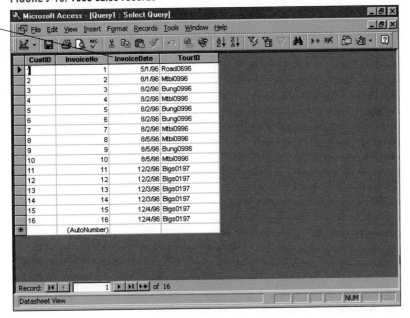

TABLE J-2: Types of action queries

type of action query	definition	use this action query to:
Delete	Deletes a group of records from one or more tables	Remove products that are discontinued or for which there are no orders
Update	Makes global changes to a group of records in one or more tables	Raise prices by 10 percent for all products
Append	Adds a group of records from one or more tables to the end of one or more tables	Merge the product table from a business you just acquired to the existing product table for the company
Make-table	Creates a new table from all or part of the data in one or more tables	Export records to another Access database, make a backup copy of a table, create a history table that contains old records, improve the performance of forms and records based on multiple-table queries, or create reports that display data from a specified point in time

Creating an Append Query

An **append query** is an action query that adds a group of records from one or more tables to the end of one or more tables. Append queries are handy when you wish to add additional records to an existing table, or when you are trying to merge the records from two tables into one. ✐ Rachel wants to back up the 1997 sales information, and decides to append the 1997 sales records to the table she just created with 1996 transactions instead of creating an entirely new table. An append query starts as a select query too, so Rachel's first step is to gather into the query design grid the fields she needs for the query.

Steps

1. Click the **Queries tab**, click **New**, click **Design View**, then click **OK**
   Again, you need only one table, Sales.

2. Double-click **Sales**, then click **Close**
   Add all of the fields of the Sales table to the query design grid.

3. Double-click the **Sales table title bar**, then drag all the **highlighted Sales fields** to the query design grid
   This time, instead of using the Zoom dialog box, add the criteria directly into the cell of the InvoiceDate field to select only those transactions that occurred in 1997.

4. Click the **Criteria cell** of the InvoiceDate field, type **>=1/1/1997 and <1/1/1998**, then click the **Datasheet View button** 📇 on the Query Design toolbar
   Notice that all of the InvoiceDate fields in the resulting datasheet now have 1997 entries. Return to Query Design View to change the query into an append query.

5. Click the **Design View button** 📐 on the Query Datasheet toolbar, click the **Query Type button list arrow** 📂▾ on the Query Design toolbar, then click **Append Query**
   The Append dialog box opens, prompting you for the name of the table to which to append the records.

6. Click the **Table Name list arrow**, then click **1996 Sales**
   The screen should look like Figure J-14. Now run the query to append the five 1997 records to the 1996 Sales table.

7. Click **OK**, click the **Run button** ❗ on the Query Design toolbar, then click **Yes** to append five rows
   Close the append query without saving it, then rename the 1996 Sales table to reflect more appropriately the records it contains.

8. Click the **Append query Close button**, click **No** when prompted to save the changes, click the **Tables tab**, right-click the **1996 Sales table**, click **Rename**, type **1996-1997 Sales**, then press **[Enter]**

> **Time To**
> ✔ Close the datasheet

9. Double-click the **1996-1997 Sales** table to view the resulting datasheet
   You should see 21 records in the datasheet, with only 1996 and 1997 dates in the InvoiceDate field, as shown in Figure J-15.

FIGURE J-14: Append dialog box

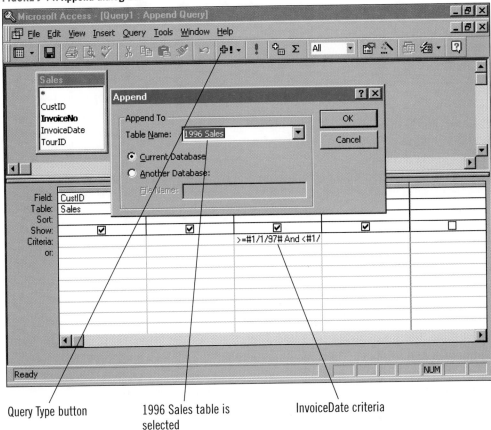

Query Type button | 1996 Sales table is selected | InvoiceDate criteria

FIGURE J-15: 1996–1997 Sales table

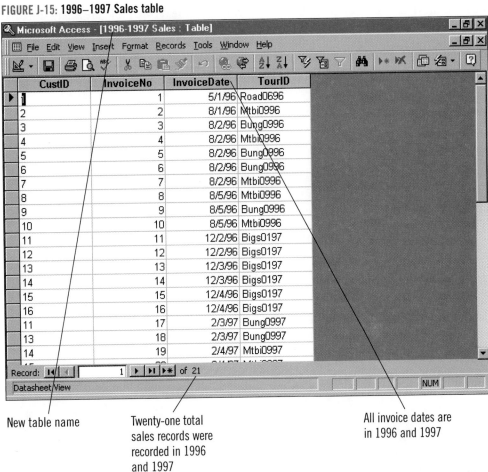

New table name | Twenty-one total sales records were recorded in 1996 and 1997 | All invoice dates are in 1996 and 1997

Creating a Delete Query

A **delete query** is an action query that deletes a group of records from one or more tables. For example, you could use a delete query to delete old records or discontinued products. A delete query always removes entire records that match the criteria within it, not just selected fields within records. Now that Rachel has safely created a 1996–1997 Sales table, she wishes to delete those old records from the Sales table. Similar to a make-table or append query, the delete query starts as a select query with criteria that identify which records to delete.

1. Click the **Queries tab**, click **New**, click **Design View**, then click **OK**
   Again, you need only one table, Sales.

2. Double-click **Sales**, then click **Close**
   Add all of the fields of the Sales table to the query design grid.

3. Double-click the **Sales table title bar**, then drag all the **highlighted Sales fields** to the query design grid
   This time, instead of using the Zoom dialog box, add directly into the cell the criteria in the InvoiceDate field to select only those transactions that occurred in 1997.

4. Click the **Criteria cell** of the InvoiceDate field, type **>=1/1/1996 and <1/1/1998**, then click the **Datasheet View button**
   The resulting datasheet should contain 21 records, the same records that are safely stored in the 1996–1997 table. Return to Query Design View to change the query into a delete query.

5. Click the **Design View button** on the Query Datasheet toolbar to return to Query Design View, click the **Query Type button list arrow** on the Query Design toolbar, then click **Delete Query**
   The Delete row is added to the query design grid.

6. Click the **Run button** on the Query Design toolbar, then click **Yes** when prompted to delete 21 rows
   Now that you have deleted the records, running the query again does not change anything. No remaining records in the Sales table meet the specified criteria of this query. You will never run this query again, so close it without saving it.

7. Click the **Delete Query Close button**, then click **No** when prompted to save the changes
   To make sure that you have actually deleted the records from the Sales table, open the Sales table in Datasheet View.

8. Click the **Tables tab**, then double-click **Sales**
   Only 10 records exist in the Sales table now, as shown in the datasheet in Figure J-16, and each has an invoice date of 1/1/98 or later.

9. Close the Sales table datasheet

Trouble?
If you start a delete query on a large table and wish to cancel the action, press [Ctrl][Break].

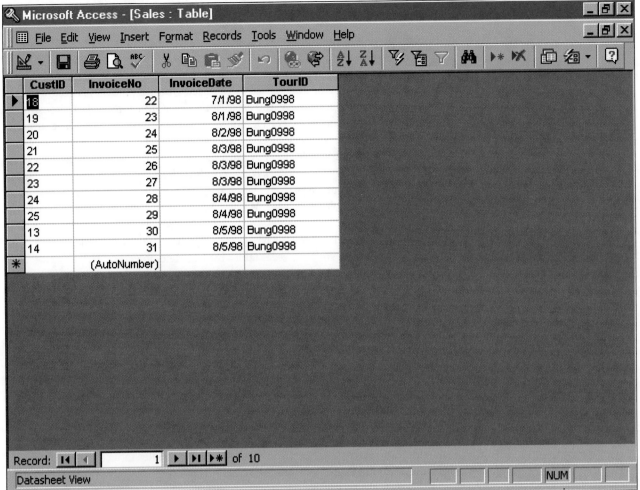

Important considerations before running delete queries

You cannot restore records that you delete using a delete query. Therefore, you should always preview the datasheet before you run the query to make sure you've selected the appropriate records to delete. You should also maintain backup copies of your data so that if you delete the wrong records, you can retrieve them from a backup copy of your database. If you enable cascading deletes in the Relationship dialog box when defining one-to-many relationships between tables, you delete all the records on a "many" side of a relationship if you delete the record that contains the "one" side.

Creating a Union Query

A union query is a type of SQL-specific query. **SQL** (Structured Query Language) is programming code that you create when building any query. You can display the SQL commands by choosing the SQL View option on the View menu in Query Design View. If you know the SQL programming language, however, you can build a query directly with SQL programming commands. Some queries, such as the union query, *require* SQL programming because you cannot create them using the query design grid. A union query combines corresponding fields from two or more tables or queries into one field and is therefore very useful when trying to combine data from two separate tables or databases into a single object. While Rachel felt that it was safe to separate the 1996 and 1997 sales transactions into two tables, she has been asked by the president of Nomad to supply a report listing sales transactions for the past three years. Rachel uses a union query to combine records from the Sales and 1996–1997 Sales tables into a single object.

Steps

1. **Click the Queries tab, click New, click Design View, then click OK**
   SQL-specific queries don't start with any tables in Query Design View. With a SQL-specific query, you enter all the SQL statements directly. Close the Show Table dialog box.

2. **Click Close**
   Specify that the query is an SQL-specific query. For more information on other types of SQL-specific queries, refer to Table J-3.

3. **Click Query on the menu bar, point to SQL Specific, then click Union**
   The blank Query Design window opens, ready to accept your SQL statements. Enter the four SQL statements to select the four fields in the 1996–1997 Sales table and the four fields in the Sales table, then display all of them in a single datasheet.

QuickTip

You can use the Copy and Paste commands to quickly copy repeated text in the SQL window.

4. **Type the following SQL statements:**

   SELECT [CustID],[InvoiceNo],[InvoiceDate],[TourID]

   FROM [1996-1997 Sales]

   UNION SELECT [CustID],[InvoiceNo],[InvoiceDate],[TourID]

   FROM [SALES]
   Your screen must look exactly as shown in Figure J-17. With the SQL statements carefully entered, view the resulting datasheet to see whether your union query worked.

QuickTip

Click the SQL View button [sql ▾] to switch to the SQL window.

5. **Click the Datasheet View button [▦] on the Query Design toolbar**
   The resulting datasheet should look like Figure J-18, with 31 records that have InvoiceDate data ranging from 1996 through 1998. Save the union query. You can use this query as part of future queries across all sales records.

6. **Click the Save button [▯], type Sales Union Query, then click OK**
   When satisfied that you can access all the sales records simultaneously, close the Sales Union Query datasheet and exit Access.

7. **Click File on the menu bar, then click Exit**

FIGURE J-17: Union query built with SQL statements

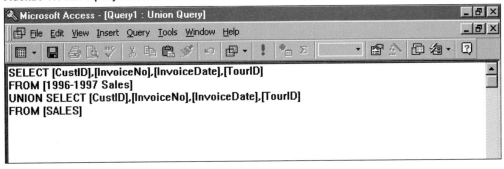

```
SELECT [CustID],[InvoiceNo],[InvoiceDate],[TourID]
FROM [1996-1997 Sales]
UNION SELECT [CustID],[InvoiceNo],[InvoiceDate],[TourID]
FROM [SALES]
```

SQL button

FIGURE J-18: Datasheet from union query

CustID	InvoiceNo	InvoiceDate	TourID
1	1	5/1/96	Road0696
10	10	8/5/96	Mtbi0996
11	11	12/2/96	Bigs0197
11	17	2/3/97	Bung0997
12	12	12/2/96	Bigs0197
13	13	12/3/96	Bigs0197
13	18	2/3/97	Bung0997
13	30	8/5/98	Bung0998
14	14	12/3/96	Bigs0197
14	19	2/4/97	Mtbi0997
14	31	8/5/98	Bung0998
15	15	12/4/96	Bigs0197
15	20	2/4/97	Mtbi0997
15	21	7/1/97	Bung0997
16	16	12/4/96	Bigs0197
18	22	7/1/98	Bung0998
19	23	8/1/98	Bung0998
2	2	8/1/96	Mtbi0996
20	24	8/2/98	Bung0998

Record: 1 of 31

TABLE J-3: Types of SQL-specific queries

type of query	description	example
Union	Combines corresponding fields from one or more tables or queries into one field or column in the query's results	Use a union query when you have several vendors that send you new inventory lists each month and you wish to combine these lists into one inventory table
Pass-through	Sends commands directly to ODBC (Open Database Connectivity) databases such as Microsoft SQL Server	Use a pass-through query to retrieve records or change data on an ODBC database
Data-definition	Creates or alters database objects, such as Microsoft Access tables or queries	Use a data-definition query when you wish to create a file of data with different data types than the original object
Subquery	Consists of a SQL SELECT statement inside another select or action query; You enter these statements in the Field or Criteria row of the query design grid	Use a subquery to calculate a result upon which a query will be run, such as when displaying products that have a unit price above the average, or finding orders with totals that are higher than the average order value

Practice

► Concepts Review

Identify each element shown in Figure J-19.

FIGURE J-19

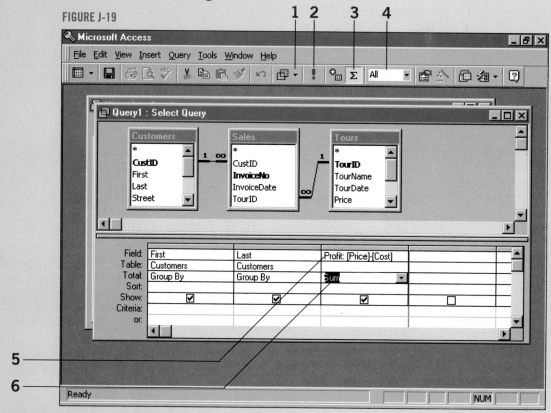

Match each term with the statement that describes its function.

7. Programming code that you create when building any query
8. Displays a dialog box prompting you for information to enter as criteria for retrieving records each time the query is run
9. The field used to link two tables together in a one-to-many relationship
10. Combines corresponding fields from two or more tables or queries into one field
11. Must contain unique data for each record in that table
12. Finds a number or percentage of top or bottom records in a resulting datasheet
13. A query that makes changes to many records in just one operation

a. Primary key
b. Action query
c. Union query
d. Parameter query
e. SQL
f. Top Values feature
g. Join field

Select the best answer from the list of choices.

14. Which of the following is *not* a datasheet-formatting option?
    a. Changing header and footer text
    b. Changing font color
    c. Changing font size
    d. Changing background color

15. Which of the following shows the proper way to enter parameter criteria in the query design grid?
    a. >=(Type minimum value here:)
    b. >={Type minimum value here: }
    c. >=[Type minimum value here:]
    d. >=Type minimum value here:

16. **You *cannot* use the Top Values feature to**
    a. Display a subset of records
    b. Show the top 30 records
    c. Update the top 10 records
    d. Show the bottom 10 percent of records

17. **A properly designed AutoLookup query depends on**
    a. The two or more tables in the underlying query
    b. Proper one-to-many relationships between the underlying tables of the query
    c. Using the "many" field of the relationship in the query design grid
    d. All of the above

18. **Which of the following is *not* an action query?**
    a. Union query
    b. Delete query
    c. Make-table query
    d. Append query

19. **Which of the following precautions should you take before running a delete query?**
    a. Check the resulting datasheet to make sure the query selects the right records
    b. Have a current backup of the database
    c. Understand the relationships between the records you are about to delete and others in the database
    d. All of the above

20. **SQL stands for:**
    a. Standard Query Layout
    b. Structured Query Language
    c. Simplified Query Layout
    d. Standard Query Language

21. **Which of the following is *not* an SQL-specific query?**
    a. Union query
    b. Pass-through query
    c. Subquery
    d. Select query

► Skills Review

1. **Query for top values**
   a. Start Access and open the Addresses-J.mdb database.
   b. Build a select query using the query design grid with the following fields in the following order:
      First, Last, Street, Zip, and Birthday from the Names table
      City and State from the Zips table
   c. Sort the query Ascending on the Birthday field.
   d. Display the top five records to display the five oldest people in the datasheet and print the datasheet.
   e. Display the top 25% of the records in a datasheet and print the datasheet.
   f. Sort the query Ascending on the Last field only.
   g. Display the top 10 records in a datasheet and print the datasheet.
   h. Save the query as "Top 10 Last records".

2. **Format data in datasheets**
   a. Display the "Top 10 Last records" datasheet.
   b. Select all the records by clicking the selector button, then format them with the following options in the Font dialog box: Font: Book Antiqua; Size:14 pts; Color: Teal.
   c. Resize all columns of the datasheet so that all of the information within every column is visible.
      Hint: Select all the columns, then right-click any selected column border to resize all the columns simultaneously.

d. Print the datasheet.

e. Save the query as "Formatted Top 10".

f. Close "Formatted Top 10".

3. Create a parameter query

a. Build a select query using the query design grid with the following fields in the following order:
First, Last, Street, Zip, and Birthday from the Names table
City and State from the Zips table

b. Add a parameter query so that the query prompts you for a new last name each time you run the query by entering =[Enter the last name:] in the Criteria cell of the Last field.

c. View the resulting datasheet and enter Baker at the prompt. Two records should appear in the resulting datasheet.

d. Print the datasheet.

e. Change the parameter query to prompt for those with birthdays between two dates by entering Between [Enter start date:] and [Enter end date:] in the Criteria cell of the Birthday field. Be sure to delete the previous parameter query.

f. Run the query, entering 1/1/1960 as the start date and 1/1/1970 as the end date.

g. Print the resulting datasheet with four records.

h. Save the query with the name "Parameter query with date prompts".

i. Close the parameter query.

4. Create an AutoLookup query

a. Open the Relationships window for the Addresses-J database.

b. Add the States table to the window, using the Show Table button on the toolbar.

c. Drag the Abbreviation field from the States table to the State field of the Zips table to create a one-to-many relationship between the tables.

d. Enforce referential integrity, then click Create.

e. Close the Relationships window and save the changes to the layout.

f. Build a select query using the query design grid with the following fields in the following order:
First, Last, and Zip from the Names table
City and State from the Zips table
StateName from the States table

g. View the datasheet for the resulting query, click the New Record button, then add the following new record (be sure to press [Tab] to move from field to field):
First: Mark
Last: Langguth
Zip: 66000

h. Be sure to press [Tab] after entering the Zip information; then print the datasheet.

i. Save the query as "Address AutoLookup".

5. Create a make-table query

a. Open Address AutoLookup in Query Design View.

b. Add criteria to display only those records that display IA in the State field.

c. Change the query to a make-table query. Name the new table Contacts in IA.

d. Run the query. You should get 14 records in the Contacts in IA table.

e. Repeat the process to make another table. Name this table Contacts in KS. You should get three records in this table.

f. Close the Address AutoLookup query *without* saving the changes.

g. Open the Contacts in IA table in Datasheet View and print the datasheet.

h. Close the Contacts in IA datasheet.

6. Create an append query
a. Open Address AutoLookup in Query Design View.
b. Add criteria to display only those records that display MO in the State field.
c. Change the query to an append query and choose the Contacts in IA table as the destination for the appended records.
d. Run the query. You should add eight rows when running the append query.
e. Rename the Contacts in IA table to Contacts in IA and MO.
f. Open the Contacts in IA and MO table in Datasheet View and print the datasheet.
g. Close the Contacts in IA and MO table.

7. Create a delete query
a. Create a new query with all the fields of the Contacts in IA and MO table.
b. Add criteria to display only those records that display MO in the State field.
c. Change the query to a delete query.
d. Run the query.
e. Close the query without saving the changes.
f. Rename the Contacts in IA and MO table to Contacts in IA.

8. Create a union query
a. Start a new query without adding any tables to the query design grid, click Query on the menu bar, point to SQL Specific, then click Union.
b. Add the following SQL statements:
SELECT [First],[Last],[Zip],[State]
FROM [Contacts in IA]
UNION SELECT [First],[Last],[Zip],[State]
FROM [Contacts in KS]
c. View the resulting datasheet and print it.
d. Save the query as Union of IA and KS.
e. Close the query datasheet and exit Access.

► Independent Challenges

1. As the president of a civic organization, you have developed a database, Cleanup-J, that tracks donations of recyclable material. You wish to query the information in several new ways.

To complete this independent challenge:

1. Start Access, then open the database Cleanup-J.
2. Create a select query that lists the following fields:
Name, City, and State from the Clubs table
Date and Weight from the Deposits table
Name from the Recycle Centers table
3. Sort the datasheet in descending order by Weight.
4. Show the top five records and print the resulting datasheet. You will see seven records in the resulting datasheet because three records have the same information in the Weight field. This results in a three-way tie for the fifth "top record."
5. Select all the records and format them with the following options on the Font dialog box:
Font: Tahoma
Font Size: 20
Color: Red

6. Resize the columns so that all the data is visible in each field.
7. Print the formatted datasheet.
8. Save the query as Top 5 Deposits.
9. Close Top 5 Deposits.
10. Open the Relationships window and add the States table to the layout.
11. Drag the Abbreviation field from the States table to the State field of the Clubs table.
12. Enforce referential integrity between the fields of the tables.
13. Reposition any or all tables so that you can clearly see the layout of the four tables and the linking lines between them.
14. Close the Relationships window, saving the layout changes.
15. Create a select query that lists the following fields in the following order:
    All the fields from the Clubs table
    Only the StateName field from the States table (add this to the fifth column, just to the right of the State field)
16. Add the following records to the query (the StateName information is automatically looked up, so you don't need to enter it):

Name	Street	City	State	StateName	Zip	Phone	Club Number
Lions	666 J Street	Omaha	NE	Nebraska	58000	612-555-2222	6
Jackson Jems	777 Elm	Olathe	KS	Kansas	66000	913-111-5555	7

17. Save the query as New Club Entry Query, print the datasheet, close the datasheet, close the Cleanup-J database, then exit Access.

2. Now that you've developed a relational database, Readings-J, that documents the books you've read, you need to use the make-table query to create another table of information for an external database requirement. Once you've determined that the make-table query is a success, you create an append query that you can use to update the extra table you created.

To complete this independent challenge:

1. Start Access, then open the Readings-J.mdb database.
2. Create a select query that lists the following fields in the following order:
   First Name and Last Name from the Authors table
   Title, Category, Rating, and Date Read from the Books table
3. Enter the criteria Crichton in the Criteria cell of the Last Name field.
4. View the datasheet to ensure that it displays only Crichton records.
5. Return to Query Design View and change the query to a make-table query using the Query button in Query Design View.
6. Give the new table the name Legal Thrillers.
7. Run the query, adding to the Legal Thrillers table all four records that match the Crichton criteria.
8. Change the query to a select query, then change the criteria to Turow in the Criteria cell of the Last Name field.
9. View the datasheet to ensure that it displays only Turow records.
10. Return to Query Design View and change the query to an append query using the Query button in Query Design View.
11. Choose the Legal Thrillers table as the location for the appended records.
12. Run the query, adding to the Legal Thrillers table the two records that match the Turow criteria.
13. Close the query without saving the changes.
14. Open the Legal Thrillers table, make sure all the information in each of the columns is visible, then print the datasheet.
15. Close the Legal Thrillers datasheet, saving the layout changes, and close Readings-J.
16. Exit Access.

3. You have recently helped the medicine director of a large internal medicine clinic put together and update a database, Doctors-J, that tracks extracurricular activities. One physician has left the clinic and one program has been eliminated, so you wish to create delete queries to remove from the database the associated records that show activity for this physician and program.

To complete this independent challenge:

1. Start Access, then open the Doctors-J.mdb database from your Student Disk.
2. Create a query with all the fields of the Activities table.
3. Enter the criteria CJ in the Criteria cell of the Physician Number field.
4. View the resulting datasheet to ensure that it displays only CJ records (there should be only one record).
5. Return to Query Design View, then change the query into a delete query using the Query button on the toolbar.
6. Run the query deleting the single CJ record.
7. Delete the CJ criteria and enter 2 in the criteria cell of the Program Number field.
8. View the resulting datasheet to ensure that it displays only those programs with a Program Number equal to 2.
9. Return to Query Design View, and make sure that the query is still a delete query.
10. Run the query deleting the two records that have a Program Number of 2.
11. Delete the 2 criteria and change the query back into a select query using the Query button in Query Design View.
12. Display the resulting datasheet, print the resulting datasheet, then close the datasheet without saving the changes.
13. Close the Doctors-J database, then exit Access.

4. You are an avid book reader and buyer and have been scouting the Web for ways to purchase books at discount prices. Your friend told you about this amazing Web site that offers great buys on terrific books. The site not only organizes titles by theme, but provides a brief description of each book.
    To complete this independent challenge:

1. Log on to the Internet and use your browser to go to http://www.course.com. From there, click Student Online Companions, click the link for this textbook, then click the Access link for Unit J.
2. Find several interesting books on the Amazon Web page, and print their descriptions. You need to print the information for at least three books.
3. Start Access, then open the Books-J.mdb database from your Student Disk. There are currently three tables in the Books-J database: Barnes (for the books you purchased from Barnes & Noble bookstore), Amazon (for the books you purchased from the Amazon Web page), and Authors (which lists all authors regardless of where you purchased the book). The Barnes and Authors tables already contain several records.
4. Open the Authors table in Datasheet View and determine whether the authors for the books you've chosen from the Amazon Web page are already entered. If not, enter the new authors using an appropriate author number that consists of their initials and the number 1 (use the number 2 if a previously recorded author has the same initials). Reference the book with only the first author's name if several authors are listed for a single work.
5. Open the Amazon table and enter the three books that correspond to the authors that you just entered in the Authors table. Leave 0 for the Rating field and do not make an entry in the Date Read field if you haven't read the book yet.
6. Create a union query that lists all the books from both the Barnes table and the Amazon table. Use the following SQL statements:
   SELECT [Title],[Category]
   FROM [Barnes]
   UNION SELECT [Title],[Category]
   FROM [Amazon]
7. View the resulting datasheet, widen each column to display all of the information within that column, then print the datasheet.
8. Save the query with the name Union of Barnes and Amazon.
9. Close the query, close the Books-J database, then exit Access.

▶ Visual Workshop

Open the VW-J database and create the datasheet shown in Figure J-21 using a select query and the fields shown. Notice that the records are sorted in descending order on Value, and that the Top 5 feature was used to display only the top records (seven records are actually displayed because there is a five-way tie for third place). The font used for the datasheet is Footlight MT Light, Italic, 14 points, and blue. Save the query as Top Contributors and print the datasheet.

FIGURE J-20

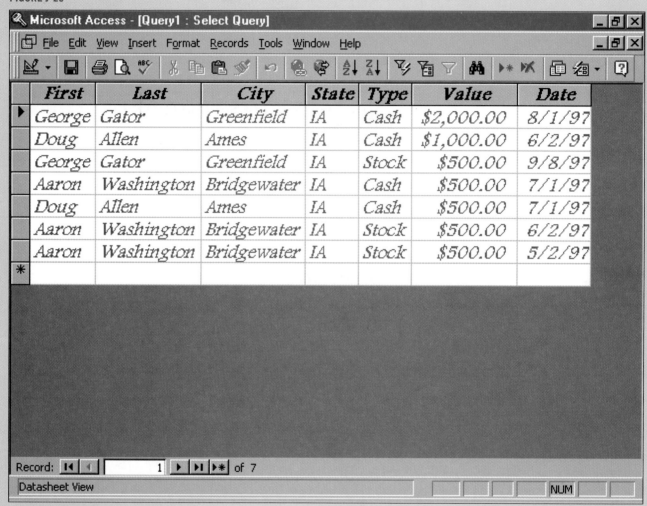

Adding
Complex Objects to a Form

Objectives

► **Add combo boxes**
► **Add check boxes**
► **Add toggle buttons**
► **Add command buttons**
► **Add option groups**
► **Add option buttons**
► **Create custom Help for a form**
► **Add pictures**

Forms are database objects that display the fields of a record. You can place fields in any order that best meets the specific needs of the form. Every element on a form is a **control**, and is either bound or unbound. **Unbound controls**, such as labels used to identify form elements or lines that enhance the design, do not change from record to record. **Bound controls** change to display the changing data contained in each record. While the most common bound control is the text box, other bound controls, such as combo boxes and check boxes, give the user an easier and more accurate way to view and enter new records because they present a limited choice of data entry options. ◄━━━ As the volume of information that has to be entered into the Nomad database increases, Rachel Best faces the task of developing productive data-entry forms to allow others to view and enter data. Rachel employs some of the more complex form bound objects, such as combo boxes and option groups, to create powerful and easy-to-use forms.

Adding Combo Boxes

A **combo box** is a powerful control that can do different tasks on a form. First, a combo box can present a list of choices from which the user can choose to *make an entry* into the underlying record. If the user wants to make an entry other than the list of choices, he or she can also type an entry into the combo box control (hence the name *combo box*). In this case, the combo box is bound to the underlying record, allowing the user to enter or edit information in the actual record. Second, you can use a combo box to *find* a record when you select a value from the list. In this case, the combo box is an unbound control used only to find a record, not to enter or edit information on a record. You can use the **Control Wizard** to help you determine which way you want the combo box to work when you add it to a form. Rachel uses the Form Wizard to build quickly a form that will display tours in a main form, and each customer who has purchased that tour in a subform. She then adds a combo box to the main form to find automatically any TourID and list the associated customers that have purchased that tour.

Steps

1. **Start Access, open the Nomad-K database, then click the Forms tab if necessary**
   Build a new order-entry form on the Customers w/n Tour Query object that was previously created. Rachel uses "w/n" as the shortcut for "within" in the query name.

2. **Click New, click Form Wizard, click the Choose the table or query where the object's data comes from list arrow, click Customers w/n Tour Query, then click OK**
   The Form Wizard's second dialog box asks which fields you want on the form. Select all of the fields in the Customers w/n Tour Query, then display the records by tour.

3. **Click the Select All Fields button** `>>`, **click** `Next >`, **click by Tours, then click** `Next >`
   Choose the Tabular layout for the form and the Standard style.

4. **Click Tabular, click** `Next >`, **click Standard, click** `Next >`, **click** `Finish` **to accept the default form names, then click the Maximize button** `□` **if necessary**
   The form opens as shown in Figure K-1. The main form displays information on the tour, and the subform lists the name of each customer and the invoice date information for each sale for each tour. Create a TourID combo box that finds tours based on the TourID selected from the list.

5. **Click the Design View button** `⊠` **on the Form View toolbar, click the Toolbox button** `⚒` **on the Form Design toolbar to open the Toolbox if necessary, click the Control Wizards button** `⊠` **if necessary, to make sure it is toggled on, click the Combo Box button** `▦`, **then click below the 4¼" mark on the ruler on the upper-right corner of the form**
   Since the Control Wizards button was toggled on when you created this control, the **Combo Box Wizard** guides the rest of your actions. You want the lookup combo box to find a record based on the value you select in the combo box.

6. **Click the Find a record on my form based on the value I selected in my combo box option button, click** `Next >`, **click TourID, click the Select Single field button** `>`, **click** `Next >`, **click** `Next >` **again, type Lookup in the text box as the label for the combo box, then click** `Finish`
   Your screen should look similar to Figure K-2. Test your lookup combo box by returning to Form View and using the new combo box control to look up specific TourIDs.

7. **Click the Form View button** `▦` **on the Form Design Toolbar, click the Lookup list arrow, then click Bung0998**
   The main form displays the Bung0998 TourID, and the subform displays the 10 associated customers who have purchased that tour, as shown in Figure K-3. Save the form.

Time To

✔ Save

FIGURE K-1: **Tours form with a subform**

Main form ——
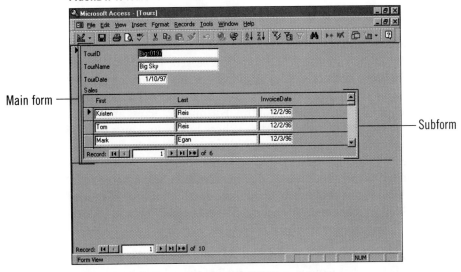
—— Subform

FIGURE K-2: **TourID lookup control added to the form**

The number on your screen may be different
Label for the combo box
New combo box control
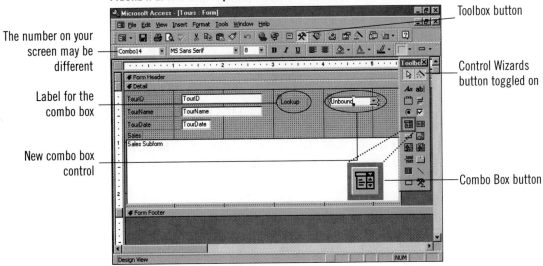
Toolbox button
Control Wizards button toggled on
Combo Box button

FIGURE K-3: **Look up the Bung0998 tour**

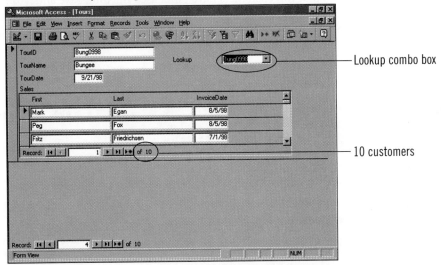
Lookup combo box
10 customers

Adding Check Boxes

A **check box** is a control that is often used to display Yes/No fields on a form because it can appear in only one of two ways: checked or unchecked. The checked state intuitively means on, yes, or true, and the unchecked state intuitively means off, no, or false. It is much easier for a user to answer questions on a form by using the mouse to click a check box control than to type the word "True" or "Yes" in a text box control. Fortunately, Access anticipates that any field with a Yes/No data type should be represented as a check box control on a form, regardless of whether the field was added to the form through the Form Wizard, AutoForm options, or in Form Design View. See Table K-1 for more information on other complex controls. ▸ Rachel needs to add the Handicap field to the Tours form. The Handicap field is part of the Tours table and has a Yes/No data type. When checked, the field indicates that the tour has made special accommodations for handicapped customers. Rachel uses Form Design View and adds the Handicap field to the form.

1. Click the Design View button 🔲 on the Form View toolbar to enter Form Design View
   The **field list window** represents all of the fields in the object upon which the form is based, regardless of whether they are all displayed on the form. Open the field list.

2. Click the Field List button 🔲 on the Form Design toolbar
   Add the Handicap field to the form below the Lookup field. Drag the field from the field list to the appropriate place on the form.

Trouble?

If the field list has a scroll bar, you can scroll to display the Handicap field or drag the ↖ on the lower-right corner of the field list to display all the fields.

3. Click the Handicap field in the field list window, then drag the Handicap field to the 4" mark on the ruler just below the lookup combo box
   The screen should look like Figure K-4. Since the Handicap field is already defined with a Yes/No data type, it was automatically added to the form as a check box control. Close the field list window.

4. Click 🔲 on the Form Design toolbar
   View the new check box control in Form View.

5. Click the Form View button 🔲 on the Form Design toolbar, click the Lookup - list arrow, then click Mtbi0997
   Your screen should look like Figure K-5. Notice that the Mtbi0997 tour is handicap-accessible and that two customers have purchased the tour. Save and close the form.

6. Click the Save button 🔲 on the Form View toolbar, then close the Tours form

CLUES TO USE

Changing controls

You can quickly change a check box control into a toggle button or option button. Right-click the check box in Form Design View, point to Change To in the menu as shown in Figure K-6, then click Toggle Button or Option Button. If you right-click a text box control, the three options are Label, Box, and Combo Box.

FIGURE K-6: Right-clicking the check box control

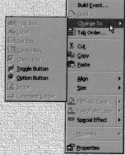

FIGURE K-4: Tours form with the Handicap check box

If your Field list has been resized, it may show all the fields and not have a scroll bar

Field List button

Check box control for handicap field

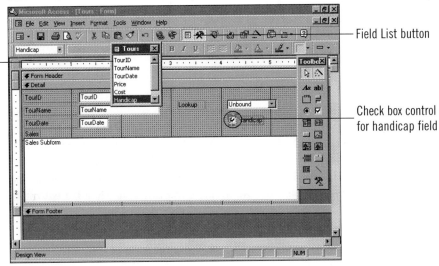

FIGURE K-5: Check box control on the Tours form

Mtbi0997 is chosen

Check box control

2 customers purchased this tour

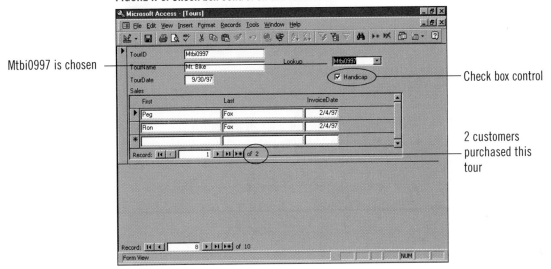

TABLE K-1: Complex controls

name	description	example
List box	Lists values that appear at all times on the form; when you're using the list box to enter or edit data, you can't add a value that's not in the list	
Combo box	Lists values that aren't displayed until you click the control; when used as a data-entry control, you can choose one of the entries in the list or enter a completely new value at the keyboard	Bung0998
Toggle button	Appears on the screen as a button that you can toggle on or off; the example shows two command buttons, one in the "off" and one in the "on" position	Referral? Referral?
Check box	Appears checked when on and unchecked when off; you can use check box controls within an option group	☑ Paid?
Command button	Executes a command or macro when clicked; Access supplies over 30 different types of command buttons with the Command Button Wizard, such as record and form navigation command buttons	
Option group	Displays a limited set of alternatives; you can select only one option button in an option group at a time	○ Single ○ Double

Access 97

Adding Toggle Buttons

Toggle buttons are another type of bound control that is commonly used for fields with Yes/No data types. The toggle button appears on the screen in a "raised" (off) or "pressed down" (on) position. When you want to give the user the look and feel of pressing a button on the screen, the toggle button control is appropriate. ➤ Rachel needs to develop a customer service form for the marketing department to record whether the customer wants to receive product information through telemarketing or mail campaigns. She has already added two Yes/No data type fields to the Customers table—Telemarketing? and Mail?—and now builds a form with toggle button controls for each of these fields to record the customers' preferences on this type of corporate communication.

1. Click the **Forms tab**, click **New**, click **Form Wizard**, click the **Choose the table or query where the object's data comes from: list arrow**, click **Customers**, then click **OK**
   You want all of the fields on the Customers table on the final form. Use the Evergreen style, and give the new form the descriptive title of "Customer Marketing Form."

2. Click the **Select All Fields button** `>>`, click `Next >`, click **Columnar**, click `Next >`, click **Evergreen**, click `Next >`, type **Customer Marketing Form** in the text box, then click `Finish`
   The final form is shown in Figure K-7. The two new Yes/No fields, Telemarketing? and Mail?, are shown on the form as check boxes. Open the form in Form Design View, delete the check box controls, and add the two fields to the form as toggle buttons.

3. Click the **Design View button** on the Form View toolbar, click the **Telemarketing? check box**, press and hold **[Shift]**, click the **Mail? check box**, then press **[Delete]**
   Widen the form to make room to add the Yes/No fields to the form as toggle buttons.

4. Position the mouse pointer on the **right edge of the form** so that it changes to a ↔, then drag it to the 5" mark on the ruler.
   Now add the fields to the form by dragging the fields from the field list.

5. Click the **Field List button** on the Form Design toolbar, click the **Toggle Button button** on the Toolbox, click **Telemarketing?** in the field list window, then drag the **Telemarketing? field** to the upper-right side of the form between the 3" and the 4" mark on the ruler, as shown in Figure K-8
   Add a label to the toggle button on the form. Click the selected button and type the text.

6. Click the **toggle button**, then type **Should we call?**
   Next, add the Mail? field in the same manner. The field list window is still open.

7. Click on the Toolbox, click **Mail?** in the field list window, then drag the **Mail? field** to just below the Should we call? toggle button
   Add a descriptive label to the second toggle button.

8. Click the second **toggle button**, type **Should we mail?**, click on the Form Design toolbar to close the field list window, click the **Save button**, then click the **Form View button** on the Form Design toolbar
   The final form should look like Figure K-9. Click both new toggle buttons to record Yes entries in the Telemarketing? and Mail? fields for Ginny Braithwaite's customer record.

9. Click the **Should we call? toggle button**, click the **Should we mail? toggle button**, then press **[Page Down]** to move to the second customer in the database
   The default value for the Yes/No field is No. In this case this value results in a toggle button that does not appear to be pressed.

Trouble?

Be sure to click the Toggle Button button first, then drag the Telemarketing? field to the form. If you perform these steps in the opposite order, the Toggle Button control might not be bound to the Telemarketing? field.

Time To

✔ Save
✔ Close the form

FIGURE K-7: Customer Marketing Form

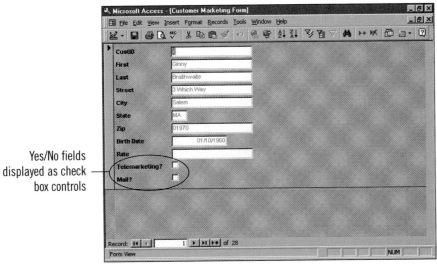

Yes/No fields
displayed as check
box controls

FIGURE K-8: Telemarketing? field added as a toggle button

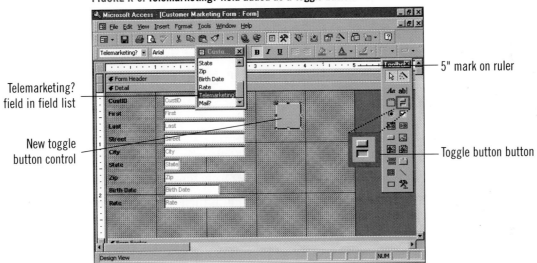

Telemarketing?
field in field list

New toggle
button control

5" mark on ruler

Toggle button button

FIGURE K-9: Customer Marketing Form with toggle buttons

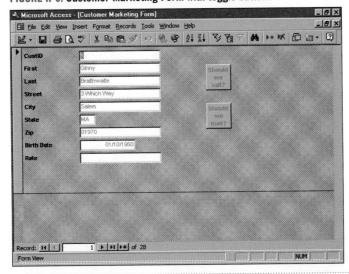

ADDING COMPLEX OBJECTS TO A FORM

Adding Command Buttons

A **command button** is a control that when clicked, immediately executes a command or a macro. A **macro** is a predefined series of commands that perform a specific task. Access supplies over 30 different command buttons that you can access with the **Command Button Wizard**. For example, the Command Button Wizard can help you put buttons on a form that add, delete, or print the current record. When clicked, the command button control executes the command it represents. If clicked twice, the command button executes the command twice. The toggle button control is usually bound to an underlying Yes/No field and therefore acts as an on/off switch. If clicked twice, the toggle button changes the data in the underlying field from "no" to "yes" and then back to "no." ✐ The Nomad travel department has asked Rachel to create an easy-to-use form for entering new tours. First, Rachel uses the Form Wizard to create a Tour Entry form then she uses Access-supplied command buttons to give users a way to add a new record.

1. Click the **Forms tab** if necessary, click **New**, click **Form Wizard**, click the **Choose the table or query where the object's data comes from: list arrow**, click **Tours**, then click **OK**

   You need all the fields of the Tours form. Because you want the users to have attractive screens to view while working, you select the Clouds style. You name the form "Tour Entry Form."

2. Click the **Select All fields button** `>>`, click `Next >`, click **Columnar**, click `Next >`, click **Clouds**, click `Next >`, type **Tour Entry Form** in the text box, then click `Finish`

   The new Tour Entry Form opens in Form View as shown in Figure K-10. The wizard does a great job, but you have to make a few modifications. Switch to Form Design View and widen the form.

3. Click the **Design View button** on the Form View toolbar, position the mouse pointer on the **right edge** of the form, then drag ✛ to the 5" mark on the ruler

   With the form widened, you have plenty of room to add a command button to help the user add new a record. You decide to use the Control Wizard to help add the control.

4. Verify that the **Control Wizards button** on the Toolbox is selected, click the **Command button** on the Toolbox, then click below the 3" mark toward the upper-right side on the form

   The Command Button Wizard dialog box opens, as shown in Figure K-11. Adding and printing records are record operation actions.

5. Click **Record Operations**, click **Add New Record**, then click `Next >`

   Next, the Command Button Wizard asks whether you want to display the button with text or with a picture. Choose an appropriate picture and complete the wizard.

6. Verify that the **Picture option button** is selected, click **Pencil (editing)**, click `Next >`, type **Add New Record Button** in the text box, then click `Finish`

   When satisfied with the look and placement of the button, switch to Form View and test the button by adding a new tour to the database.

7. Click the **Form View button** on the Form Design toolbar, click the **Add Record command button**, then enter the following new tour information:

Tour ID	TourName	TourDate	Price	Cost	Handicap	Difficulty
Ragb0798	Ragbrai	7/16/98	$150	$50	no	1

   The completed form is shown in Figure K-12. The new tour form makes data entry easy.

Trouble?

If the Command Button Wizard dialog box does not open, delete the command button control you just added to the form, click the Control Wizards button on the Toolbox to make sure that the button is toggled on, then repeat step 4.

Time To

✔ Save
✔ Close

FIGURE K-10: **Tour Entry Form**

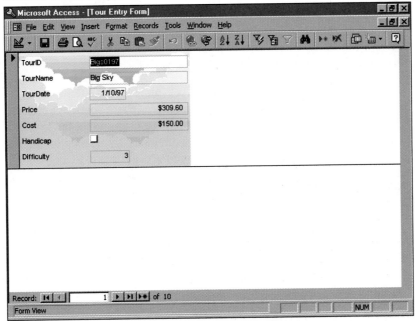

FIGURE K-11: **Command Button Wizard**

Sample of the command button picture for the action chosen

Action categories

Actions within each category

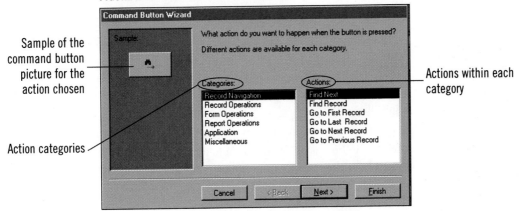

FIGURE K-12: **Tour Entry Form with command button**

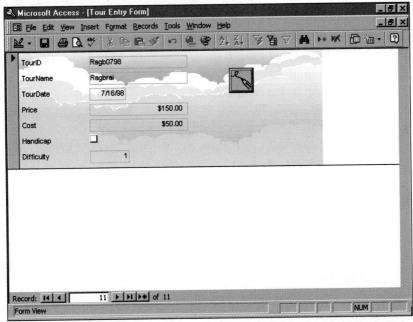

Adding Option Groups

An **option group** is a control used to display a limited set of alternatives for a single field. An option group consists of a **group frame** and option buttons, check boxes, or toggle buttons within the frame. The group frame is usually bound to an underlying field, and the buttons within the frame represent a limited set of numeric values that the field can hold. Only one option button within a group frame can be selected at a time. ✏ The accounting department decides to implement a new tour pricing policy that gives loyal customers a discount when purchasing additional tours. Rachel added a field called Rate to the Customers table to handle this data. The Rate field holds only one of three values (1, 2, or 3) identifying whether the customer is a "Preferred" (1), "Normal" (2), or "Late-Paying" (3) customer. First, Rachel creates an option group in the customer entry form to represent the Rate field. Later, she adds option buttons inside the option group control to represent these three values.

1. **Click the Forms tab if necessary, click New, click Form Wizard, click the Choose the table or query where the object's data comes from: list arrow, click Customers, then click OK**

   You need all the fields from the Customers form. Use the Standard style, and name the form Customer Entry Form.

2. **Click the Select All Fields button [>>], click [Next >], click Columnar, click [Next >], click Standard, click [Next >], type Customer Entry Form in the text box, click [Finish], then maximize the form if necessary**

   The new Customer Entry Form opens in Form View as shown in Figure K-13. Next, switch to Form Design View, then widen the form to make room for the new control.

3. **Click the Design View button [⬚] on the Form View toolbar, position the mouse pointer on the right edge of the form, then drag ↔ to the 6" mark on the ruler**

   With the form widened, there is plenty of room to add an option group control on the right side of the form to help the user identify which rate each customer should receive. First, delete the existing Rate text box, then open the field list window.

4. **Click the Rate text box, press [Delete], then click the Field List button [⬚] on the Form Design toolbar**

   Next, add the Rate field to the form as an option group control.

5. **Verify that the Control Wizards button [⬚] on the Toolbox is toggled "off", click the Option Group button [⬚] on the Toolbox, click the Rate field in the field list, then drag the Rate Field from the field list window to the upper-right corner of the form near the 4" mark on the ruler**

   Now that the Rate field is added back to the form as an option group control, you modify it by making changes in its property sheet. First, make sure that the default value for the control is 1 and also specify the control to appear "sunken" on the form.

6. **Click the Properties button [⬚] on the Form Design toolbar, click the Data tab in the Option Group Rate property sheet, click the Default Value text box, type 1, click the Format tab, click the Special Effect text box, click the Special Effect list arrow, then click Sunken**

   Close the property sheet and field list, then view the control in Form Design View.

7. **Click [⬚] to close the property sheet, then click [⬚] on the Form Design toolbar to close the field list**

   Now that the Rate option group control is added to the form as shown in Figure K-14, you're ready to start adding option buttons inside it.

Trouble?

If the Option Group Wizard dialog box opens, or you get an error message that you do not have the Wizard installed, delete the option group you just added to the form, click [⬚] on the Toolbox to make sure it is toggled off, then repeat step 5.

FIGURE K-13: **Customer Entry Form**

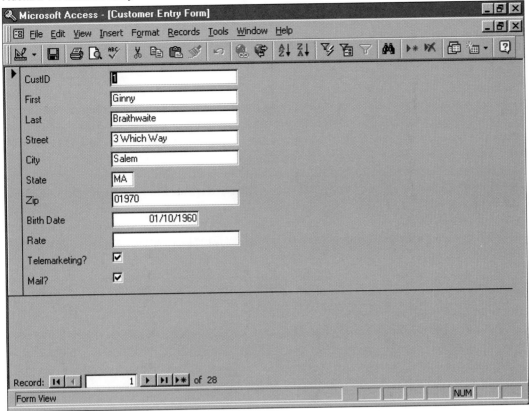

FIGURE K-14: **New Option Group in Form Design View**

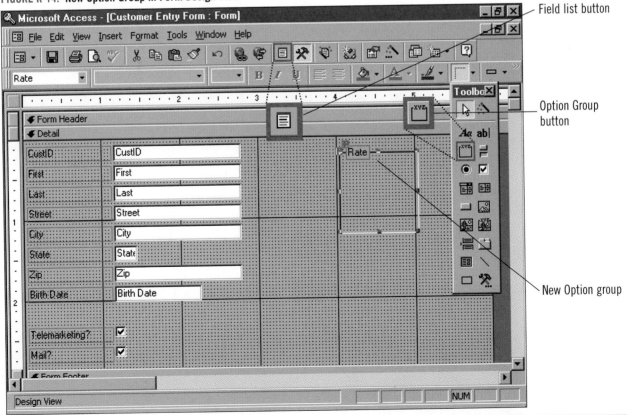

Field list button

Option Group button

New Option group

Adding Option Buttons

In the previous lesson, you added an option group to the form to represent the Rate field. If you use the advanced Option Group Wizard to add an option group control, you can create the Option Group and then automatically add the option buttons inside the group by answering the interactive questions presented by the wizard. However, you can add the option buttons separately, after the control for the option group is placed on the form. When used within an option group, option buttons are not bound to a field, but instead, represent a numeric value that the user can enter in the field to which the option group control is bound. ![arrow] Rachel isn't finished with the Rate option group control yet. Because the Rate field can contain three numeric entries (1, 2, or 3) the Rate option group must contain three option buttons to represent these values. In order to use the control to enter data into the Rate field, she adds three option buttons inside the Rate option group control and modifies their accompanying labels.

Steps

QuickTip

The name "Optionxx" where xx is a sequential number represents the number of labels on the form.

1. Click the **Option Button button** ⊙ on the Toolbox, then click in the upper-left corner of the Rate option group.
   When adding an option button to an option group, a label is automatically placed to the right of the button. The number on your screen might be different from that shown in Figure K-5. By default, option buttons represent the values of the order in which they are added to the form. The first option button added to the option group represents the number 1 when clicked in Form View. The second option button represents the number 2 when clicked, and so on.

2. Click the **Option25 label** to the right of the option button, click the **Properties button** 🖼 on the Form Design toolbar, click the **Format tab** if necessary, double-click the **Option25 label** in the Caption property text box, type **Preferred**, then click 🖼
   Next, add two more option buttons to the group below the "Preferred" option button.

3. Click the **Option Button button** ⊙ on the Toolbox, click below the **Preferred option button**, click ⊙ again, then click in the **option group** below the second option button
   With the three option buttons in place, change the Caption properties of the accompanying labels on their respective properties sheets to identify what each option button represents.

4. Click the **Option26 label** to the right of the second option button, click 🖼, click the **Format tab** if necessary, double-click the **Option26 text** in the Caption property text box, type **Normal**, click the **Option27 label**, double-click the **Option 27label** in the Caption property text box, type **Late**, then click 🖼
   The screen should look like Figure K-16. It's difficult to precisely place controls in alignment when using the mouse. Align the option buttons and then the accompanying labels with respect to each other.

5. Click the **first option button**, press and hold [Shift], click the **second option button**, click the **third option button**, release [Shift], click **Format** on the menu bar, point to **Align**, then click **Left**
   Now that the option buttons are precisely aligned, do the same to the accompanying labels.

6. Click the **Preferred label**, press and hold [Shift], click the **Normal label**, click the **Late label**, release [Shift], click **Format** on the menu bar, point to **Align**, then click **Left**
   Test the form by recording Late in Virginia Rodarmor's record.

Time To

✔ Save

7. Click the **Form View button** 🖽 on the Form Design toolbar, click the **Next Record navigation button** ▶ to move to record 2, then click the **Late option button**
   Your screen should look like Figure K-17.

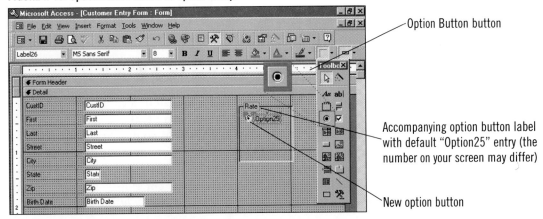

FIGURE K-15: Option Button added to Option Group

Option Button button

Accompanying option button label with default "Option25" entry (the number on your screen may differ)

New option button

FIGURE K-16: New Option Buttons and labels

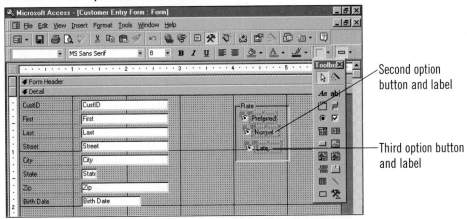

Second option button and label

Third option button and label

FIGURE K-17: Three option buttons in the Rate Option Group

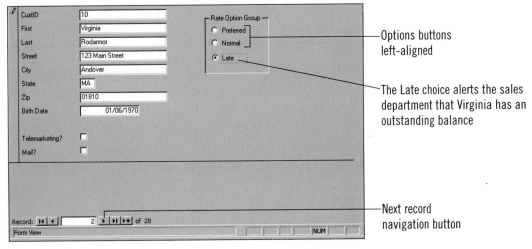

Options buttons left-aligned

The Late choice alerts the sales department that Virginia has an outstanding balance

Next record navigation button

CLUES TO USE

Considerations when adding option buttons to option groups

Each option button added to an option group contains a default option value property that corresponds to the order in which the button was added to the group. For example, the third option button added to the option group contains the value of 3 in its option value property. This means that when clicked, the third option button enters a 3 in the field bound to the surrounding option group. You can change this property to any numeric integer between -2 billion to +2 billion by accessing the option button's property sheet in Form Design View and changing the option value property on the Data tab to the value desired.

Creating Custom Help for a Form

You can create several types of custom Help for a form or a control on a form. If you want to display a tip that pops up over a control when you point to it, use the **ControlTip Text** property for that control. Or, use the **Status Bar Text** property to display helpful information about a form or control in the status bar. Although the accounting department understands the purpose for and choices available in the Rate option group, other Nomad employees have had questions regarding which option to choose when entering a new customer. Rachel adds ControlTip and status bar Help text to the control to clarify its purpose.

Steps

Trouble?

Be sure to click the option group frame to access the properties for the option group itself. You know that you've selected the right control if the property sheet title bar displays "Option Group."

1. Click the **Design View button** 📐 on the Form View toolbar, click the **Rate Option Group control**, then click the **Properties button** 🗐 on the Form Design toolbar

The property sheet for the option group opens. The Status Bar Text and ControlTip Text properties are found on the Other tab.

2. Click the **Other tab**, click the **Status Bar Text property text box**, then type **Choose one option to identify the customer's tour rate status**

The screen should look like Figure K-18. First move the property sheet to the left side of the screen so that the three option buttons are visible. Then change the ControlTip Text property for the first of the three option buttons within the option group. Preferred-rate customers have 3 or more sales, and Normal customers have 1-2 sales.

Trouble?

Be sure to click the option button itself rather than the label to the right of the option button.

3. Drag the **property sheet title bar** to the left so that the three option buttons are visible, click the **Preferred first option button**, click the **ControlTip Text property text box**, then type **3 Sales = Preferred Rate**

With the first ControlTip in place, add descriptive tips to the second button.

4. Click the **Normal second option button**, click the **ControlTip Text property text box**, then type **1-2 Sales = Normal Rate**

Finish the ControlTips by adding the third tip to the last button.

5. Click the **Late third option button**, click the **ControlTip Text property text box**, then type **Overdue Accounts = Late Rate**

The change to the third option button is shown in Figure K-19. Close the field property sheet, then close the Toolbox.

6. Click 🗐, then click the **Toolbox button** 🛠 on the Form Design toolbar

Test the new tips in Form View by pointing to the four controls you have modified.

Time To

✔ Save
✔ Close

7. Click the **Form View button** 🖼 on the Form Design toolbar, click the **Next Record navigation button** ▶ twice to move to record 3 for Kristen Reis, then click the **Preferred option button**

Refer to Figure K-20. Notice the text in the status bar as well as the ControlTip Help text.

Adding extensive Help to a form

Add Help to any form or control and access it by clicking the What's This button ᴺ?, then clicking the control. Use a word-processing program to create the Help text, then save the file with a Rich Text Format file type. Compile the Help file with the Windows Help Compiler, then attach the file to the control using the control's Help properties (HelpFile and HelpContextID). The Windows Help Compiler is included with Microsoft Office 97 Developer Edition as well as other Microsoft programming products.

FIGURE K-18: Modifying the Status Bar Text property

This number may differ on your screen

"Option Group" in title bar of property sheet

The field list is a valuable reference and may be displayed while adding controls to the form if you choose

Rate option group is selected

Other tab

Status Bar Text property

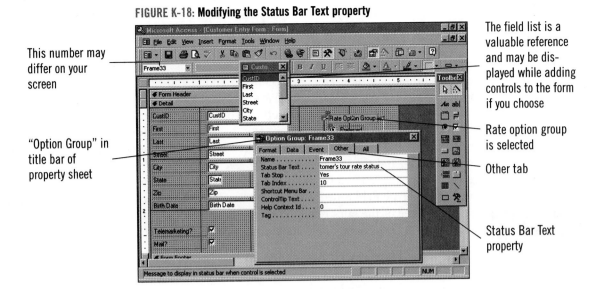

FIGURE K-19: Modifying the ControlTip Text property

This number may differ on your screen

ControlTip Text property

Third option button is chosen

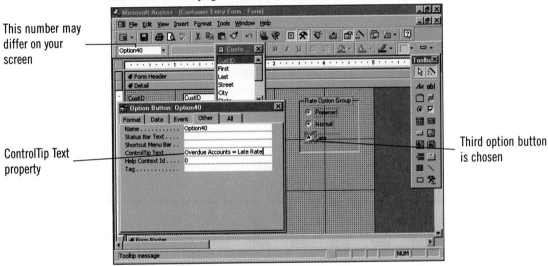

FIGURE K-20: Displaying Help text on a form

ControlTip Help text

Status Bar Help text

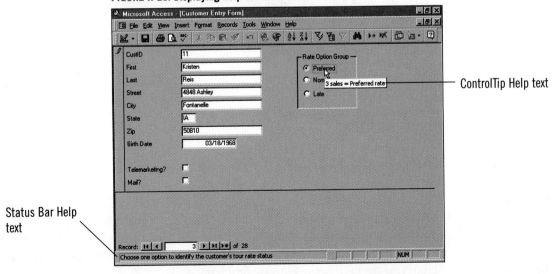

Access 97

Adding Pictures

Forms can display many types of pictures, including Microsoft-supplied clip art, scanned images, and bitmap files. The **OLE** (Object Linking and Embedding) field data type allows a field to store data such as Microsoft Word or Microsoft Excel documents, pictures, sound, and other types of binary data created in other programs. To insert in a form an OLE field such as a picture, you must add a **bound object frame** control to the form. Refer to Table K-2 for more information on the differences between the bound object frame control, the unbound object frame control, and the image control. ✎ In response to a sales contest, all Nomad sales representatives were asked to pick a sports team to represent themselves. For fun, Rachel added an OLE data type field called Team to the Reps table and inserted a bitmap image of the team logo into three of the sales representatives' Team fields. Now she needs to add a bound object frame control to the Sales Rep Data Form to display the chosen team for each representative.

1. **Click the Forms tab if necessary, click Sales Rep Data Form, then click Design**
   The Sales Rep Data Form opens in Form Design View. Add the bound object frame control, linked to the Team OLE field. You need the Toolbox and the field list window.

2. **Click the Toolbox button ✹ on the Form Design toolbar, if necessary click the Field list button ▣ on the Form Design toolbar, click the Bound Object Frame button on the Toolbox, click the Team field in the field list, then drag the Team field from the field list to the right side of the form**
   The screen should look like Figure K-21. The bound object frame control automatically expands to be large enough to display the entire bitmap of the first record.
   The Team label to the left of the bound object frame is unnecessary, so you decide to delete it.

3. **Click the Team label, press (Delete), click the Properties button 🖹 on the Form Design toolbar, click the Format tab, click the Size Mode property list arrow, click Zoom, then click the Properties button 🖹 to toggle off the property sheet**
   The **Size Mode** property controls the way the image appears within the bound object frame. **Clip** (the default) displays the object at the actual size. **Zoom** displays the entire object, resizing it without distorting its proportions. **Stretch** sizes the object to fill the control, and may distort its proportions if the frame has different proportions than the image.

4. **Click the Form View button ▣ on the Form Design toolbar**
   Your screen should look like Figure K-22. The team logos for three of the sales representatives are in the database. Move to the second and third records to view these teams.

Time To
- ✔ Save
- ✔ Close
- ✔ Exit

5. **Click the Next Record navigation button ▶ to move to record 2, which displays the Iowa State Cyclones logo, then click ▶ again to move to record 3, which displays the logo**
   When satisfied with your changes, save the form.

Linking versus inserting

When you insert an object in a form or report, Access stores the object in your database. If you modify the object, it is changed in your database file. For this reason, an inserted object is always available. On the downside, an inserted object is actually a duplicated object, totally separate from the original information, so changes made to one copy do not affect the other. When you link to an object, you can look at the object and make changes to it from your form or report, but there is actually only one copy of the object, and the changes are stored in the original object file (such as Word, Excel, or Paint), not in your database file. Linking to an object is useful for very large files that you don't want to include in your database file, and for files that you want to use in several forms and reports.

FIGURE K-21: Bound object frame added to the Sales Rep Data Form

Team field

Team label

— Image button

Bound Object Frame button

Unbound Object Frame button

Bound object frame control

FIGURE K-22: Sales Rep Data Form with the Team OLE field

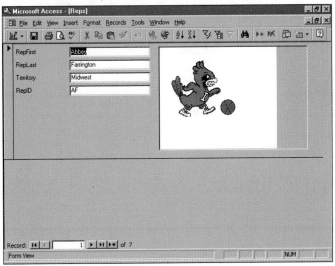

TABLE K-2: Differentiating between image controls

type of control	definition	could be used to
Image control	Adds a static picture to a form or report; an object added with the image control cannot be edited in Access	Add the corporate logo to the header section of a form or report; image controls not bound and therefore display the same image regardless of which record is displayed on the form
Unbound object frame	Adds a picture to a form or report that you expect to update frequently	Add to the footer section of a form or report an Excel graph or worksheet that summarizes current sales activity and therefore changes over time; because the unbound object frame is not bound to an underlying field, it remains the same regardless of which record is displayed; an unbound object frame can be linked or inserted on a form or report.
Bound object frame	Adds an OLE object field to a form or report	Insert an employee picture on a form that is stored as an OLE field in the underlying employee record; because the bound object frame is bound to an underlying field, it changes from record to record; a bound object frame can be linked or inserted on a form or report

ADDING COMPLEX OBJECTS TO A FORM

Practice

► Concepts Review

Identify each element shown in Figure K-23.

FIGURE K-23

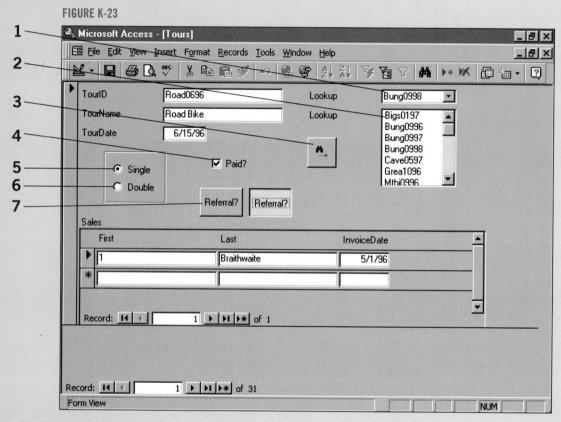

Match each term with the statement that describes its function.

8. A control that appears on the screen as a button that can be toggled on or off
9. A field data type that allows the field to store data such as documents, pictures, or sound clips
10. A control that, when clicked, immediately executes a command or macro
11. A control for adding an OLE object field to a form or report
12. A control that usually contains option buttons and is used to display a limited set of alternatives
13. When used within an option group, this control represents a numeric value that can be entered in the field bound to the option group
14. A control that presents a list of choices or allows the user to make an entry from the keyboard

a. Command button
b. Option group
c. Option button
d. Combo box
e. OLE data type
f. Toggle button
g. Bound object frame

Select the best answer from the list of choices.

15. Which of the following controls would you most likely use to represent a Yes/No field?
   a. Combo box
   b. List box
   c. Option group
   d. Check box

16. **The combo box control is a combination of which two controls?**
    a. List box and text box
    b. List box and check box
    c. Option group and check box
    d. Option group and option button

17. **Which control would most likely be used to execute a macro when clicked?**
    a. Check box
    b. Command button
    c. Option button
    d. Image control

18. **Which of the following types of data would you store in an OLE field?**
    a. Images
    b. Sounds
    c. Documents
    d. All of the above

19. **Which of the following controls would you most likely use to display a corporate logo at the top of a form?**
    a. Bound object frame
    b. Unbound object frame
    c. Option group frame
    d. Image control

20. **When using option buttons within an option group, what is usually bound to the underlying field?**
    a. The option buttons
    b. The option group frame
    c. The form itself
    d. Check boxes within the option group

21. **Which of the following is *not* a type of Help text you can add to a control?**
    a. Help Wizard text
    b. ControlTip text
    c. Status bar text
    d. What's This text

22. **The default values for three option buttons placed within an option group would be**
    a. Whatever values the first three records contain
    b. Whatever text you specify in the property sheet
    c. 1, 2, and 3
    d. Nonexistent, because option buttons do not have default values when placed within an option group

▶ Skills Review

1. **Add combo boxes**
   a. Start Access and open the Addresses-K.mdb database.
   b. Use the Form Wizard to create a form based on the Names Ascending query.

   c. Add the following fields to the form: First, Last, Street, Zip, and Birthday.

   d. Use a Columnar layout and a Standard style, and title the form "Name Lookup Form".

   e. Widen the form in Form Design View to the 5" mark on the ruler.

   f. Open the field list window if necessary and add the Last field to the upper-right corner of the form as a combo box using the Contol Wizard that finds records based on the value you select.

   g. Give the combo box the label "Name Lookup", then widen the label on the form so that it is clearly visible.

   h. View the form in Form View, look up the last name Dostart, then print the record.

   i. Save the form.

2. Add check boxes

   a. Return to Form Design View for the Name Lookup Form.

   b. Use the field list window to add the Pledge? field as a checkbox under the Last combo box control.

   c. View the form in Form View, look up the Hennigraf record, then print the record.

   d. Save the form.

3. Add toggle buttons

   a. Return to Form Design View for the Name Lookup Form.

   b. Use the field list window to add the Reunion field as a toggle button below the Pledge? check box on the right side of the form.

   c. Enter the caption "Attending Reunion?" to the command button.

   d. Resize the command button to display the caption clearly.

   e. View the form in Form View, look up the Brayton record, then print the record.

   f. Save the form.

4. Add command buttons

   a. Return to Form Design View for the Name Lookup Form.

   b. Lengthen the form to the 3" mark on the vertical ruler.

   c. Add a command button control using the Control Wizard below the Birthday text box that prints a record, using the picture option for the button.

   d. The last question of the Command Button Wizard asks you to give a name to the button. Label the control "Print Command Button".

   e. View the form in Form View, look up the "Baker" record, then use the new command button to print the record.

   f. Save the form.

5. Add option groups

   a. Return to Form Design View for the Name Lookup Form.

   b. Open the field list window and add the Level field as an option group to the bottom-middle section of the form, just to the right of the print command button. Note: These steps assume you do not have the Option Group Wizard installed.

   c. Open the Option Group's property sheet and make sure that the following properties are entered: Format tab: Special Effect=Shadowed; Data tab: Contol Source=Level; Default Value=1. Change the label at the top of the option group to "Level of Giving."

   d. View the form in Form View, look up the "Boysen" record, then use the print command button to print the record.

   e. Save the form.

6. Add option buttons
a. Return to Form Design View for the Name Lookup Form.
b. Add three option buttons to the option group. The labels to the right of the option buttons should be named "Gold Club", "Silver Club", and "Bronze Club" respectively.
c. Align the option button controls with each other (if necessary) within the "Level of Giving" option group.
d. View the form in Form View, look up the first "Brayton" record, then print the record.
e. Save the form.

7. Create custom Help for a form
a. Return to Form Design View for the Name Lookup Form.
b. Open the Level of Giving option group's property sheet and click the Other tab.
c. Enter "Choose the appropriate scholarship contribution pledge" in the Status Bar Text property.
d. Open the Gold Club option button's property sheet and enter "$1,000 and above" in the ControlTip Text property.
f. Open the Silver Club option button's property sheet and enter "$500 to $999" in the ControlTip Text property.
g. Open the Bronze Club option button's property sheet and enter "$1 to $499" in the ControlTip Text property.
h. View the form in Form View, look up the Iceberg record, make sure that the status bar and ControlTip text properties work, then print the record.
i. Save the form.

8. Add pictures
a. Return to Form Design View for the Name Lookup Form.
b. Add the Profession field to the lower-right corner of the form as a bound object frame control.
c. Move the Profession label so that all of the controls fit on the form without overlapping.
d. View the form in Form View, look up the first Brayton record, then print the record.
e. Save and close the form.
f. Close the Addresses-K.mdb database.
g. Exit Access.

▶ Independent Challenges

If you complete all of the exercises in this unit, you may run out of space on your Student Disk. To make sure you have enough disk space, please copy the files Clubs-K, Readings-K, Doctors-K, Novell-K, and VW-K onto a new disk, and use the new disk to complete the rest of the exercises in this unit.

1. As the president of a civic organization, you have developed a database, Clubs-K, that tracks charitable clubs in your area. You need to develop a form with some complex objects to make it easy to enter new clubs into the database.
   To complete this independent challenge:

1. Start Access, then open the database Clubs-K.
2. Use the Form Wizard to create a new form based on the Clubs table.
3. Select the following fields for the form: Name, Street, City, State, and Zip.
4. Use a Columnar layout and a Pattern style.
5. Title the form "Club Entry Form".
6. Open the form in Form Design View, then widen the form to the 5" mark on the ruler.
7. Add to the upper-right corner of the form a combo box control that finds records based on the Name field.
8. Label the combo box "Club Lookup".

9. Widen the Club Lookup label so that it is entirely visible.

10. Open the Club Entry Form in Form View, use the Club Lookup combo box to find the Teen Helpers club, then print the record.

11. Return to Form Design View, then add the Nonprofit? field as a check box control immediately beneath the Club Lookup combo box.

12. Also in Form Design View, add the Affiliated? field as a toggle button control immediately below the Nonprofit? check box.

13. Add the caption "Affiliated with United Way?" to the Affiliated? toggle button.

14. Resize the toggle button so that the entire caption is visible.

15. View the form in Form View, look up the Jackson Jems record, then print the record.

16. Save the Club Entry Form, close the form, then close the Clubs-K database.

2. Now that you've developed a relational database, Readings-K, that documents the books you've read, you wish to create a form with a command button to help you add and print records faster, and an option group to give you three choices for a numeric rating of the book.

To complete this independent challenge:

1. Start Access, then open the Readings-K.mdb.

2. Use the Form Wizard to create a new form based on the Books table.

3. Select all fields, a Columnar layout, and a Stone style.

4. Title the form "Book Entry Form".

5. View the form in Form Design View, then widen the form to the 5" mark on the ruler.

6. Add a command button in the upper-right corner to print a record. The command button should display a picture of a printer and be called "Print Command Button".

7. Add a command button just below the Print Command Button to delete a record. The command button should display a picture of a toilet and be called "Delete Command Button".

8. Expand the bottom edge of the form to the 2.5" mark on the vertical ruler.

9. Delete the existing Rating text box and Rating label.

10. Add the Rating field to the form below the Author Number field as an option group.

11. Add three option buttons with the labels Great, Good, and Fair within the option group.

12. On the Data tab of the property sheet of the option group, set the default value to 1. Be sure the Contol Source property is the Rating field.

13. Change the label at the top of the option group to "Rating".

14. View the Book Entry Form in Form View and use the Delete Record button to delete the first record, *Rocks Are Great*.

15. Give the second book, *You and Rocks*, a Fair rating, then use the Print Record button to print the record.

16. Save the form, close the form, then close the Readings-K.mdb database.

17. Exit Access.

3. You have recently helped the medical director of a large internal medicine clinic put together and update a database, Doctors-K, that tracks extracurricular activities. You wish to create a program entry form that contains status bar and ControlTip Help text as well as a bound image control for the program's symbol.

To complete this independent challenge:

1. Start Access, then open the Doctors-K.mdb database.

2. Use the Form Wizard and the Programs object to create a new form.

3. Add the following fields: Name, State?, and Federal?.

4. Use a Tabular layout and a Flax style, and title the form "Outreach Programs Form".

5. View the form in Form Design View, then widen it to the 5" mark on the ruler.

6. Add the text "Does this program receive state aid?" to the Status Bar Text property in the State? check box's property sheet. The Status Bar Text property is on the Other tab.

7. Add the text "Does this program receive federal aid?" to the Status Bar Text property in the Federal? check box's property sheet.

8. Add the text "Type complete program name" to the ControlTip Text property in the Name text box control's property sheet.

9. Add the Symbol field as a bound object frame control to the right side of the Detail section of the form.

10. Move the Symbol label as necessary so that no controls on the form overlap.

11. View the form in Form View and print the Elderly Outreach record.

12. Save and close the Outreach Programs form and close the Doctors-K database.

13. Exit Access.

4. The college campus has hired you to build a database of worldwide vendor contact numbers. The database will enable campus personnel to search for vendor telephone numbers across the world at any time. You already started the database, but haven't entered all the records yet. Connect with the Novell Web site, add several records to the database, then develop a form for easy data entry.

To complete this independent challenge:

1. Log on to the Internet, use your browser to go to http://www.course.com, click Student Online Companions, click the link for this text book, then click the Access link for Unit K.

2. Print the Novell: Education: Worldwide Contact List Web page that lists the countries and telephone contact information, then log off the Internet.

3. Open Novell-K.mdb.

4. Click the Forms tab, then use the Form Wizard to create a new form based on the Contact List table.

5. Select all the fields, use the Columnar layout, use the Colorful 1 style, then give the form the title "Contact List Form".

6. Enter Form Design View and widen the form to the 5" mark on the ruler.

7. Add to the upper-right corner of the form a combo box control that finds records based on the country chosen.

8. Name the label "Country Lookup" and widen as necessary.

9. Enter Form View, look up the Austria record, then print the record.

10. Change the Novell Toll Free? and Sylvan Toll Free? check boxes into toggle buttons by right-clicking the check boxes in Form Design View.

11. Add the caption "Yes/No" to each toggle button and resize them to fit within the current space on the form.

12. Enter Form View, then print the Austria record.

13. Enter at least three new records into the Contact List Form. Pay particular attention to the Yes/No fields that indicate whether the telephone calls are toll free.

14. Save the form.

15. Exit Access.

▶ Visual Workshop

Open the VW-K database and create the form shown in Figure K-24. Use the Form Wizard based on the Alumni/Donations query, select all the fields, view the data by alumni, choose a Tabular layout, use the International style, then accept the default titles.

FIGURE K-24

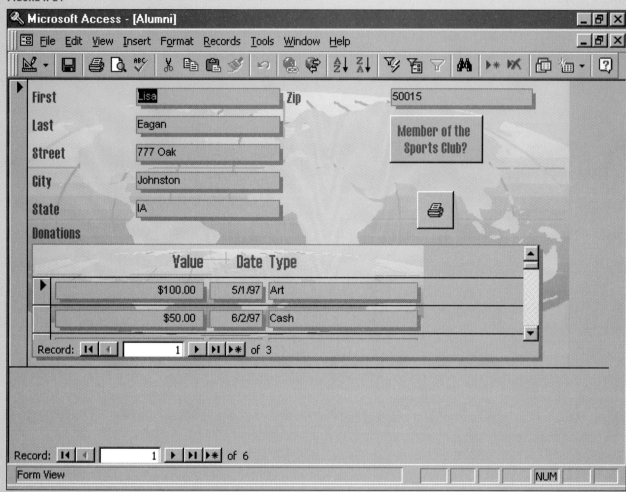

Managing
Database Objects

Objectives

- ► **Copy database objects**
- ► **Rename database objects**
- ► **Delete database objects and compact the database**
- ► **Use the Documenter**
- ► **Print the Relationships window**
- ► **Create a switchboard**
- ► **Modify a switchboard**
- ► **Change startup options**

Once you've developed a working database with several table, query, form, and report objects, it is critical that you protect your company's data and hard work. While many people may use, update, and enter data, it is often the task of a **database manager** to change or add objects. For example, a database manager might create and test queries or reports in a "test" database, then copy them to the database they use for the business. Other database manager activities include documenting and securing the database. In this unit, you learn how to create paper documentation for the entire database as well as create a **switchboard**, an opening form that gives the user access to only those objects that he or she actually uses. As the information in Nomad's database has become more valuable throughout the company, Rachel Best's duties and responsibilities have grown as well. Rachel now develops new objects in a test database, and copies them to the production database when she knows they are ready. She has also developed extensive documentation of the Nomad database, and has created a switchboard form to protect and enhance the database.

Copying Database Objects

Access allows you to copy objects from one database to another using simple copy and paste commands. Access features an application window that allows you to have only one file open at a time. You cannot copy information from one document to another without loading the application program twice. Although the Window menu option of Access doesn't allow you to switch between open files, it allows you to switch between open objects of the current file, the database.

Steps Rachel has been asked to create a quick printout of fields from several tables. She uses a test database called Nomad-Test to create the query, and then copies the query and pastes it into the production database, Nomad-L.

1. **Start Access, open Nomad-Test, click the Queries tab, click New, click Design View, then click OK**
   The Show Table dialog box opens with the new query window. The research department has requested information showing the number of tours sold and profit by state to start analyzing whether new campaigns should be targeted based on geographic factors. To find this information, you need access to fields from the State, Customers, Sales, and Tours tables.

2. **Double-click States, double-click Customers, double-click Sales, double-click Tours, then click Close**
   The specific fields required to answer this question include StateName from the States table, TourID from the Sales table, and a calculated Profit field based on data from the Tours table.

3. **Double-click StateName in the States table, double-click TourID in the Sales table, click the Field cell of the third column in the query design grid, type Profit:[Price]-[Cost], then maximize the query datasheet window**
   Figure L-1 shows the grid with the formula. While no fields are specifically used from the Customers table, the table is still required in the query to provide a link to the States table, which contains the entire state name in the StateName field. The query also has to summarize the data by TourID within StateName. Add the Total row to the query design grid and sum on the Profit field.

4. **Click the Totals button [Σ] on the Query Design toolbar, click the Profit field cell of the Total row, click the Group By list arrow, then click Sum**

5. **Click the Datasheet View button [▦] on the Query Design toolbar**
   The datasheet shows the total profit for sales grouped by TourID within StateName; see Figure L-2. The Profit field summarizes the profit for all TourIDs sold within that StateName.

6. **Click the Save button [💾], type Research Query in the Query Name text box, click OK, click File on the menu bar, then click Close to close the datasheet**
   The Research Query object, with 24 records, appears selected on the Queries tab of the Nomad-Test Database window. Next, copy and paste the query into the Nomad-L database.

7. **Click the Copy button [▣], click Start on the Taskbar to start a second version of Access, open the Nomad-L database, click the Paste button [▣], type Research Query in the Query Name text box, then click OK**
   To make sure the query was copied successfully, open it in Datasheet View to verify that the same 24 records appear.

8. **Double-click Research Query on the Query tab**
   The datasheet displays 24 records. Close the datasheet and close the extra Access application window. From now on, the lessons require only one Access window with the Nomad-L database.

Time To
- ✔ Close the datasheet
- ✔ Close the Nomad-Test database
- ✔ Exit the second Access application
- ✔ Empty the Clipboard

FIGURE L-1: Query Design View

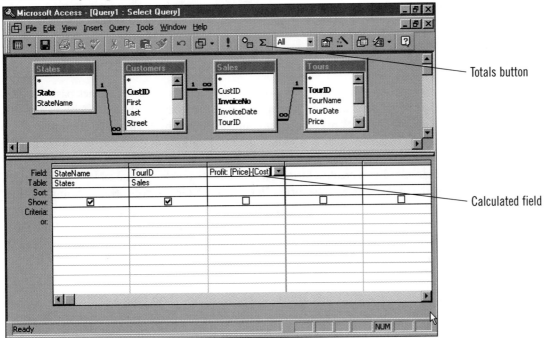

Totals button

Calculated field

FIGURE L-2: Datasheet View

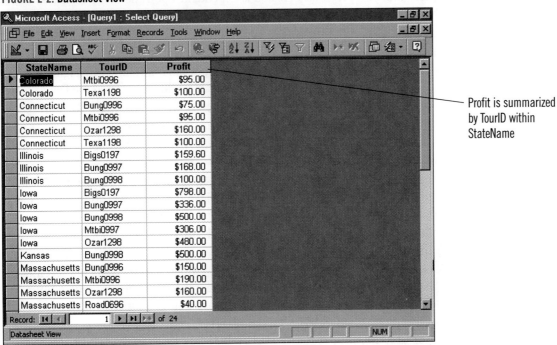

Profit is summarized
by TourID within
StateName

CLUES TO USE

Saving an object to an external file

To copy a database object to another file that is not currently open, click File on the menu bar, click Save As/Export, click To an External File or Database in the Save As dialog box, then choose the file to receive the object in the dialog box. Using this technique, you can save an Access database table to another file in one of many application formats: Microsoft FoxPro, dBASE, Paradox, Excel, Lotus, several text formats, or any program or database that supports the ODBC (open database connectivity) protocol.

Renaming Database Objects

While database managers may have extensive Access knowledge, they sometimes lack basic business process knowledge. When this happens, the database manager may build objects with names that appear clear and descriptive, but are complex or confusing to the user. Therefore, it's important to know how to rename database objects as well as the ramifications of doing so. If you rename an object, you also need to update any reference to the object in other database objects, such as forms or reports. For example, if you create a form that is bound to a table and the table's name changes, you also need to change the entry in the form's **Record Source** property. ◀▬▬ Nomad decides to offer more products than bicycle tours. The marketing department plans to call its products Events and has asked Rachel to update the name of the Tours table to Events and the Tour Entry Form to Event Entry Form. Rachel can do this, but she also has to change the references to the existing Tours table in other objects of the Nomad-L database.

Steps 1 2 3 4

1. **Click the Tables tab, right-click Tours, click Rename, then type Events**
   Although changing the name of a database object is relatively easy, you must also consider the effect this change has on every other object that is dependent upon the Tours table. The Research Query that you previously created is dependent upon the Tours table and therefore must be changed.

2. **Click the Queries tab, click Research Query, click Design, click OK to acknowledge the error message, then maximize the Query Design window**
   Query Design View opens displaying an empty Tours table as shown in Figure L-3. To restore the query, you must delete the empty Tours table field list and add the Events table.

3. **Click the Tours table title bar, press [Delete], click the Show Table button 📇 on the Query Design toolbar, double-click Events, then click Close**
   The Query Design View now displays the accurate table names in the upper portion of the screen, and the query is restored.

4. **Close the Research Query window, then click Yes when prompted to save the changes**
   In addition to changing the reference to the Tours table in the query, you also need to change the reference to the Tours table in the Tour Entry Form.

5. **Click the Forms tab, click Tour Entry Form, click Design, then click the Properties button 📰 on the Form Design toolbar**
   The form's property sheet opens. The Record Source property on the Data tab specifies the source of the underlying data for the form. The current value for the property is Tours, but since that table object was renamed Events, the Record Source property for this form currently points to a nonexistent object. Correct this error.

6. **Click the Data tab, click the Record Source text box if necessary, click the Record Source list arrow, then click Events**
   Figure L-4 shows the revised property sheet. Close the property sheet, then test the property change by opening the form in Form View to view the records within the form.

7. **Click the Properties button 📰 on the Form Design toolbar, click the Form View button 📰**
   The form has 13 records, as shown in Figure L-5. To give the form the name Event Entry Form, use the Save As/Export command from the File menu, then close the form.

8. **Click File on the menu bar, click Save As/Export, type Event Entry Form in the New Name text box, then click OK**

9. **Close the Tour Entry Form window**
   The database window shows both the original Tour Entry Form object as well as the new Event Entry Form object.

FIGURE L-3: Query Design View with the empty Tours table

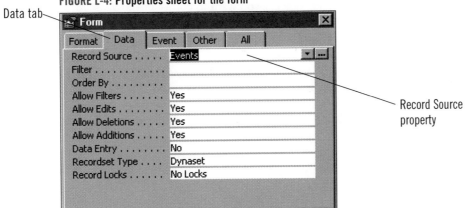

Empty Tours table

Show Table button

FIGURE L-4: Properties sheet for the form

Data tab

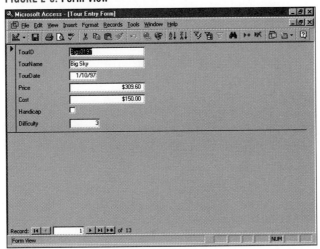

Record Source property

FIGURE L-5: Form View

CLUES TO USE

Guidelines for naming fields, controls, and objects

When developing a database, try to use descriptive yet concise and consistent naming conventions for fields, controls, and objects. The following rules apply: 1. Names can be up to 64 characters long. 2. Names can include any combination of characters except a period (.), an exclamation point (!), an accent grave (`), or brackets ([]). 3. Names can't begin with leading spaces, nor can they include control characters such as [Ctrl] or [Alt]. 4. Avoid using names that Access already uses as property names, such as Format, Control Source, Name, or Caption. While use of such names is allowed, this sometimes produces unexpected behavior or extra programming effort.

Deleting Database Objects and Compacting the Database

In a perfect world, you would never create a database object that wasn't first carefully designed on paper. To keep the wheels of progress moving forward, however, you often must create objects knowing that they will be heavily modified or deleted. End users are often unwilling to design a form or report from scratch, but are happy to critique an existing one. Once you've determined which objects will be used and which will be scrapped, you can quickly delete the unwanted objects. If you've deleted table objects, you want to **compact** the database to rearrange efficiently how the database file is stored on disk. ✒ Rachel used the Save As/Export command to save another copy of the Tours Entry Form quickly with the new name of Event Entry Form. Now that the new form has been successfully saved, she needs to delete the original Tours Entry Form to avoid any confusion created by the two form objects. Also, she found out that the Reps table is really unneeded, so she deletes the table and then compacts the database.

1. **Click the Forms tab**, if necessary, then right-click **Tour Entry Form**

   When you right-click an object in the database window, the menu shown in Figure L-6 appears listing the available commands. Notice that many of the commands are available as menu options (the Save As/Export command is also on the File menu), as toolbar buttons (the Cut and Copy commands are also buttons on the Database toolbar), as quick keystrokes (you can also invoke the Delete command by pressing the [Delete] key), or as buttons within the database window itself (the Open and Design commands are also buttons on the right side of the database window).

2. **Click Delete**, then click **Yes** when prompted to delete the form permanently

   The dialog box warns you that you cannot undo the deletion. The database window returns displaying only one form object, the Event Entry Form. Now delete the Reps table.

3. **Click the Tables tab, click Reps, press [Delete], then click Yes**

   With the two objects deleted, you're ready to close and then compact the **Nomad-L** database.

Trouble?

Don't close the entire Access application, only the Nomad-L database.

4. **Click File on the menu bar, click Close, click Tools on the menu bar, point to Database Utilities, then click Compact Database**

   The Database to Compact From dialog box opens, requesting information on which database to compact. First note the original size of the database, which is 208K.

5. **Click the Look in: list arrow to point to your Student Disk if necessary, click the Details button ▦, click Nomad-L.mdb, notice the file size in the dialog box, then click Compact**

   The Compact Database Into dialog box opens as shown in Figure L-7. You have to enter a filename for the compacted file. If you enter the same filename, you can overlay the original file with the new, compacted file.

6. **Type Nomad-L, click Save, then click Yes to confirm that you want to replace the original Nomad-L file with the compacted one**

   The status bar indicates that the file is being compacted.

7. **Click the Open button 🖿 on the Database toolbar, then click Nomad-L**

   The size of the Nomad-L file is now reduced, saving you valuable space on your disk.

FIGURE L-6: Right-clicking an object

FIGURE L-7: Compacting a database

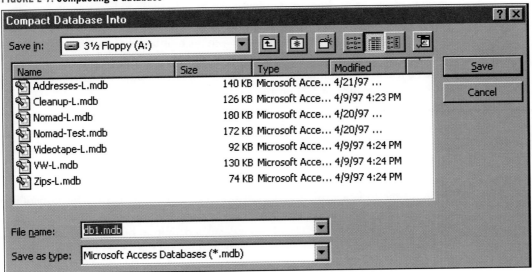

Undoing actions in Access

The Undo button's main purpose is to help you undo data-entry additions or changes. For example, you can click the Undo button 🔄 to remove any entry or change to the current record whether you are working in a datasheet or in a form. You can undo only your last action, so once you begin editing another record, the Undo button applies to that record. You *can't* undo actions that result in file saves to disk, such as changing and saving queries, forms, or reports in Design View, deleting objects, or renaming objects.

Access 97

Using the Documenter

There are several types of documentation that you may want to print and keep handy when working on an Access database. The Access **Documenter** feature prints the relationships between the tables and provides additional information about the linkage itself. The Documenter also allows you to print the property definitions of any or all of the objects of a database. These paper documents are very helpful when building objects based on fields from multiple tables, communicating the structure and design of the database to others, or analyzing and troubleshooting problems. Finally, the Documenter can save the definitions of any object as a table within the database or as an external file. ✎ Rachel is attending an Access database convention, and plans on sharing information about the Nomad database with various consultants. Instead of taking an expensive laptop and the entire database to the show, Rachel prints a few pages of critical documentation that she can share with the experts, but first she needs to make sure that the relationships between the tables are intact.

1. Click **Open** to open the Nomad-L database, click **Tools** on the menu bar, point to **Analyze**, then click **Documenter**

   The Documenter dialog box opens as shown in Figure L-8. It contains one tab for each object type as well as a tab titled Current Database and a tab titled All Object Types. You can print documentation for one or many objects by choosing them in the appropriate tab.

2. Click the **Current Database tab**, click the **Relationships check box**, click **OK**, then maximize the Print Preview window

   The documentation displays in Print Preview mode. As you scroll through the report, see Figure L-9, notice that all three relationships between the four tables of the database are documented, including the table names, linking field, type of link (one-to-many), and enforced attribute, which refers to the fact that in each of these linkages, referential integrity has been enforced.

3. Click the **Print button** 🖨 on the Print Preview toolbar

4. Click the **Close button** on the Print Preview toolbar

   Complete relationships information about the tables of your database is often referred to as the **database schema** and is extremely important when examining the relationships between the tables of your database. Without proper relationships between the tables, the other objects of your database may not provide consistent or accurate results. Therefore, the relationships printout is the most valuable piece of information regarding the design and integrity of your overall database. The Documenter feature can also provide detailed information about a particular object within the database. Next print a detailed definition of each of your table's properties. Some database experts call these detailed descriptions of the fields of a table a **data dictionary**.

5. Click **Tools** on the menu bar, point to **Analyze**, then click **Documenter**

   The Documenter dialog box opens, allowing you to choose what types of documentation you wish to view or print.

> **QuickTip**
>
> Click Select All to select all the options on my tab in the Documenter dialog box.

6. Click the **Tables tab** (if necessary), click the **Customers check box**, click the **Events check box**, click the **Sales check box**, click the **States check box**, then click **OK**

   The documentation displays in Print Preview mode as shown in Figure L-10. Not only does it include information about the properties of the table as a whole, the documentation also lists the properties of each field within the table. The documentation for the four tables prints on 14 pages. Before printing documentation for a large number of objects, you should click the Last Page navigation button to determine how many pages the printout comprises. Print the first four pages of the documentation and close the Print Preview window.

7. Click **File** on the menu bar, click **Print**, click **Pages option button**, type 1, press **[Tab]**, type 4, then click **OK**

8. Click the **Close button** on the Print Preview toolbar

FIGURE L-8: Documenter dialog box

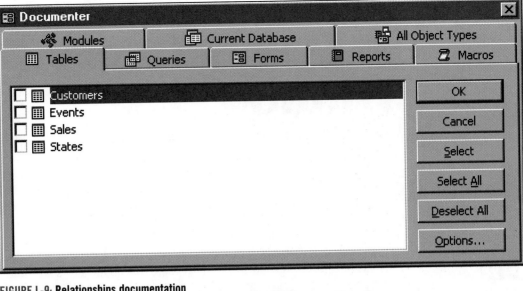

FIGURE L-9: Relationships documentation

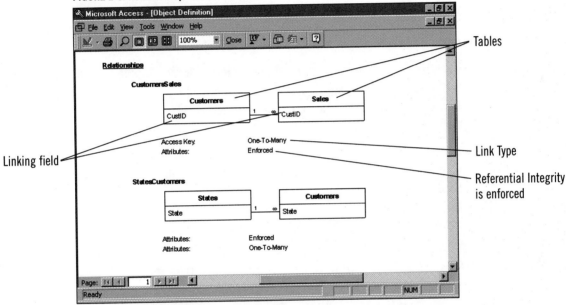

FIGURE L-10: Table definitions

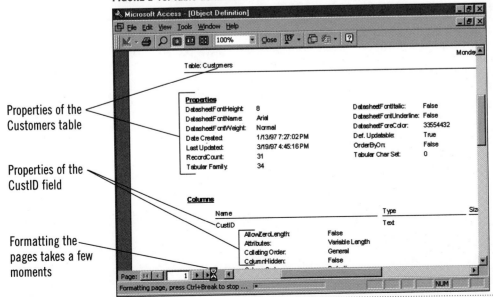

Printing the Relationships Window

While the Documenter feature is an excellent tool to view, print, or save the design characteristics of database objects, it doesn't provide an image of how the tables are linked together. This is shown in the Relationships window. To print this important picture, you can press the [Print Screen] key while viewing the Relationships window to place a copy of the screen on the Windows Clipboard, then paste the image into an image processing program such as Paint. After you paste the image to a program, you can print for easy reference. ➤ While the relationships documentation printed by the Documenter feature provides linkage information between the tables, Rachel also wants to print the Relationships window image to study and use at the Access trade show. First she opens the Relationships window and makes sure that all the tables are clearly displayed.

Steps 1 2 3 4

1. Click the **Relationships button** 🔗 on the Database toolbar
   The Relationships window opens, showing you three tables in the database and the relationship lines between them. Add the Events table to the window.

2. Click the **Show Table button** 🔲 on the Relationship toolbar, double-click the **Events** table, then click **Close**
   Resize the field lists so that all the tables in the database and all the fields within the tables are visible.

3. Drag the bottom edge of the **Events field list** down so that all the field names are visible, then drag the bottom edge of the **Customers field list** down so that all the field names are visible
   The screen should look like Figure L-11. See Table L-1 for information about the Relationships window and toolbar. With the screen arranged so that all the tables and fields are visible, you are ready to copy the screen image to the Clipboard.

4. Press **[Print Screen]** to place a copy of the screen image on the Clipboard
   Start the Paint program that is provided with Windows 95 as part of the Accessories package.

5. Click **Start** on the Taskbar, point to **Programs**, point to **Accessories**, then click **Paint**
   The Paint program opens.

6. Click **Edit** on the menu bar, click **Paste**, then maximize the Paint window if necessary
   The screen image of the Access Relationships window is pasted into the Paint program.

7. Click **File** on the menu bar, click **Print**
   The screen image prints as a single page. Since you can copy and paste the Relationships window at any time as fields or tables are added to the database, it isn't necessary to save the Paint file. Close the Paint file without saving it.

8. Click **File** on the menu bar, click **Exit**, then click **No**
   Close and save the Relationships window, then return to the opening Nomad-L database window.

9. Close the Relationships window, then click **Yes** when prompted to save the changes

QuickTip

You can delete extra field lists in the Relationships window by clicking the list, then pressing [Delete]. You can move the field lists by dragging their title bars.

FIGURE L-11: Relationships window

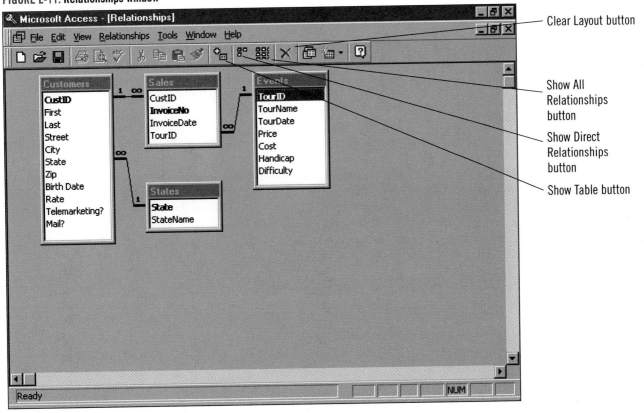

Clear Layout button

Show All Relationships button

Show Direct Relationships button

Show Table button

TABLE L-1: Buttons on the Relationship toolbar

button	name	description
	Show Table	Opens the Show Table dialog box, which allows you to add table or query objects to the Relationships window
	Show Direct Relationships	Shows only the relationships defined for the tables visible in the Relationships window
	Show All Relationships	Shows all the relationships defined in the database
	Clear Layout	Removes all tables and relationships from the Relationships window (but not from the database)

Creating a Switchboard

A **switchboard** is a special Access form that contains command buttons that open or print specified database objects such as forms and reports. Because a switchboard form can open immediately when the database opens, switchboards are created to give end users easy access to the objects they use, and shield users from the complexity of underlying objects they don't directly use, such as tables and queries. In this way, switchboards also provide a certain layer of security to a database, giving users access to only those objects they need. You can create switchboards through the **Switchboard Manager**. A database can contain more than one switchboard, and once created, you can modify the Switchboards in Form Design View. ▰▰▰ Nomad has hired a new employee in the Events department to add and enter events into the Nomad database. Unfortunately, he has no Access training. Rachel creates a switchboard with command buttons to add and update events using the Event Entry Form, the only object that he needs.

Steps

1. Click **Tools** on the menu bar, point to **Add-ins**, click **Switchboard Manager**, then click **Yes** when prompted to create a new switchboard

   The Switchboard Manager dialog box opens, displaying the switchboard pages within the database. Since this is your first switchboard, you need to edit and name the switchboard.

2. Click **Edit**, then click **New** to accept the default name of Main Switchboard

   The Edit Switchboard Item dialog box opens, prompting you to enter the name of the first switchboard button, the command that this button executes, and the name of the switchboard where this button should appear (there can be multiple switchboards). Your first switchboard button opens the Event Entry Form to add a new event.

3. Type **Add New Event** in the Text: text box, click the **Command: list arrow**, click **Open Form in Add Mode**, click the **Form: list arrow**, then click **Event Entry Form**

   Your screen should look as shown in Figure L-12. Add this command button to the switchboard, then add another button to open the Event Entry Form in edit mode.

4. Click **OK**, click **New**, type **Edit Existing Events** in the Text: text box, click the **Command: list arrow**, click **Open Form in Edit Mode**, click the **Form: list arrow**, click **Event Entry Form**, then click **OK**

   The Edit Switchboard Page dialog box now shows the two items you added to the switchboard as shown in Figure L-13. Change the name of the switchboard to Event Switchboard in case you wish to add more switchboard pages later.

5. Double-click **Main** in the Switchboard Name: text box, type **Event**, click **Close**, then click **Close**

   If you developed multiple switchboard pages, you could link them together. The Switchboard Manager dialog box would list each page and identify which page was the **default switchboard**, which appears when you open the database. Open and test the switchboard.

6. Click the **Forms tab**, then double-click **Switchboard**

   The Event Switchboard opens as shown in Figure L-14, displaying the two command buttons that you added in the Edit Switchboard Item dialog box. Next, test the buttons.

7. Click the **Edit Existing Events button**

   The 1998 Bungee tour has been enhanced to allow handicap access.

8. Press **[Page Down]** three times to move to the fourth record for the Bung0998 tour, then click the **Handicap check box**

   The button is working very well. Rachel is confident that the switchboard works well to enter and edit events.

9. Close the Event Entry Form

   The Event Switchboard reappears, ready to help you navigate to a different object of the database.

FIGURE L-12: **Edit Switchboard Item dialog box**

Text that displays
on the switchboard

Command button's
function

Object that the
command button
acts upon

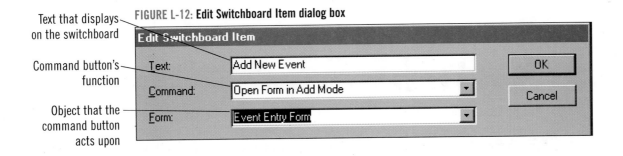

FIGURE L-13: **Edit Switchboard Page dialog box**

Command buttons
added to this
switchboard

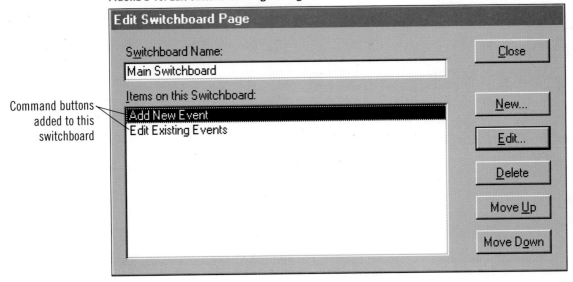

FIGURE L-14: **The Switchboard**

Command
buttons

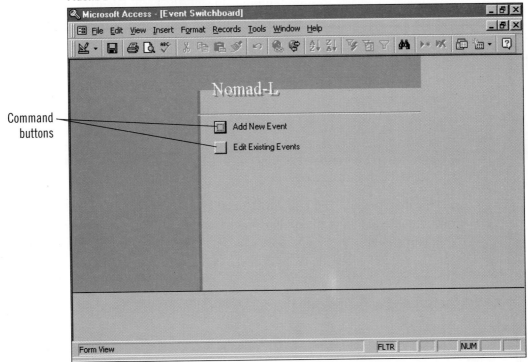

Modifying a Switchboard

As you've seen, a switchboard is a special form that allows quick and easy navigation through the objects of a database. You can modify switchboards in Form Design View to make formatting changes to unbound controls. Access documentation recommends that if you expect to customize the command buttons of the form extensively, however, it's better to create the switchboard form from scratch or use the Switchboard Manager to add or remove command buttons. ◆━━ Rachel wants to change the Nomad-L label at the top of the event switchboard, so she uses Form Design View to modify this unbound control. She also wants to use the Switchboard Manager to add a command button to the form that opens a report.

Steps

1. Click the **Design View button** 🖉, click the **Nomad-L label**, click the **Bold button** **B** on the Formatting (Form/Report) toolbar, then click the **Font/Fore Color button** **A** ▾ to make the label red
   Return to Form View to observe the change, then save the form.

2. Click the **Form View button** 📧, then click the **Save button** 💾

3. Close the switchboard form
   To add or modify the command buttons on the switchboard form, use the Switchboard Manager.

4. Click **Tools** on the menu bar, point to **Add-Ins**, click **Switchboard Manager**, then click **Edit**
   The Edit Switchboard Page dialog box opens, allowing you to add, delete, move, or edit the command buttons on the event switchboard. To add, delete, or edit buttons on a switchboard, it is much easier to use the Switchboard Manager than Form Design View. Use the Switchboard Manager to add a button that prints the Event Report.

5. Click **New**, type **Open Events Report** in the Text: text box, click the **Command: list arrow**, click **Open Report**, click the **Report: list arrow**, then click **Event Report**
   Your screen should look like Figure L-15. Finish adding the command button to open the Event Report, then change the order of the buttons on the switchboard so that the Open Tours Report button is first.

6. Click **OK**, click **Open Events Report**, click **Move Up**, then click **Move Up** again
   The Edit Switchboard Page dialog box should look like Figure L-16. Of the three command buttons, the first corresponds to the Open Events Report command. Close the dialog box, then view the modified switchboard.

7. Click **Close** to close the Edit Switchboard Page dialog box, click **Close** to close the Switchboard Manager dialog box, then double-click the **Switchboard object** to open it in Form View
   The modified Event Switchboard opens in Form View as shown in Figure L-17.
   When satisfied with your changes, save and close the switchboard.

8. Click the **Save button** 💾, then close the switchboard form

FIGURE L-15: **Adding a new button to the switchboard**

New command
added to the
Events Switchboard

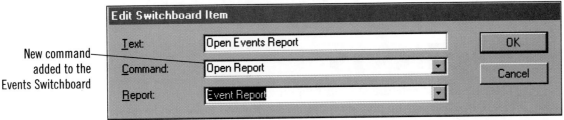

FIGURE L-16: **Changing the order of buttons on a switchboard**

Open Events Report
command will be
the first button on
the Event
Switchboard

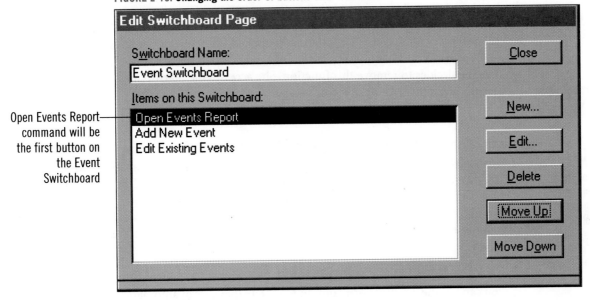

FIGURE L-17: **Final Event Switchboard**

New Command
button

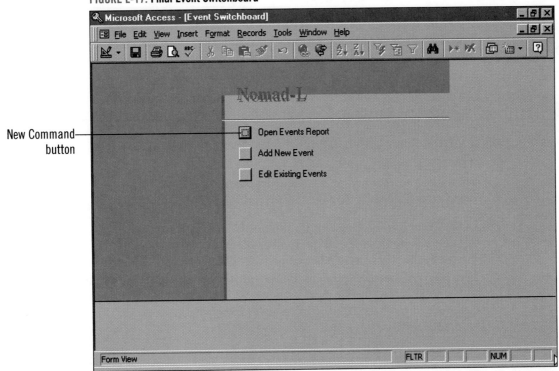

Changing Startup Options

There are several database **startup properties** that control what happens as soon as the database is opened. Startup properties are used mainly to make the database easier to use, and to protect it from improper modifications. For example, one of the most popular startup options is to specify that the default switchboard open automatically when the database opens. Other startup options specify what Access elements—such as the database window or status bar—are displayed, as well as what options you allow the user to modify, such as menu or toolbar changes.

Rachel wants to make sure that the default switchboard, the Event Switchboard, opens automatically when the Nomad-L database is opened. Also, one of her advanced users tried to create his own customized toolbar and inadvertently deleted the Save button from the Database toolbar. She decides to remove this function. She accesses the Startup dialog box and indicates her startup preferences to make these changes.

Steps

Trouble?

Be sure to uncheck the Allow Toolbar/Menu Changes option and *not* uncheck the Allow Built-in Toolbars option. Unchecking Allow Built-in Toolbars removes all Access-supplied toolbars from the screen.

1. Click **Tools** on the menu bar, then click **Startup**

The Startup dialog box opens as shown in Figure L-18. The Application Title and Application Icon options allow you to change the title and icon in the title bar. The four "Allow" check boxes at the bottom of the dialog box turn on and off database privileges such as allowing full use of all the menu options, or allowing the user to change toolbars and menu options. Remove the checks, which allow toolbar and menu changes, so that these items cannot be modified.

2. Click the **Allow Toolbar/Menu Changes check box** to remove the check

You can use the Display Form: option to specify that a form automatically display when the database is opened. Because switchboard forms contain only command buttons that allow you to navigate through the database, this option is often changed to "Switchboard" so that the default switchboard page automatically displays upon opening the database.

3. Click the **Display Form:** list arrow, then click **Switchboard**

Your Startup dialog box appears as shown in Figure L-19. Test the startup options by closing the Startup dialog box, closing Nomad-L, and then opening the Nomad-L database from your Student Disk. The changes to the Startup dialog box do not take effect until the database is closed, then reopened.

4. Click **OK**, click **File** on the menu bar, then click **Close**

5. Click the **Open button** 📂 on the Database toolbar, click the **Nomad-L database**, then click **Open**

You should be viewing the default switchboard, Event Switchboard, which you specified in the Startup dialog box. Test the toolbar modification startup change too.

6. Click **View** on the menu bar, then point to **Toolbars**

Because you disabled the Allow Toolbar/Menu Changes option in the Startup dialog box, the Toolbars option on the View menu isn't available to you within this database. Of course, you could recheck this option in the Startup dialog box, then close and reopen the database to restore this feature, but most users would probably think twice about modifying menu options and toolbars if they had to go to these lengths to do so. Done for the day, close Nomad-L and Access.

7. Click **File** on the menu bar, then click **Exit**

FIGURE L-18: Startup dialog box

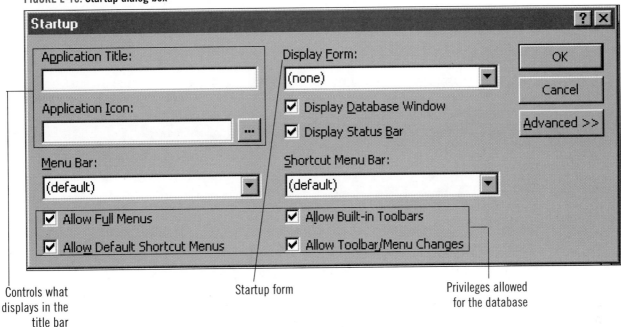

Controls what
displays in the
title bar

Startup form

Privileges allowed
for the database

FIGURE L-19: Startup dialog box after specifying changes

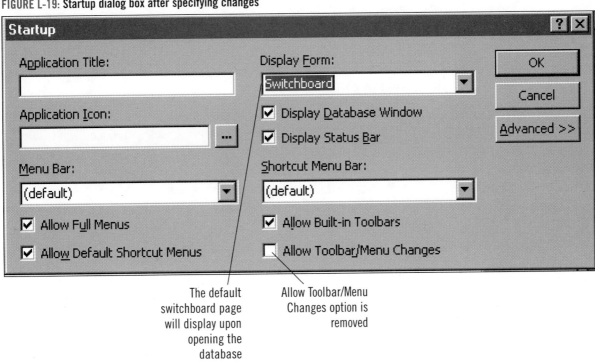

The default
switchboard page
will display upon
opening the
database

Allow Toolbar/Menu
Changes option is
removed

Practice

► Concepts Review

Identify each element shown in Figure L-20.

FIGURE L-20

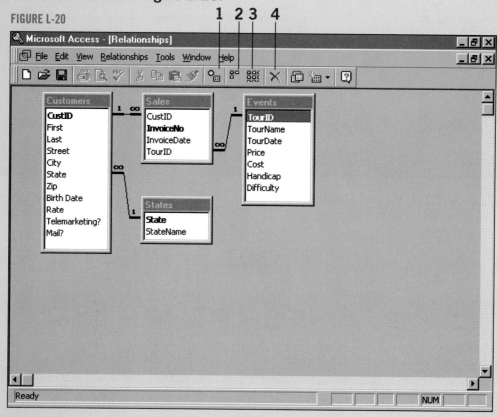

Match each term with the statement that describes its function.

5. A special Access form that gives the user access to only those objects needed

6. Options which control what happens as soon as a database is opened

7. The person who often modifies, adds, and creates database objects

8. Allows you to print object properties and relationship information about the database

9. Detailed descriptions regarding the fields of a table

10. Efficiently rearrange how a database is stored on disk

11. A feature that helps you create and edit switchboard pages

12. The switchboard that automatically displays when the database opens

13. Relationships information about the tables in your database

a. compact
b. Documenter
c. startup properties
d. switchboard
e. database schema
f. Switchboard Manager
g. default switchboard
h. data dictionary
i. database manager

Select the best answer from the list of choices.

14. **Which of the following is *not* one of the main jobs of a database manager?**
    a. Changing objects in an existing database
    b. Entering most of the data into a database
    c. Testing new objects in a database
    d. Developing new objects for a database

15. **Which property identifies the source of the underlying data for a form?**
    a. Source
    b. Table/Query
    c. Record Source
    d. Object Source

16. **Which of the following is *not* a valid name for a report in a database?**
    a. Lisa's Report
    b. 1997-1998 Crosstab Report
    c. Customer Profitability Report!
    d. $1,000 Orders Report

17. **You can find the Compact Database feature by clicking which menu option on the Tools menu?**
    a. Database Utilities
    b. Startup
    c. Option
    d. Security

18. **You can find the Documenter feature by clicking which menu option on the Tools menu?**
    a. Database Utilities
    b. Option
    c. Security
    d. Analyze

19. **Which key(s) do you press to put a copy of the entire current screen on the Clipboard?**
    a. [Alt][Print Screen]
    b. [Ctrl][Print Screen]
    c. [Shift][Print Screen]
    d. [Print Screen]

20. **In Access, how should you modify the command buttons on a switchboard?**
    a. in Form Design View
    b. using the Switchboard Manager
    c. using the Documenter
    d. using the Command Button Wizard

21. **Which of the following is *not* a startup option?**
    a. Allow Toolbar/Menu Changes
    b. Opening Display Form
    c. Display Database Window
    d. Allow Internet access

Skills Review

1. Copy database objects
   a. Start Access, then open Addresses-L.mdb.
   b. Open Zips-L.mdb into a second Access applications window.
   c. Click the NewZips table in the Zips-L database, then click the Copy button to place a copy of the NewZips table on the Clipboard.
   d. Switch to the Addresses-L database and click Paste. Name the table "NewZips" and be sure to paste both the structure and the data.
   e. Close the Zips-L.mdb database and the Access window.

2. Rename database objects
   a. Rename the NewZips table to "Zip Code."
   b. Open the Zip Code Form in Form Design View, open the property sheet for the form, then change the Record Source property on the Data tab to "Zip Code."
   c. Save the changes to the Zip Code Form, then close the form.

3. Delete database objects and compact the database
   a. Delete the Zips table.
   b. Delete the relationships between the Zips table and the other tables of the database. (Note: You will be deleting both the relationship between the Zips table and the Names table and the Zips table and the States table. In step 4c, you reestablish these table relationships with the new Zip Code table.)

4. Use the Documenter
   a. Open the Relationships window.
   b. Add all three tables to the Relationships window (if necessary).
   c. Drag the Zip5 field from the Zip Code table to the Zip field of the Names table. Enforce referential integrity.
   d. Drag the Abbreviation field from the States table to the State field of the Zip Code table. Enforce referential integrity.
   e. Click Tools on the menu bar, point to Analyze, then click Documenter.
   f. Click the All Object Types tab, then select Names, States, Zip Code, and Relationships chart boxes
   g. Click OK to preview the report. You should have built a 10-page report showing the data dictionaries documenting the Names, States, and Zip Code tables, as well as the database schema for the database.
   h. Print the first four pages of documentation, then close the Print Preview screen.

5. Print the relationships window
   a. Return to the Relationships window.
   b. If necessary, move and resize the field list windows so that the linking lines and field names within the windows are completely visible.
   c. Press [Print Screen] to capture a picture of the Relationships window on the Clipboard, then start Paint and click Paste.
   d. Print the Paint document that contains the image of the Access Relationships window, then close Paint without saving the changes.
   e. Return to the Addresses-L Relationships window and close the Relationships window, saving the changes.

6. Create a switchboard
a. Click Tools on the menu bar, point to Add-Ins, then click Switchboard Manager.
b. Edit the main switchboard page, and change its name to "Zip Code Switchboard."
c. Edit the Zip Code Switchboard and add the following command buttons to the switchboard:

Text	Command	Form
Add New Zip Code	Open Form in Add Mode	Zip Code Form
Edit Existing Zip Codes	Open Form in Edit Mode	Zip Code Form

d. Make sure that you specify the Zip Code Switchboard as the default switchboard in the Switchboard Manager dialog box.

7. Modify a switchboard
a. Add the following command buttons to the switchboard:

Text	Command	Report
Open Zip Code Report	Open Report	Zip Code Report

b. Move the Open Zip Code Report option button to the top item on the switchboard in the Edit Switchboard Page dialog box.

8. Change startup options
a. Click the Tools menu, then the Startup option to open the Startup dialog box.
b. Specify that the switchboard be the opening display form.
c. Remove the user's ability to allow toolbar or menu changes.
d. Close Addresses-L.
e. Reopen Addresses-L. You should be viewing the default switchboard startup form, the Zip Code Switchboard.
f. Click the Open Zip Code Report button, then print the three-page report.
g. Close the Zip Code Report.
h. Close Addresses-L and exit Access.

▶ Independent Challenges

1. As the outgoing president of a citywide civic organization, you have developed a database, Cleanup-L, that tracks deposits of recyclable materials to recycling centers by charitable clubs. The new president will be handling the database soon, and you wish to change some of the objects of the database before you step down.

To complete this independent challenge:

1. Start Access, then open the database Cleanup-L.
2. Rename the Clubs table "Organizations."
3. Rename the Club Entry Form "Organization Entry Form."
4. Change the Record Source property of the Organization Entry Form's property sheet to "Organizations," then save the form.
5. Open the Organization Entry Form in Form View, print the first record, then close the form.
6. Rename the Club Report "Organization Report."
7. Open the Organization Report in Report Design View and change the label in the Report Header from "Clubs" to "Organizations."
8. Change the Record Source property of the report's property sheet to "Organizations," then save the report.
9. Open the Organizations Report in Print Preview, then print and close the report.

10. Click the Substances table, then click the Copy button. Since you no longer need this table in the database, you delete it. First, however, you paste it to a Word document and print the records.

11. Open an empty Word document, click Paste, then print the image with the Substances table records.

12. Close Word without saving the changes to the document.

13. Return to Cleanup-L and delete the Substances table.

14. Close Cleanup-L.

15. Click Tools on the menu bar, click Database Utilities, then click Compact Database. Choose the Cleanup-L database on your Student Disk to compact, and name the final database Cleanup-L.

16. Complete the database compact and exit Access.

2. In addition to making the object name changes and deleting the Substances table from the Cleanup-L database, you wish to print documentation on the database schema and data dictionaries before you leave.
To complete this independent challenge:

1. Start Access and open the Cleanup-L database.

2. Click Tools on the menu bar, point to Analyze, then click Documenter to open the Documenter dialog box.

3. Click the All Object Types tab, then click each of the table objects as well as the Relationships check box to choose all of the data dictionaries and the database schema for your documentation report.

4. Preview, then print, the first five pages of the report.

5. Close the report, then open the Relationships window for the database.

6. Use the [Print Screen] technique to capture an image of the Relationships window on the Clipboard.

7. Open an empty Word document, click the Paste button, then print the image of the Cleanup-L Relationships window.

8. Close the Word document without saving changes, then return to Cleanup-L.

9. Close the Relationships window of Cleanup-L, saving the changes if prompted, then exit Access.

3. You've decided to add an opening switchboard form to the Cleanup-L database as your last contribution to the database.
To complete this independent challenge:

1. Start Access, then open the Cleanup-L.mdb database.

2. Click Tools on the menu bar, point to Add-Ins, then click Switchboard Manager to build the first switchboard for the database.

3. Edit the Main Switchboard, adding two new items to it as follows:

Text	Command	Form:/Report
Add Organizations	Open Form in Edit Mode	Organization Entry Form
Open Organization Report	Open Report	Organization Report

4. Name the switchboard Organization Switchboard in the Edit Switchboard Page dialog box, then make sure you identify it as the default in the Switchboard Manager dialog box.

5. Click Tools on the menu bar, then click Startup to open the Startup dialog box.

6. Choose Switchboard for the startup Display Form.

7. Close Cleanup-L to save the startup changes.

8. Open Cleanup-L. The switchboard should be displayed.

9. Click the Open Organization Report button, preview the report, and print the report.

10. Close the Organization Report as well as Cleanup-L, then exit Access.

4. You've volunteered at your local library to start a database called Videotape-L that tracks library videotapes. The library just gained access to all of the Discovery Channel's programs. You will go to the Discovery Channel's Web site, print today's program schedule, and add the records to your Videotape-L database. Once you've updated the database, you create a switchboard to make it easy for others to update the videotape records as well.

To complete this independent challenge:

1. Log on to the Internet and use your browser to go to http://www.course.com. From there, click Student Online Companions, click the link for the book you are using, then click the Access link for Unit L.

2. Click the Discovery Channel Program Schedules hyperlink, then print the schedule for today's programs.

3. Log off the Internet, start Access, then open Videotape-L.

4. Open the Series form, then add five of today's shows to the database. Notice that the form is a form/subform combination, and that the series title might already be entered into the database in the main form. The show times must be added in the 24-hour clock format to avoid confusing AM and PM showings. If the series title is entered, add only today's episode information in the subform. If the series title has not yet been added to the database, add both the series title as well as the episode information.

5. Create a switchboard with the following three items:

Text	Command	Form:/Report
Edit episodes	Open Form in Edit Mode	Series
Add new episodes	Open Form in Add Mode	Series
Open series report	Open Report	Series Report

6. Specify that the switchboard be the opening Display Form in the Startup dialog box.

7. Close Videotape-L to save the startup options.

8. Open Videotape-L to make sure that the switchboard is the opening form.

9. Preview and print the series report, close the report, then close Videotape-L, and exit Access.

▶ Visual Workshop

Open the VW-L database and create the switchboard shown in Figure L-21.

FIGURE L-21

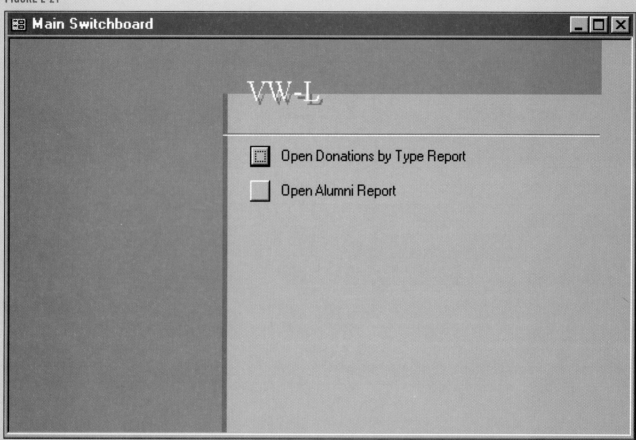

Creating Macros

Objectives

► **Understand macros**
► **Create a macro**
► **Add actions and arguments**
► **Create a macro group**
► **Set conditional expressions**
► **Assign a macro to a command button**
► **Customize toolbars with macros**
► **Troubleshoot macros**

A **macro** is a database object that stores Access actions which perform a particular task. When you run a macro, you execute the stored set of actions. A macro can automate almost any Access action such as printing a report, opening a form, or exporting data to a different file format. Any task that is repetitive and requires several clicks or keystrokes is a good candidate for a macro because automating routine and complex tasks builds efficiency, accuracy, and flexibility into your database. After using the Nomad database for some time, Rachel noticed that several tasks are completed on a regular basis and could be automated with macros. Although she hasn't worked with macros before, Rachel recognizes their benefits and is excited to get started.

Access 97

Understanding Macros

A macro may contain one or more **actions**, the tasks that you want Access to perform. When you **run** a macro, the actions execute in the order in which they are listed in the **Macro window**. Access provides a list of actions such as OpenTable or OpenForm for you to choose from as you create the macro. Think of actions as menu options you would choose or buttons you would click to get something done. Each action has a specified set of **arguments** which provide additional information on how to carry out the action. For example, if the action were OpenForm, the arguments would include specifying the Form Name, the View (Form or Design) in which you wish to open the form, and whether you want to apply any filters when you open the form. ◄━━━ Rachel is looking forward to building macros to automate the repetitive tasks of the Nomad database, but is somewhat overwhelmed by the new terminology surrounding this new database object. She decides to take a short course at the local college to help her understand this powerful feature. The final exam included three questions. Rachel's answers are summarized as follows:

Details

Identify the major benefits of using macros

- Save time by automating routine tasks.
- Increase accuracy by ensuring that tasks are executed consistently.
- Make forms and reports work together by providing command buttons that represent macros and that enable users to jump back and forth between the objects.
- Make the database easier to use by providing command buttons that represent macros to filter and find records automatically.
- Ensure data accuracy in forms by responding to types of data entry with different messages.
- Automate data transfers such as exporting data to an Excel workbook.
- Create your own customized working environment by automatically opening certain objects and customizing menu bars.

Define the following macro terminology

- **macro:** An Access object that stores a series of actions that perform a series of tasks.
- **action:** Each task that you want the macro to perform.
- **arguments:** Properties of an action that provide the action with additional information regarding how it should execute.
- **macro group:** An Access object that stores one or more macros together. The macros in a macro group run independently of each other. Macro groups are used to organize multiple macros that have similar characteristics, such as all the macros that print reports, or all the macros that are added as command buttons to a form. Macro group objects appear on the Macros tab of the Database window just as macros do.
- **expression:** A combination of values, identifiers (such as the value in a field), and operators that result in a value.
- **conditional expression:** An expression that is often used in a complex macro to make it behave differently based on the current situation. If the result of the conditional expression is true, a series of macro actions are executed. If the result of the conditional expression is false, the series of actions are not executed.
- **event:** Something that happens on a form, window, or datasheet—such as the click of a command button or a move from one record to another—that can be attached to or evaluated by a macro.

Identify the major components of the Macro window shown in Figure M-1. Refer to Table M-1 for a brief description of each component

FIGURE M-1: Macro window with several macros

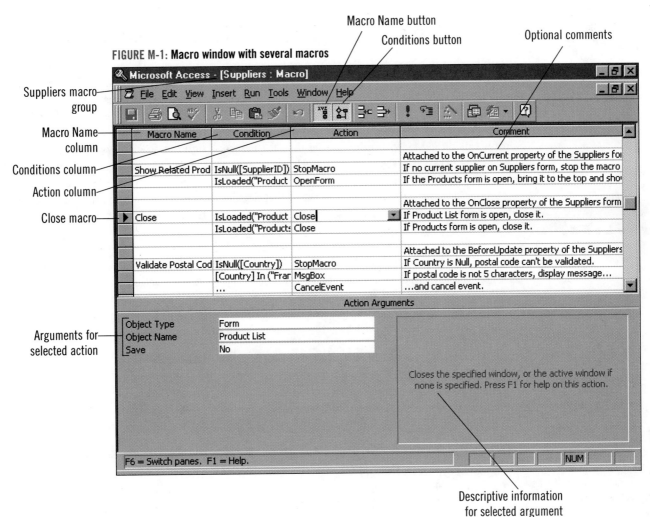

Macro Name button

Conditions button

Optional comments

Suppliers macro group

Macro Name column

Conditions column

Action column

Close macro

Arguments for selected action

Descriptive information for selected argument

TABLE M-1: Macro window components

component	description
Macro Name column	Contains several macros identified by their macro names. If you are developing a single macro, it isn't necessary to view the Macro Name column, and you can toggle it off by clicking the Macro Name button
Conditions column	Contains condition expressions which make the macro behave differently based on the current situation. You can toggle off this column by clicking the Conditions button if the macro doesn't contain any conditional expressions
Action column	Is the heart of the macro. These are the steps, or actions, that the macro executes when it runs. When developing a macro, you choose from a limited list of macro actions that appear in the list
Close Macro	Is only two actions long. Both macro actions are Close actions and are executed only if the conditional expression is "true"
Comment column	Is a place to add explanatory text for each macro action. Entries in the Comment column are optional
Action Arguments	Display values that further define the macro action that is chosen in the upper part of the Macro window. In Figure M-1, the Close macro action has three arguments to define further what object will be closed and how it will be closed. The Action Arguments change based on the action

Creating a Macro

In some programs, you can create a macro by having a "macro recorder" monitor and save your keystrokes and mouse clicks while you perform a series of actions. In Access, you create a macro in the Macro window, by specifying the actions, arguments, and conditions that you want the macro to execute. The Macro window is analogous to the Query, Form, or Report Design View; it's the window in which you define and modify the object. In this case, however, the window is simply called the Macro window rather than the macro design window. ◀━━━ Rachel did very well on the Access macros course and feels confident about developing macros for Nomad. After observing that Nomad users waste time closing the Customers Form to open and print the Customers Report several times a week, Rachel decides to create a macro to automate this task. She opens the Nomad-M database and adds the macro actions directly in the Macro window.

Steps

1. Start Access, open the Nomad-M database, click the Macros tab, then click New

The Macro1: Macro window opens, ready to accept your first action statement. By default, the Macro Name and the Condition columns are not visible. They have been toggled off. Develop the macro to simply print the Customers Report, an object that has already been created. The cursor is positioned in the Action cell of the first row.

2. Click the Action list arrow, then scroll and click OpenReport

The OpenReport action is added as the first line of the Macro window, and the arguments that further define the action display in the Action Arguments panel. The OpenReport action has two required arguments: the name of the report on which you wish to act, and the view in which you wish to open the report. Refer to Table M-2 for a listing of some macro actions.

QuickTip

Set action arguments in the order they are listed, because choices for one argument may be dependent upon earlier arguments.

3. Click the Report Name argument text box, click the Report Name list arrow, then click Customers Report

As you might suspect, all of the report objects in the database display in the Report Name list so that you can choose which report you want to act upon with this macro action. Instead of viewing the report on the screen, you want to print the report immediately. Choose the Print value for the View argument to carry out this action.

4. Click the View argument text box, click the View list arrow, review the options, then click Print

Your screen should look like Figure M-2. Macros can be one or many actions long. They can contain conditional expressions which execute only if the result of the conditional expression is true. In this case, the macro is only one action long and there are no conditional expressions. Save the macro and close the Macro window.

5. Click the Save button 🔲 on the Macro Design toolbar, type Print Customers Report in the Macro Name text box, then click OK

6. Close the Print Customers Report: Macro window

Test your new macro. The Print Customers Report is already selected on the Macros page.

7. Click Run

One copy of the Customers Report is sent to the default printer.

FIGURE M-2: **Macro window**

OpenReport Action

Optional comments column

Report Name

"View" in which to open the report

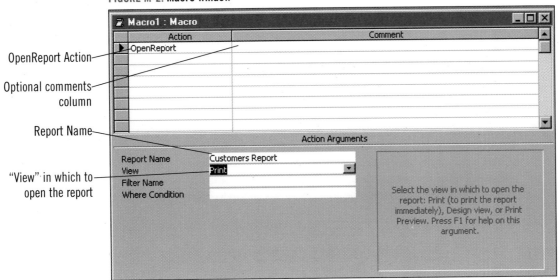

TABLE M-2: **Common macro actions**

subject area	macro action	description
Handing data in forms and reports	ApplyFilter	Restricts the number of records that appear in the resulting form or report by applying limiting criteria
	FindRecord	Finds the first record that meets the criteria
	GoToControl	Moves the focus (where you are currently typing or clicking) to a specific field or control
	GoToRecord	Makes a specified record the current record
Executing menu options or running objects	DoMenuItem	Carries out a specified menu option
	RunCode	Calls a Visual Basic function (a series of programming statements that do a calculation or comparison and return a value)
	RunMacro	Runs a macro or attaches a macro to a custom menu command
	StopMacro	Stops the currently running macro
Importing/Exporting data	TransferDatabase TransferSpreadsheet TransferText	Imports, links, or exports data between the current Microsoft Access database and another database, spreadsheet, or text file
Manipulating Objects	SetValue	Sets the value of a field, control, or property
	Close	Closes a window
	OpenForm	Opens a form in Form View, Design View, Print Preview, or Datasheet View
	OpenQuery	Opens a select or crosstab query in Datasheet View, Design View, or Print Preview; runs an action query
	OpenReport	Opens a report in Design View or Print Preview, or prints the report
	OpenTable	Opens a table in Datasheet View, Design View, or Print Preview
	PrintOut	Prints the active object in the open database, such as a datasheet, report, form, or module
	Maximize	Enlarges the active window to fill the Access window
	MsgBox	Displays a message box containing a warning or an informational message
	SendKeys	Send keystrokes directly to Microsoft Access or to an active Windows-based application
	Beep	Sounds a beep tone through the computer's speaker

Access 97

Adding Actions and Arguments

Macros can contain as many actions as necessary to complete the process that the user wants to automate. Each action is evaluated in the order in which it appears in the Macro window, starting at the top. While some macro actions manipulate data or objects, others are used only to make the database easier to use. Many miscellaneous macro actions such as MsgBox, which shows an informational message box, and Beep, which sounds a beep, fall into this category. Rachel decides to add an action to the Print Customers Report macro to clarify what is happening when the macro runs. She adds a MsgBox action to display a descriptive message for the user.

Steps

1. Click **Print Customers Report** if necessary, then click **Design**

The Print Customers Report macro opens in Design View. Add the two actions with their respective arguments.

2. Click the **Action cell** just below the OpenReport action, click the **Action list arrow**, scroll, then click **MsgBox**

With the appropriate action chosen, you are ready to specify the arguments for the action.

3. Click the **Message argument text box**, then type **Customers Report has been sent to the printer**

The Message argument is the most important argument for the MsgBox action because it determines what text displays in the message box. Notice that a description of the current argument displays in the lower-right corner of the Macro window. Pressing [F1] displays Help text for the action and argument chosen. Make sure that you properly define the other arguments for the MsgBox action.

4. Click the **Beep argument text box**, click the **Beep list arrow**, click **Yes**, click the **Type argument text box**, click the **Type list arrow**, click **Information**, click the **Title argument text box**, then type **Important Information!**

Your screen should look like Figure M-3. Save the macro.

5. Click the **Save button** 🖫 on the Macro Design toolbar

Close the Macro window.

6. Close the **Print Customers Report: Macro window**

Test the new macro action.

7. Click **Run**

First, you should hear a beep, then the middle of your screen should display the message box shown in Figure M-4. Finally, the Customers Report should print. Notice that the arguments you specified for the MsgBox action correspond to the characteristics of the message box. Respond to the message box by clicking the OK button.

8. Click **OK**

The macro accomplishes your goal. It prints the Customers Report and gives the user an audible cue and a valuable message too.

FIGURE M-3: **Print Customers Report macro with an additional MsgBox action**

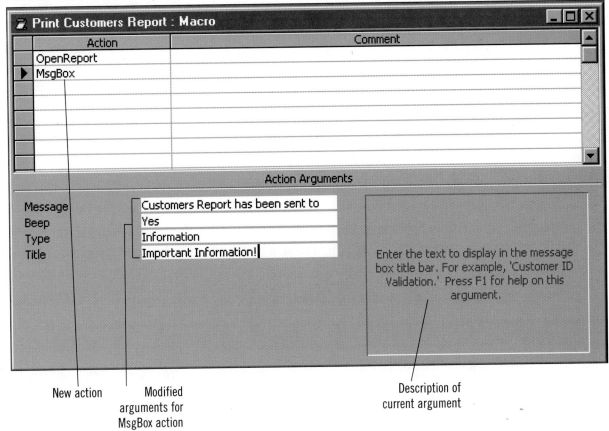

New action

Modified
arguments for
MsgBox action

Description of
current argument

FIGURE M-4: **Message Box**

Title argument
determines this text

Information
argument places
this icon in the
message box

Message argument
determines this text

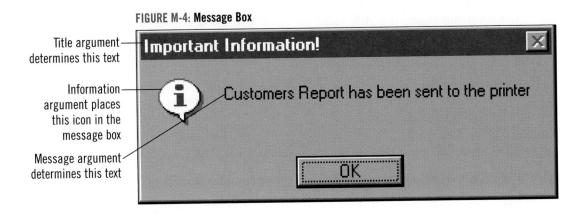

Creating a Macro Group

A **macro group** stores several macros together in one macro object. Macro groups are used to organize multiple macros that have similar characteristics, such as all the macros that print reports, or all the macros that are represented as command buttons on a form. When you create macro groups and put several macros in the same Macro window, you must enter a unique name in the Macro Name column to identify where one macro starts and one stops in the macro group. You must open the Macro Name column in the Macro window, and must enter the macro name on the row where the macro actions start. Open the Macro Name column by clicking the Macro Names button on the Macro Design toolbar. ◢◣ Rachel expects to create several macros to print reports, so she changes the Print Customers Report macro into a Print Macro Group, and adds to the group another macro that prints the Tours Report.

Steps 1 2 3 4

1. Click **Print Customers Report** if necessary, click **Design**, then click the **Macro Names button** 🔳 on the Macro Design toolbar, then maximize the window
   The Macro Name column opens in the Macro window. Enter the appropriate macro name in the first cell of the Macro Name column to identify the first two macro actions. Then position the insertion point in the Macro Name cell of a blank row.

2. Type **Print Customers Report**, then press ↓ twice
   Enter the macro name and macro actions for your next macro, which will print the Tours Report.

3. Type **Print Tours Report**, press **[Tab]**, click the **Action list arrow**, scroll, click **OpenReport**, click the **Report Name argument text box**, click the **Report Name list arrow**, then click **Tours Report**
   The Macro window should look like Figure M-5. Return to the Database window.

4. Click the **Save button** 🔳 on the Macro Design toolbar, then close the Print Customers Report: Macro window
   Rename the macro group as Print Macro Group.

5. Right-click the **Print Customers Report macro object** on the Macros tab in the Database window, click **Rename**, type **Print Macro Group**, then press **[Enter]**
   When you combine two or more macros within the same macro group object, to test them you must run them separately using the Tools command on the Access menu. Test the macros within the Print Macro Group to make sure that both of the macros within the group work properly.

6. Click **Tools** on the menu bar, point to **Macro**, click **Run Macro**, click the **Macro Name list arrow**, click **Print Macro Group.Print Customers Report**, click **OK**, then click **OK** to respond to the message box
   One copy of the Customers Report was sent to the default printer. Test the Print Tours Report macro too.

7. Click **Tools** on the menu bar, point to **Macro**, click **Run Macro**, click the **Macro Name list arrow**, click **Print Macro Group.Print Tours Report**, then click **OK**
   One copy of the Tours Report was sent to the default printer. Once you start creating macros, you'll find macro groups a very handy way to organize several individual macros that do similar tasks.

FIGURE M-5: **Macro group window**

Macro Name button ——

Two macros are stored in this macro group

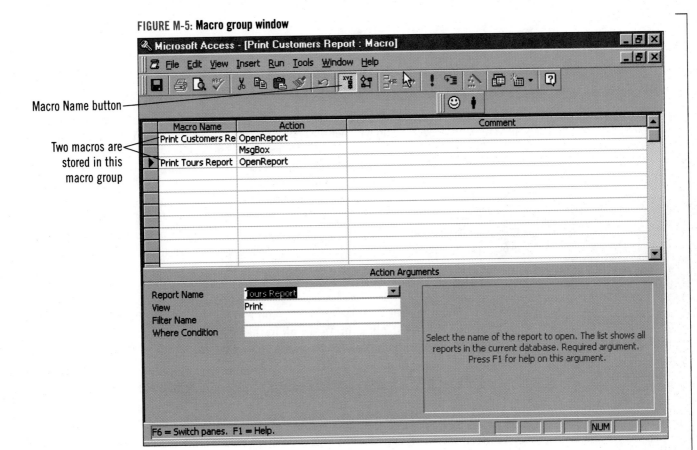

CLUES TO USE

Assigning a macro to a key combination

You can assign a macro to a specific key combination by creating an AutoKeys macro group. When you press the key or key combination, Access executes the macro. To do this, type the key combination to which you want to assign the macro actions in the Macro

Name column of the Macro window. If you assign a set of actions to a key combination that Access is already using (for example, [Ctrl][C] is the key combination for Copy), the actions you assign this key combination replace the Access key assignment.

Setting Conditional Expressions

You can use **conditions**, logical expressions that result in a true or false value, to allow a macro to fol-low different paths depending on whether the condition evaluates true or false. You enter conditions in the Conditions column in the Macro window. If a condition evaluates true, Access executes the action in that row. If a condition evaluates false, the macro skips that action. Conditional expressions often compare values of a specific control on a form or a report to a date, number, or constant to determine whether the expression is true or false. To refer to a value of a control on a form in a macro, you must use the following syntax: [Forms]![*formname*]![*controlname*]. To refer to a control on a report, the syntax is [Reports]![*reportname*]![*controlname*]. Nomad is selling tours to cus-tomers 60 years of age and older. The marketing department has asked Rachel whether there is an easy way to determine who is 60 years or older in the Customers Form, and to assign a value of 1 to the Rate field when this is true. Rachel develops a conditional macro to handle this request.

QuickTip

You can also press [Shift][F2] to open the Zoom dialog box to enter long expressions.

1. **Click New, click the Conditions button** **on the Macro Design toolbar to open the Condition column, right-click the first cell in the Condition column, click Zoom, then type [Forms]![Customers Form]![Birth Date]<Date()-(60*365)**
   Your screen should look like Figure M-6. This conditional expression says "Check the data in the Birth Date field on the Customers Form and determine whether the date is less than 60 years before today's date."

2. **Click OK to close the Zoom dialog box, press [Enter] point to the Column heading separa-tor between the Condition column and the Action column, double-click ++ to widen the Condition column, click the first Action cell, click the list arrow, scroll, then click SetValue**
   Change both of the SetValue's arguments to assign the Rate field a value of 1 when the expression is true.

3. **Click the Item argument text box, type [Forms]![Customers Form]![Rate], click the Expression Action Argument text box, type 1, then maximize the Macro window**
   Refer to Figure M-7. The object type is the first component of the entry, the object name is the second component, and the control is the third component. Save the macro.

4. **Click the Save button** , **type Over 60 Macro in the Macro Name text box, click OK, then close the Over 60 Macro: Macro window**
   To test the macro, you must open the Customers Form and run the macro against a record with an "over 60" birth date and one with an "under 60" birth date.

5. **Click the Forms tab, double-click the Customers Form, then maximize the Customers Form**
   The record for Ginny Braithwaite, the first customer in the database, opens in Form View. Ginny's birth date is 1/10/1960, so she is obviously not 60 years old. Note too that Ginny's Rate entry is 3. When you run the Over 60 Macro against this record, you should not see the value of the Rate field change to 1.

6. **Click Window on the menu bar, click Nomad-M: Database, click the Macros tab, click Over 60 Macro, then click Run**
   Switch back to the Customers Form to make sure the macro did not change the Rate field. To Test the macro against a true value, change the birth date to 1/10/1930.

Trouble?

You must press [Tab] or click outside the Birth Date text box for the data to be recorded for that field and the macro to work correctly.

7. **Click Window on the menu bar, click Customers, click the Birth Date text box, change the date to 1/10/1930, press [Tab], click Window on the menu bar, click Nomad-M: Database, click Over 60 Macro if necessary, then click Run**
   Switch back to the Customers Form to see whether the macro changed Ginny's record this time.

8. **Click Window on the menu bar, then click Customers**
   The screen should look like Figure M-8. Notice that the Rate field has changed to 1 based on the fact that the conditional expression in the Over 60 Macro resulted in a true value, thus executing the SetValue action. The Over 60 Macro works correctly.

FIGURE M-6: **Zoom dialog box**

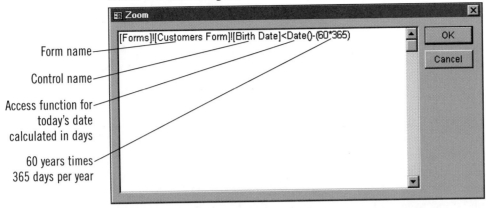

Form name
Control name
Access function for today's date calculated in days
60 years times 365 days per year

FIGURE M-7: **Final macro**

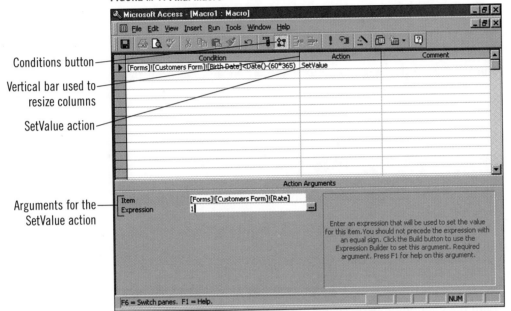

Conditions button
Vertical bar used to resize columns
SetValue action
Arguments for the SetValue action

FIGURE M-8: **Updated Customers Form**

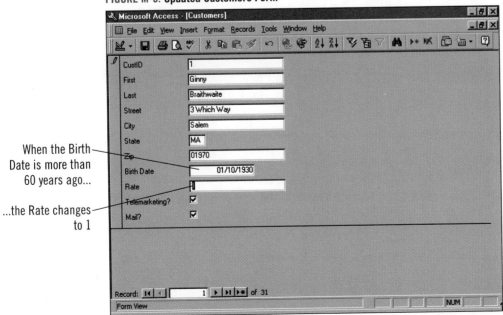

When the Birth Date is more than 60 years ago...
...the Rate changes to 1

Assigning a Macro to a Command Button

In previous lessons, you learned that you can add command buttons to forms to automate common tasks such as adding or printing a record. You can also use a command button to represent a macro object. If you add the command button control to the form, you won't need to jump back to the Macros page of the Database window each time you want to run a macro. Instead, you can run the macro directly from Form View by clicking the command button. Rachel is pleased that the Over 60 Macro automated the tedious task of determining whether a customer is over 60 years old and if so, automatically changing his or her Rate value to 1. Still, she found it inconvenient to jump back to the Database window to run the macro when she was working on a record in Form View. To address this concern, Rachel adds a command button to the Customers Form that represents the Over 60 Macro.

Steps

1. Click the **Design View button** 📐 on the Form View toolbar, point to the right edge of the form until the mouse pointer changes to ↔, then drag to the 5⅛" mark on the horizontal ruler
   Add a command button to the upper-right corner of the form.

2. Click the **Toolbox button** 🔨 on the Form Design toolbar if necessary, click the **Command Button button** 🔲 on the Toolbox, click ⁺🔲 below the 3½" mark near the top of the form, then click **Cancel** if the first Command Button Wizard dialog box opens
   The Command Button Wizard is helpful for adding Access-supplied actions to the button. However, in this case, because you want to attach a user-created macro to the button, you use the command button's property sheet instead of the Command Button Wizard. Use the property sheet to modify the text on the button through the Caption property.

3. Click the **Properties button** 🔲 on the Form Design toolbar, click the **Format tab**, verify that the text in the Caption property text box is selected, then type **Over 60 Rate?**
   With the Caption property changed to a more descriptive label, you're ready to attach the button to the Over 60 Macro.

4. Click the **Event tab**, click the **On Click text box**, click the **list arrow**, click the **Over 60 Macro**, then click 🔲 on the Form Design toolbar
   The command button in Form Design View is shown in Figure M-9. View the form in Form View. You decide to test the macro with the customer in the second record.

5. Click the **Form View button** 📋 on the Form Design toolbar, then click the **Next Record navigation button** ▶
   Virginia Rodarmor, the second customer, is over 60 because her birth date is 1/6/1935. The value in the Rate field is currently 3. Test the Over 60 Rate? command button.

6. Click the **Over 60 Rate? command button**
   Virginia's record has been updated and the new Rate value is 1 as shown in Figure M-10. Close the Customers Form and save the changes.

7. Click **File** on the menu bar, click **Close**, then click **Yes**

FIGURE M-9: Adding a command button to run a macro

New command button

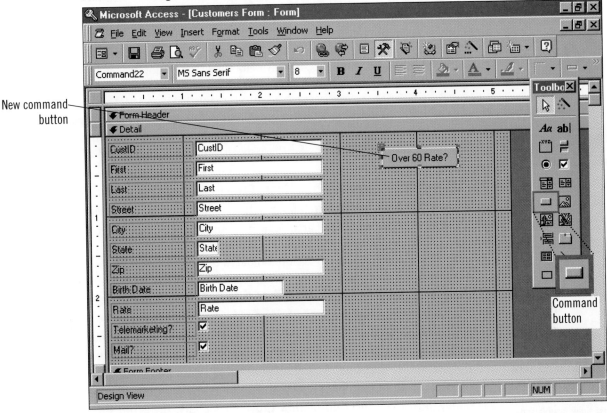

FIGURE M-10: Using a command button to run a macro

Command button

Rate value changed from 3 to 1

Next record button

Record 2

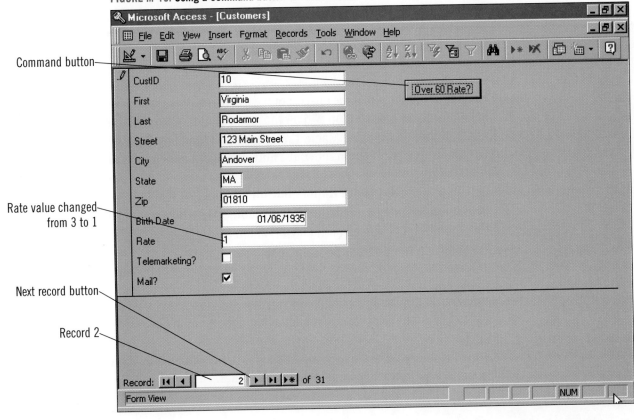

Customizing Toolbars with Macros

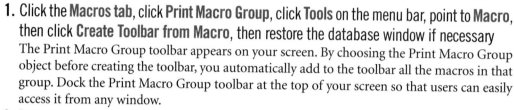

In Access, you can run macros many different ways. You found that assigning a macro to a command button on a form is handy when you want to run the macro against the data displayed in the form. When you want macros to be available at all times, however, assigning the same macro to a command button on every form is unproductive. Fortunately, Access also allows you to run macros from existing or user-created toolbars, menu bars, and shortcut menus. Using these techniques, you can make the macro available to the user at all times. ✐ Rachel notices that the Customers Report and Tours Report macros are used often each week, and decides to create a new toolbar with buttons for these macros that can be displayed at all times.

1. **Click the Macros tab, click Print Macro Group, click Tools on the menu bar, point to Macro, then click Create Toolbar from Macro, then restore the database window if necessary**
The Print Macro Group toolbar appears on your screen. By choosing the Print Macro Group object before creating the toolbar, you automatically add to the toolbar all the macros in that group. Dock the Print Macro Group toolbar at the top of your screen so that users can easily access it from any window.

2. **Drag the Print Macro Group toolbar title bar to the top of the screen, then release it just below the Database toolbar as shown in Figure M-11**
Since this toolbar only has two macros associated with it, the entire name of the macro can comfortably appear on the toolbar. If you add several more macros to the toolbar, however, you quickly run out of room. To remedy that, change the macro buttons from text to pictures.

3. **Right-click the Print Macro Group toolbar, click Customize to open the Customize dialog box, click the Commands tab if necessary, drag the Customize dialog box title bar to the left so that the entire macro toolbar is visible, right-click the Print Customers Report button on the Print Macro Group toolbar, then point to the Change Button Image option on the shortcut menu**
The screen should look like Figure M-12. The options on the shortcut menu allow you to modify the button image and text in many ways. Choose the second picture on the last row, that of a woman's head, to represent the Print Customers Report macro. You also have to choose the Default Style option so that the image, not the macro name, appears on the button.

4. **Click the Woman's head icon 🔘 on the icon palette, right-click the Print Customers Report button on the Print Macro Group toolbar, then click Default Style**
The Default Style for a button shows the button image, not the text. Change the Print Tours Report button to an appropriate image as well.

5. **Right-click the Print Tours Report button on the Print Macro Group toolbar, point to Change Button Image, click the Runner icon 🏃 on the icon palette, right-click the Print Tours Report button on the Print Macro Group toolbar, click Default Style, then click Close on the Customize dialog box**
The screen should look similar to Figure M-13. Like all Access toolbar buttons, the macro buttons display a ScreenTip when you point to them with the mouse. For macro buttons, the ScreenTip displays the macro name.

6. **Point to 🏃 on the Print Macro Group toolbar, then point to 🔘 on the Print Macro Group toolbar**
Review the ScreenTips on the toolbar. Adding macros to toolbars gives your database a fast and easy way to execute powerful macro commands.

Trouble?

The Print Macro Group toolbar might be in the lower-right corner of your screen. You need good mouse skills to place toolbars. If the toolbar doesn't dock correctly the first time, drag it and try again.

Trouble?

If your macro buttons don't display ScreenTips when you point to them, you should make sure that the Show ScreenTips on toolbars check box is selected on the Options page of the Customize dialog box. Open the Customize dialog box by right-clicking any toolbar, then click Customize.

FIGURE M-11: **New macro toolbar**

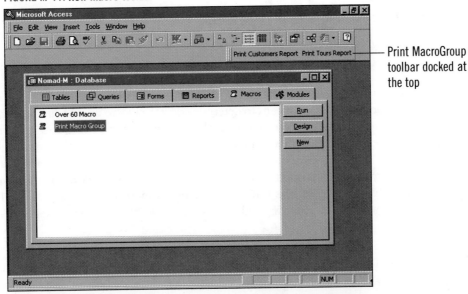

Print MacroGroup toolbar docked at the top

FIGURE M-12: **Changing the image of the macro buttons on the macro toolbar**

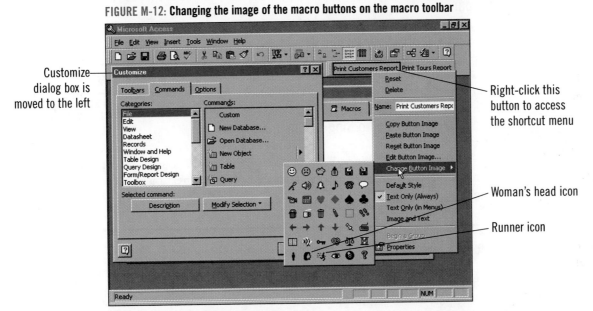

Customize dialog box is moved to the left

Right-click this button to access the shortcut menu

Woman's head icon

Runner icon

FIGURE M-13: **Macro toolbar with icons**

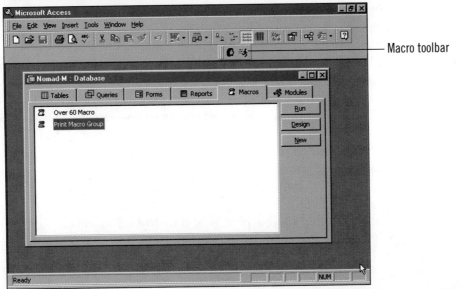

Macro toolbar

Troubleshooting Macros

When macros don't execute properly, Access supplies several techniques to allow you to **debug** the macro. Debugging means to determine why the macro doesn't run properly. **Single stepping** is to run a macro one line at a time, observing the effect of each macro action as it is executed. Another technique to debug a macro is to disable a macro action temporarily by entering False in the Condition cell in the row of the action that you wish to ignore temporarily. Rachel plans to build more sophisticated macros, and decides to learn how to debug them before she actually runs into serious problems. She opens the Macro window of the Print Macro Group object and learns debugging techniques using the Print Customers Report.

Steps

1. **Click Print Macro Group if necessary, click Design, click the Single Step button on the Macro Design toolbar, then click the Run button on the Macro Design toolbar**

   The screen should look like Figure M-14, with the Macro Single Step dialog box open. This dialog box displays information about the macro, such as its name, whether it is being executed (the Condition is True) or not (the Condition is False), the macro action name, and the arguments specified for that action. From the Macro Single Step dialog box, you can step into the next macro action, halt execution of the macro, or continue running the macro actions without single stepping. Step into the next macro action, the MsgBox action.

2. **Click Step in the Macro Single Step dialog box**

   Once again, the Macro Single Step dialog box displays descriptive information about the action. Since the first action was supposed to print the Customers Report, the report should be ready for you to retrieve on the printer. Step into the next macro action.

3. **Click Step**

   The MsgBox action executes and displays a message box stating that the Customers Report has been sent to the printer. Respond to the message box.

4. **Click OK**

   You want to suspend the OpenReport action temporarily so that the report doesn't print each time you run the macro. Enter False in the Condition cell for the action row with the OpenReport macro action.

5. **Click the Conditions button on the Macro Design toolbar, click the Print Customers Report Condition cell of the OpenReport action, then type False**

   The screen looks like Figure M-15. To see the effect of the False condition, run the macro in single-step mode again. The Single Step button is still selected.

6. **Click the Run button, then click Yes when prompted to save the macro changes**

   The Macro Single Step dialog box still displays descriptive information about the action, but since the Condition value is False, the OpenReport macro action that actually prints the report does not execute. Now that you know how to enter false conditions to skip macro actions temporarily, halt the single-step action, then remove the False condition.

7. **Click Halt, double-click False in the Conditions cell, then press [Delete]**

   Close the Macro window.

8. **Click File on the menu bar, click Close, then click Yes when prompted to save the changes**

   When satisfied that you can now use the false condition to skip a macro action temporarily during execution to debug problems, close Nomad-M and exit Access.

9. **Click File on the menu bar, then click Exit**

QuickTip

To halt a macro while it's running and then single step through it, press [Ctrl][Break].

FIGURE M-14: Macro Single Step dialog box

Run button

Single Step button

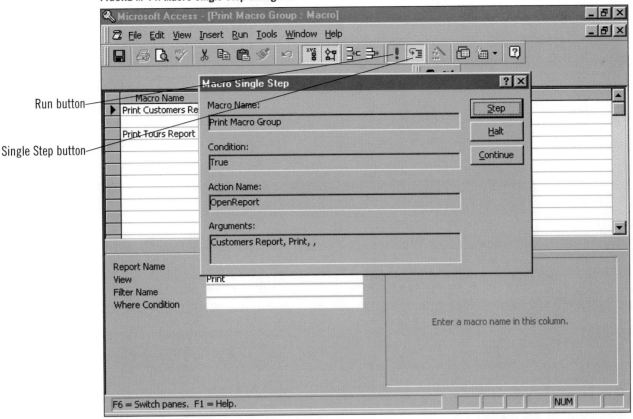

FIGURE M-15: Using a False condition in a macro action

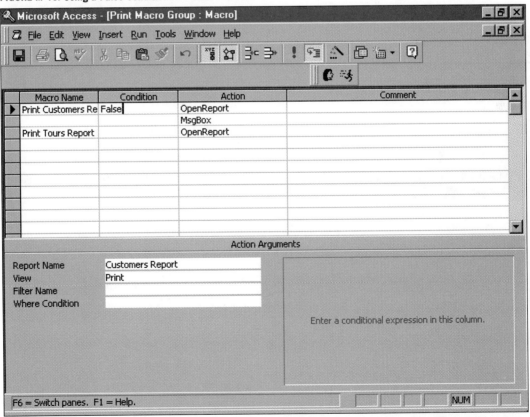

Practice

► Concepts Review

Identify each element shown in Figure M-16.

FIGURE M-16

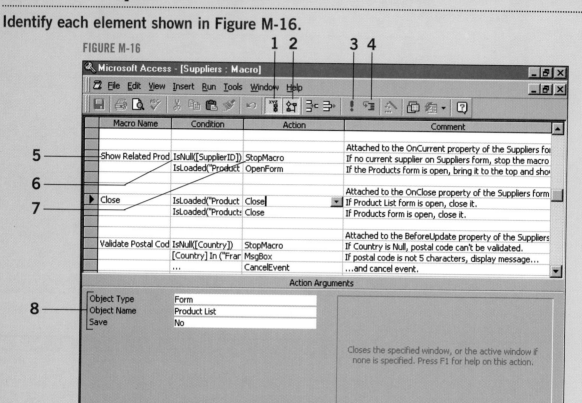

Match each term with the statement that describes its function.

9. macro
10. conditional expression
11. arguments
12. debugging
13. actions

a. Individual tasks that you want the Access macro to perform
b. An Access object that stores a series of actions that perform a series of tasks
c. Determining why a macro doesn't run properly
d. Provide additional information to define how an Access action will perform
e. Results in a true or false answer, directing Access either to execute or not execute a series of macro actions

Select the best answer from the list of choices.

14. Which of the following is *not* a major benefit of using a macro?

   a. To save time by automating routine tasks
   b. To ensure consistency in executing routine or complex tasks
   c. To make the database more flexible by adding macro command buttons to forms
   d. To redesign the relationships among the tables of the database

15. Which of the following *best* describes the process of creating an Access macro?

   a. Use the macro recorder to record clicks and keystrokes as you complete a task
   b. Use the single-step recorder feature to record clicks and keystrokes as you complete a task

c. Use the macro wizard to determine which tasks are done most frequently

d. Open the Macro window and add actions, arguments, and conditions to accomplish the task desired

16. **Which of the following does *not* run a macro?**

    a. Click the macro name on the Macros page of the Database window, then click Run

    b. Attach the macro to a command button on a form

    c. Add the macro to a toolbar

    d. Add the macro as an entry in the title bar

17. **Which is *not* a reason to run a macro in single-step mode?**

    a. You want to disable OpenReport actions temporarily

    b. You want to observe the effect of each macro action individually

    c. You want to debug a macro that isn't working properly

    d. You want to run only the first three actions of a six-action macro

18. **Which is *not* a reason to use conditional expressions in a macro?**

    a. More macro actions are available when you are also using conditional expressions

    b. Conditional expressions allow you to skip over actions when the expression evaluates to false

    c. You can enter "False" in the Conditions column of the Macro window to skip that action temporarily

    d. Conditional expressions give the macro more power and flexibility

19. **Which example illustrates the proper syntax to refer to a specific control on a form?**

    a. {Forms}!{*formname*}!{*controlname*}

    b. [Forms]![*formname*]![*controlname*]

    c. (Forms)!(*formname*)!(*controlname*)

    d. Forms!*formname*!*controlname*

20. **Which of the following is an Access-supplied function that returns to today's date?**

    a. Date!

    b. [Date]

    c. Date[]

    d. Date()

▶ Skills Review

1. **Understand macros**

    a. Start Access and open the Addresses-M.mdb database.

    b. Open the Macro window of the Preview Large Donors macro and record your answers to the following questions on a plain sheet of paper:

       1. Which macro action is in this macro? What conditional expression does this macro contain?

       2. What arguments does the first action in this macro contain? What values were chosen for those arguments?

       3. Is this macro in a macro group?

    c. Close the Macro window for the Preview Large Donors macro.

2. **Create a macro**

    a. Click the New button on the Macros page to open an empty macro window and start a new macro.

    b. Specify the OpenReport action in the first row, and use the following values for the first two arguments. Don't make any entries in the last two arguments.

       Report Name: Zip Code Report   View: Print Preview

    c. Save the macro with the name "Preview Zip Code Report."

    d. Run the macro using the Run button on the Macro window.

    e. The macro should place the Zip Code Report in Print Preview mode. Print the report, then close the report.

3. **Add actions and arguments to a macro**

    a. Open the Macro window of the Preview Zip Code Report macro (if necessary).

    b. Add a MsgBox action to the second action row, and use the following values for the four arguments:

       Message: This report may be several pages long.   Type: Warning!

       Beep: Yes   Title: Print Warning

c. Save the macro, then run it again.

d. Click OK to respond to the message box, view the report, then close the report without printing it.

4. Create a macro group

a. Open the Macro window of the Preview Zip Code Report macro (if necessary).

b. Open the Macro Names column by clicking the Macro Names button on the Macro Design toolbar.

c. Enter "Preview Zip Code Report" in the first Macro Name row.

d. Add another macro to the macro group starting on the third row of the Macro window. Enter "Preview Names Report" in the Macro Name column.

e. Add two actions to the Preview Names Report macro as shown below:

1. Action: OpenReport   **2**. Action: MsgBox

    Arguments: Report Name: Names Reports   Arguments: Message: This report contains sensitive information.

    View: Print Preview   Beep: Yes

                                        Type: Critical

                                        Title: Critical Message

f. Close the Macro window, saving the changes.

g. Rename the Preview Zip Code Report macro to "Preview Macros."

h. Click Tools on the menu bar, point to Macro, then click Run Macro to view the Run Macro dialog box.

i. Click the Preview Macros.Preview Names Report macro, then click OK to run that macro.

j. Click OK to respond to the message box, then print and close the report

5. Set conditional expressions for a macro

a. Click the New button on the Macros page to start a new macro.

b. Click the Conditions button to open the Condition column.

c. Enter the following condition in the first condition cell: [Forms]![Name Form]![Pledge Amount]>1000. The condition checks whether the Pledge Amount is greater than or equal to 1000. If it is, the Level control is updated to a value of 1. Use the Zoom dialog box or widen the Condition column.

d. Enter the following action and corresponding arguments in the first row:

Action: SetValue   Arguments: Item: [Forms]![Name Form]![Level]

                                  Expression: 1

e. Save the macro with the name "Check Giving Level," then close the Macro window.

f. Open the Name Form and run the Check Giving Level macro against the first record by clicking Tools on the menu bar, clicking Run Macro, choosing Check Giving Level as the macro name, then clicking OK. The Level field value shouldn't change, because the Pledge Amount is less than 1000.

g. Move to the second record and run the macro again. This time, the Level field should be updated to 1 because the Pledge Amount is over 1000.

6. Assign a macro to a command button

a. Open the Name Form in Design View, and widen the form so that the right edge is at the 5" mark.

b. Add a command button to the upper-right corner of the form.

c. Change the following properties on the command button:

Format tab, Caption property: Check Pledge Level   Event tab, On Click property: Check Giving Level

d. Open the Name Form in Form View and navigate to the third record, that of Sara Dostart.

e. Click the Check Pledge command button. Because the giving level was equal to 1000 rather than greater than 1000, the value of the Level field should *not* have changed.

f. Navigate to the 15th record, that of Colleen Armstrong.

g. Click the Check Pledge command button. The value of the Level field should have changed to 1.

h. Print the Name Form displaying the updated Colleen Armstrong record.

i. Close the Name Form, saving changes when prompted.

7. Customize toolbars with macros

   a. Click the Macros page of the Database window, then click the Preview Macros object. The Preview Macros object is a macro group that contains two individual macros: the Preview Zip Code Report macro and the Preview Names Report macro.

   b. Click Tools on the menu bar, point to Macro, then click Create Toolbar from Macro.

   c. Dock the new toolbar at the top-right edge of the screen (just under the Database toolbar), right-click the new toolbar, then choose Customize.

   d. Move the Customize dialog box to the left side of the screen so that you can see as much of the new macro toolbar as possible, right-click the Preview Zip Code Report button, point to Change Button Image, then click the happy face icon (the first one on the first row).

   e. Right-click the Preview Zip Code Report button again, then click Default Style so that only the happy face icon is visible on the toolbar to represent the Preview Zip Code Report macro.

   f. Right-click the Preview Names Report button, point to Change Button Image, then click the single standing person icon (the first one on the last row).

   g. Right-click the Preview Names Report button again, then click Default Style so that only the single standing person icon is visible on the toolbar to represent the Preview Names Report macro.

   h. Close the Customize dialog box.

8. Troubleshoot macros

   a. Open the Preview Macros object in the Macro window.

   b. Click the Single Step button on the Macro Design toolbar, then click the Run button.

   c. Click Step twice to step through the two actions of this macro, then click OK on the resulting message box.

   d. Close the Zip Code Report Preview screen and return to the Macro window.

   e. Open the Condition column by clicking the Conditions button on the Macro Design toolbar.

   f. Add the value False as a condition to the first row. You'll be modifying the first action (the OpenReport action) of the first macro (the Preview Zip Code macro).

   g. Click the Run button to start the macro, save the macro when prompted, click Step twice to move through the actions of this macro, then click OK when prompted with the message box. The Zip Code Report should *not* be previewed, because you chose to ignore this macro action with the False condition.

   h. Delete the False condition in the first row of the Macro window, save the macro, then close the Macro window.

   i. Close the database and Exit Access.

▶ **Independent Challenges**

1. As the president of a civic organization, you have developed a database, Cleanup-M, that tracks deposits of recyclable materials. You wish to develop a macro to automate the printing of the Organization Report. After developing the macro, you add a command button to the Organization Entry Form that executes the macro.

   To complete this independent challenge:

1. Start Access, then open the database Cleanup-M.

2. Click the Macros tab, click New, then enter the OpenReport macro action into the first row.

3. Modify the arguments of the OpenReport action so that the Report Name value is Organization Report, and the View value is Print. (*Note:* The last two arguments remain blank.)

4. Save the macro with the name "Print Organization Report Macro," then close the Macro window.

5. Open the Organization Entry Form in Form Design View, widen the form to the 5" mark on the ruler, then add a command button in the upper-right corner of the form.

6. Open the property sheet of the command button and make these property changes:
Caption: Print Organization Report (found on the Format page)
On Click: Print Organization Report Macro (choose this macro from the On Click list found on the Event page)

7. Resize the command button so that the entire caption "Print Organization Report" is visible, then view the form.
8. Click the Print Organization Report command button to execute the command, then review the report that is sent to the default printer.
9. Save and close the Organization Entry Form, close the database, then exit Access.

2. The chamber of commerce has asked you to analyze the total membership of each of the organizations in the Cleanup-M database and record the appropriate annual dues for each organization based on its membership. For organizations with less than 150 members, annual dues are $100. For organizations of 150 or more members, annual dues are $200. You use an Access macro to automate this process, then you attach the macro to a button on the Organization Entry Form.

To complete this independent challenge:

1. Start Access, then open the Cleanup-M database.
2. Click the Macros tab, then click New to start a new macro.
3. Specify that SetValue be the first macro action, then modify the arguments as follows:
Item: [Forms]![Organization Entry Form]![Rate]   Expression: 100
This action sets the Rate value to 100.
4. Move to the second row of the Macro window, click the Conditions button on the Macro Design toolbar to open the Condition column, then enter the following condition in the Condition column of the second row:
[Forms]![Organization Entry Form]![Membership]>=150
This condition executes only if the value in the Membership field is greater than or equal to 150.
5. Specify that SetValue also be the second macro action, then modify the arguments as follows:
Item: [Forms]![Organization Entry Form]![Rate]   Expression: 200
This action sets the Rate value to 200, but only if the condition evaluates True. Otherwise, the Rate value remains at 100 as specified by the first macro action.
6. Save the macro, naming it "Calculate Chamber Dues Macro," then close the Macro window.
7. Open the Organization Entry Form in Form Design View, then add another command button in the upper-right corner of the form, just below the existing Print Organization Report command button.
8. Open the property sheet of the new command button and make these property changes:
Caption: Calculate Chamber Dues (found on the Format page)
On Click: Calculate Chamber Dues Macro (choose this macro from the On Click list found on the Event page)
9. Resize the command button so that the entire caption "Calculate Chamber Dues" is visible, then view the form.
10. Click the Calculate Chamber Dues command button to execute the command, then review the Rate to make sure that it calculated correctly. Those organizations that have memberships of less than 150 should have a Rate of 100. Those organizations that have memberships equal to or greater than 150 should have a Rate of 200.
11. Go through each of the seven records in the Organization Entry Form, and click the Calculate Chamber Dues command button to update the seven records.
12. Save the Organization Entry Form, then close the form and exit Access.

3. The macros you have written for the Cleanup-M database have worked well, and you have decided to build a toolbar that represents macro buttons that print the Organization Report and Recycle Centers Report. First you rename the Print Organization Report Macro so that it represents all print macros, then you add macro commands to print the Recycle Centers Report. Finally, you create a toolbar to represent both printing macros.

To complete this independent challenge:

1. Start Access, then open the Cleanup-M.mdb database.
2. To rename the Print Organization Report Macro to something more descriptive, click the Macros tab, right-click the Print Organization Report Macro, click Rename, then type "Print Macro Group."
3. Open the Print Macro Group in Design View, then click the Macro Names button on the toolbar to open the Macro Name column. Type "Print Organization Report" as the first macro name, then press the down arrow key to move into the second row of the Macro window.

4. Type "Print Recycle Centers Report" as the second macro name, then press [Tab] to move into the Action cell for the second row.

5. Choose the OpenReport action for the second row, then change the arguments to the following:
   Report Name: Recycle Centers Report   Filter Name: (leave blank)
   View: Print   Where Condition: (leave blank)

6. Save and close the Print Macro Group Macro window.

7. With the Print Macro Group object still selected, choose the following menu options to create quickly a toolbar with the macros in this macro group: Tools, Macro, then Create Toolbar from Macro. The new Print Macro Group toolbar is probably located in the lower-right corner.

8. Drag up the title bar of the Print Macro Group toolbar to dock the toolbar at the top-right corner of the screen, just below the Database toolbar.

9. Right-click the macro toolbar, click Customize to open the Customize dialog box, then drag the Customize Dialog box to the left side of the screen so that both buttons on the macro toolbar are visible.

10. Right-click the Print Organization Report button, point to Change Button Image, then click the club icon (the club icon looks like a club from a deck of cards, but this "club" represents a club such as an organization).

11. Right-click the Print Organization Report button again, then click Default Style so that only the club icon is visible, not the macro text. Right-click the Print Recycle Center Report button, point to Change Button Image, then click the garbage can icon (the garbage can icon is the third icon in the fourth row).

12. Right-click the Print Recycle Center Report button again, then click Default Style so that only the garbage can icon is visible, not the macro text.

13. Close the Customize dialog box, close Cleanup-M, then exit Access.

4. Your grandmother has given you a collection of M. I. Hummel figurines. Some of them are quite valuable and you have developed a database, Hummel-M.mdb, to track this precious inventory. You use the M. I. Hummel Internet Web site to keep up-to-date on the collection's retail value, build a macro to automate the printing of a report, and attach the macro as a command button to a form.

To complete this independent challenge:

1. Log on to the Internet and use your browser to go to http://www.course.com. From there, click Student Online Companions, then click the link for the book you are using, then click the Access link for Unit M.

2. Find the price list for the "Friendship" collection, print the page, then log off the Internet.

3. Start Access, then open Hummel-M.mdb.

4. Open the Figurines Form in Form View, then record the Retail Price for each Hummel figurine.

5. Click the Macros tab, then click New to open the Macro window.

6. Add the OpenReport action in the first row with the following arguments:
   Report Name: Figurines Report   View: Print   Filter Name: (leave blank)   Where Condition: (leave blank)

7. Save the macro with the name "Print Figurines Report Macro," then close the Macro window.

8. Open the Figurines Form in Design View, then widen the form to the 5" mark on the ruler.

9. Add a command button to the upper-right corner of the form.

10. Change the following properties of the command button:
    Format page, Caption property: Print Figurines Report
    Event page, On Click property: Choose the Print Figurines Macro option from the drop-down list

11. Resize and move the command button so that the entire caption, "Print Figurines Report," is clearly visible.

12. Open the Figurines Form in Form View, then click the new command button to print the report.

13. Close the Figurines Form, saving the changes when prompted.

14. Close the Hummel-M database, then exit Access.

▶ Visual Workshop

Open the VW-M database and add the command button to the Alumni Form shown in Figure M-17. The command button is attached to a macro that prints the Alumni Report. Test your command button to make sure that it prints the Alumni Report.

FIGURE M-17

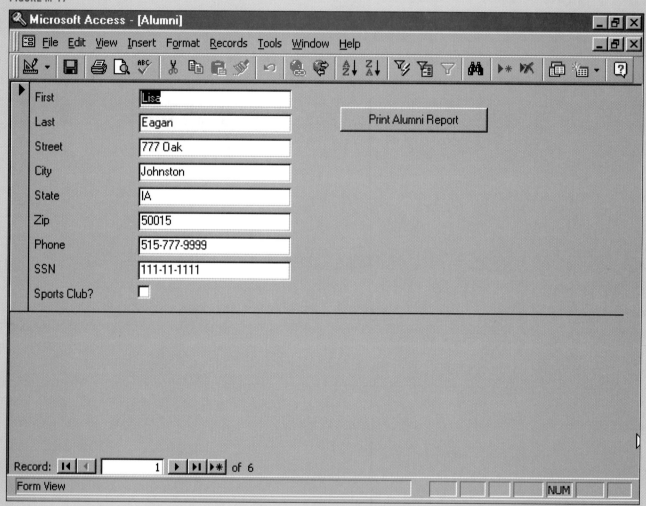

Creating
Modules

Objectives

▶ **Understand modules**
▶ **Understand when to use macros versus modules**
▶ **Create a Function procedure**
▶ **Document a procedure**
▶ **Test a procedure**
▶ **Use If statements**
▶ **Create a class module**
▶ **Troubleshoot module problems**

Access is an extremely robust and easy-to-use relational database. Reports and screens that took hours to create using earlier DOS-based programs by entering complex programming code are now created using wizards, graphical tools, and property sheets. Macros that formerly took hours to debug can now be written, tested, and attached to a command button in minutes. Because Access provides so many user-friendly tools to accomplish tasks, many database administrators don't need to work with the Access programming language, **Visual Basic**, to meet the needs of the users. When programming is required, however, the Visual Basic code is stored in a database object called a **module**. This unit introduces you to the reasons for using modules and gives you practice writing Visual Basic code and storing it as a module. Rachel Best learns about and creates an Access module to enhance the capabilities of the Customer Entry Form in the Nomad-N database.

Understanding Modules

A **module** is an Access object that contains Visual Basic programming code. A module is named just like the other objects in the database. The programming code contained within the module is executed in several ways—as command buttons placed on forms, in response to events (such as printing a report), or from anywhere in the database. A database can contain two kinds of modules: **class modules**, which are stored as part of the form or report object and respond to events that occur on that specific form or report, and **standard modules**, which are stored on the Modules tab of the opening Database window and contain code that can be executed from anywhere in the database application. 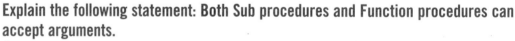 Although she does not have a programming background, Rachel wants to learn more about Visual Basic and Access modules. Modules are often discussed at her Access users' group meetings, and she is confident that this knowledge will help her enhance the Nomad-N database. Rachel decides to return to the local college and take a short course on modules to help her understand. One quiz included the following questions. Rachel's answers are summarized as follows.

What does a module contain?

A module contains Visual Basic programming code organized in units called procedures. A procedure may be a few or several lines long. Modules also contain **comment lines** to document the code. Comment lines in Visual Basic are preceded by a single apostrophe.

What is a procedure?

A **procedure** is a series of Visual Basic statements that perform an operation or calculate a value. There are two types of procedures: Function procedures and Sub procedures. You use **declaration statements** to name and define procedures as well as to set rules for how the statements in a module are processed.

What is a Function procedure, and why would you use it?

A **function** is a series of programming statements that return a value. Access supplies many built-in functions, such as Count, which returns the number of records in a specified group, Sum, which returns a total of the values in the specified field, and Now, which returns the current date and time. The user can also create functions. For example, you might wish to create a function called FirstOfNextMonth to return the date of the first day of the month following the current date.

What is a Sub procedure, and why would you use one?

A **Sub procedure** performs a series of programming statements, but does not return a value. For example, you might create a Sub procedure to set the focus to a School's Name text box when the user selects a College Graduate check box.

QuickTip

On a form, focus refers to the control that is currently selected.

Explain the following statement: Both Sub procedures and Function procedures can accept arguments.

Arguments are constants, variables, or expressions passed to a procedure to define further how it should execute. Arguments are specified immediately after the Sub procedure or function. When used in functions, arguments are surrounded by parentheses. For example, the full syntax for the Sum function, including its arguments, is Sum(*expr*), where *expr* is a placeholder that represents the field or expression that should be summarized.

Explain the following statement: Objects can perform methods.

A **method** is an action that an object can perform. For example, the GoToPage method moves the focus to the first control on a specified page in the active form. The syntax for this line of code is *form*.GoToPage *pagenumber*, where *form* is a placeholder for an actual form object within the database, and *pagenumber* is a valid page number for the form.

Identify the parts of the Module window displayed in Figure N-1.

FIGURE N-1: Module window

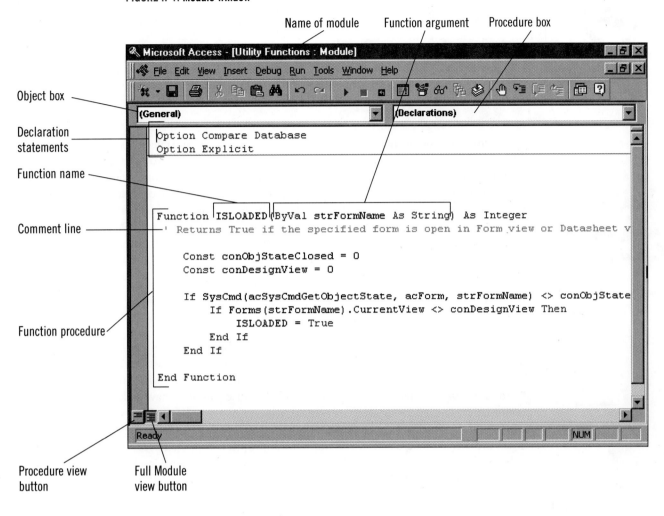

Name of module   Function argument   Procedure box

Object box

Declaration statements

Function name

Comment line

Function procedure

Procedure view button

Full Module view button

TABLE N-1: Components of the Module window

component	description
Procedure View button	Shows the statements that belong only to the current procedure
Full Module View button	Shows all lines of Visual Basic in the module
Declaration statements	Name and define procedures, variables, and constants. For example, the Option Compare Database statement helps the module determine how to sort records. The Sub statement declares the name of a new Sub procedure
Object box	In standard modules, lists the object as well as its controls, so that procedures can be written that apply to that specific object or control
Procedure box	In standard modules, lists the procedures that have been defined in the module
Comment line	Descriptive text that serves as guiding documentation. Comment lines in modules start with a single apostrophe (')

Understanding When to Use Macros Versus Modules

Both macros and modules help run your database more efficiently and effectively. Both require some understanding of programming concepts, an ability to follow a process through its steps logically, and a bit of patience. Some tasks can be accomplished using either an Access macro or module, but there are definitely some guidelines and rules that will help guide your choice of which object is best for the task. The following second quiz is for the Access modules class that Rachel took at the local college along with Rachel's answers. This quiz focused on the question, "When should I use a macro, and when should I use a module to accomplish a task in Microsoft Access?"

Details

 For what types of tasks are macros best suited?

Macros are an easy to way handle repetitive, simple details such as opening and closing forms, showing and hiding toolbars, and printing reports.

 Which is easier to create, a macro or a module, and why?

To create a module, you must know the correct syntax for each line of code. Modules consist of Visual Basic programming code, a robust programming language with endless possibilities. Macros are usually easier to create than modules because you don't have to know as much programming syntax, and you aren't presented with as many options. For example, to make a macro do something, you choose a macro action from a list of predefined choices. Once you've chosen the specific macro action you want, the appropriate arguments for that macro appear at the bottom of the Macro window. The choices for actions, arguments, and values are limited to what appears on the screen.

 Is there ever a situation when I must use a macro?

Yes, you must use macros to make global shortcut key assignments. You can also use an automatic macro that, when the database first opens, carries out a series of actions that are beyond the capabilities of the startup options.

 When should I use a module?

There are at least five reasons to use a module rather than a macro:

- **Class modules** are stored as part of the form or report object in which they are created. Therefore, if you develop forms and reports in one database and copy them to another, class modules are always moved with the object to which they pertain.
- You must use modules to store unique function procedures. For instance, you might wish to create a function called COMMISSION that calculates the appropriate commission on a sale using your company's unique commission formula.
- Modules can contain procedures that mask error messages. Access error messages can be confusing to the user, but using Visual Basic procedures, you can detect the error when it occurs and display your own message or take some action.
- You can't use a macro to accomplish many tasks outside of Access, but Visual Basic code stored in modules works with the other products in the Microsoft Office suite to pass information back and forth between the programs.
- Macros work with entire sets of records at once, but Visual Basic code stored in modules can step through a set of records one record at a time, and perform an operation on each record.

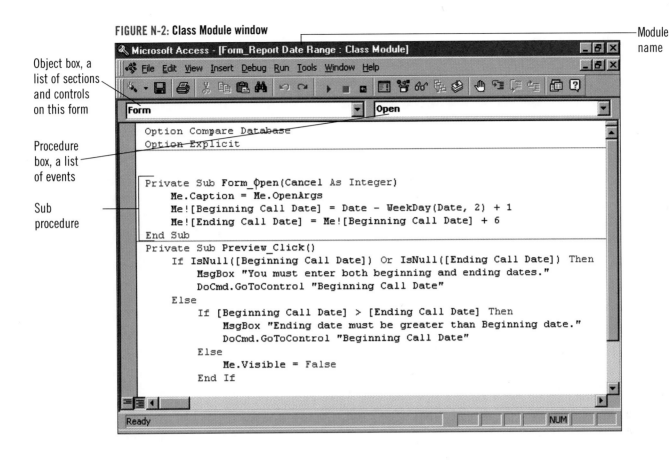

Object box, a list of sections and controls on this form

Module name

Procedure box, a list of events

Sub procedure

```
Option Compare Database
Option Explicit


Private Sub Form_Open(Cancel As Integer)
    Me.Caption = Me.OpenArgs
    Me![Beginning Call Date] = Date - WeekDay(Date, 2) + 1
    Me![Ending Call Date] = Me![Beginning Call Date] + 6
End Sub
Private Sub Preview_Click()
    If IsNull([Beginning Call Date]) Or IsNull([Ending Call Date]) Then
        MsgBox "You must enter both beginning and ending dates."
        DoCmd.GoToControl "Beginning Call Date"
    Else
        If [Beginning Call Date] > [Ending Call Date] Then
            MsgBox "Ending date must be greater than Beginning date."
            DoCmd.GoToControl "Beginning Call Date"
        Else
            Me.Visible = False
        End If
```

TABLE N-2: Components of the Class Module window

component	description
Sub procedure	Performs a series of programming statements, but does not return a value
Object box	In class modules, lists the object as well as its sections and controls, so that procedures can be written that apply to that specific object, section, or control
Procedure box	In class modules, lists the events with which you can associate the procedure
Module name	Located in the title bar

Access 97

Creating a Function Procedure

While there are hundreds of Access-supplied functions, there may be times when you want to create a unique function to accomplish a specific task. You can create a Function procedure in a module that uses arguments to return a value that you can then display or use in an expression.  Some Nomad database users prefer to enter all the data with the Caps Lock key in its locked position. This creates situations where customers have been added to the database in the following manner: NANCY NORTHEY. While this isn't a problem for internal reports, it presents an unprofessional image when using the data for executive reports or customer letters. Rachel creates a Function procedure called NAMECAP in a module object to convert a text entry so that the first letter is capitalized, but the rest of the letters are lowercase, regardless of how the text was entered. By creating a Function procedure for this purpose, she can quickly convert entries in name fields using the NAMECAP function without retyping the long expression that NAMECAP represents. Rachel can use the NAMECAP function procedure in the Customer Entry Form and other forms to handle the uppercase data-entry problem.

1. **Start Access, open Nomad-N, click the Modules tab, then click New**
   The Module window opens with two declaration statements already entered at the top of the screen. The Option Compare Database statement is used to declare the default comparison method to use when string data is compared. The Option Explicit statement requires that you explicitly declare all variables used in the module, which helps you avoid typing errors when entering variable names into the Visual Basic statements. Start a Function procedure by typing the word *function*, the name of the function in uppercase letters, and then any arguments the function needs to use in the calculation. Function arguments are entered inside parentheses.

2. **Type Function NAMECAP(UserEntry), then press [Enter]**
   As soon as you enter the Function statement followed by an appropriate function name and any trailing arguments and then press [Enter], Access automatically adds the End Function statement to mark the end of the Function procedure, and lists NAMECAP as a function of this module in the Procedure box. If you had multiple procedures in this module, you could quickly go to each one by choosing it from the Procedure box list. Access attempts to increase your productivity by adding as many Visual Basic lines of code as it can anticipate. Add the statement that makes the actual conversion of the UserEntry argument.

3. **Maximize the Module 1: Module window, type NAMECAP, then press [Spacebar]**
   As you type a statement that includes a function name such as NAMECAP, the arguments of the function name appear as a ScreenTip as shown in Figure N-3, which helps you enter the function. You'll see ScreenTips appear for other Access-defined functions that are used in the NAMECAP function, such as Ucase, Left, Lcase, Right, and Len.

4. **Type =Ucase(Left(UserEntry,1))&Lcase(Right(UserEntry,Len(UserEntry)-1))**
   The statement to convert the UserEntry argument so that the first character is uppercase and the rest of the characters are lowercase is quite long and scrolls off the right side of the screen. Add a blank line between the NAMECAP statement and the End Function statement.

5. **Press [Enter]**
   The screen should look like Figure N-4. Print the module to keep a record of what you have done.

6. **Click the Print button 🖨 on the Visual Basic toolbar**

7. **Click the Save button 💾 on the Visual Basic toolbar, type Functions in the Module Name text box, then click OK**
   You are finished with the module, close the Module window.

8. **Click the Module window Close button**

QuickTip

Functions do not need to be entered in all uppercase letters, but this convention is often followed to make the function easier to read.

Trouble?

An entry displayed in red indicates that Access has detected a syntax error. Recheck your entry and correct the errors.

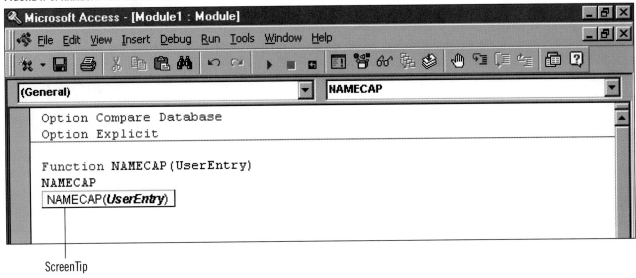

ScreenTip

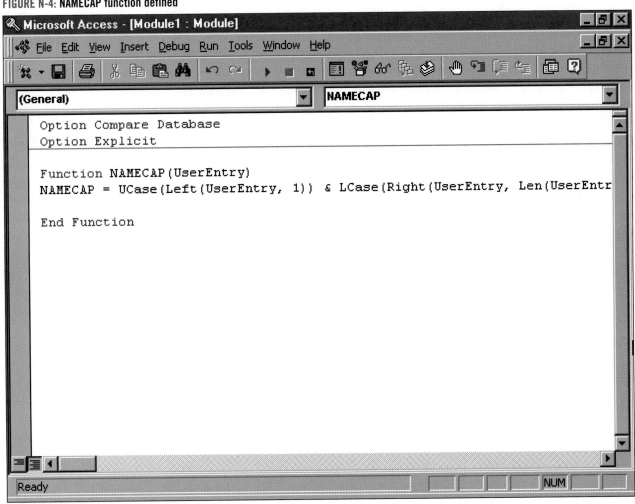

Testing a Procedure

Functions stored within modules cannot be used or tested independently. Rather, you call or execute such functions from controls on forms or reports. Once the Function procedure is defined in the module, it can be used over and over again, just as you would use the Access-supplied SUM, COUNT, or NOW functions. The benefit of defining new functions in modules is that if you edit the definition of the function within the module, every form and report that calls the function automatically updates as well. ◄━━━━ Rachel tests the NAMECAP function in the Customer Entry Form by using it in a new text box control so that any first name entry is automatically converted to the proper capitalization.

Steps 1 2 3 4

1. **Click the Forms tab, click Customer Entry Form if necessary, then click Design**
   You have to widen the form to the 5" mark on the ruler.

2. **Place the insertion point on the right edge of the form so that it changes to a ✛, then drag to the 5" mark on the ruler**
   To use the NAMECAP function, add an unbound text box control to the right side of the First text box on the form.

3. **Click the Toolbox button 🛠 on the Form Design toolbar if necessary, click the Text Box button [abl] on the Toolbox, click to the right of the First text box at the 3" mark on the ruler, click inside the text box control, then type =NAMECAP([First])**
   With the new control added to the form, delete the unnecessary label that was automatically inserted on the form when you added the text box control.

4. **Click the Text22 label, then press [Delete]**
   The screen should look like Figure N-5. Test the NAMECAP function within the new text box control by entering Form View and modifying a record.

5. **Click the Form View button [▦] on the Form Design toolbar, double-click Ginny in the First text box, press [Caps Lock], type GINNY, then press [Tab]**
   Notice that the NAMECAP function displays Ginny properly as shown in Figure N-6, with only the first letter capitalized. Save and close the Customer Entry Form.

6. **Click the Save button [💾] on the Form View toolbar**

7. **Close the Customer Entry Form**

FIGURE N-5: **NAMECAP function added to the Customer Entry Form**

NAMECAP function

New control

Argument

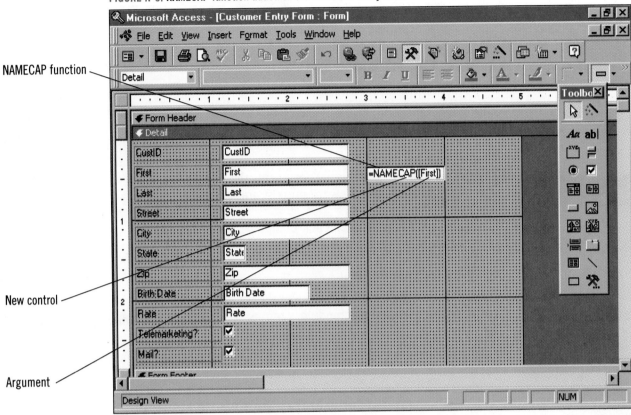

FIGURE N-6: **NAMECAP function working in the Customer Entry Form**

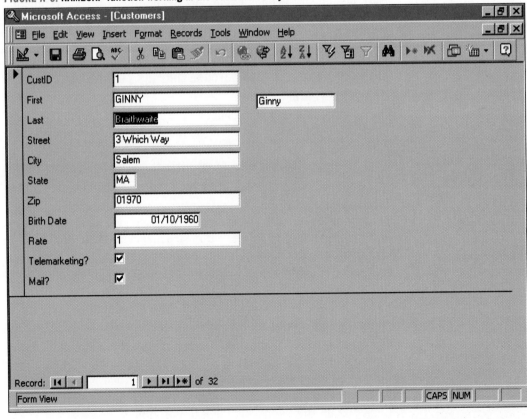

Documenting a Procedure

Writing a module that works properly is a challenge, so it would be poor practice not to protect your hard work with proper documentation. The best way to document a module is to add descriptive comment lines within the module to help you and others understand what has been written, who wrote the code, and when the code was written. A few comments sprinkled within the lines of code are extremely valuable at a later time when you or someone else is trying to modify the module.  Rachel documents the Functions module with descriptive comments so that she can easily follow the purpose and logic of the function.

1. **Click the Modules tab, then click Design**
   The Functions module opens in Design View. Position the insertion point before the Function statement.

2. **Click the blank line just above the Function statement**
   Next, create a new blank line, then enter the comment.

QuickTip

Add comments on the same line as Visual Basic code by preceding the comment with a single apostrophe. The comment must be to the right of the module statement.

3. **Press [Enter], type 'This module creates a new function called NAMECAP, then press [Enter]**
   Comment lines start with a single apostrophe ['] and are displayed in green in the Module window. They are skipped when the module is executed and exist only to make the module easier to read and follow.

4. **Type 'This module was created by *Your Name*, press [Enter], type 'The function statement identifies the name and arguments for the function, then press [Enter]**
   Your screen should look like Figure N-7. Blank lines are another useful way to separate sections of a module and are simply skipped when executing the lines of code in a module. Next, document the line of code that defines the NAMECAP function itself. Position the insertion point before the NAMECAP line, create a new blank line, then enter the comment.

5. **Click before the NAMECAP = statement, press [Enter], press the [Up arrow] to move above the NAMECAP line, type 'NAMECAP converts the UserEntry argument so that the first character is uppercase and the rest of the characters are lowercase, then press [Enter]**
   The fact that that your comment and the next line of Visual Basic code have scrolled off the right edge of the screen doesn't affect the program; however, these long lines make the code harder to read. Shorten both lines so that you can clearly see them on the screen.

Trouble?

If you have a syntax error in any line, it will be red. Carefully check to make sure that there is a space before the underscore character. Error-free Visual Basic appears black; statements and functions appear blue; comments are in green; and variables and arguments supplied by the user are shown in black.

6. **Click to place the insertion point after the word character in the comment line you just entered, press [Enter], then type ' (apostrophe)**
   Breaking long comment lines into two comment lines is straightforward. Just add a single apostrophe to the beginning of the line. When you want to break an actual line of Visual Basic code into two lines to see the entire statement on the screen, insert the line-continuation characters, a space followed by an underscore character [_], then press [Enter] to break the entry into two lines. See Table N-3 for information on other important keys and key combinations within the Module window.

7. **Click after & in the NAMECAP line, press [Spacebar], type _ (underscore), then press [Enter]**
   The long NAMECAP line breaks into two lines that are visible on the screen. Your screen should look like Figure N-8. Not only is the module well documented, each line is completely visible on the screen without scrolling. When pleased with your changes, close the Module window and save the changes.

8. **Click File on the menu bar, click Close, then click Yes**

FIGURE N-7: Adding comments to a function

Green comment
lines start with a
single apostrophe

Your name
appears here

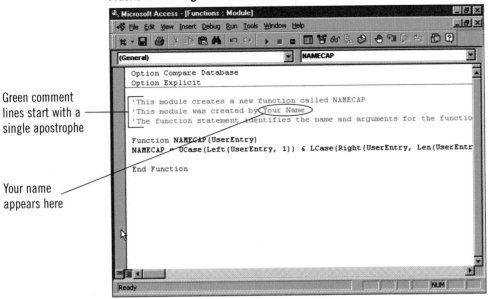

FIGURE N-8: Using the continuation character for long lines of code

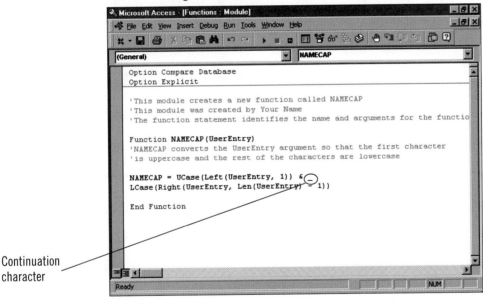

Continuation
character

TABLE N-3: Module shortcut keys

key	action
[Ctrl][Y]	Cuts the current line and places it onto the Clipboard
[F2]	Displays the Object Browser, a dialog box you can use to examine the contents of the object library to get information about the objects provided
[Ctrl][A]	Selects all visible code in the Module window
[Tab] or [Shift][Tab]	Indents or removes indentation from selected lines
[Ctrl][G]	Displays the Debug window
[F9]	Toggles a breakpoint at the selected line
[Ctrl][Break]	Halts execution of code or a macro

Using If Statements

The **If . . . Then . . . Else** statement allows you to test a logical condition and execute commands only if the condition is true. The If . . . Then . . . Else statement can be one or several lines of code, depending on how many conditions you want to test, and how many answers the result can be. See Table N-4 for more information on this popular statement. ◄ Rachel's NAMECAP function works well to convert first name entries to the proper capitalization for every existing record in the database. When you are entering new records using the Customer Entry Form, however, the NAME-CAP function doesn't work properly because it doesn't accommodate a situation in which no entry is in the First control. In other words, when the UserEntry argument of the NAMECAP function is nothing, the function doesn't run properly. Rachel uses the If . . . Then statement first to check whether the UserEntry argument contains an entry. (Recall that in this case, the UserEntry argument has been defined as the First field in the form's Design View.) If information has been entered in the First field, the NAMECAP function executes. If the First field is empty, the NAMECAP function does not execute.

Steps

1. Click **Design** to open the Functions Module window, then click the blank line after the last comment line
   You add three lines of documentation to explain the If statement.

2. Press **[Enter]**, type **'This If statement will check to see if the UserEntry argument is empty**, press **[Enter]**, type **'If it is empty, NAMECAP will not execute**, press **[Enter]**, type **'if it is NOT empty, NAMECAP will execute**, then press **[Enter]**
   Your screen should look like Figure N-9. Now add the appropriate If statement programming code.

3. Press **[Enter]**, type **If UserEntry <> "" Then**, then press **[Enter]**
   Translated, the line of code reads "If the UserEntry argument is not empty, then do the next statement. If the UserEntry argument *is empty*, skip the next statement." In other words, the NAMECAP function is evaluated only if the UserEntry argument contains an entry. The greater-than and less-than signs together mean "not equal to." The two double quotes with nothing in between them represent "empty" or "nothing." For each If statement started, you must identify where the If statement ends because you must identify where the execution of the function continues if the result of the If statement is false.

4. Press **[Down Arrow]** three times, press **[Enter]**, type **End If**, press **[Enter]**, then press **[Down Arrow]**
   The screen should look like Figure N-10. Notice that Visual Basic words If, Then, and End If are in blue, and that the variable information you type is in black. This is one way Access helps you read and follow the logic of Visual Basic code. Save and test the If statement.

5. Click the **Save button** 🖫 on the Visual Basic toolbar, click the **Functions Module window Close button**, click the **Forms tab**, double-click **Customer Entry Form** to open it in Form View, then click the **New Record button** ▸* on the Form View toolbar
   The NAMECAP function text box added to the form to display the First name entry properly appears blank. Without the If statement in the Function procedure, it would have returned an error message because you had not yet supplied the argument. Add a new record to test the NAMECAP function further.

6. Type **33**, press **[Tab]**, type **NANCY**, then press **[Tab]**
   The text box to the right of "NANCY" should be capitalized correctly as "Nancy." Fill out the rest of the record for this new customer.

7. Type **Kent**, press **[Tab]**, type **90 Poplar Street**, press **[Tab]**, type **Ames**, press **[Tab]** twice, type **50010**, press **[Tab]**, type **8/20/57**, press **[Tab]**, type **1** for the Rate field, then click **the check boxes Yes** for both the **Telemarketing?** and **Mail?**
   When satisfied that the If statement works correctly, close the Customer Entry Form.

8. Click **File** on the menu bar, then click **Close**

FIGURE N-9: Documenting an If statement

New documentation ———

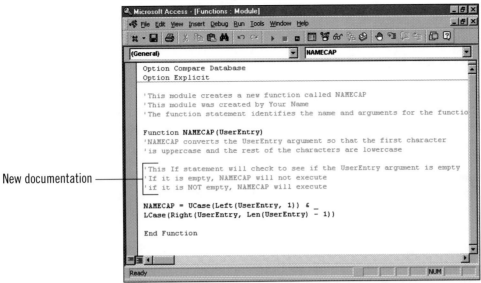

FIGURE N-10: The completed If statement

If statement ———

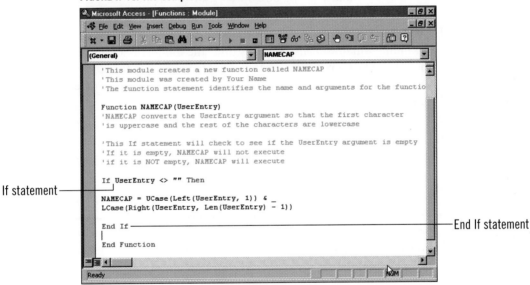

End If statement

TABLE N-4: If . . . Then . . . Else statement syntax

type of if . . . then . . . else statement	example	type of if . . . then . . . else statement	example

Running a single statement if a condition is true	If myDate < Now Then myDate = Now	**Running certain statements if a condition is true and others if it is false**	If value = 0 Then
			    AlertLabel.ForeColor = "Red"
			    AlertLabel.Font.Bold = True
			Else
			    AlertLabel.ForeColor = "Blue"
			    AlertLabel.Font.Bold = False
			End If

Running more than one line of code if a condition is true	If value = 0 Then
	    AlertLabel.ForeColor = "Red"
	    AlertLabel.Font.Bold = True
	End If
		Testing a second condition if the first condition is false	If performance = 1 Then
			    Bonus = salary * 0.1
			Else If performance = 2 Then
			    Bonus = salary * 0.09
			Else
			    Bonus = 0
			End If

Creating a Class Module

Class modules are form or report modules that are associated with a particular form or report. Form and report modules often contain event procedures that run in response to an event on the form or report. An **event procedure** is a procedure run in response to an action performed by the user, such as clicking a command button or changing data. Event procedures can help your users avoid common data-entry errors and draw their attention to important information. ▶ Rachel uses an event procedure to create a beep if the data in the CustID text box changes in the Customer Entry Form. She stores the event procedure as a class module in the Customer Entry Form.

Steps

1. Click **Design** to open the Customer Entry Form in Design View, double-click the **CustID text box** to open the CustID property sheet, click the **Event tab**, click the **On Change property text box**, then click the **Build button** [...]
   The Choose Builder dialog box opens, asking whether you wish to build an expression, a macro, or Visual Basic code. You have to use the Code Builder.

2. Click **Code Builder**, then click **OK**
   A Module window opens, only this time, the module is a class module, applicable only for the CustID text box on the Customer Entry Form. Add the appropriate line of code to produce a sound through the computer's speaker when the data in the CustID text box changes.

3. Type **Beep**
   The Module window should look like Figure N-11. Save and close the Module window.

4. Click the **Save button** 🖫 on the Visual Basic toolbar, click the **Module window Close button**, click the **Form View button** 🖽, click the **New Record button** ▶＊ on the Form View toolbar, then type **1**
   As soon as you type any information in the CustID field, you should hear a beep. If your PC's speaker isn't turned on, however, this event procedure doesn't alert you that changes have been made to the CustID field. Modify the event procedure to display a dialog box also.

5. Press **[Esc]** twice to remove the entry in the CustID field as well as stop editing the record, click the **Design View button** 🖳 on the Form View toolbar, then click the **Code button** 🗔 on the Form Design toolbar
   The Class Module window opens. Add the statement to display a dialog box after the Beep statement.

6. Click after the **Beep statement**, press **[Enter]**, type **MsgBox**, then press **[Spacebar]**
   The Module window should look like Figure N-12. As soon you type the MsgBox function and press the Spacebar, the ControlTip help text appears indicating the possible arguments for the function. Only one function is required, the Prompt argument, which is why it appears bold. Enter the rest of the statement.

7. Type **("Customer number has been updated or changed.")**
   The screen should look like Figure N-13. Close the Class Module window, saving the changes to the module, then add a new record to the Customer Entry Form.

8. Click the **File** on the menu bar, click **Close**, click 🖽, click ▶＊, then type **1**
   A message box appears with the text that was entered as the Prompt argument in the MsgBox function. Satisfied that the event module works as planned, close the message box, then close the Customer Entry Form without saving the changes to the new record.

9. Click **OK**, press **[Esc]** twice, click **File** on the menu bar, click **Close**, then click **No**

FIGURE N-11: Creating an event procedure in a class module

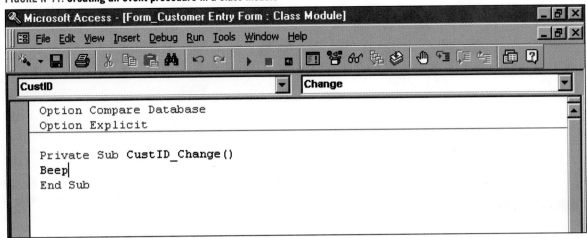

FIGURE N-12: Entering the MsgBox function

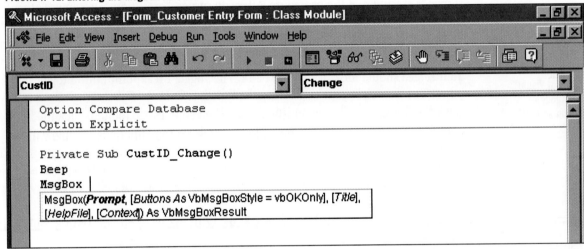

FIGURE N-13: Editing an event procedure in a class module

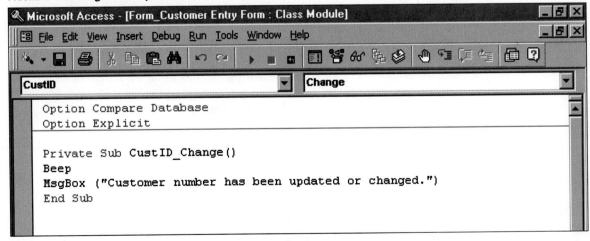

Troubleshooting Module Problems

Debugging is a process you use to find and resolve errors in your Visual Basic code. There are three types of errors you may encounter as your code runs, and Access provides several techniques to help you debug them. **Compile-time** errors occur as a result of incorrectly constructed code. For example, you may have forgotten to balance pairs of statements such as If and End If, or you may have a programming mistake such as an incorrect number of arguments for a function. **Run-time** errors occur after the code starts to run and include attempting an illegal operation such as dividing by zero. **Logic** errors occur when the code runs, but doesn't produce the expected results.  Although Rachel doesn't have problems with her current module, she wants to learn debugging techniques.

1. Click the Modules tab, then click Design

The Functions module opens in the Module window. The first step in determining what is happening at any point in the procedure is to set a **breakpoint**, a line of code that automatically suspends execution of the procedure. After you suspend execution, you can use other tools to determine what is happening at that exact point in time. Toggle a breakpoint at the If statement.

QuickTip

Click in the gray bar to the left of the line of Visual Basic code to toggle breakpoints on and off.

2. Click the If UserEntry line, then click the Toggle Breakpoint button 🖐 on the Visual Basic toolbar

Your screen should look like Figure N-14. The Toggle Breakpoint button toggles the breakpoint. Test the breakpoint by running the function from the Customer Entry Form.

3. Click the Database Window button 📇 on the Visual Basic toolbar, click the Forms tab, double-click Customer Entry Form, then maximize the Functions Module window

When the Customer Entry Form opens in Form View, it immediately runs the NAMECAP function. Since you set a breakpoint at the If statement, that statement is highlighted, as shown in Figure N-15, indicating that the code has been suspended at that point. Open the Debug window to analyze the code.

QuickTip

The Debug Window button 🔲 on the Visual Basic toolbar also displays the Debug window.

4. Click View on the menu bar, click Debug Window to open the Debug window, then click the Locals tab if necessary

The screen should look like Figure N-16. The Debug window tells you that the NAMECAP function is currently empty. You can click the plus and minus signs to the left of the entries in the expression column can be clicked to expand or collapse the property list for that item, so you can track exactly when and how properties change based on the line of Visual Basic code you are analyzing. Use the **immediate pane**, a scratch pad window in which statements are evaluated immediately, to determine what is happening at that line of code. Determine the value of the UserEntry argument.

5. Type ? UserEntry, then press [Enter]

Since the NAMECAP function is evaluating the data in the First field of the first record in the Customer Entry Form, the UserEntry argument of the NAMECAP function currently holds the value "GINNY." Close the Debug window, remove the breakpoint, then close the Module window.

6. Close the Debug window, close the Functions module window, then click Yes when asked whether you want to stop running the code

The breakpoints work as intended, remove the breakpoint from the module.

Time To

✔ Exit

7. Close the Customer Entry Form, click the Modules tab, click Design, click the If UserEntry statement, click 🖐, then close the Functions Module window

Now that you've learned a few techniques for debugging Visual Basic code, you're ready to close the Nomad-N database and exit Access.

FIGURE N-14: **Setting a breakpoint**

Toggle Breakpoint
button

Database Window
button

Step Into
button

Debug Window
button

Toggle breakpoint

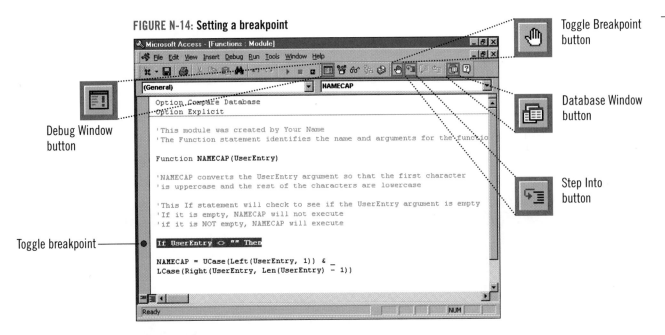

FIGURE N-15: **Running a function with a breakpoint**

Breakpoint highlighted

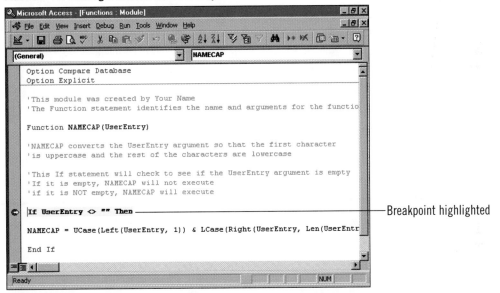

FIGURE N-16: **Debug window**

Immediate pane

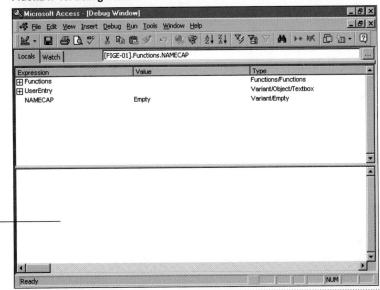

Access 97

Practice

► Concepts Review

Identify each item shown in Figure N-17.

FIGURE N-17

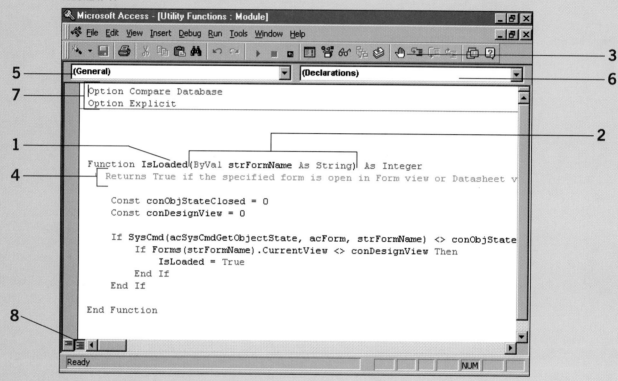

Match each term with the statement that describes its function.

9. **Procedure**
10. **If . . . Then . . . Else statement**
11. **Debugging**
12. **Class modules**
13. **Visual Basic**
14. **Function**
15. **Arguments**
16. **Breakpoint**
17. **Module**

a. Allows you to test a logical condition and execute commands only if the condition is true
b. The programming language used in Access modules
c. A line of code that automatically suspends execution of the procedure
d. A procedure that returns a value
e. Constants, variables, or expressions passed to a procedure to further define how it should execute
f. Stored as part of the form or report object in which they are created
g. The Access object where Visual Basic code is stored
h. A series of Visual Basic statements that perform an operation or calculate a value
i. A process you use to find and resolve errors in your Visual Basic code

Select the best answer from the list of choices.

18. The Access object that contains Visual Basic programming code is the
    a. Module.
    b. Macro.
    c. Procedure.
    d. Function.

19. A module contains Visual Basic programming code organized in units called
    a. Macros.
    b. Arguments.
    c. Breakpoints.
    d. Procedures.

20. **Which type of procedure does _not_ return a value?**
    a. Sub procedure
    b. Function
    c. Module
    d. Macro

21. **Which type of modules are stored as part of the form or report object in which they are created?**
    a. Object modules
    b. Standard modules
    c. Class modules
    d. Global modules

22. **Which of the following is _not_ a reason to use modules rather than macros?**
    a. Modules must be used to store unique function procedures
    b. Visual Basic code stored in modules works with the other products in the Microsoft Office suite to pass information back and forth between the programs
    c. Modules can contain procedures that mask error messages
    d. Modules are usually easier to create than macros

23. **Event procedures are often developed to**
    a. Help your users avoid common data-entry errors and draw users' attention to important information.
    b. Automate printing tasks.
    c. Create startup options.
    d. Make Visual Basic programming code easier to debug.

▶ Skills Review

1. **Understand a module.**
    a. Start Access and open the Addresses-N.mdb. Click the Modules tab, click Design to open the Module window of the Fahrenheit to Celsius converter module, then maximize the window.
    b. Record your answers to the following questions on a plain sheet of paper:
        1. What does each line of code that begins with a ' (single apostrophe) represent?
        2. If the last three lines did not start with a ' (single apostrophe), what type of procedure would they be?
        3. If the last three lines did not start with a ' (single apostrophe), how many arguments would be declared in the function?
        4. If the last three lines did not start with a ' (single apostrophe), what would the name of the function be?
        5. Why are the lines of code that start with a ' (single apostrophe) in green?

2. **Understand when to use macros rather than modules.**
    a. If the window is not already opened, open the Module window of the Fahrenheit to Celsius converter module in the Addresses-N database.
    b. Record your answers to the following questions on a plain sheet of paper:
        1. If the last three lines did not start with a ' (single apostrophe), why would they be entered in a module window rather than a Macro window?
        2. If the last three lines did not start with a ' (single apostrophe), what type of procedure would they represent?

3. **Create a Function procedure.**
    a. If the window is not already opened, open the Module window of the Fahrenheit to Celsius Converter module in the Addresses-N database.
    b. Edit the last three lines of the module, deleting the leading ' (single apostrophe).
    c. There should be only one End Function line of code, as only one function has been defined. Delete any extra End Function lines of code that are generated. The last three statements should look like the following:
    Function Celsius(Fahrenheit)
    Celsius = (Fahrenheit -32) * 5/9
    End Function

d. Save the function, then print the function by clicking the Print button on the Visual Basic toolbar.

e. Close the Module window

4. **Test a function.**

    a. Open the States Form in Design View.

    b. Change the text box to the right of the Average Temp C label so that the Control Source property is =Celsius([Average Temp]).

    c. Display the form in Form View, display the first record for Alaska, enter 38 as the average temperature next to the Average Temp F label, and watch the Celsius function convert the Fahrenheit temperature to the Celsius equivalent in the next text box.

    d. Print the Alaska record, then close the form, saving the changes.

5. **Document a procedure.**

    a. Open the Fahrenheit to Celsius Converter Module window in Design View, then modify the top three comments to read as follows:

    'This module creates a function called Celsius.

    'Celsius converts Fahrenheit temperatures to the Celsius scale.

    'The lines of Visual Basic code required to do this are shown below.

    b. Delete any extra lines so that only one blank line separates the three comment lines from the three Visual Basic programming statements.

    c. Save the function, then print the function by clicking the Print button on the Visual Basic toolbar.

6. **Use If statements.**

    a. In the Fahrenheit to Celsius Converter Module window, add another function to the bottom of the Module window with the following statements. Press [Tab] to indent the statements between the If and End If statements.

```
Function ClimateAnswer(Result)
'If Celsius < 10, the ClimateAnswer should be set to "Cold."
'Else, ClimateAnswer should be set to "Moderate."
If Result < 10 Then
    ClimateAnswer = "Cold"
    Else: ClimateAnswer = "Moderate"
End If
End Function
```

    b. Save and close the module.

    c. Open the States Form in Design View and display the property sheet for the fourth text box, the one to the right of the Average Temp C label.

    d. Change the Name property on the Other tab to read Ctemp.

    e. Click the fifth text box, the one to the right of the Climate label, to display its property sheet.

    f. Change the Control Source property on the Data tab to read =ClimateAnswer([Ctemp]).

    g. Display the form in Form View. The first record is AK, Alaska.

    h. Type 45 in the Average Temp F text box.

    i. The Average Temp C text box should display 7.22, and the Climate text box should display Cold.

    j. Print the Alaska record.

7. **Create a class module.**

    a. Open the States Form in Design View, then click the Average Temp F text box.

    b. Click the Event tab in the property sheet, click the On Lost Focus property, click the Build button, click Code builder, then click OK.

    c. Type MsgBox ("You have just changed the average temperature.") in the line between the Private Sub and End Sub commands.

    d. Save and close the Class Module window.

    e. Close the text box property sheet, then open the form in Form View.

f. Type 70 for the Average TempF for Alaska, then press [Tab].

g. Click OK to respond to the dialog box created by the MsgBox statement.

h. Print the Alaska record. The Climate text box should now display Moderate.

i. Save and close the States Form.

8. **Troubleshoot module problems.**

a. Open the Fahrenheit to Celsius Converter Module window.

b. Set a breakpoint at the If Result < 10 line, then save and close the module.

c. Open the States Form to display the Alaska record. You should be immediately returned to the Module window with the breakpoint statement highlighted.

d. Open the Debug window by clicking the Debug Window button on the Visual Basic toolbar or by clicking View on the menu bar, then clicking Debug Window.

e. Type ? result, then press [Enter]. The answer should be displayed as 21.11111111.

f. Close the Debug window, then close the Module window, responding Yes to the question about halting execution of the code.

g. Close the States Form window, return to the Fahrenheit to Celsius Converter Module window, remove the breakpoint from the If statement, then save and close the module.

h. Close the database, then exit Access.

▶ Independent Challenges

1. You have been hired as a marketing representative for an exciting company called Product. Product sells women's clothing to upscale retail outlets. You have developed a database called Product-N to record the store locations that carry Product clothing, the dollar amount of merchandise they have purchased from Product, and your resulting commission.

To complete this independent challenge:

1. Start Access, then open the database Product-N.

2. Open a new Module window and enter the following module statements to develop a function called COMMISSION which calculates your commission on total sales.

'Commission is 25% of the SalesFigure argument.

Function Commission(SalesFigure)

Commission = SalesFigure * 0.25

End Function

3. Save the module, naming it Commission Function, then close the Module window.

4. Open the Store Entry Form in Design View, then click the Commission text box.

5. Open the Commission text box's property sheet, modify the Control Source property on the Data tab so that it reads =Commission([Sales]), then close the property sheet.

6. Display the Store Entry Form in Form View, then print the first record for the Arizona Dept. Stores.

7. Save the Store Entry Form, close the form, close the database, then exit Access.

2. You have been hired to work on a database for a company called Clothing. Clothing wants its sales representatives to focus on the high dollar accounts, and has created a Commission formula to reflect this goal. Clothing pays 25 percent commission only if the sales are greater than $5,000 to the store. You create a Commission function to handle this policy, then add a class module to sound a beep when sales have been modified on the Store Entry Form.

To complete this independent challenge:

1. Start Access, open the Clothing-N database, then open a new Module window.

2. Enter the following statements so that they contain the If statements to accommodate the commission policy.

'Commission is 25% of the SalesFigure argument.

'The SalesFigure must be > 5000 for commissions to be paid.

Function Commission(SalesFigure)

If SalesFigure > 5000 Then

```
Commission = SalesFigure * 0.25
Else: Commission = 0
End If
End Function
```

3. Save the module, naming it Clothing Commission, then close the Module window.

4. Open the Store Entry Form in Design View, then click the Commission text box.

5. Open the Commission text box's property sheet, modify the Control Source property on the Data page so that it reads =Commission([Sales]), then close the property sheet.

6. Open the Store Entry Form in Form View and print the first two records. The commission for the first record, the Arizona Dept. Stores, should now be $0, but the commission for the second record, Barney's in Beverly Hills, should be $12,500.

7. Open the Store Entry Form in Design View, click the Sales text box, then click the Properties button.

8. Click the After Update property on the Event page, click the Build button, then select the Code Builder.

9. Enter the following Visual Basic statements to cause the computer to beep if the value in the Sales text box is greater than $5,000: If Sales > 5000 then Beep.

10. Save the class module, then close it.

11. Close the property sheet of the Sales text box, then open the form in Form View.

12. Modify the Sales entry of the first record, the Arizona Dept. Stores, to $10,000 by entering 10000, then pressing [Tab]. You should see the Commission calculate as well as hear a beep from the computer.

13. Save the Store Entry Form, then print the first record.

14. Close the Store Entry Form, close Product-N database, then exit Access.

3. You are working with a college's records department, maintaining student information in an Access database called Students-N.mdb. Your school offers a two-year program that feeds into a four-year degree from a neighboring school. Your school uses a 4.0 scale to determine the grade point average (GPA), but the neighboring school uses a 5.0 scale. Your current challenge is to determine an easy way to convert the student's current GPA on a 5.0 scale, then display this value in the Student Information Form.

To complete this independent challenge:

1. Start Access, then open Students-N.mdb from the Student Disk.

2. Click the Modules tab, then enter the following Function procedure, which converts a 4.0 GPA to a 5.0 scale.
```
'This function converts a GPA
'on a 4.0 scale to a GPA on a 5.0 scale.
Function GPA5SCALE(GPA4scale)
GPA5SCALE = GPA4scale *5/4
End Function
```

3. Save the function, naming it GPA Converter, then close the Module window.

4. Open the Student Info Form in Design View, then add an unbound text box control to the right of the GPA text box at about the 3" mark on the ruler.

5. Modify the Caption property of the Text22 label (which you created when you added the unbound text box control) to "GPA on 5.0 scale:". Resize the control as needed.

6. Modify the Control Source property of the unbound text box control to =GPA5SCALE([GPA]).

7. View the form in Form view, print the first three records, then close the form saving the changes to the design.

8. Open the GPA Converter Module window, then modify the module so that the additional three statements starting with the If statement are added as follows. This modification causes a message box to appear if the student has a low GPA:
```
'This function converts a GPA on a 4.0 scale to a GPA on a 5.0 scale.
Function GPA5SCALE(GPA4scale)
If GPA4scale < 2 Then
MsgBox ("Conditional Student")
End If
```

GPA5SCALE = GPA4scale * 5/4
End Function

9. Save, print, then close the module.
10. Open the Student Info Form in Form View. Since the first student's GPA is below 2.0, you should see the Conditional Student message box. Click OK to close the message box.
11. Close the Student Info form, close the database, then exit Access.

4. You work for a retailer that sells products to women's clothing stores. You have been asked to handle three new stores in California, and wish to add them to your current Access database called ProductNet-N. You'll access the appropriate Internet Web site to locate the stores in California, choose three for your territory, then use the Access database to determine commissions on sales. To complete this independent challenge:

1. Log on to the Internet and use your browser to go to http://www.course.com. From there, click Student Online Companions, click the link for the book you are using, then click the Access link for Unit N.
2. Print the Web pages that list the stores in the state of California.
3. Log off the Internet.
4. Start Access, then open the ProductNet-N database.
5. Open the Store Entry Form, then add the three new stores. Sales for the three stores should be $4,000, $6,000, and $10,000, respectively.
6. Save and close the Store Entry Form.
7. Management has changed the Commission function. They have decided to add a $1,000 bonus to the commission for each sale that is $10,000 or greater. Open the Module window for the Commission function and enter the following code to accommodate this policy.

'Commission is 25% of the SalesFigure argument.
'The SalesFigure must be > 5000 for commissions to be paid.
'If the SalesFigure is > = 10000, a 1000 bonus is applied.
Function Commission(SalesFigure)
If SalesFigure > =10000 Then
Commission = SalesFigure * 0.25 +1000
ElseIf SalesFigure > 5000 Then
Commission = SalesFigure * 0.25
Else: Commission = 0
End If
End Function

8. Save the module as Commission Function, then close the module window.
9. Open the Store Entry Form, then print the last three store records. These should be the same store records that you entered in step 5.
10. Save and close the Store Entry Form.
11. Open the Commission Function Module window, then set a breakpoint at the first If statement.
12. Open the Store Entry Form, which will immediately attempt to process the Commission function with the breakpoint.
13. Click the Debug Window button or click View from the menu bar, then click Debug Window to open the Debug window.
14. Type ?SalesFigure, then press [Enter]. The first store's sales figure of 5,000 should appear because this record is currently being processed by the Commission function.
15. Close the Debug window, close the Module window, answering Yes to halting execution of the module, then close the Store Entry form.
16. Open the Commission Function Module window, remove the breakpoint at the first If statement, then save and close the Commission Function Module window one last time.
17. Close ProductNet-N, then exit Access.

▶ Visual Workshop

Open the VW-N database and create the module shown in Figure N-18. This module creates a function called QUARTERLY that you can use in forms to calculate a quarterly pledge amount based on the argument called pledge. Save the module as Quarterly Function, then print it. Open the Donations form, which displays a text box that uses the Quarterly function, then print the first record.

FIGURE N-18

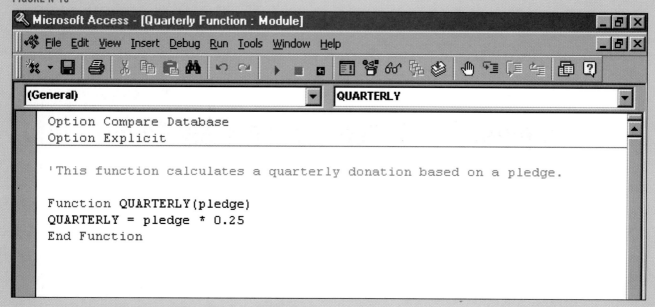

Creating
Graphical Reports

Objectives

▶ **Use AutoFormat and the Format Painter**
▶ **Add subreports**
▶ **Create column charts**
▶ **Create line charts**
▶ **Create pie charts**
▶ **Add background pictures**
▶ **Add page breaks**
▶ **Keep records in groups together**

Reports are database objects which give you maximum flexibility regarding how you summarize, print, and format groups of records on **hard copy** (paper) output. For example, a report can present summary information such as subtotals on groups of records as well as present custom headers and footers for different sections of the report. You design reports much like you develop forms, using Report Design View with bound and unbound controls. Bound controls can be as simple as text boxes representing information within an underlying record, or as complex as a column chart that graphically displays numeric information summarized across groups of records. You can preview reports on the screen, but you cannot edit data displayed in a report as you can data in a form. As the information in Nomad's database has grown, so has management's appetite for summarized and graphic analysis of the data. Rachel uses Access report objects to create professional and powerful reports that not only present individual records similar to datasheet printouts, but also analyze and graph groups of records. Rachel also uses the powerful report-formatting features to make the reports look more professional and the information within them easier to read and understand.

Using AutoFormat and the Format Painter

You can use the **AutoFormat** feature to automate formatting for an entire report after you create it. **Formatting** refers to changing a report's colors, lines, fonts, and other appearance properties. Access supplies several AutoFormat choices, and you can create your own. After you apply formatting properties to an individual control within a report, you cannot save them individually, but you can use the **Format Painter** feature to copy formatting characteristics of an individual control to another control. ✏ Management asked Rachel to create a report to summarize 1998 sales. She uses the Report Wizard, then uses the AutoFormat and Format Painter features to apply formatting styles.

QuickTip

Rachel used the shortcut w/n for the word *within* when naming this query.

1. **Start Access, open the Nomad-0 database on your Student Disk, then click the Reports tab**
   Build a new report based on the Customers w/n Tour Query object.

2. **Click New, click Report Wizard, click the Choose the table or query where the object's data comes from list arrow, click Customers w/n Tour Query, then click OK**
   The Report Wizard displays a series of dialog boxes that walk you through the process of creating a report. Select all of the fields, then display the records by tour.

3. **Click the Select All fields button ➤➤ , click Next > , click by Tours, then click Next >**
   Grouping means to sort records according to a specified field. You've grouped the records by the TourID field. Access refers to this sorting capability as "grouping" rather than "sorting," because report groups give you the additional ability to insert a **group header** or **group footer** above or below the individual records in the group. Sort the records for this report by the Last field.

4. **Click Next > , click the first sort list arrow, click Last, then click Next >**
   Next specify how to format the report. The wizard presents a list of predeveloped Access AutoFormats that you can apply now or later.

Trouble?

The Font/Fore Color button default is red but will display the last font color you chose. Click the Font/Fore Color list arrow and click the red button to return to the default.

5. **Click the Outline 1 option button, click the Landscape option button, click Next > , click Corporate, click Next > , type Sales by Tour Report, click Finish , then maximize the Sales by Tour Report window**
   The new report opens in Print Preview. Scroll down to see the report as shown in Figure O-1. You decide to add some red accents to help distinguish the information for each group of records. Switch to Form Design View and format the controls in the TourID header to red.

6. **Click the Design View button 📐 , click the TourID label in the TourID Header section, then click the Font/Fore Color button A ▾ on the Formatting (Form/Report) toolbar**
   The screen should look like Figure O-2. Apply the TourID label's formatting characteristics to the other labels in the TourID Header section.

7. **Double-click the Format Painter button 🖌 on the Report Design toolbar, click the TourName label, click the TourDate label, click the Last label, click the First label, click the InvoiceDate label, then press [Esc] to release the Format Painter mouse pointer**
   Save these formatting changes so that you can apply them to a different report object.

Trouble?

If "Corporate with red text" style exists on your computer, click Format, click AutoFormat, click the style, click Customize, click Delete style, then click OK.

8. **Click Format on the menu bar, click AutoFormat, click Customize, click Create a new AutoFormat based on the Report 'Sales by Tour Report' option button, click OK, type Corporate with red text in the Style Name text box, then click OK**
   The AutoFormat dialog box reappears with a sample of the new formatting options you have just defined, as shown in Figure O-3.

9. **Click Close, click the Save button 💾 , then close the Sales by Tour Report**

FIGURE O-1: Sales by Tour Report

Report Header ——

TourID group Header ——

Detail records ——

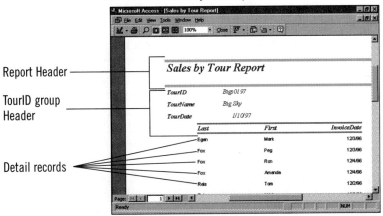

FIGURE O-2: Sales by Tour Report in Report Design View

Object indicator button

TourID label is selected and formatted

TourID Header section

Format Painter button

Font/Fore Color button

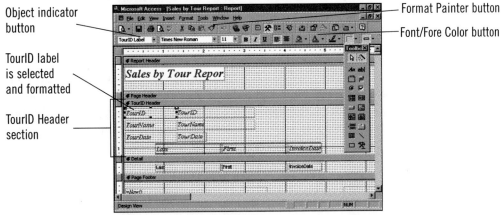

FIGURE O-3: AutoFormat dialog box

New AutoFormat ——

Preview of 'corporate with red text' AutoFormat

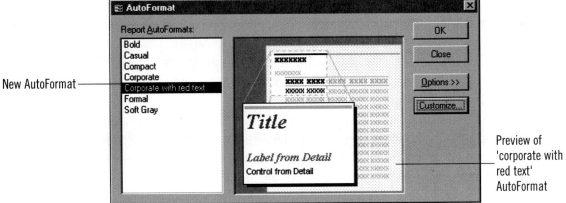

CLUES TO USE

Summary controls in headers and footers

Group header and group footers are excellent locations to add summary controls to a report. These controls can add, count, or average a field in the group of records to which they refer. Specify multiple groups (for example, a Zipcode group within a State group) if you wish to add summary statistics on more than one field. If you grouped records on Zipcode within State, you could count the number of records within State, you could count the number of records with the same Zipcode in the Zipcode group footer, and also count the total number of records with the same State in the State group footer. You can also sort records within a group. While sorting records also places them in a certain order, it does not provide for group header and footer report sections as grouping does.

Adding Subreports

A **subreport** is a report that is added as a control within another report in the same manner that subforms are added to forms. The first report is called the **main report**, and the report that is placed as a control on the main report is the subreport. Use subreports when you want to combine or print two or more reports in a single report object, or when you cannot accomplish the report layout you desire with a single report object. An example of the latter might be when you want the first or last page of a report to contain summarized information that you would normally calculate in a group header or footer section, and you want the rest of the report pages to show detail records. In this case, you would need to develop two separate reports and put them together in a report/subreport combination. ⟍ Management has asked Rachel to add another page to the Sales by Tour Report, a summarization of the number of sales transactions for each TourID. To accomplish this, she starts a report called Summary Sales Report that counts the number of sales made for each tour. She adds the Summary Sales Report as a subreport control to the Report Footer section of the Sales by Tour Report; therefore, the Summary Sales Report prints at the end of the Sales by Tour Report. First, however, she finishes the Summary Sales Report to count the sales transactions for each TourID.

1. Click **Summary Sales Report**, then click **Design**

    The report opens in Report Design View. The Tour ID Header section contains label and text box controls that identify each tour, and there are no controls in the Detail section.

2. Click the **Toolbox button** 🛠 on the Report Design toolbar if necessary, click the **Text Box button** 🔲 in the Toolbox, then click the **1" mark** in the TourID Header section below the TourID text box as shown in Figure O-4.

    With a text box control added to the TourID header section, you can now modify the text box to count the number of tours within each group.

3. Click the **unbound text box** in the TourID Header section, then type **=Count([TourID])**

    Now modify the label to the left of the text box.

QuickTip

You can also modify a label by double-clicking it to open its property sheet, then changing its caption property directly on the Format tab.

4. Click the **new label control** in the TourID Header section, double-click the existing **Text44: label**, then type **Count**

    The screen should look like Figure O-5. Save and close the Summary Sales Report. This report will then be a subreport in the Sales by Tour Report.

5. Click the **Save button** 💾 on the Report Design toolbar, close the Summary Sales Report, click the **Sales by Tour Report** on the Reports tab of the database window, then click **Design**

    Open the Report Footer section, then add the subreport control to that section.

6. Scroll to the bottom of the Sales by Tour Report to display the **Report Footer section**, position the mouse pointer on the **bottom edge of the Report Footer section** so that it changes to a ⥮, then drag down about 1"

    Now add the subreport control to the Report Footer section.

QuickTip

See Table O-1 for more information on Access Wizards.

7. Verify that the Control Wizards button 📐 on the Toolbox is selected, click the **Subform/Subreport button** 🖼 on the Toolbox, then click the upper-left corner of the opened Report Footer section

    The Subform/Subreport Wizard opens, requesting information about the control.

Time To

✔ Save
✔ Print
✔ Close

8. Click the **Reports and forms option button**, click the list arrow, click **Summary Sales Report**, click [Next >] scroll the **Select one of these links:** list box, click **None**, click [Next >], verify **Summary Sales Report** as the default subreport name, click [Finish], then maximize the Sales by Tour Report

    The Summary Sales Report control is added to the Report Footer section of the Sales by Tour Report as shown in Figure O-6.

FIGURE O-4: Summary Sales Report in Report Design View

1" mark on ruler

TourID Header section

Label control

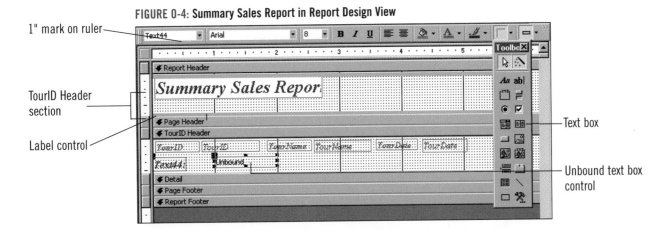

Text box

Unbound text box control

FIGURE O-5: Summary Sales Report with the count calculation

Count label added

Count statistic added

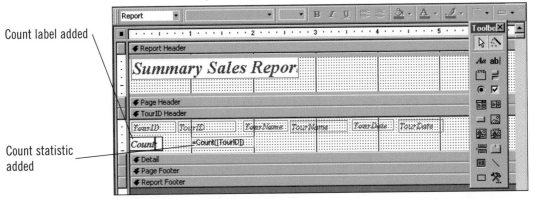

FIGURE O-6: Sales by Tour Report with a subreport control

Report Footer section

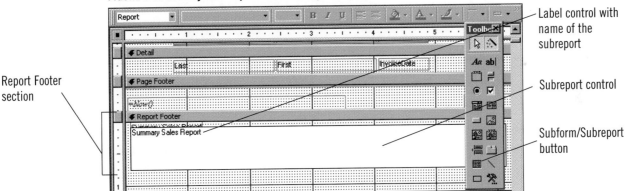

Label control with name of the subreport

Subreport control

Subform/Subreport button

TABLE O-1: Wizard installation options

install option	wizards installed
These wizards are always installed, regardless of Setup choices	Color Builder, Expression Builder, Field Builder, Query Builder, Subform/Subreport Field Linker
Wizards installed when you select the Wizards option in Setup	AutoForm, AutoReport, Combo Box, Command Button, Crosstab Query, Database Wizard, Export Text, Form, Import HTML, Import Spreadsheet, Import Text, Label, Link HTML, Link Spreadsheet, Link Text, List Box, Lookup, Microsoft Word Mail Merge, Picture Builder, PivotTable, Publish to the Web, Report, Simple Query, Switchboard Manager, Table
Wizards installed when you select the Advanced Wizards option in Setup	Add-in Manager, Chart Wizard, Conflict Resolver, Database Splitter, Documenter, Find Duplicates Query, Find Unmatched Query, Input Mask, Linked Table Manager, Macro to Module Converter, ODBC Connection String Builder, Option Group, Performance Analyzer, Subform/Subreport, Table Analyzer, User-Level Security

Creating Column Charts

Charts graphically display numeric information. Bars and lines are often easier to understand than columns or rows of numbers. Charts can be an extremely powerful and effective way to present information. The most common types of business charts include column, line, and pie charts. You can quickly add these powerful visuals to a report by using the **Chart Wizard** feature. To use the Chart Wizard, you must have **Microsoft Graph 97** installed. Access does not install Microsoft Graph in a Typical setup. You must use a Custom installation. A chart control that is bound to an underlying record changes as you move from record to record, displaying a graphic view of the data within that record. The marketing department requested a report that details information for each tour as well as graphically shows the difference between each tour's price (to the customer) and cost (to Nomad).

1. Click the **Reports tab** if necessary, click **New**, click **AutoReport: Columnar**, click the **Choose the table or query where the object's data comes from:** list arrow, click **Tours**, then click **OK**

   The new Tours report is automatically developed with the same formatting choices made the last time you used the Reports Wizard. Open the report in Report Design View and use the Chart Wizard to build a column chart to display graphically the difference between the Price and Cost fields for each record.

Trouble?

If the Chart menu option is not available, see your instructor. Before you can use the Chart Wizard, you must choose Graph 97 and the Advanced Wizard installation option.

2. Click the **Design View button** 🖉, click **Insert** on the menu bar, click **Chart**, then click just to the right of the TourID text box in the Detail section as shown in Figure O-7

   The Chart Wizard opens. Chart the Price and Cost fields for each TourID in the Tours table.

3. Click **Tours**, click [**Next >**], click **TourID**, click the **Select Single field button** [**>**], click **Price**, click [**>**], click **Cost**, click [**>**], then click [**Next >**]

   Choose the Column Chart style, then specify how to display the data within the column chart. See Table O-2 for more information on different chart types.

QuickTip

The chart type name appears in the right pane in this wizard dialog box.

4. Click the **Column Chart button** 📊 (the first button), click [**Next >**], then drag the **Cost field button** to the field box in the middle of the chart, just below the **SumOfPrice field**

   See Figure O-8. Next, specify what data to display on the chart. You want the chart to change from record to record, showing one bar for each TourID's Price data and one bar for the Cost data.

5. Click [**Next >**], click [**Next >**] to accept the TourID link between the Report Fields and the Chart Fields, type **TourID Column Chart** in the title of the chart text box, then click [**Finish**]

   A sample chart object is inserted in the Detail section of the form. Use Print Preview to see the actual report with a column chart that displays each TourID's Price and Cost data.

Trouble?

A Yes/No field appears either as Yes and No on a report, or as a check box, depending on the Display Control property setting.

6. Click the **Print Preview button** 🔍 on the Report Design toolbar, then scroll so that you can clearly see the chart for the first record, Bigs0197

   The chart is shown in Figure O-9. The chart changes for each TourID, as the columns are bound to the underlying Price and Cost fields for that record.

7. Click **File** on the menu bar, click **Save**, type **Column Chart by TourID**, click **OK**, then click the **Print button** 🖨 on the Report Design toolbar

   Review the printout. When satisfied with the chart, you can close the Tours report.

8. Close the report

FIGURE O-7: Inserting a chart

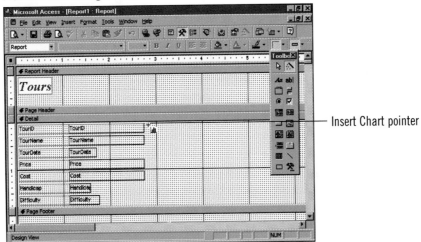

Insert Chart pointer

FIGURE O-8: Laying out the data in the chart

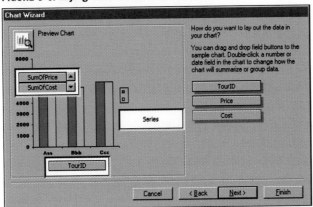

FIGURE O-9: Tours report with column chart bound to each record

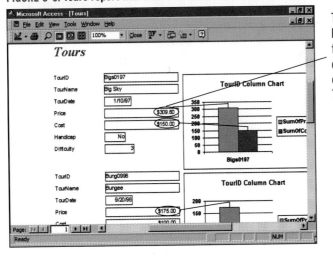

The data in the Price and Cost fields is displayed on the column chart for each TourID

TABLE O-2: Common chart types

chart type	description	examples
Column/Bar	Uses vertical/horizontal bars to show variation over a period of time or comparisons among items	
Area Chart	Displays the cumulative change over time by plotting data points on top of one another and filling the area beneath the data points	
Line Chart	Compares values over time using a line to connect the data points; excellent for showing trends over time	

CREATING GRAPHICAL REPORTS AC O-7

Creating Line Charts

A **line chart** uses a line to connect the data points. Line charts are excellent for showing trends over time. A line chart's **axes** (scales by which information is measured and plotted) are extremely important when developing a line chart. The horizontal axis is the **x-axis**, and the vertical axis is the **y-axis**. An appropriate line chart might show sales (measured in dollars or units on the y-axis) over time (measured in months or years on the x-axis). To modify or format any element of an existing chart on a report—including its overall size, axes, colors, chart type, legend, or titles—double-click the chart control in Report Design View and use the Graph 97 program to make the appropriate changes. Table O-3 lists several common Graph 97 commands.

Management has asked Rachel to chart the success of Nomad's tour offerings over time. To do this, she charts sales on the y-axis against a time frame on the x-axis using a line chart. The time period starts before the first tour date and ends after the last tour date. Rachel prepared a query called TourIDs Sold that consists of two fields: the TourID field from the Sales table (to determine how many sales were made for each TourID) and the TourDate field from the Tours table (to determine when the tour occurred). This query is the source of the line chart data. Rachel uses the Chart Wizard to create the report with the appropriate line chart object.

1. Click the **Reports tab** if necessary, click **New**, click **Chart Wizard**, click the **Choose the table or query where the object's data comes from:** list arrow, click **TourIDs Sold**, then click **OK**

   Next, specify which fields from the query contain the data you want in the chart, and what type of chart you want to create on the report.

2. Click the **Select all fields button** `>>`, click `Next >`, click the **Line Chart button** (third row, third button), then click `Next >`

   You want to plot the total number of TourIDs sold on the y-axis, and the TourDates in monthly increments on the x-axis.

   > **QuickTip**
   >
   > Double-click a field button in the chart to change how the chart summarizes or groups data.

3. Drag the **TourID button** from the Axis (x-axis) position to the Data position, then drag the **TourDate by month button** from the Series position to the Axis position

   You screen should look like Figure O-10.

4. Click `Next >`, type **Line Chart of Tours Sold** in the title of the chart text box, then click `Finish`

   The final report with the single chart object opens in preview mode. Scroll to display the report as shown in Figure O-11. The report shows a modest increase in the number of tours sold over time. Save and close the report.

5. Click **File** on the menu bar, click **Save**, type **Line Chart of Tours Sold** as the report name, click **OK**, then close the report

   The report object appears in the Database window on the Reports tab. The Line Chart of Tours Sold report consists of one control, a chart control, that displays data from all the fields in the underlying TourIDs Sold query in a global chart. Graphical reports, like all reports, always display current data. As you record more sales over time and the number of records in the TourIDs Sold query grows, the Line Chart of Tours Sold report also changes to reflect the current data supplied by the query.

Preview the chart while still using the Chart Wizard

If you are unsure how your chart is developing while you work through the Chart Wizard, you can click the Preview Chart button in the Chart Wizard dialog box to preview how the chart will appear on the report. When finished viewing the preview, close the sample preview dialog box and continue through the last step of the wizard.

FIGURE O-10: **Data layout for a line chart**

Preview Chart button —

Data position —

y-axis —

Series position —

Your sample may appear slightly different —

x-axis —

Axis position —

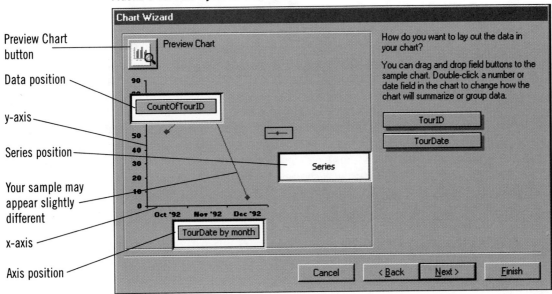

FIGURE O-11: **Line Chart of Tours Sold**

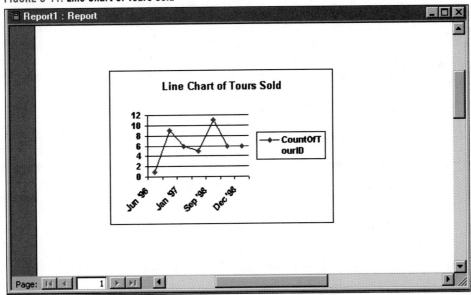

TABLE O-3: **Graph 97 Commands**

to:	do this:
Widen the chart	Widen the border of the sample chart window as well as the chart object in Report Design View
View or edit all data series formatting options	Click the data series in the sample chart window, then click the Format Data Series button 📊
Change the chart type	Click the desired choice from the Chart Type list 📈 ▾
Change bar colors	Click the data series in the sample chart window, then click the Fill Colors list 🎨 ▾
Change the chart title	Click the title in the sample chart, then edit or format the text as you would edit or format a report label
Change or format the x- or y-axis	Double-click the axis in the chart window to open the Format Axis dialog box and make the appropriate changes

Creating Pie Charts

A **pie chart** is a common business graphic that shows the relationship of parts to a whole. For example, you can graph each department's expenses as a wedge in a total expenses pie chart, or graph each sales representative's sales as a wedge in a total sales pie chart. Pie charts can represent only one data series, such as expenses or sales. In addition, the wedges of the pie must add up to 100 percent. Otherwise, the graph does not accurately represent all the data. For example, you don't want to plot only three of the four departments' expenses as a whole pie because the three departments' expenses don't represent *all* of the expenses. ◄■■■ Top management asked Rachel to represent graphically which tours have contributed to Nomad's 1998 total profit. She uses a pie chart to answer this question, using each wedge of the pie to represent the slice of profits created by each tour. Rachel prepared a query called 1998 Profits by TourID that contains the two fields she needs: TourID from the Sales table and a calculated Profit field from the Tours table.

Steps

1. Click the **Reports tab**, click **New**, click **Chart Wizard**, click the **Choose the table or query where the object's data comes from: list arrow**, click **1998 Profits by TourID**, then click **OK**
   The Chart Wizard's next two questions ask which fields from the query contain the data you want in the chart, and what type of chart you want to create on the report. You need only the TourID and Profit fields to create the pie chart.

2. Click the **TourID field**, click the **Select Single field button** `>`, click the **Profit field**, click `>`, click `Next >`, click the **Pie Chart button** `●`, then click `Next >`
   Next, the Chart Wizard requests information about the layout of the pie, as shown in Figure O-12. Access sets up the pie chart to summarize the profit of each tour in the pie wedges, and shows TourID information in the legend. This is the layout that you want, so continue with the next Chart Wizard question.

3. Click `Next >`, type **1998 Profits** as the title of the chart, then click `Finish`
   The pie chart report opens in preview mode. The Tour ID information in the legend identifies the wedges of the pie. The pie shows that the Bung0998 and Ozar1298 tours contributed most to Nomad's 1998 profits. To add data labels so you can see the numbers that make up the wedges of the pie, you enter Report Design View and use Microsoft Graph.

4. Click the **Design View button** `📐`, double-click the **chart control** to open a Microsoft Graph window, point to **Chart** on the menu bar, click **Chart Options**, click the **Data Labels tab**, click the **Show value option button**, then click **OK**
   Close the Graph window, then view the report in Print Preview mode.

5. Click **File** on the Microsoft Graph menu bar, then click **Exit & Return to Report 1: Report**

6. Click **File** on the menu bar, click **Save**, type **Pie Chart of 1998 Profits** in the Report Name text box, then click **OK**

7. Click the **Print Preview button** `🔍` on the Report Design toolbar, then scroll to get the full view of the chart
   The updated pie chart should look like Figure O-13.

8. Click **File** on the menu bar, then click **Close**
   The report object appears in the Database window on the Reports tab. The Pie Chart of 1998 Profits report consists of one control, a chart control, that displays data from all the fields in the underlying 1998 Profits by TourID query in a global chart.

FIGURE O-12: Pie Chart data layout

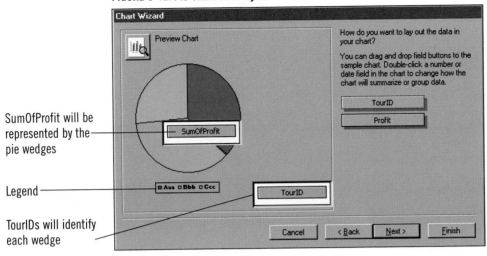

SumOfProfit will be represented by the pie wedges

Legend

TourIDs will identify each wedge

FIGURE O-13: 1998 Profits Pie Chart

Data labels

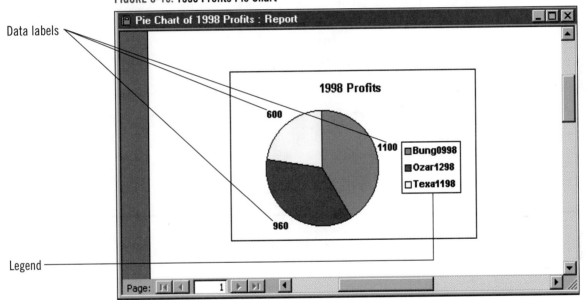

Legend

TABLE O-4: Common chart types

chart type	description	examples
Pie Chart	Shows the relationship of parts to a whole; capable only of plotting one data series	
3-D Pie Chart	Creates a pie chart with the appearance of a third dimension, a "depth" to the slices of the pie	
Bubble Chart	Creates a type of XY scatter chart that uses bubble markers to indicate the relative size of the concentration of data points at that location	
3-D Bubble Chart	Creates a bubble chart with the appearance of a third dimension, a "depth" to the bubbles in the chart	
Doughnut Chart	Shows the relationship of parts to a whole, but can plot more than one data series, each as a ring around the center	

Adding Background Pictures

You used image controls to add bound and unbound clip art images to different sections of a report. You can also add pictures to the background of a report or form. These background pictures are sometimes called **watermark** pictures. You add them by using the Picture property of the report's property sheet. Historically, watermarks were preprinted images added to expensive corporate stationery. The image, such as a logo or symbol, was usually very light but still visible even when text was typed or printed on the paper. With Access, a background picture added as a report property works the same way: The report prints on top of the image. Therefore, be careful to choose images that don't interfere with the text of the report. ⬤⬤⬤ Rachel decides to add a background picture to the Summary Sales Report. She adds the picture to the report's property sheet, then works with the other picture properties to size and position the picture precisely.

Steps 123 4

1. Click **Summary Sales Report** on the Reports tab, click **Design**, maximize the report window, click the **Report Selector button** 🔲 in the report window, click the **Properties button** 📇 on the Report Design toolbar, then click the **Format tab** on the property sheet if necessary

   The Summary Sales Report opens in Design View with the report's property sheet displayed as shown in Figure O-14. To add a background picture, you use the Build button on the Picture property to locate and insert the picture. The Picture property is on the Format tab of the report's property sheet.

2. Click the **Picture property text box**, click the **Build button** 📇, click the **Look in: list arrow** and click the folder and drive of your Student Disk if necessary, click **sportsbackground.bmp**, then click **OK**

   The path and filename of the sportsbackground image are inserted in the Picture property text box. Now you change a few of the other picture properties to improve the placement and size of the image on the report. Properties that affect background pictures are described in Table O-4.

3. Click the **Picture Size Mode property text box**, click the **Picture Size Mode list arrow**, then click **Zoom**

   The Zoom property extends the size of the clip art image, but maintains its original proportions. Now move the picture to the bottom-right corner of the report.

4. Click the **Picture Alignment property text box**, click the **Picture Alignment list arrow**, then click **Bottom Right**

   This moves the image from the center of the report to the bottom-right corner. Since the data on this report doesn't fill an entire page, moving the image to the bottom-right corner gives the final report a more balanced look. Close the property sheet.

5. Click 📇 on the Report Design toolbar

   Preview the report to view the updated report, then print the report.

6. Click the **Print Preview button** 🔍 on the Report Design toolbar, click the **Zoom list arrow** on the Print Preview toolbar, then click **Fit**

   Your screen should look like Figure O-15. When satisfied with the way the picture enhances the report, print the report.

7. Click the **Print button** 🖨 on the Print Preview toolbar

   Save and close the report.

8. Click **File** on the menu bar, click **Save**, then close the report

FIGURE O-14: Summary Sales Report in Design View

Report Selector button

Format tab

Picture properties

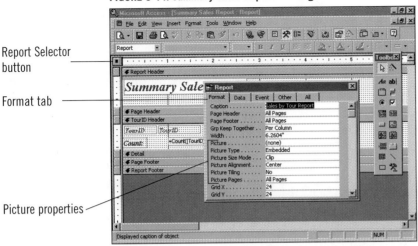

FIGURE O-15: Summary Sales Report with background picture

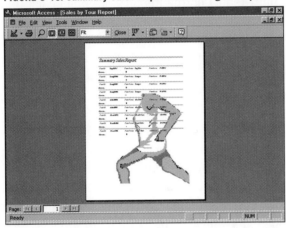

TABLE O-5: Picture properties

property	values	specifies that the picture is
Picture Type	Embedded (Default)	Embedded in the report and part of the Access database file
	Linked	Linked to the object; Microsoft Access stores a pointer to the location of the picture rather than to the picture itself
Picture Size Mode	Clip (Default)	Displayed in its actual size; if the picture is bigger than the report, the picture is clipped
	Stretch	Stretched horizontally and vertically to fill the entire report, even if its original ratio of height to width is distorted
	Zoom	Enlarged to the maximum extent possible while keeping its original ratio of height to width
Picture Alignment	Center (Default)	Centered in the report
	Top Left/Right	Displayed in the top-left (or -right) corner of the report
	Bottom Left/Right	Displayed in the bottom-left (or -right) corner of the report
Picture Tiling	No (Default)	One image of the picture displays on the report
	Yes	Tiled across the entire report
Picture Pages	All Pages (Default)	Displayed on all pages of the report
	First Page	Only on the first page of the report
	No Pages	Not on the report

Adding Page Breaks

In reports, you can use a **page break control** to identify where you want to start a new page within a section. For example, you might want to print a report's title page and an introductory message on separate pages, but unless you insert a page break control both will print on the same page because the controls for each are in the report header section. Sometimes you want to print each record or group of records on a separate page; to do so, you would change the **ForceNewPage** property of the detail or group header section. Table O-6 describes the values for the ForceNewPage property. To print each record on a separate page, set the ForceNewPage property of the detail section to After Section. To print each group of records on a separate page, set the ForceNewPage property of the group header to Before Section. After reviewing the Sales by Tour Report, Rachel decides to print each TourID on its own separate page. She also adds an unbound label containing explanatory text after the Summary Sales Report subreport control in the Report Footer, and adds a page break control between the subreport and the unbound label so that the label prints on its own page.

Steps 1 2 3 4

1. Click the **Sales by Tour Report** on the Reports tab, then click **Design**
   To make sure that each new TourID is printed on a separate page, change the ForceNewPage property of the TourID Header section.

2. Double-click the **TourID Header section bar**, click the **Format tab** if necessary, click the **Force New Page text box**, click the **Force New Page list arrow**, then click **Before Section**
   Your screen should look like Figure O-16. This property change ensures that each TourID starts printing at the top of a new page. Now close the property sheet, then add the explanatory text to the end of the report.

3. Click the **Properties button** on the Report Design toolbar, scroll to display the **Report Footer section**, click the **Label button** Aa on the Toolbox, click at the left edge and below the **Summary Sales Report subreport control**, then type **To request changes to this report call Rachel Best at extension 444**
   You want to print the label on its own separate page at the end of the report, so add a page break control between the subreport and the new label.

4. Click the **Page Break button** on the Toolbox, click **between the subreport and label control**, then click **below the report** to deselect the new page break control as shown in Figure O-17
   Next, preview the report to make sure that each TourID is printed at the top of a new page, and also check to make sure that the explanatory label prints by itself on the final page of the report. You view one entire page of the report.

5. Click the **Print Preview button** on the Report Design toolbar, click the **One Page button** on the Print Preview toolbar if necessary, then click the **Next Page Navigation button** several times
   Observe that each TourID prints on a separate page. To view the effect of the page break control in the report footer section, quickly move to the last page of the report. Your report should now be twelve pages long.

6. Click the **Last Page Navigation button**, then position the **increase magnification mouse pointer** over the **To request changes to this report call Rachel Best at extension 444 label**, then click
   You see that the message appears on the last page. This will be very helpful to the Nomad users. When satisfied with the changes, print and save the report.

7. Click the **Print button** on the Print Preview toolbar, then click the **Save button**

FIGURE O-16: Changing the Force New Page property

Format tab

TourID Header section bar

Before Section setting

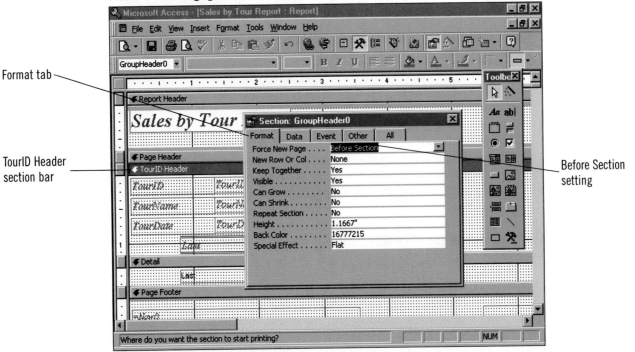

FIGURE O-17: Adding a page break control

Label button

Page break control

Label control

Area to click to deselect the page break control

Page Break button

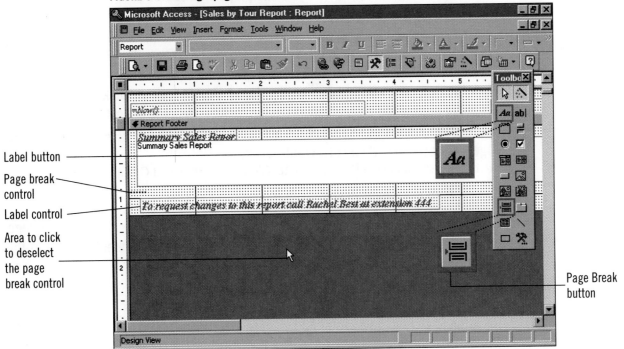

TABLE O-6: ForceNewPage property settings

setting	description
None (Default)	Prints the section on the current page
Before Section	Prints the section at the top of a new page
After Section	Prints the following section at the top of a new page
Before & After	Prints the section at the top of a new page, and prints the following section at the top of a new page

Keeping Records in Groups Together

Sometimes you want to allow more than one group of records to print on a page, but you don't want a group's detail records to span more than one page. In this case, the **KeepTogether** property for a group helps keep parts of a group together on the same page, and also allows more than one small group to be printed on a page. If the detail records within the group are too numerous to print on the same page, the KeepTogether property is ignored for that group.

Rachel decides that since the Sales by Tour report has several short groups that could print together on one page, she wants to remove the ForceNewPage property on the TourID header section, and enforce the KeepTogether property on the detail section. This change keeps the records of one section printing on the same page, but allows multiple groups of records to print on the same page if they fit. This change also allows the first group of records to print immediately after the report header section on the first page.

Steps 1 2 3 4

1. Click the **Design View button** 📐 to return to Design View, then double-click the **TourID Header section bar** to open the property sheet for the section
   The first thing you need to do is to change the Force New Page property to None for the TourID Header section.

2. Click the **Format tab** if necessary on the property sheet, click the **Force New Page text box**, click the **Force New Page list arrow**, then click **None**
   Now you need to keep the detail records within each TourID group together on the same page. To do this, close the property sheet, then open the Sorting and Grouping dialog box for the TourID group section.

3. Click the **Properties button** 📄 on the Report Design toolbar, click the **Sorting and Grouping button** 🔢 on the Report Design toolbar, click the **Keep Together text box** in the Group Properties section of the Sorting and Grouping dialog box, click the **Keep Together list arrow**, then click **Whole Group**
   Your screen should look like Figure O-18. Close the Sorting and Grouping dialog box.

4. Click 🔢 on the Report Design toolbar

5. Click the **Print Preview button** 🔍 on the Report Design toolbar, click the **One Page button** 🔲 on the Print Preview toolbar if necessary to view one entire page of the report, then press **[Page Down]** several times
   Observe that the records of each TourID are kept together on the same page, but that multiple TourID groups can be printed on each page. Return to the first page of the report.

6. Click the **first page navigation button** ⏮
   Observe that the first group of records for the first TourID were allowed to print immediately beneath the report header section, as shown in Figure O-19, because the Force New Page property was removed for each group header. Save and close the report.

7. Click **File** on the menu bar, click **Close**, then click **Yes** to save the report
   The reports are going to help the staff at Nomad tremendously. Exit Access.

8. Click **File** on the menu bar, then click **Exit**

FIGURE O-18: **Sorting and Grouping dialog box**

Sorting and
Grouping button

TourID group
is chosen

Keep Together
property

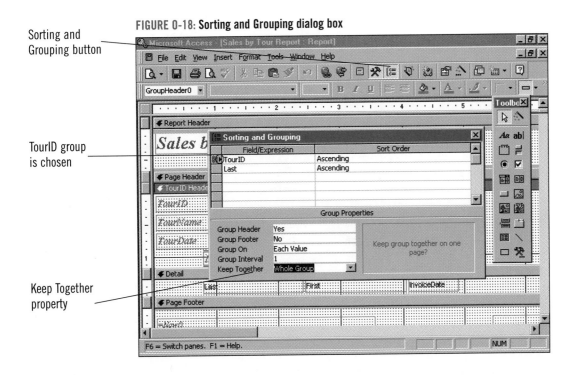

FIGURE O-19: **Final Sales by Tour Report**

Two groups of
records printed
on the first page

Page 1

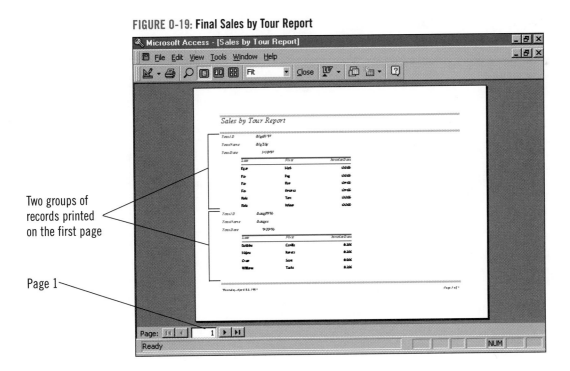

Practice

► Concepts Review

Identify each element shown in Figure O-20.

FIGURE O-20

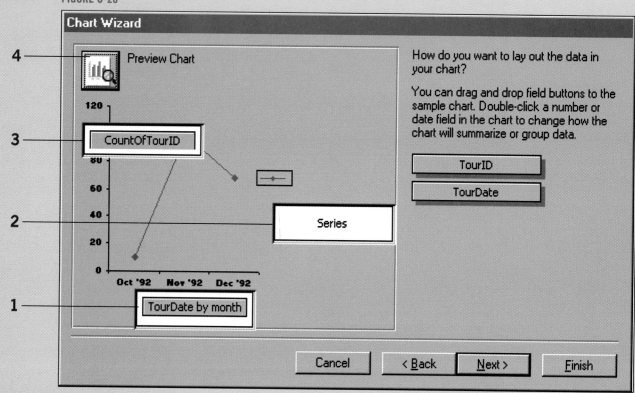

Match each term with the statement that describes its function.

5. A report that is added as a control within another report
6. Graphically displays numeric information
7. Scale by which information is measured and plotted on a chart
8. A background picture on a report or form
9. Must be installed before you can use the Chart Wizard feature
10. A common business graphic that shows the relationship of parts to a whole
11. An automated way to format an entire report after it is created
12. Can contain a subreport control in Report Design View
13. Used to copy formatting characteristics of an individual control to another control

a. Microsoft Graph 97
b. AutoFormat
c. Axis
d. Pie chart
e. Subreport
f. Watermark
g. Format Painter
h. Main report
i. Chart

Select the best answer from the list of choices.

14. **The AutoFormat feature can *not* do which of the following?**
    a. Add lines to report sections
    b. Change text color on a report
    c. Change text font size on a report
    d. Add calculated controls to group footers

15. **The Format Painter can *not* be used to copy which of the following?**
    a. Large font sizes from one label to another
    b. A combo box control from one section to another
    c. A line or border color from one control to another
    d. An alignment property from one control to another

16. **What does it mean to group on a report?**
    a. Sort records according to a specified record
    b. Sort records according to a specified field and provide a group header and footer section if desired
    c. Group fields together in the page header and footer sections
    d. Group and sort fields alphabetically in the report detail section

17. **Which of the following is *not* a reason to use subreports?**
    a. You wish to add calculations to group footer sections
    b. You want the group footer sections to print together on the first page of the report
    c. You want to view two or more reports by viewing a single report object
    d. You want to print two or more reports by printing a single report object

18. **Which graph type is best described as vertical bars showing variation over a period of time or comparisons among items?**
    a. Line
    b. Area
    c. Pie
    d. Bar

19. **Which graph type is best for showing trends over time?**
    a. Line
    b. Area
    c. Pie
    d. Bar

20. **Which graph type is best for showing cumulative totals?**
    a. Line
    b. Area
    c. Pie
    d. Bar

21. **If you want the detail records of a group to print on the same page, you should do which of the following?**
    a. Insert a page break control in the detail section of the report
    b. Insert a page break control in the group header section of the report
    c. Set the ForceNewPage property of the detail section to Before Section
    d. Set the KeepTogether property of the group header to Whole Group

▶ Skills Review

1. Use AutoFormat and the Format Painter
a. Start Access and open Addresses-O.mdb.

b. Use the Report Wizard to build a report from the Names Ascending query.

c. Include all of the fields in the query, group the records by Zip, and sort ascending by Last.

d. Use a Stepped layout and a landscape orientation.

e. Use a Soft Gray style and title the report "Names within Zip Codes Report."

f. View the report in Design View and make the following three changes to the Zip label in the Page Header section: center-align, bright blue text color, and black border color.

g. Double-click the Format Painter and paint each of the labels within the Page Header section with three formatting changes from the Zip label.

h. Resize the Pledge?, Level, and Reunion labels in the Page Header section so that the entire label is visible.

i. Move the Pledge? check box, Level text box, and Reunion check box in the Detail section as necessary so that they remain centered under their respective labels in the Page Header section.

j. Delete the Profession label in the Page Header section and the Profession control in the Detail section, then resize the Detail section so that the bottom of the section is immediately below the text box controls it contains.

k. Click Format on the menu bar, then click AutoFormat to create a new AutoFormat based on the changes you've made to this report. Click the Customize button on the AutoFormat dialog box, create a new AutoFormat based on the Names within Zip Codes Report, and name the style Soft Gray with Blue Labels.

l. Save, print, and close the Names within Zip Code Report.

2. Add subreports
a. Open the Names within Zip Codes Report in Design View, then use the Save As/Export option on the File menu to save the report with the new name of Count of Zip Codes Report.

b. Delete all the controls in the Detail section, then resize the Detail section so that it is completely closed.

c. Delete all the labels in the Page Header section except for the first, the Zip label.

d. Add an unbound text box control to the right of the Zip text box in the Zip Header section with the following Control Source property: =Count([Zip]).

e. Delete the unnecessary label to the left of the new text box. (*Hint:* The unnecessary label will display Text25 or something similar.)

f. Change the label control in the Report Header to read Count of Zip Codes Report.

g. Save and close the report.

h. Open the Names within Zip Codes Report in Design View.

i. Open the Report Footer section about ½"and place a Subform/Subreport control in the upper-left corner of the section. (*Hint:* Be sure that the Control Wizards button on the Toolbox is toggled on before adding the control.)

j. Use the Subform/Subreport Wizard to specify that the Count of Zip Codes Report should be the source of the subreport control.

k. Choose None when asked which fields link the two reports together, and use the default name of Count of Zip Codes Report as the name for the subreport.

l. Preview the report to make sure that the Count of Zip Codes Report prints as the last page.

m. If necessary, narrow the left and right margins so that the report fits across a regular piece of paper. (*Hint:* In Report Design View, use the Page Setup command from the File menu and narrow the left and right margins to 0.5".)

n. Save, print, and close the report.

3. **Create column charts**
   a. Create a new report using the Chart Wizard option, and base the report on the Names table.
   b. Select the Zip and Pledge Amount fields from the Name table. Your goal is to create a column chart that shows the total amount pledged by zip code.
   c. Choose a Column Chart Type, choose Zip for the x-axis position, and SumofPledge Amount for the Data position.
   d. Title the chart Total Pledge Amount by Zip Code, and click the "No, don't display a legend" check box in the last wizard dialog box.
   e. View the report in Print Preview mode and notice that the x-axis doesn't show every zip code.
   f. To widen the graph, view the report in Report Design View and drag the sizing handles to widen the graph control so that the right edge of the control is at the 5" mark on the ruler.
   g. Notice that the labels on the x-axis are too wide to display in the chart. Open the Microsoft Graph application to widen the chart. Double-click the chart control, then drag the lower-right corner of the window to widen the Report1 : Report - Chart window by at least 1".
   h. Close the Microsoft Graph windows and preview the report. If all of the zip codes appear on the x-axis, print and save the report. Name the report Column Chart of Pledges by Zip Code. If not, repeat step g until the graph window is wide enough to accommodate the zip code labels displaying on the x-axis, then print and save the report.
   i. Close the Column Chart of Pledges by Zip Code report.

4. **Create line charts**
   a. Create a new report using the Chart Wizard option, and base the report on the Names table.
   b. Select the Pledge Amount and the Pledge Date as the fields for the chart.
   c. Choose a Line Chart type, choose Pledge Date by Month for the x-axis position, and SumofPledge Amount for the Data position.
   d. Double-click the Pledge Date by Month button and choose Quarter instead of Month grouping.
   e. Title the chart Quarterly Pledge Amounts.
   f. Preview, print, and save the report, naming it Line Chart of Quarterly Pledge Amounts.
   g. Close Line Chart of Quarterly Pledge Amounts.

5. **Create pie charts**
   a. Create a new report using the Chart Wizard option, and base the report on the Names table.
   b. Select the Pledge Amount and the Pledge Date as the fields for the chart.
   c. Choose a Pie Chart type, choose Pledge Date by Month for the Series (legend) position, and SumofPledge Amount for the Data position.
   d. Double-click the Pledge Date by Month button and choose Quarter instead of Month grouping.
   e. Title the chart Quarterly Pledges.
   f. Preview, print, and save the report, naming it Pie Chart of Quarterly Pledges.
   g. Close Pie Chart of Quarterly Pledges.

6. **Add background pictures**
   a. Open the Count of Zip Codes Report in Report Design View.
   b. Click the Report selector to select the entire report, click the Properties button, then modify the Picture property on the Format tab to add a background picture.
   c. Use the Compass.wmf file on your Student Disk as a background picture for the report.
   d. Change the Picture Size Mode property to Zoom, and the Picture Alignment property to Bottom Right.
   e. Preview, print, save, and close the Count of Zip Codes Report.

7. **Add page breaks**
   a. Open the Names within Zip Codes Report in Design View.
   b. Change the Force New Page property of the Zip Header section to After Section.
   c. Add a page break control before the Count of Zip Codes Report subreport control in the Report Footer section.

    d. Preview the report. You should have a 10-page report.

    e. Print, save, and close the Names within Zip Codes Report.

8. Keep records in groups together

    a. Return to Design View of the Names within Zip Codes Report.

    b. Change the Force New Page property of the Zip Header section to None.

    c. Open the Sorting and Grouping dialog box, and change the KeepTogether property of the Zip field to Whole Group.

    d. Preview the report. You should have a four-page report because several groups are printing on the same page.

    e. Print, save, and close the Names within Zip Codes Report.

    f. Close the Address-O database, then exit Access.

▶ Independent Challenges

1. As the president of a civic organization, you have developed a database, Cleanup-O, that tracks charitable clubs in your area. You wish to develop a professionally formatted report with a custom style that prints the records of each group on a separate page.

    To complete this independent challenge:

1. Start Access, then open the database Cleanup-O.

2. Use the Report Wizard to create a new report based on the Deposit Dates and Weights query.

3. Use all the fields in the report and view the data by Name.

4. Do not add any more grouping levels, but sort ascending by Date.

5. Use an Outline 1 layout and a portrait orientation.

6. Use a Corporate style and name the report Club Deposits.

7. Format the label in the Report Header with a green, 24-point Arial font.

8. Format the Name, Date, and Weight labels in the Name Header to a green Arial font.

9. Format the Name text box in the Name Header to a red Arial font.

10. Save the style with the name Arial Green Style.

11. Open the property sheet for the Name Header section and change the Force New Page property to Before Section.

12. Print preview the report, print the first page of the five-page report, then save and close the report.

13. Close the database, then exit Access.

2. After submitting the Club Deposits report from the Cleanup-O database to the board, you have been asked to present a graphical analysis of the information for the next board meeting.

    To complete this independent challenge:

1. Start Access and open the Cleanup-O database.

2. Using the Chart Wizard, create a report based on the Deposit Dates and Weights query.

3. Use the Name and Weight fields and choose a Column chart.

4. Use the bars to represent the SumOfWeight data, and use the x-axis to show the Name information.

5. Title the chart Deposit Dates and Weights, then remove the legend.

6. In Report Design View, widen both the chart control as well as the chart window (double-click the chart control to access the chart window) to expand the room for the labels on the x-axis.

7. When you can clearly see the four club name labels on the x-axis, print and save the report, naming it Bar Chart of Deposit Weights.

8. Close the Bar Chart of Deposit Weights report.

9. Using the Chart Wizard, create a report based on the Deposit Dates and Weights query.

10. Use the Weight and Date fields and choose a Line Chart.

11. Use the line to represent SumOfWeight data, and use the x-axis to show Date by Month labels.

12. Title the chart Deposit Dates and Weights. Use the sizing handles to resize the chart control to best display the report.

13. Save the report as Line Chart of Deposit Dates and Weights, print the report, then close both the report and the Cleanup-O database.

14. Exit Access.

3. You have recently helped the medical director of a large internal medicine clinic put together and update a database, Doctors-O, that tracks extra-curricular activities. You wish to create a couple of sophisticated reports that show where the physicians have spent their time.

To complete this independent challenge:

1. Start Access, then open the Doctors-O.mdb database.
2. Using the Report Wizard, create a new report based on the Physician Activity query.
3. Use all the fields and view the data by Programs (Name).
4. Do not add any more grouping levels, but sort the data ascending by Date.
5. Use an Outline 2 layout and a portrait orientation.
6. Use a Formal style, and title the report Program Activity Report.
7. Open the Program Activity Report in Design View, then use the Save As/Export option on the File menu to save the report as the Program Activity Summary Report.
8. Delete all the controls from the Detail section of the Program Activity Summary Report, and delete the Date, Last Name, and Hours labels from the Name Header section.
9. Add an unbound text box to the Name Header section, just below the Name text box, then change the Control Source property to =sum([Hours]) to add up the total number of hours for each program name.
10. Change the label to the left of the calculating text box to Total Hours.
11. Change the label in the Report Header section to read Program Activity Summary Report, then save and close the report.
12. Open the Program Activity Report in Report Design View, expand the Report Footer section, then add a subform/subreport control to the upper-left corner of the Report Footer section that is based on the Program Activity Summary Report.
13. Do not link the fields between the main report and subreport, and accept the default name for the subreport. Use the sizing handles to resize the chart control to best display the report.
14. Delete the extra label in the upper-left corner of the Report Footer, then print, save, and close the Program Activity Report.
15. Close the database, then exit Access.

4. You have volunteered to help create some reports from the Fine Arts Museums of San Francisco's membership database. To get a better understanding of the organization's membership process, you access and print its web page application form and use this information to update the organization's database.

To complete this independent challenge:

1. Log on to the Internet and use your browser to go to http://www.course.com. From there, click Student Online Companions, click the link for the book you are using, then click the Access link for Unit O.

   WEB PAGE http://www.thinker.org/fam/membership/application
2. Once connected to the Membership Application for the Fine Arts Museums of San Francisco, print the Web page and log off the Internet.
3. Start Access, open the Museum-O.mdb database, then examine the Members table in either Design View. The museum wants to track membership levels as identified by its Web page, but failed to add a field to the Members table to handle this data. Add to the table a field called Level with a Currency Data Type.
4. Open the Members table in Datasheet View and enter the dollar amount in the Level field for the four members who are currently in the database. The first two members joined at the Participating level, and the last two members joined at the Donor level.
5. Close the Members table and use the Chart Wizard to create a pie chart report based on the Members table.
6. Select only the Level field, then select a Pie Chart type.
7. Call the report Contribution Breakout and display a legend.
8. Preview the pie chart, print the report, save the report with the name Pie Chart of Contribution Breakout, close the report, then close the database
9. Exit Access.

▶ Visual Workshop

Open the VW-O database and create the report shown in Figure O-21. Use the Chart Wizard based on the Alumni/Donations query, selecting the Value and Type fields to create the column chart. Notice that there is no legend showing and that the title of the chart is Donations by Type.

FIGURE O-21

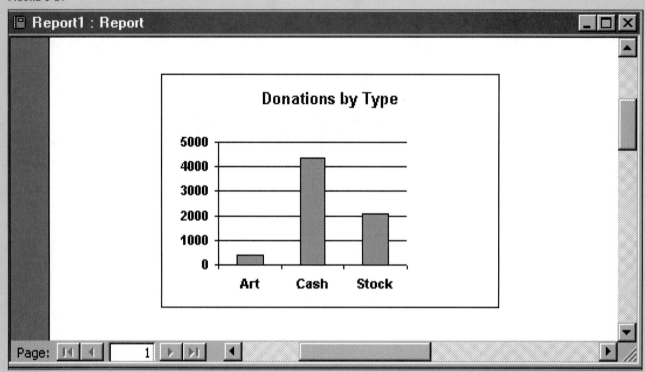

Maintaining
the Database

Objectives

- ► Back up a database
- ► Set a database password and encrypt the database
- ► Secure a database with startup command-line options
- ► Repair a damaged database
- ► Replicate a database using the Briefcase
- ► Synchronize a database using the Briefcase
- ► Split a database
- ► Analyze performance

Once you've put months of effort into developing an Access database, spending a few hours protecting it is a practical and wise investment of time. Protecting an Access database becomes even more critical when you realize that the database often represents the lifeblood of your business—information about your customers, products, and sales. It's not uncommon for businesses to develop mission-critical applications in Access. **Mission critical** means that the application and data within the application are critical to the survival (the mission) of the business. Losing mission-critical information can often mean losing or severely hampering the business. ◢— This unit introduces you to some of the database administration issues that you must consider to protect, share, and repair an Access database.

Backing Up a Database

One of the most important and universal tasks of a database administrator is that of backing up the database. **Backing up** means making a duplicate copy of the database on a medium physically separated from the primary location of the database. The backup **medium** might be a floppy disk, tape drive, recordable CD device, or separate hard drive. The medium you choose depends on many factors, including the size of your database, the frequency of your backups, and the financial resources of your company. See Table P-1 for more information on choosing an appropriate backup medium. ━━━ Rachel has been backing up the Nomad database regularly, but realizes that this important task needs to be documented, and that she also needs to cross-train another employee on how to use it. She has written the following steps as a "how-to" manual for backing up the Nomad-P database. She uses the Explorer program of Windows 95 to back up the database.

Steps

Trouble?

It is very important that you complete this unit with the Student Files on a floppy disk in drive A:. If you have been storing your files on a hard disk, copy the Unit P files to a floppy for this unit, then have an extra blank floppy disk available for this lesson.

1. Click the **Start button** on the **Taskbar**, point to **Programs**, then click **Windows Explorer**
The Explorer program starts as shown in Figure P-1. The folder tree on the left represents the drives and folders on the PC. The folders and files on your screen will be different than Figure P-1 because your computer has different programs loaded on its hard drive. If you have two floppy disk drives on your computer, you could back up the Nomad-P database, which is on a Student Disk in one drive, directly to the other drive. Copy the entire contents of the Student Disk to a blank disk. Explorer makes this possible *without* the use of two disk drives. When backing up a single database file from one floppy disk to another disk on a machine that has only one floppy disk drive, you can use the hard drive as a temporary storage location.

2. If the Explorer toolbar is not visible, click **View** on the menu bar, then click **Toolbar**, click the **3½ Floppy A: drive** on the folder tree, then click the **Details button** 🔳 on the toolbar to display four columns of information about each file
The files on the disk appear on the right side of the screen. You should see the Nomad-P database along with the other student files for this unit.

3. Right-click **3½ Floppy A:**, then click **Copy Disk**
The Copy Disk dialog box opens as shown in Figure P-2. Your Copy Disk dialog box will have more or fewer entries in the Copy from: and Copy to: text boxes based on the drives that are present on your computer. The 3½ Floppy A: drives should already be selected in both windows by default, so you are ready to start the copying process.

4. Click **Start**
The Copy Disk program copies the contents of the entire disk to a temporary location on the computer. You have to replace the disks when prompted to do so.

5. Remove the Student Disk from the A: drive and insert a blank disk in the drive, then click **OK**
The Copy Disk process continues, placing all the copied database files for Unit P on the blank disk. You are notified when the copying process has been completed successfully.

6. Click **Close**
You should still have the 3½ Floppy A: drive chosen on the left side of the folder tree within Explorer. You should see all of the student files from the original disk now safely copied to the new disk on the right side of the screen. You should store this backup or **archive** copy in a separate and safe place.

7. Close the **Explorer window**

FIGURE P-1: Explorer

Chosen drive or folder

Floppy disk drive

Hard drive

Folder tree of C: hard drive

Details button

Contents of chosen drive or folder

Details columns

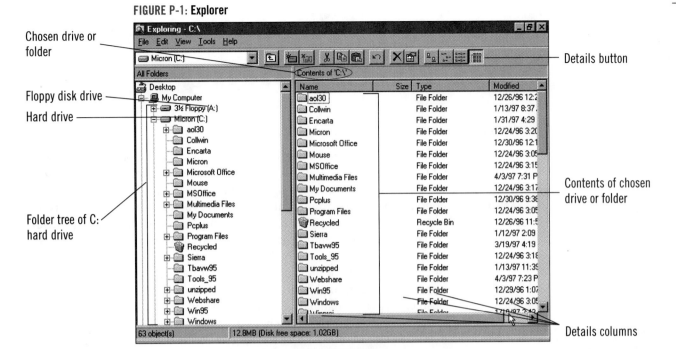

FIGURE P-2: Copy Disk dialog box

Listed drives may be different on your computer

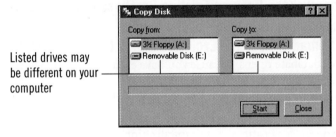

TABLE P-1: Backup media

media	advantages	disadvantages
3½" disk	• Most PCs have a disk drive • 3½" disks are cheap and readily available • Disks can be moved easily to an off-site location	• One 3½" disk can only hold 1.44 MB of information; most working Access databases cannot fit on a single disk, and you cannot put a portion of a file on a disk • Disks are easily lost, stolen, and mislabeled • Disks can be easily ruined by exposure to heat, moisture, or magnets
Tape cartridge	• Tape cartridges generally hold between 100 and 250 MB per cartridge • Tape cartridges and tape drives are fairly inexpensive • Tapes can be moved easily to an off-site location	• Tapes can be easily ruined by exposure to heat, moisture, or magnets • Tapes are easily lost, stolen, and mislabeled • Tapes store information sequentially; which makes them cumbersome and slow when restoring information • Special tape management software is often required to run the tape drive
Compact disc	• CDs hold over 600 MB per disc • Per megabyte, CDs are one of the least expensive storage devices • CDs are extremely durable and withstand exposure to heat and moisture much better than disks and tapes • CDs cannot be erased by exposure to magnets • CDs can be easily moved to an off-site location	• Recordable CD devices are about as expensive as a PC itself • CDs are easily lost, stolen, and mislabeled
Hard drive	• The capacity of a hard drive is almost unlimited • Per megabyte, hard drives are the least expensive storage device • Hard drives are very reliable and extremely fast	• Hard drives cannot be easily moved to an off-site location

Setting Passwords and Encrypting a Database

A database can be password-protected so that only those who know the password can open the database. **Encrypting** a database compacts and scrambles a database file so that it is indecipherable when opened by a utility program or word processor. **Decrypting** a database reverses the encryption process. You might want to encrypt a database before you back it up so that it is smaller and more secure on the backup medium. Also, you probably want to encrypt a database before sending it over unsecured networks, to frustrate any potential outsiders from reading the data in a simple word-processing program. Finally, encrypting is a good idea if you have used passwords to protect the database or attached tables. ◀━━ To provide an additional layer of security, Rachel wants to password-protect the database. She also encrypts the database. To create a database password, she must have exclusive rights to the database. Therefore, Rachel opens the Nomad-P database in **exclusive mode**, which ensures that no other users have access to the database while it's open.

Steps

1. Start **Access**, click the **Open an Existing Database option button** if necessary, click **OK**, click the **Look in: list arrow**, click the drive and folder location of your Student Files, click **Nomad-P**, click the **Exclusive check box**, then click **Open**
   The Nomad-P database opens. Because you have exclusive rights to it, you can set a database password.

2. Click **Tools** on the menu bar, point to **Security**, then click **Set Database Password**
   The Set Database Password dialog box opens as shown in Figure P-3. Passwords are case-sensitive, so you must pay attention to capitalization when you enter and verify the password.

3. Type **Atlantic**, press [Tab], type **Atlantic**, then click **OK**
   Now that the database is password-protected, you may wish to encrypt it. You can't encrypt or decrypt a database when it is open, so you close the Nomad-P database.

4. Click **File** on the menu bar, then click **Close**
   In a **multiuser environment**, such as a database that permits more than one person to enter or modify the same set of data at the same time, all users need to close the database before it can be encrypted.

5. Click **Tools** on the menu bar, point to **Security**, then click **Encrypt/Decrypt Database**
   The Encrypt/Decrypt Database window opens, displaying the database files in the currently selected folder, which should be the files on your Student Disk.

6. Click **Nomad-P**, then click **OK**
   A password is required to get back into the database; the Password Required dialog box opens.

7. Type **Atlantic**, then press [Enter]
   The Encrypt Database As dialog box opens, prompting you for a new filename for the encrypted database. If you specify the name of the database file that you chose to encrypt, Access automatically replaces the original file with the encrypted version. If an error occurs, Access doesn't delete the original file.

8. Type **Nomad-P** in the File name text box, click **Save**, then click **Yes** when prompted to replace the existing file
   The database has been given a password and has also been encrypted. To decrypt the file, you click Tools on the menu bar, point to Security, then click Encrypt/Decrypt. If you choose an encrypted file in the Encrypt/Decrypt Database window, Access automatically assumes that you wish to decrypt rather than encrypt the file.

QuickTip

Asterisks, not characters, display in the Password text box to protect your password further. Therefore, you must be careful when typing your password since you cannot verify your typing on the screen.

FIGURE P-3: Set Database Password dialog box

Set Database Password   [?] [X]

Password:

[   ]   [OK   ]

Verify: [Cancel]

[   ]

Password Tips

Access passwords are case-sensitive, so the "Atlantic" password is different from "atlantic," which is different from "ATLANTIC." Passwords should be unique, but not so cryptic that you can't remember them. Don't use obvious passwords that anyone could guess, like your name, your initials, the name of the database, or the name of the company. If you change passwords often, think of a series of things like the oceans, the planets, or the starters for the Chicago Bulls, then move through the series in some organized way so you won't forget the password. If you create passwords that combine text and numbers or spell something backwards, you add another level of complexity to confuse would-be intruders. If you lose or forget the database password, it can't be recovered and you won't be able to open your database. You can "unset" the Access database password by clicking Tools on the menu bar, pointing to Security, clicking Unset Database Password, and then entering the current password.

Access 97

Securing a Database with Startup Command-Line Options

You can automatically open a database for exclusive access, run a macro, or compact a database when you start Access by specifying options on the command line. **Command-line** refers to the fact that these instructions are entered as text commands, similarly to how commands were entered and executed on a PC with the DOS operating system. The entire command line has three parts: the **full file specification** (drive and folders) for the MSAccess.exe file surrounded by double quotes, the full file specification for the database file that you wish to open surrounded by double quotes, and the command-line option itself preceded by a forward slash. You can specify command-line options for Access on the Windows Start menu or on a shortcut icon. See Table P-2 for a list of the Access command-line options. Rachel finds herself compacting the Nomad-P database on a regular basis. She cannot automate this task with a macro, because a macro can be executed only when the database that contains the macro object is open, and a database cannot be compacted if it is open. Rachel creates a shortcut icon on the desktop that uses the compact command-line option to start Access, compact the Nomad-P database, and exit Access.

Steps 1234

Trouble?

If the Compact Nomad-P icon is on the desktop, right-click the icon, click Delete, then click Yes to remove it.

Trouble?

If you aren't sure about the path to the Msaccess.exe file, you can click the Browse button in the Create Shortcut dialog box and browse for the full file specification of this file. If you browse for the Msaccess.exe file, you still have to make sure double quotes surround it, type the "A:\Nomad-P.mdb" part of the command-line entry, then type /compact to finish the entry.

1. Click **File** on the menu bar, click **Exit**, then minimize all other open windows
   The Windows 95 Desktop is displayed on your screen. Create a shortcut icon to open Access.

2. Right-click the **Desktop**, point to **New**, then click **Shortcut**
   The Create Shortcut dialog box opens as shown in Figure P-4, prompting you for the command-line entry. By the time you type all three parts of the command-line entry, it is quite long. Therefore, special attention is required to type it precisely as shown.

3. Type **"C:\Program Files\Microsoft Office\Office\Msaccess.exe" "A:\Nomad-P.mdb" /compact**
   With the command line entered successfully, you're ready for the next Create Shortcut Wizard question.

4. Click [Next >], type **Compact Nomad-P** in the Select a name for the shortcut text box, then click [Finish]
   It might take Windows 95 a few seconds to build the icon on the desktop, but an Access icon appears with the title Compact Nomad-P under it.

5. Double-click the **Compact Nomad-P** icon on the desktop
   Access starts and prompts you for the password to the Nomad-P database.

6. Type **Atlantic**, then press **[Enter]**
   Access completes the compact instructions on the startup command line and closes Access. To review the command-line options for the icon, you view the icon's properties.

7. Right-click the **Compact Nomad-P** on the desktop, click **Properties**, then click the **Shortcut tab**
   The Compact Nomad-P Properties dialog box opens as shown in Figure P-5. This dialog box shows general information about a shortcut icon, such as the date it was created on the General tab and specific startup command-line information on the Shortcut tab. If you need to modify the command-line properties later, you can use this dialog box to do so rather than re-create the shortcut from scratch. Since you made no changes, cancel the dialog box.

8. Click **Cancel**
   If you are working on a lab computer, you should delete the Access shortcut you just created.

9. Right-click the **Compact Nomad-P shortcut** on the desktop, click **Delete**, then click **Yes**

FIGURE P-4: Create Shortcut dialog box

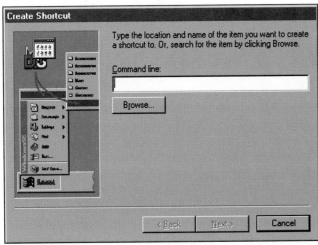

FIGURE P-5: Compact Nomad-P Properties dialog box

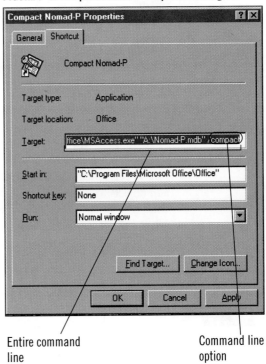

Entire command line

Command line option

TABLE P-2: Startup command-line options

option (variables appear in italics)	result
/excl	Opens the specified database for exclusive access
/ro	Opens the specified database for read-only access
/user *username*	Opens the specified database using the specified user name
/pwd *password*	Starts Microsoft Access using the specified password
/profile *userprofile*	In a multiuser environment, starts Access using the options in the specified user profile instead of the standard Windows Registry settings created when Access was installed
/compact *target database*	Compacts the database and closes Access; use the *target database* variable when you want the compacted database to have a different name than the original
/repair	Repairs the database and closes Access
/convert *target database*	Converts a database from an earlier version (1.x or 2.0) to a Microsoft Access 97 database and then closes Access; use the *target database* variable when you want the converted database to have a different name than the original
/x *macro*	Runs the specified macro
/nostartup	Starts Access without displaying the Startup dialog box
/wrkgroup *workgroup information file*	In a multiuser environment, starts Access using the specified workgroup information file

Repairing a Damaged Database

You need to **repair** a database if it becomes corrupted or unstable. How does a database become damaged? Often, damage occurs when a power outage suddenly halts the operations of Access. See Table P-3 for other examples of how databases get damaged. When damage occurs, the best-case scenario is that the current record you are updating in the form or datasheet is lost, and any design changes not saved to objects such as forms and reports are lost. In the worst-case scenario, the database is corrupted and unusable. The repair feature attempts to reestablish the data, relationships, and objects to an earlier, stable state. In most cases, Access detects that a database is damaged when you try to open, compact, encrypt, or decrypt it. On detecting such damage, Access gives you the option to repair the database. Occasionally, however, Access may not detect that a database is damaged and you initiate the repair option to attempt to fix a database that is behaving unpredictably. Nomad's office building has been under constant renovation the past few weeks, and there have been many brief power interruptions and outages. While Rachel hasn't noticed any specific loss of data or functionality of the forms and reports she has developed, she has decided to repair the database to make sure none of the information linking the objects has been lost.

1. **Start Access, then open the Nomad-P database**
   The Nomad-P database is still password-protected.

2. **Type Atlantic in the Enter the password for the database text box, then press [Enter]**
   You can start Access and then specify which database you wish to repair in the Repair Database dialog box, or you can repair an open database.

3. **Click Tools on the menu bar, point to Database Utilities, then click Repair Database**
   You may have to wait a few seconds while Access determines the current state of the Nomad-P database on your Student Disk and restores any missing pieces to an earlier state. When finished, Access displays a dialog box indicating that the database has been repaired, as shown in Figure P-6.

4. **Click OK**
   The Nomad-P database has now been through the repair process and you can be reasonably sure that Access has done its best to restore any missing remnants of information or object functionality. Close the Nomad-P database.

5. **Click File on the menu bar, then click Close**

FIGURE P-6: **Message indicating that Access has repaired the database**

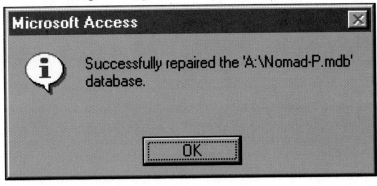

TABLE P-3: **Database damage**

incident	what can happen	appropriate action
Virus	Viruses can cause a vast number of damaging actions to occur, ranging from idiotic or profane messages occurring at unexpected times, to actual destruction of data or software	Purchase the leading virus-checking software and load it on each machine; keep the virus-checking software current by updating regularly; use the Access repair option to repair lost data or information
Power outage	Power outages, "brown-outs" (a dip in power), and power spikes (a surge in power) can cause the computer to halt suddenly	Purchase a **UPS** (Uninterruptable Power Supply) to maintain constant power to the file server (if networked); purchase a "surge protector" power strip for each end user; use the Access repair option to repair lost data or information
Theft or intentional damage	Expensive computer equipment is a constant target for computer thieves or other scoundrels	Place the file server (if networked) in a room that can be locked after hours; consider motion alarms for individual PCs that set off an alarm if the equipment is moved; back up the most important element of the database, the Nomad-P file in this case, to an off-site location on a regular basis; the Access repair option *cannot* repair inaccurate data that is intentionally deleted or purposely modified, but a recent complete backup can

Replicating a Database Using the Briefcase

If your computer is connected to a network, you can share data from an Access database in a multi-user environment in at least four different ways. First, you can put the entire database in a shared folder, probably on a dedicated file server. Second, you can share only the tables in the database by putting a database with only the table objects on the network server that everyone updates, and a database with the other database objects on the users' computers. Later you learn how to make the two databases work together—you simply put links in the user's database to the actual tables in the database on the file server. Third, you can share the database on the Internet by turning your Access objects into World Wide Web pages. Fourth, you can replicate the database on an office and portable computer, and then use the **Windows Briefcase** program to keep those replicas synchronized. ✏ Rachel uses the Windows Briefcase to **replicate** (make special copies of) the Nomad-P database that will be loaded on both on her laptop and Nomad's file server. Then she **synchronizes** (reorganizes) the replicas so that they are all updated with the latest information. You cannot replicate a database that is password-protected, so Rachel's first step is to open the Nomad-P database in exclusive mode so that she can remove the "Atlantic" password.

Steps

1. Click the **Open Database button** 🖾 on the toolbar, point to the Student Disk, click **Nomad-P**, click the **Exclusive check box**, click **Open**, type **Atlantic**, then press **[Enter]**
   Now that the database is opened exclusively, you can remove the password.

2. Click **Tools** on the menu bar, point to **Security**, then click **Unset Database Password**
   The Unset Database Password dialog box opens, prompting you for the current password.

3. Type **Atlantic**, then press **[Enter]**
   With the password removed, Rachel can replicate the Nomad-P database using the My Briefcase icon. Close the Nomad-P database, then exit Access to return to the Windows Desktop.

4. Click **File** on the menu bar, click **Exit**, then minimize all open windows
   The Windows 95 Desktop is displayed on your screen. To keep both versions of your database synchronized— the Nomad-P database that you take home and modify on your laptop, and the Nomad-P database on the computer network—you use the Windows Briefcase program. The copy of the Nomad-P database that is on your Student Disk represents the corporate network copy of the database. Copy that file to the Briefcase. Figure P-7 illustrates this scenario.

5. Click the **Start button** on your Taskbar, point to **Programs**, then click **Windows Explorer**
   In this simulation, the corporate Nomad-P database is stored on A:.

Trouble?
If you receive an error message indicating that My Briefcase already contains a file named Nomad-P, click Yes to replace it.

6. Click **3½ Floppy A:** at the top of the folder tree on the left side of the window, right-click the **Nomad-P database** on the right side of the window, point to **Send To**, then click **My Briefcase**
   The Nomad-P database is copied to My Briefcase. The Updating Briefcase dialog box opens, showing progress on the task. You are also presented a series of dialog boxes briefly explaining what is happening. Figure P-8 shows the first dialog box, which explains that the replication process may increase the size of your database. The second dialog box explains that you should create a backup of the database in the file Nomad-P.bak before starting this process. You need not back up the database again now.

7. Click **Yes,** then click **No**
   The final Briefcase dialog box determines which copy of the Access database will serve as the Design Master, as shown in Figure P-9. The **Design Master** is the only copy of Nomad-P that allows you to enhance and develop objects. The original copy of Nomad-P that is synchronized with the Design Master is called the **replica**.

8. Click the **Briefcase Copy option button**, then click **OK**
   Now that the Design Master of Nomad-P is in the Briefcase, close Explorer.

9. Click **File** on the menu bar, then click **Close**

FIGURE P-7: Synchronizing two database files with the Briefcase

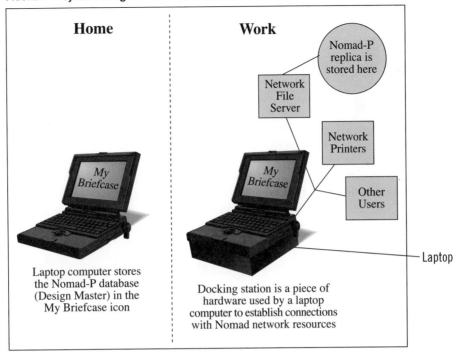

FIGURE P-8: First Briefcase dialog box

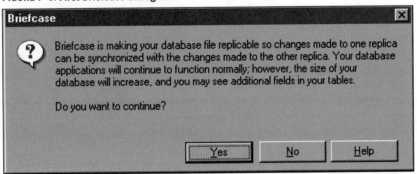

FIGURE P-9: Final Briefcase dialog box

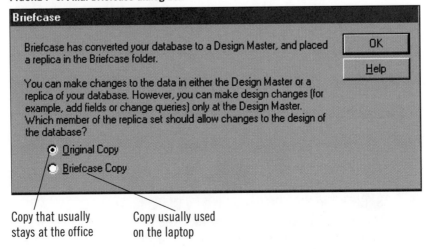

Access 97

Synchronizing a Database Using the Briefcase

Once you have replicated the database, you can use either the replica or the Design Master to enter data. Only the Design Master, however, can be used to update and enhance the objects of the database. The **synchronization process** updates both copies of the database with any new data that was added in either database. Plus, the synchronization process copies changes made to objects in the Design Master to the other replicas of the Design Master. ◀──── Rachel creates a new report from the Nomad-P Design Master database stored in the My Briefcase icon. She then synchronizes her updated Nomad-P database with one stored on the corporate network.

Steps

1. **Double-click the My Briefcase icon on the desktop, then double-click the Nomad-P database**

   Access starts and opens the Nomad-P database. The title bar tells you this database is the Design Master. The new object icons represent replicated objects as shown in Figure P-10. For steps 1 through 4, you are at the laptop computer away from the office.

2. **Click the Reports tab, click New, click AutoReport Columnar, click the Choose the table or query where the object's data comes from: list arrow, click Customers, then click OK**

   The new report opens in Print Preview mode. Close the preview and save the report object.

3. **Click the Customers Report Close button, click Yes when prompted to save the changes, type Columnar Customers Report in the Report Name text box, click the Make Replicable option box so that the report can be replicated to other databases, then press [Enter]**

   The new report is added to the Design Master. The copy of the Nomad-P database back at work, however, does not contain this object. Moreover, the office has probably entered new customer and sales records that are not in the Design Master copy of Nomad-P on the laptop. Close Nomad-P and exit Access. You also want to return to the Windows Desktop with all windows closed.

4. **Click File on the menu bar, click Exit, click File on the Briefcase window menu bar, then click Close**

   You return to work and use the Briefcase icon on the desktop to resynchronize the laptop copy of the Nomad-P database with the office copy of the Nomad-P database.

5. **Double-click My Briefcase**

   The window shown in Figure P-11 opens. The Status column indicates that this copy of the Nomad-P file has been changed and needs to be resynchronized with replicas. To resynchronize the two copies of Nomad-P, use the menu options in the My Briefcase window.

6. **Click Nomad-P in the My Briefcase window, click Briefcase on the menu bar, then click Update Selection**

   The Update My Briefcase dialog box opens indicating that the Nomad-P file in the Briefcase will replace the Nomad-P file in the A:\ drive. If changes had been made to the Nomad-P file on the A:\ drive (such as the addition of several new customer records), Access would prompt you to **merge** the files instead of replacing one with another. You can change the type of update by right-clicking the action arrow (Replace in this case) and choosing another action.

7. **Click Update**

   The synchronization is finished, you can see the status is changed to Up-to-date; see Figure P-12.

8. **Click the My Briefcase window Close button**

   You need to resynchronize the files whenever you want the replica to contain the objects that were modified in the Design Master, or want the Design Master to contain the records that were updated in the replica.

Trouble?

If the Update My Briefcase dialog box shows the Merge action instead of the Update action, right-click Merge action and choose Update.

FIGURE P-10: Replicated objects

This is the Design Master

Replicated object icon

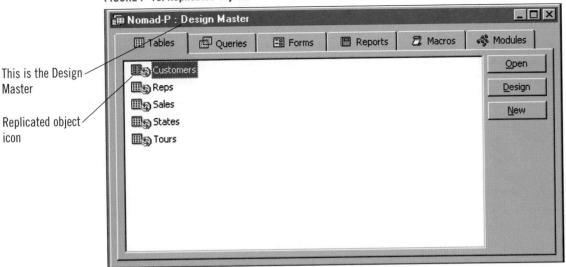

FIGURE P-11: Contents of My Briefcase before the update

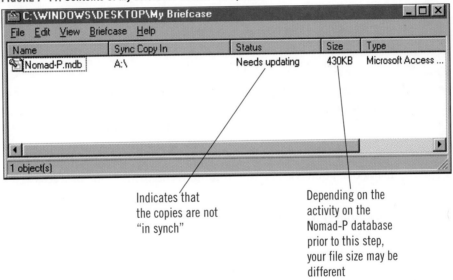

Indicates that the copies are not "in synch"

Depending on the activity on the Nomad-P database prior to this step, your file size may be different

FIGURE P-12: Contents of My Briefcase after the update

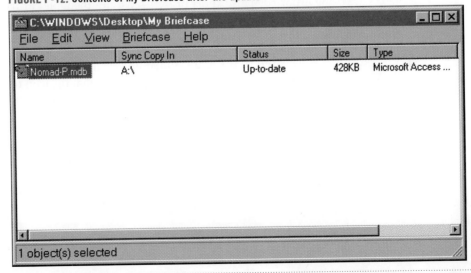

Splitting a Database

A successful database grows in many ways. As information within the database grows, users "invent" new and exciting ways to use the database. These new ideas create the need for new database objects, higher levels of security, and higher levels of database organization. **Local area networks** (LANs) are often installed to link multiple PCs together to share the same database. In a short time, reluctant users have become advocates of sophisticated information systems. The Access **Database Splitter** feature handles some of these multiuser issues by allowing you to split a database into two files: the **back-end database**, which contains the actual table objects, and the **front-end database**, which contains the other objects as well as links to the back-end database tables. This example of **client/server computing** allows the database with the table objects to be stored on the **file server** (a PC that is accessible by each user PC on a LAN) and the database with the other objects to be stored on the user PCs. In this scenario, users can customize their own queries, forms, and reports while working together to maintain a single source of data on the file server. ◄▬▬ Rachel uses the Database Splitter, an advanced wizard, to split the Nomad2-P database into two databases. That way, she can load the database with the tables onto the new file server being installed at Nomad, and the database with the objects on the user PCs. Later, she customizes the database with the objects at each PC to fit the needs of each particular user.

Steps 1 2 3 4

1. Start Access, then open the Nomad2-P database
The Nomad2-P database loads into memory. Before you can use the Database Splitter, the database that you want to split must be open.

2. Click Tools on the menu bar, point to Add-Ins, then click Database Splitter
You must use the Nomad2-P file, as the Database Splitter will not work on Nomad-P, a replicated file. The Database Splitter dialog box opens as shown in Figure P-13. It explains some of the benefits of splitting the database and encourages you to make a backup copy of the database before splitting it. Making a backup copy of a production database before any major operation is a matter of common sense. This lesson proceeds as if you've already completed this step.

3. Click Split Database
The Create Back-end Database dialog box opens, prompting you for a name of the back-end database, the one that will hold the data. The default name of Nomad2-P_be.mdb is appropriate, so accept this suggestion.

4. Click Split
As the Database Splitter is working on your database, notice that the status bar indicates that tables are being exported. This export process separates the tables of data from the rest of the objects of the database. When the task is completed, the Database Splitter displays a dialog box indicating that it is finished.

5. Click OK to acknowledge that the database has been successfully split
Nomad2-P now appears as shown in Figure P-14. Notice that the icon to the left of the table objects has changed. No longer do the table objects physically exist in the Nomad2-P database. Rather, they are linked to the Nomad2-P database and exist only in the Nomad2-P_be database.

Trouble?
The Database Splitter is an advanced wizard that is available only if Access was installed using the Custom Installation feature. If this feature is not installed on your system, skip to the next lesson.

FIGURE P-13: **Database Splitter dialog box**

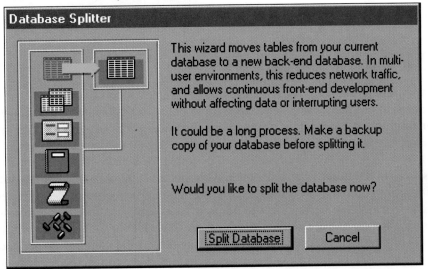

FIGURE P-14: **The tables in the Nomad2-P database after using the Database Splitter**

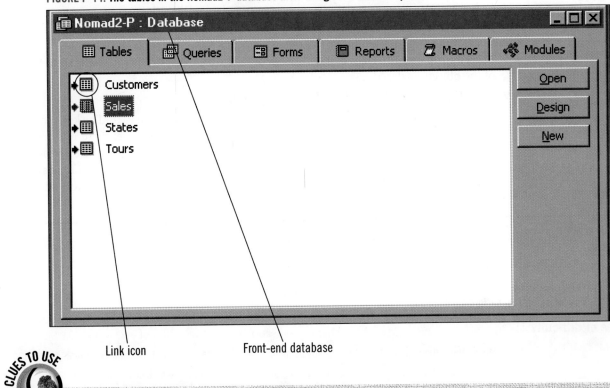

Link icon   Front-end database

Client/Server Computing

Client/server computing can be defined as two or more information systems cooperatively processing to solve a problem. One of the most common models of client/server computing involves a file server and several user PCs tied together through a local area network. The file server PC serves data or application files to the PC to process at a local level. Another common model of client/server computing involves the Internet and user PCs. When surfing the Web, the local PC is using a browser such as Netscape Navigator to access the Web pages stored on Internet

Web server computers. The browser was first loaded on the PC's local hard drive and must reside in the PC's memory to surf. The Web pages displayed by the browser are loaded hundreds or thousands of miles away on the Web server computer. The Web server might be another PC or even a huge mainframe. The point of client/server computing is that both the client and the server are independent information systems, but to complete the specific task at hand, they must cooperatively handle the processing chores.

Analyzing Performance

Whether your Access database runs in a single-user or complex multiuser environment, you want it to run as fast as possible. Fortunately, Access provides extensive documentation in the on-line Help manual to assist you in this process. Also, Access provides a powerful tool called the **Performance Analyzer** that studies the structure and size of your database and makes a variety of recommendations on how you could improve its performance. Usually, fixing performance problems boils down to two issues: time and money. With adequate time and knowledge of Access, you can alleviate many performance bottlenecks by using the software tools provided by Access. With a bit of extra money, however, you can also purchase faster hardware, specifically processors and more memory, that can usually do the same thing. See Table P-4 for more tips on increasing the performance of your Access database. ✍ Now that Rachel has split the Nomad2-P database and it is being run across a local area network, she's concerned that the overall performance could get sluggish and that the users might become frustrated. Before she dips into her budget to purchase additional hardware, she uses the Performance Analyzer, an advanced wizard, to see whether Access has any easy recommendations on how to maintain peak performance.

Trouble?

The Database Performance Analyzer is an advanced wizard that is available only if Access was installed using the Custom Installation feature.

1. **Click Tools on the menu, point to Analyze, then click Performance**
   The Performance Analyzer dialog box opens as shown in Figure P-15. You wish to have all of the objects analyzed.

2. **Click the All tab, click Select All, then click OK**
   The results of the Performance Analyzer appear as shown in Figure P-16. The key shows that the analyzer gives four levels of information regarding performance: mere ideas, suggestions, strong recommendations, and even areas that were fixed. In this case, the Performance Analyzer had only one idea for improving your database performance. As you click an entry in the Analysis Results, the Analysis Notes section of the dialog box gives you additional information regarding that specific result.

3. **Click Close to close the Performance Analyzer dialog box**
   Close the Nomad2-P database and exit Access.

4. **Click File on the menu bar, then click Exit**

TABLE P-3: **Tips for optimizing performance**

degree of difficulty	tip
Easy	Close all applications that you aren't currently using on your PC to free up memory and other computer resources
Easy	Eliminate memory-resident programs if they can be run safely on an "as-needed" basis
Easy	If you are the only person using a database, open it in exclusive mode
Easy	Periodically compact your database
Moderate	Add more memory to your computer; memory is the single biggest determinant of overall performance
Moderate	If others don't need to share the database, load it on your local hard drive instead of the network's file server
Moderate	Split the database so that only the table objects are being stored on the file server, and the other database objects are stored locally on your hard drive
Moderate to difficult	Eliminate disk compression software, or move the database to an uncompressed drive
Moderate to difficult	If you've recently added another local hard drive to your system, check and change the virtual memory parameters so that your virtual memory space is being directed to the free drive
Moderate to difficult	Run the Performance Analyzer; make sure each entry in the Analysis Results window is handled correctly
Moderate to difficult, depending on your budget	Make sure that all PCs are running the latest versions of Windows 95 and Access 97; this may involve purchasing more software or upgrading hardware to support these robust software products properly

FIGURE P-15: **Performance Analyzer dialog box**

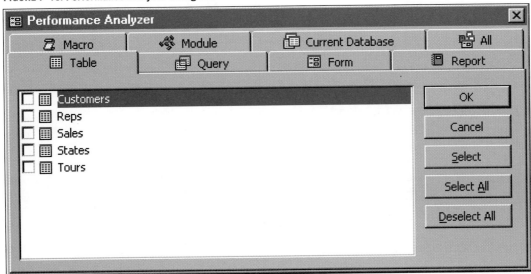

FIGURE P-16: **Performance Analyzer results**

Ideas   Analysis results   Explains icons

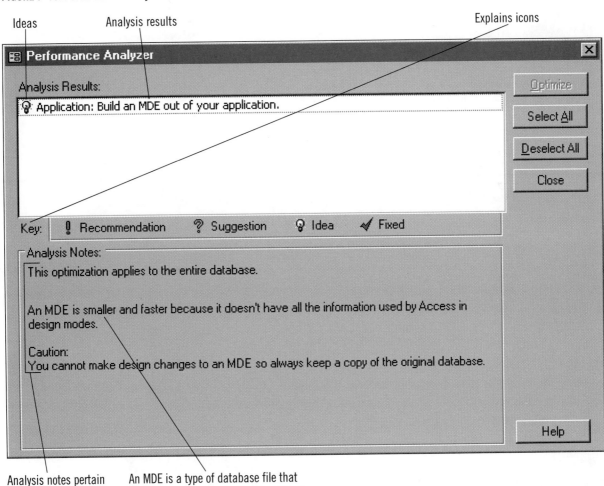

Analysis notes pertain
to the selected entry
in the analysis results
panel

An MDE is a type of database file that
compiles and compacts the Visual Basic
code so that it runs more efficiently

Practice

► Concepts Review

Identify each item shown in Figure P-17.

FIGURE P-17

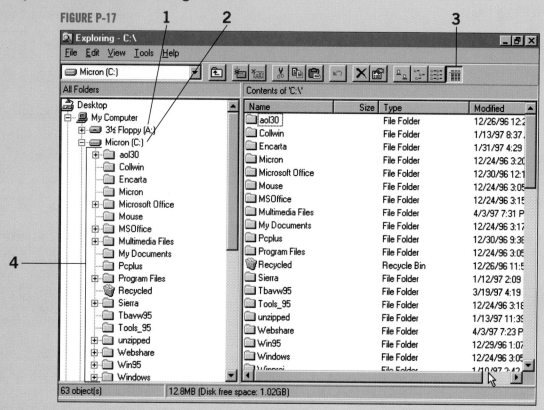

Match each term with the statement that describes its function.

5. Means that the application and data within the application are critical to the survival (the mission) of the business

6. Means that no other users will have access to the database file while it's open

7. Refers to the fact that instructions are entered as text commands

8. Studies the structure and size of your database and makes a variety of recommendations on how you can improve its speed

9. Making a duplicate copy of the database on a medium physically separated from the primary location of the database

10. Breaks the database into two files, one that holds the physical table objects and one that contains the rest of the database objects

11. Compacts and scrambles a database file so that it is indecipherable when opened by a utility program or word processor

12. Reorganizes the Design Master and replicas of a database file so that they are all updated with the latest information

13. A special piece of hardware that a laptop computer uses to establish connections with resources at the office

a. Exclusive mode
b. Command-line
c. Mission-critical
d. Database Splitter
e. Encrypting
f. Backing up
g. Docking station
h. Performance Analyzer
i. Synchronization process

Select the best answer from the list of choices.

14. **Which of the following is probably not a practical backup medium for a small company with limited financial resources?**
    a. Floppy disk
    b. Tape drive
    c. Recordable CD device
    d. Separate hard drive

15. **Floppy disks, tape drives, and hard drives all have which disadvantage in common?**
    a. They are all limited to less than 100 MB
    b. They are all susceptible to damage by magnets
    c. They are all extremely expensive
    d. They are all extremely slow

16. **Which of the following is *not* true about backing up important database files?**
    a. You should back up your database files on a regular basis
    b. You should take the backup copy off-site
    c. The sole purpose of the My Briefcase program is to help you create backup copies of your database
    d. Compacting or encrypting files before backing them up helps manage their size

17. **You must open the database in exclusive mode to**
    a. Compact it.
    b. Encrypt it.
    c. Decrypt it.
    d. Set a database password.

18. **Which character precedes a command-line option?**
    a. \
    b. |
    c. /
    d. "

19. **C:\Program Files\Microsoft Office\Office\MSAccess.exe is an example of a**
    a. Full file specification.
    b. File location.
    c. Path.
    d. Command-line option.

20. **Which of the following is *not* an advantage of splitting the database using the Database Splitter?**
    a. It is the first step when backing up a database
    b. It keeps the data centralized in one database
    c. It gives the users local control over form and report objects
    d. It helps increase the overall performance of a local area network

21. Both the Database Splitter and the Performance Analyzer are considered what type of Access feature?
  a. Advanced add-Ins
  b. Advanced wizards
  c. Exclusive options
  d. Exclusive multiuser features

 # Skills Review

If you complete all of the exercises in this unit, you may run out of space on your Student Disk. To make sure you have enough disk space, please copy the files Addresses-P, Addresses2-P, Cleanup-P, Doctors-P, Books-P, Fastfood-P, and VW-P onto a new disk and use the new disk to complete the rest of the exercises in this unit.

1. Back up a database
  a. Have your Student Disk and another 3½" blank disk handy.
  b. Insert your Student Disk into the 3½" A: disk drive of your PC.
  c. Click Start, point to Programs, then click Explorer from the cascading menu.
  d. Within Explorer, right-click the 3½ floppy A: disk drive on the left, then click Copy Disk.
  e. When prompted, remove the Student Disk from the A: drive and insert the blank disk.
  f. Click Close when finished with the copying process, then close Explorer.

2. Set a database password and encrypt the database
  a. Start Access, open Addresses-P, being careful to check the Exclusive option in the Open dialog box.
  b. Click Tools on the menu bar, point to Security, then click Set Database Password.
  c. Enter, then confirm the password "Pacific" for this database.
  d. Close Addresses-P, but do not close Access.
  e. Click Tools on the menu bar, point to Security, then click Encrypt/Decrypt Database.
  f. Encrypt the Addresses-P database, replacing the original with the encrypted version.

3. Secure a database with startup command-line options
  a. Close Access and minimize all open windows so that the Windows 95 Desktop is displayed on your screen.
  b. Create a shortcut icon to open Access by right-clicking the desktop, pointing to New, then clicking Shortcut.
  c. Type "C:\Program Files\Microsoft Office\Office\Msaccess.exe" "A:\Addresses-P.mdb" /compact in the command line.
  d. Click the Next button to finish creating the shortcut, type "Compact Addresses-P" as the name of the shortcut, then click Finish.
  e. Test your shortcut by double-clicking the icon, then enter the "Pacific" password when prompted.

4. Repair a damaged database
  a. Start Access, then open the Addresses-P database.
  b. Type "Pacific" for the password.
  c. Click Tools on the menu bar, point to Database Utilities, then click Repair Database.
  d. Click OK to respond to the database repair message, then close Addresses-P.

5. **Replicate a database using the Briefcase**
   a. Open Addresses-P in Exclusive mode so that you can unset the password (you cannot replicate a database that is password-protected).
   b. Enter "Pacific" for the password.
   c. Click Tools on the menu bar, point to Security, then click Unset Database Password, then type Pacific to unset the password.
   d. Close Addresses-P, close Access, then minimize all open windows so that the Windows 95 Desktop is displayed on your screen.
   e. Click the Start button on your Taskbar, point to Programs, then click Windows Explorer.
   f. Click 3½ floppy A: on the left, click the Addresses-P database on the right side of the window, then click the Copy button on the toolbar.
   g. Minimize Explorer, right-click My Briefcase, then click Paste.
   h. Click Yes twice to indicate that you wish to continue this replication process, click Briefcase Copy to make the Design Master, then click OK.

6. **Synchronize a database using the Briefcase**
   a. Double-click the My Briefcase icon, then double-click the Addresses-P database to open it.
   b. Create a new object in this copy of Addresses-P, the Design Master. Click the Reports tab, then create an AutoReport: Tabular report from the Zips table.
   c. Name the report "Zips Listing".
   d. Close Addresses-P and close Access.
   e. Double-click the My Briefcase icon to open the My Briefcase window.
   f. Click Addresses-P in the My Briefcase window, click Briefcase on the menu bar, then click Update Selection.

7. **Split a database**
   a. Start Access, then open the Addresses2-P database.
   b. Click Tools on the menu, point to Add-Ins, then click Database Splitter.
   c. Click Split Database.
   d. Accept the default back-end database name and click Split.
   e. Click OK to acknowledge that the database has been successfully split.

8. **Analyze performance**
   a. Click Tools on the menu, point to Analyze, then click Performance.
   b. Click the All tab, click Select All, then click OK.
   c. Click each of the entries to observe the Analysis Notes at the bottom of the dialog box.
   d. Click Close to close the Performance Analyzer dialog box.
   e. Close Addresses2-P, then exit Access.

Independent Challenges

If you complete all of the exercises in this unit, you may run out of space on your Student Disk. To make sure you have enough disk space, please copy the following files onto a new disk: Cleanup-I.mdb, Toxic.xls, Deposit Analysis.xls, Readings-I.mdb, Review.doc, Doctors-I.mdb, Policy.doc, Peds.doc, Careers.mdb, and VW-I.mdb. Use the new disk to complete the rest of the exercises in this unit.

1. As the president of a civic organization, you have developed a database, Cleanup-P, that tracks deposits of recyclable materials by charitable clubs. Because there are many volunteers who work on this database, you wish to back up, password-protect, and encrypt this database.

To complete this independent challenge:

1. Have your Student Disk and another 3½" blank disk handy.
2. Insert your Student Disk into the 3½" A: disk drive of your PC.
3. Click Start, point to Programs, then click Explorer from the cascading menu.
4. Within Explorer, right-click the 3½" Floppy A: disk drive on the left, then click Copy Disk.
5. When prompted, remove the Student Disk from the A: drive and insert the blank disk.
6. Click Close when finished with the copying process, then close Explorer.
7. To set a database password and encrypt the database, open Cleanup-P from your Student Disk, being careful to check the Exclusive option in the Open dialog box.
8. Click Tools on the menu bar, point to Security, then click Set Database Password.
9. Enter, then confirm the password "Indian" for this database.
10. Close Cleanup-P, but do not close Access.
11. Click Tools on the menu bar, point to Security, then click Encrypt/Decrypt Database.
12. Encrypt the Cleanup-P database, replacing the original version with the encrypted version.
13. Exit Access.

2. You have developed a database, Doctors-P, that tracks volunteer activities for a medical clinic. The physicians themselves have enjoyed working with the database, and several have created and then deleted various reports and queries over time. Because so many people use this database, create objects for special needs, and then delete the objects, you wish to create an icon on the desktop with the /compact command-line option to keep the database compacted as small as possible, then repair the database just as a precaution.

To complete this independent challenge:

1. Close Access and minimize all open windows so that the Windows 95 Desktop is displayed on your screen.
2. Create a shortcut icon to open Access by right-clicking the desktop, pointing to New, then clicking Shortcut.
3. Type "C:\Program Files\Microsoft Office\Office\Msaccess.exe" "A:\Doctors-P.mdb" /compact in the command line.
4. Click the Next button to finish creating the shortcut, type Compact Doctors-P as the name of the shortcut, then click Finish.
5. Test your Compact Doctors-P shortcut by double-clicking the icon.
6. Start Access, then open the Doctors-P database from your Student Disk.
7. Click Tools on the menu bar, point to Database Utilities, then click Repair Database.
8. Click OK to respond to the database repair message, then close Doctors-P.
9. Exit Access.

3. You have developed a database called Books-P that logs books and authors. You wish to update it at both the office, where you hold your regular Book Club meetings after work, and at home. You'll use the My Briefcase icon to keep the two copies of the Books-P database synchronized.

To complete this independent challenge:

1. Click Start, point to Programs, then click Explorer to start the Windows Explorer program.
2. Click 3½" Floppy A: on the left, click the Books-P database on the right side of the window, then click the Copy button on the toolbar.
3. Minimize Explorer, right-click My Briefcase, then click Paste.
4. Click Yes twice to indicate that you wish to continue this replication process, click Briefcase Copy to make it the Design Master, then click OK.
5. Add an object to the copy of Books-P in the Briefcase, the Design Master, by double-clicking the My Briefcase icon, then double-click the Books-P database to open it.
6. Click the Reports tab, then create an AutoReport: Tabular report from the Authors table.
7. Name the report Authors Report.
8. Close Books-P and exit Access.
9. Double-click the My Briefcase icon to open the My Briefcase window.
10. Click Books-P in the My Briefcase window, click Briefcase on the menu bar, then click Update Selection.
11. Exit My Briefcase and close all open windows.

4. For a project in a nutrition class, you created a database called Fastfood-P that tracks the nutritional value of several types of fast food. Based on this information, other members of the class can query the database for items with less than a given number of calories or grams of fat.

To complete this independent challenge:

1. Log on to the Internet and use your browser to go to http://www.course.com. From there, click Student Online Companions, then click the link for the book you are using, then click the Access link for Unit P.
2. Survey the Web site for foods with more than 350 calories at Burger King, then print the Web page that displays the results.
3. Log off the Internet, then open Fastfood-P from your Student Disk.
4. Add the Burger King records to the database.
5. Create a query that lists all the foods in your database with more than 350 calories. Make sure the records are sorted from the most calories to the fewest calories. Name the query "High Calorie Fast Foods."
6. Create a form for future data entry with the AutoForm: Columnar feature, based on the Foods table.
7. Use the AutoReport: Columnar feature to create a report to print your findings of the High Calorie Fast Foods query.
8. Use the Access Splitter to split the Fastfood-P database so that you can keep the data on the file server in one department of the college, but allow other interested departments connected to this file server to keep their own form and report objects at a local level. To do this, click Tools on the menu, point to Add-Ins, then click Database Splitter.
9. Click Split Database.
10. Accept the default back-end database name and click Split.
11. Click OK to acknowledge that the database has been successfully split.
12. Analyze the performance of the Fastfood-P database using the Performance Analyzer by clicking Tools on the menu, pointing to Analyze, then clicking Performance.
13. Click the All tab, click Select All, then click OK.
14. Click each of the entries to observe the Analysis Notes at the bottom of the dialog box.
15. Click Close to close the Performance Analyzer dialog box.
16. Close Fastfood-P, then exit Access.

▶ Visual Workshop

Open the VW-P database and create the Performance Analysis as shown in Figure P-18 by analyzing all options on the All tab.

FIGURE P-18

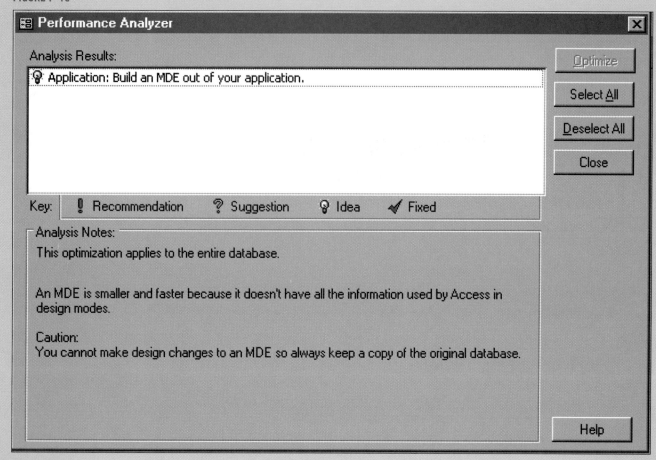

Glossary

Accessories Built-in programs that come with Windows 95 that you can use for day-to-day tasks.

Active program The program that is running (that is, open).

Active window A window that you are currently using. If a window is active, its title bar changes color to differentiate it from other windows and its program button in the taskbar is highlighted.

Check box Clicking this square box in a dialog box turns an option off or on.

Click To press and release the left mouse button once quickly.

Clipboard Temporary storage space that contains information that has been cut or copied.

Close Use to quit a program or remove a window from the desktop. The Close button usually appears in the upper-right corner of a window.

Command Directive that provides access to a program's features.

Command button In a dialog box, a button that carries out an action. A command button usually has a label that describes its action, such as Cancel or Help. If the label is followed by an ellipses, clicking the button displays another dialog box.

Context-sensitive help Information related to your current task. An example of context-sensitive help in Windows is the What's This? feature.

Control Panel A Windows utility for changing computer settings, such as desktop colors or mouse settings.

Copy To copy information in a file and place it on the Clipboard to be pasted in another location.

Cursor The blinking vertical line in a document window such as WordPad, which indicates where text will appear when you type. Also known as the insertion point.

Cut To remove information from a file and place it on the Clipboard.

Cut and paste To move information from one place to another using the Clipboard as the temporary storage area.

Desktop An on-screen version of a desk that provides workspace for different computing tasks.

Dialog box A window that opens in which you enter information needed to carry out a command. Many commands display dialog boxes in which you must select options before Windows can carry out the command.

Disk label Name that you assign to a disk using the Properties dialog box.

Document window Displays the current document.

Double-click To press and release the left mouse button twice quickly.

Drag To move an item by pressing and holding the left mouse button to select it, moving the mouse to a new location, then releasing the mouse button.

Drive Device which reads and saves files on a disk. Floppy drives read and save files on floppy disks. Hard drives read and save files on your built-in hard disk.

Edit To change the contents of a file without having to recreate it.

File A collection of information that has a unique name, distinguishing it from other files.

File hierarchy A logical order for folders and files that mimics how you would organize files and folders in a filing cabinet.

File management A skill to organize and keep track of files and folders.

Folder A collection of files and other folders that helps you organize your disks.

Font The design of a set of characters (i.e., Times New Roman).

Format Change the appearance of information but not the actual content.

Graphical user interface (GUI) An environment made up of meaningful symbols, words, and windows in which you can control the basic operation of a computer and the programs that run on it.

Help button A button in a Help window that when clicked jumps to a dialog box or opens a program to answer your question.

Highlight When an icon is shaded differently indicating it is selected. See also Select.

Horizontal scroll bar Moves your view from side to side in a window.

Icon Graphical representation of files and other screen elements.

Insertion point The blinking vertical line in a document window such as WordPad, which indicates where text will appear when you type. Also known as the cursor.

Keyboard shortcut A keyboard alternative for executing a menu command (i.e., [Ctrl][X] for Cut).

List box A box in a dialog box containing a list of items. To choose an item, click the list arrow, then click the desired item.

Maximize To enlarge a window so it takes up the entire screen. There is usually a Maximize button in the upper-right corner of a window.

Menu A list of available commands in a program.

Menu bar Provides access to most of a program's features through commands.

Minimize To reduce the size of a window. There is usually a Minimize button in the upper-right corner of a window. Clicking the Minimize button shrinks the window to an icon.

Mouse A hand-held input device that you roll on your desk to position the mouse pointer on the Windows desktop. See also Mouse pointer.

Mouse buttons The two buttons on the mouse (right and left) that you use to make selections and issue commands.

Mouse pointer The arrow-shaped cursor on the screen that follows the movement of the mouse as you roll the mouse on your desk. You use the mouse pointer to select items, choose commands, start programs, and edit text in applications. The shape of the mouse pointer changes depending on the program and the task being executed.

My Computer Use to view the files that are available on your computer and how they are arranged. The icon appears on the desktop.

Object An item (such as a file or folder) in a window. In task-oriented programs, objects are also graphics or text from another program.

Open Action which describes starting a program or displaying a window that was previously closed. Also used to describe a program that is currently running, but not necessarily displayed in an active window.

Operating system Controls the basic operation of your computer and the programs you run on it.

Option button A small circle in a dialog box that you click to select an option. Also known as a radio button.

Pattern A design that will display as your desktop background.

Point To move the mouse pointer to position it over an item on the desktop. Also a unit of measurement used to specify the size of text.

Pop-up menu The menu that appears when you right-click an item on the desktop. Also known as a shortcut menu.

Program Task-oriented software that you use for a particular kind of work, such as word processing or database management. Microsoft Access, Microsoft Excel, and Microsoft Word are all programs.

Program button The button that appears on the taskbar, representing a minimized (but still running) program.

Properties The characteristics of a specific element (such as the mouse, keyboard, or desktop display) that you can customize.

Radio button A small circle in a dialog box that you click to select an option. Also known as an option button.

RAM (random access memory) The memory that programs use to perform necessary tasks while the computer is on. When you turn the computer off, all information in RAM is lost.

Recycle Bin An icon that appears on the desktop that represents a temporary storage area for deleted files. Files will remain in the Recycle Bin until you empty it.

Restore To reduce the window to its previous size before it was maximized. There is usually a Restore button in the upper-right corner of a window.

Right-click To press and release the right mouse button once quickly.

Run To operate a program.

Screen saver A moving pattern that fills your screen after your computer has not been used for a specified amount of time.

Scroll bar A bar that appears at the bottom and/or right edge of a window whose contents are not entirely visible. Each scroll bar contains a scroll box and two scroll arrows. You click the arrows or drag the box in the direction you want the window to move.

Scroll box Located in the vertical and horizontal scroll bars and indicates your relative position in a window. See also Horizontal scroll bar and Vertical scroll bar.

Select When you click and highlight an item in order to perform some action on it. See also Highlight.

Shortcut A link that you can place in any location that gives you instant access to a particular file, folder, or program on your hard disk or on a network.

Shortcut menu The menu that appears when you right-click an item on the desktop. Also known as a pop-up menu.

Shut down The action you perform when you have finished your Windows work session. After you perform this action it is safe to turn off your computer.

Start button A button on the taskbar that you use to start programs, find files, access Windows Help, and more.

Taskbar A bar at the bottom of the screen that contains the Start button and shows which programs are running

Text box A box in a dialog box in which you type text.

Title bar The area along the top of the window that contains the filename and program used to create it.

Toolbar Contains buttons that allow you to activate a command quickly.

ToolTip A description of a toolbar button that appears on your screen.

Triple-click To press and release the left mouse button three times quickly. In some programs, this action causes an entire line to be selected.

Vertical scroll bar Moves your view up and down through a window.

Wallpaper An image that is in the same format as Windows 95 Paint files that will display as your desktop background.

Window A rectangular frame on a screen that might contain icons, the contents of a file, or other usable data.

Windows Explorer Use to manage files, folders, and shortcuts; more powerful than My Computer and allows you to work with more than one computer, folder, or file at once.

Glossary

Actions query A query that makes changes to many records in just one operation. Make-table, delete, append, and update are all action queries.

Actions Tasks that you want Access to perform and which are specified on each line of an Access macro object.

Aggregate functions Functions such as Sum, Avg, and Min that are used in the Query Design grid to calculate statistics across several records.

AND query A query in which more than one criteria must be satisfied for the record to be displayed in the resulting datasheet. AND criteria are placed in the same row of the Query Design grid.

Append query An update query used to add records to an existing table.

Arguments Constants, variables, or expressions passed to a procedure to further define how it should execute; arguments provide additional information on how to carry out a macro action.

AutoForm Wizards Options in the New Form dialog box that allow quick creation of tabular, columnar, or datasheet AutoForms.

AutoFormat Feature An automated way to format an entire report after it is created.

AutoKeys To assign a macro to a specific key combination, you create an AutoKeys macro group.

AutoLookup query A multiple-table query that automatically fills in certain field values for a new record.

AutoReport A report created with the New Object button on the toolbar. Access displays all fields and records in the selected table or query with field names used as labels.

AutoReport Wizard Two options in the New Report dialog box that allow quick creation of tabular or columnar AutoReports.

Axes Scales by which information is measured and plotted on a chart, usually called the x-axis and y-axis.

Backing up Making a duplicate copy of the database on a medium physically separated from the primary location of the database.

Backup medium Backup medium might be a floppy disk, tape drive, recordable CD device, or separate hard drive. It is the physical device that stores the backup.

Bitmap A clip art or image file format that is made up of patterns of individual dots. The file type for bitmap files is usually .BMP.

Bound control A control on a form or report that is linked to a field in an underlying table or query.

Bound object frame control A control on a form or report that is linked to information from an OLE field.

Calculated expressions Bound report controls that total groups of records and are most likely placed in the group footer section of the report.

Calculated field Created in the Query Design grid by entering a field name followed by a colon in the Field cell followed by an expression such as New Price:[Price]*1.1.

Cascading deletes An option in the Relationship dialog box when defining one-to-many relationships between tables, that allows you to delete all the records on a "many" side of a relationship if you delete the record that contains the "one" side.

Cell The intersection of a row and a column.

Chart An object which graphically displays numeric information.

Check box A square box on a dialog box or form used to indicate whether an option is selected (checked) or cleared (unchecked). Also used to indicate yes/no choices.

Class modules Modules that are stored as part of the form or report object and respond to events that occur on that specific form or report.

Client/Server computing Two or more information systems cooperatively processing to solve a problem.

Column A vertical stack of cells, usually representing the values for a database field.

Combo box A list box with the additional capability of allowing the user to type an entry from the keyboard.

Command button A control on a form that executes a command or macro when clicked. Access supplies over 30 different types of command buttons with the Command Button Wizard such as record and form navigation commands.

Command Line Option Text instructions that further define how an Access database will be opened.

Comment line A descriptive line of text that serves as guiding documentation.

Compact a database A technique to efficiently rearrange how the database file is stored on disk.

Compile-time errors When running procedures, compile-time errors occur as a result of incorrectly constructed code.

Conditional expression An expression that is often used in complex macros which make the macro behave differently based on the current situation. If the result of the conditional expression is true, a series of macro actions are executed. If the result of the conditional expression is false, the series of actions are not executed.

Control A graphical object used on a form or report that displays data or other information.

Control Wizard An Access wizard which helps you add and make property changes to controls on forms and reports.

ControlTip A tip that pops up when you move the mouse pointer over a control is called a ControlTip. A ControlTip is a type of ScreenTip. Other ScreenTips include ToolTips that pop up when you move the mouse pointer over a button in a toolbar.

Criteria A set of conditions used in a filter or query that selects a particular group of records.

Crosstab query A query that presents information in a cross-tabular report, usually with one field counted or summarized by rows and columns within the body of the report.

Data   The information stored in a database.

Data definition query   An SQL-specific query that creates or alters database objects, such as Microsoft Access tables or queries.

Data Dictionary   Detailed descriptions regarding the fields of a table.

Data source   In Word, the document or object (such as an Access table or query) that contains variable information, such as addresses and names, to be merged into the main document to create the multi-page merged document.

Data type   A specification that controls what kind of data a field can contain.

Database   An organized collection of data for a specific purpose.

Database management system   A computer program that organizes and manages data.

Database schema   Complete relationships information about the tables of your database.

Database Splitter Feature   Feature that allows you to split a database into two files: one that contains the actual table objects called the back-end database, and one that contains the other objects as well as links to the back-end database tables called the front-end database.

Database window   The window that opens when you start an Access database. It lists all the objects contained in the database.

Dataset   A set of records retrieved by applying a filter or running a query.

Datasheet   Data from a table, form, or query displayed as rows and columns.

Debug   Determine why a macro or procedure doesn't run properly.

Declaration statements   Lines of Visual Basic used to name and define procedures as well as to set rules for how the statements in a module process.

Decrypting   Reversing the encryption process.

Default Switchboard   The default switchboard automatically displays when you open the database.

Delete query   An update query used to delete a chosen subset of records.

Design grid   The grid that you use to design a query or filter.

Design view   A window that shows the structure of a table, form, query, or report.

Destination program   The program that receives information from an external source. For example, if you link or import a table of information from Excel into an Access database file, Access is the destination program.

Detail section   The section of the report that prints once for each record in the underlying record set.

Documenter   An Access feature that prints the relationships between the tables as well as provides additional information about the linkage itself.

Drag and drop   A method to copy an Access table to a Word document that requires excellent mouse skills. To drag and drop an Access table to a Word document, click any table or query name in the Access Database window, then drag the object to a visible edge of an open Word window or to the Word button displayed in the Taskbar.

Encrypting   Compacts and scrambles a database file so that it is indecipherable when opened by a utility program or word processor.

Event   Something that happens on a form, window, or datasheet that can be attached to or evaluated by a macro, such as the click of a command button or moving from one record to another.

Event procedure   A procedure run in response to an action performed by the user such as clicking on a command button or changing data.

Exclusive Mode   A way to open an Access database in which no other user will have access to it while it's open.

Export   An Access feature that automatically copies information from any Access datasheet to an Excel spreadsheet.

Expression   A combination of values, identifiers (such as the value in a field), and operators that result in a value.

External source   The application that provides the information to the destination application. For example, if you link or import a table of information from Excel into an Access database file, Excel is the external source.

Field   The part of a table that contains a particular type of data. Also used to name the column of cells containing a particular type of data.

Field list   A window available in Design view to display all the fields in a table or query being used.

Field properties   The qualities of a field that affect how it appears or what type of data it receives.

Field selector   The gray bar at the top of a field column that selects the entire column.

Filter   Criteria used to retrieve a specific set of records.

Find   A feature that allows you to search for a string of characters in one or many fields.

Footer   The text that appears at the bottom of each page in printed output.

Foreign key   The field in the table on the "many" side of a one-to-many relationship.

Form   An object, resembling a paper form, used for entering and editing single records.

Form view   A window that displays the contents of a database in a form.

Format Painter   A feature that can be used to copy formatting characteristics of an individual control to another control.

Formatting   Changing a report's colors, lines, fonts, and other appearance properties.

Formula   An entry in an Excel workbook that automatically updates when any of the values in the cell addresses contained in the formula change.

Full File Specification   The drive and folders that specify where a file is stored.

Function   A series of programming statements that returns a value.

Graphics   Any nontext or nonnumeric element such as lines, clip art, or boxes placed in the report.

Group footer   A section of a form or report that appears on its own line on a report just after the Detail section of a new group of records. Group footer sections are often used to add summary statistics to groups of records.

Group frame   An option group consists of a group frame and option buttons, check boxes, or toggle buttons within the frame.

Group header   A section of a form or report that appears on its own line on a report just before the Detail section of a new group of records.

Grouping   The sorting of records according to a specified field. Grouping provides a way to sort records so that summary statistics can be applied to a group of records that meet a certain criteria.

Handle   A small black square used to move or resize controls in Design View.

Hard copy   Paper output.

Header   The text that appears at the top of each page in printed output.

Help   An online collection of information about Access that you reach from the Help menu.

Hide Duplicates property   Hides multiple occurrences of the same data for the fields in the Detail section of the report.

HTTP   *See* Hypertext Transfer Protocol.

Hyperlink   Controls added to Access forms or reports that, when clicked, dynamically open documents created with different programs such as Word, Excel, PowerPoint, or World Wide Web pages.

Hyperlink address   The hyperlink address contains three parts: the displaytext (the text that appears in the field), the path to the file—the URL or UNC for the file or page (optional), and the subaddress—a tag which identifies the specific location within the file or page (optional).

Hyperlink field   A field created with a hyperlink data type. A hyperlink field is used to store hyperlink addresses for each record that point to local, intranet, or Internet resources such as documents, Web pages, or e-mail addresses.

Hypertext   A textual hyperlink.

Hypertext Transfer Protocol   A set of rules for moving hypertext files (Web pages) across the Internet.

Icon   A small graphical representation of an object.

If . . . Then . . . Else statement   Visual Basic statement that allows you to test a logical condition and execute commands only if the condition is true.

Image control   A control that is used to add the corporate logo to the header section of a form or report.

Immediate Pane   A scratch pad window at the bottom of the debug window in which Visual Basic statements are evaluated immediately, to determine what is happening at that line of code.

Imported table   A new Access table in your database created from information copied from an external file.

Internet   A global network of computer networks that links the mainframes of business, government, and education, as well as Internet-connected microcomputers together to share information and ideas.

Intranet   Internal subsets of the Internet, generally secured for a single company's employees or those with a "need to know."

Join field   The field used to link the two tables in the query together in a one-to-many relationship.

Key field   A field that contains unique information for each record.

Key field combination   Using two or more fields together as the key field for a record.

Label   A control that displays unbound text on a form or report.

Line chart   A chart that compares values over time using a line to connect the data points.

Linked table   A table created in Excel or other database product that is stored in a file outside the open database.

List box   A box that displays a list of choices.

Local Area Network (LAN)   Connects local resources that can be connected via a direct cable.

Logic errors   When running procedures, logic errors occur when the code runs, but doesn't produce the expected results.

Macro   An object that represents a predefined series of actions that perform a specific task.

Macro group   An Access object that stores one or more macros together (the macros still run independently of each other). Macro group objects appear on the Macros tab of the Database window just as macros do.

Macro window   The design window in which you specify a macro's actions, and the arguments for each action.

Mail Merge Helper   A valuable Word feature used to complete a mail merge and is found on the Tools menu.

Main document   In Word, the main document is the document that contains standard text that will be merged to a list of names and addresses, for example, to create a multi-page merged document. The main document is sometimes called the form letter.

Main report   The report on which a subreport control is placed.

Make-Table query   A query that creates a new table from all or part of the data in one or more tables.

Menu   A list of related commands displayed by clicking a menu name.

Menu bar   The row at the top of a window that contains menu names.

Metafile   A clip art or image file format that is made up of lines. The file type for metafiles is often .WMF or .EMF.

Method   An action that an object can perform.

Mission critical   Term used to describe programs and/or data that are critical to the survival (the mission) of the business.

Module   An Access object where Visual Basic code is stored.

Move handle   The large black square in the upper-left corner of a selected control that you drag to reposition the control.

Navigation buttons   The arrows in the lower-left corner of a datasheet or form that are used to move through records.

Object The principal component of an Access database. Tables, forms, queries, reports, macros, and modules are all referred to as "objects" in Access.

Object linking and embedding (OLE) field data type A field data type that allows a field to store data such as Microsoft Word or Microsoft Excel documents, pictures, sound, and other types of binary data created in other programs.

ODBC *See* Open Database Connectivity Protocol.

OLE *See* Object linking and embedding.

One-to-many relationship The link between two tables in which the "one" side of the relationship is a key field and the "many" side of the relationship allows the data in that field to be entered many times in that table.

Open Database Connectivity Protocol (ODBC) A protocol that lets you save an Access database table to another file in one of many application formats: Microsoft FoxPro, dBase, Paradox, Excel, Lotus, several text formats, or any program or database that supports the protocol.

Operators Instructions added to criteria to create new criteria conditions. Mathematical operators such as + (add), and * (multiply) can be used to calculate new criteria. Logical operators such as AND and OR can be used to create more complex criteria expressions.

Option button A button, typically part of a group, that selects an option. Only one option can be selected at a time.

Option group A control on a form that displays a limited set of alternatives. Only one option button in an option group can be selected at a time.

OR query A query in which only one of two or more criteria rows must be satisfied for the record to be displayed in the resulting datasheet. OR criteria are placed on different rows in the Query Design grid.

Page Break control Control added to a report or form to identify where you want to start a new page within a section.

Parameter query A query that displays a dialog box prompting you for information to enter as criteria for retrieving records.

Pass-Through query An SQL-specific query that sends commands directly to ODBC (Open Database Connectivity) databases such as Microsoft SQL Server.

Performance Analyzer Feature An Access feature that studies the structure and size of your database and makes a variety of recommendations on how you could improve its performance.

Pie chart A common chart that shows the relationship of parts to a whole.

Pointer Used to select items; repositioned by movement of the mouse.

Primary key A field whose value uniquely identifies each record.

Print Preview An on-screen view of how an item will appear on paper.

Procedure A series of Visual Basic statements that perform an operation or calculate a value; a procedure is stored in a module object.

Property An attribute of an object that you can change to control the object's appearance or behavior.

Property sheet The window that displays all the properties for the chosen control on a form or report.

Query A set of instructions used to extract specific records from a database. A "question" asked to the database.

Record All the pieces of information (fields) about one item. A row composed of fields in a datasheet.

Record number box The small box that displays the current record number in the lower-left corner of a datasheet or form.

Referential integrity A set of rules to help maintain the accuracy of a database. For example, enforcing referential integrity will not allow entry of records with data on the "many" side of a one-to-many relationship before the data is first recorded for the "one" side.

Relational database A database where information is stored in tables that can be related to one another.

Relationship The connection between two or more tables established by fields common to two or more tables.

Replace A feature that allows you to search for a string of characters and replace it with a different entry.

Replicate Make special copies of an Access database using the Windows Briefcase program.

Report An Access object that presents data selected and formatted for printed output.

Report window The window that presents reports in Design View.

Row A horizontal grouping of a record's data fields in a datasheet.

Row selector A gray box at the left edge of a datasheet that is used to select an entire row.

Run A command or button used to run a query.

Run-time errors When running procedures, run-time errors occur after the code starts to run and include attempting an illegal operation such as dividing by zero.

Section A designated area of a form or report in which controls can be placed. For example, a Page Header section displays/prints at the top of every page, but a Report Header section displays/prints only at the top of the entire report.

Select query A query that creates a record set without changing any of the affected records.

Shortcut key A key or key combination that lets you carry out a command without opening a menu or using a button.

Shortcut menu A floating menu that opens when the right mouse button is clicked. Menu contents vary, depending on the task in process.

Single-step The ability to run a macro one line at a time, observing the effect of each macro action as it is executed.

Size Mode A property that controls the way an image appears within a bound object frame.

Sizing handle A small black square at the edge of a selected control that you drag to resize the control.

Sorting Placing the records in a certain order (such as ascending order) according to the data in a particular field.

Sort order The order that records are displayed in—either Ascending (A-Z) or Descending (Z-A).

Special effects Raised, sunken, shadowed, etched, or chiseled effects added to controls on forms or reports.

SQL *See* Structured Query Language.

Standard Modules Modules that are stored on the modules tab of the opening database window and contain code that can be executed from anywhere in the database application.

Startup Properties Control what happens as soon as the database is opened.

Status bar The gray bar across the bottom of the screen that shows supplementary information about commands or actions.

Status Bar Text Property Property to display helpful information about a form or control in the status bar.

Structured Query Language (SQL) Programming code that is created when you build any query.

Sub Procedure A procedure that performs a series of programming statements but does not return a value.

Subform A form contained inside another form.

Subquery An SQL SELECT statement inside another select or action query. These statements are entered in the Field or Criteria row of the query design grid.

Subreport A report that is added as a control within another report in the same manner that subforms are added to forms.

Switchboard An opening form that gives the user access to only those objects that he or she actually uses.

Switchboard Manager A feature that can be used to create switchboards.

Synchronize To update the replicated copies of a database.

Text box The most common type of bound control on a form or report. When using a form, the text box allows the user to make an entry for a record by typing information at the keyboard. When reading a report, the text box displays the information in the field on the report.

Toggle button A form control that appears as a button on the screen which can be toggled on or off.

Toolbar The row of buttons just below the menu bar that provides shortcuts for frequently-used commands.

Toolbox The tools used to place controls on a form or report in Design view.

ToolTip The short description of a button name or purpose that appears when you point at a toolbar button.

Top Values Access feature that allows you to list the 5 (or any number you designate) highest or lowest values or highest or lowest 10 percent (or any percent you designate) for a specific field in a query datasheet.

Unbound control A control that is stored entirely in the design for a form or report. There is no link to data in a table.

Unbound object frame A frame containing an image that is stored entirely in the design for a form or report. There is no link to an image stored in the database.

UNC *See* Universal Naming Convention.

Uniform resource locator Is an address to a resource on the Internet such as a Web page, newsgroup, or e-mail address. A URL expresses the protocol to be accessed as well as where the resource is located. Web page URLs start with http such as the following: http://www.ibm.com.

Union query An SQL-specific query that combines fields from two or more tables or queries into one field and is therefore very useful when trying to combine data from two separate tables or databases into a single object.

Universal Naming Convention The standard format for paths that include a local area network file server. The protocol for a UNC is \\server\share\path\filename.

Update query A query that updates the information in the resulting datasheet.

URL *See* uniform resource locator.

Validation properties Properties of a field that help you eliminate unreasonable entries in a field at the point of data entry.

Value The contents of a field.

View A window that lets you work with Access objects in a specific way including Form View, Design View, and Report View.

Visual Basic The programming language used to write Access procedures stored in module objects.

Watermark A background picture added to a report on which text and numbers print.

Web Server A computer that serves Web pages on the World Wide Web.

What-if analysis An Excel feature that allows the user to interactively apply assumptions to a set of numbers and watch the resulting calculated formulas update instantly.

Wide Area Network (WAN) Connects computer resources across public thoroughfares which usually requires connecting with existing public communications networks through telecommunications hardware and software.

Windows Briefcase A program used to replicate a database on an office and portable computer, and to keep those replicas synchronized.

Wizard A tool that helps you create objects such as tables, queries, and forms.

Zoom box A dialog box that lets you view and edit the full contents of an entry that is too large to be viewed in a single cell.

Index

Index

Index

Index

Index